EUROPEAN FEDERAL CRIMINAL LAW

EUROPEAN FEDERAL CRIMINAL LAW

The Federal Dimension of EU Criminal Law

Carlos Gómez-Jara Díez

intersentia
Cambridge – Antwerp – Portland

Intersentia Ltd
Sheraton House | Castle Park
Cambridge | CB3 0AX | United Kingdom
Tel.: +44 1223 370 170 | Fax: +44 1223 370 169
Email: mail@intersentia.co.uk
www.intersentia.com | www.intersentia.co.uk

Distribution for the UK and Ireland:
NBN International
Airport Business Centre, 10 Thornbury Road
Plymouth, PL6 7PP
United Kingdom
Tel: +44 1752 202 301 | Fax: +44 1752 202 331
Email: orders@nbninternational.com

Distribution for Europe and all other countries:
Intersentia Publishing nv
Groenstraat 31
2640 Mortsel
Belgium
Tel.: +32 3 680 15 50 | Fax: +32 3 658 71 21
Email: mail@intersentia.be

Distribution for the USA and Canada:
International Specialized Book Services
920 NE 58th Ave Suite 300
Portland, OR 97213
USA
Tel.: +1 800 944 6190 (toll free) | Fax: +1 503 280 8832
Email: info@isbs.com

European Federal Criminal Law. The Federal Dimension of EU Criminal Law

ISBN 978-1-78068-120-7
NUR 824

British Library Cataloguing in Publication Data. A catalogue record for this book is available from the British Library.

Dedicated to my son Máximo

PREFACE

There is no United States of Europe. There is no federal criminal law of the United States of Europe. This should be clear from the beginning. This book is not about trying to convince the reader of the existence of such institutions. The EU has not (yet) evolved into a federal state; and it may never turn into such a structure. Nevertheless, the development of the various treaties signals without a doubt a tendency towards federalism. Federalism has many faces, and so does federal criminal law. This book aims to shed some light into the federal nature of the current system of EU criminal law. In fact it will be argued that some EU institutions of criminal law are more "federal" than their counterparts in consolidated federal systems.

In this sense, the following pages must begin with a fair warning: the more the European discussion is reluctant to acknowledge the federal dimension contained in certain criminal law related institutions, the more the dangers embedded in the nature of federal criminal law are likely to appear and spread all over. An adamant recognition from the outset that the EU has similar problems to the ones faced by federal states will enable a better and more reasonable solution to these problems. Stressing the need for harmonization curtails the legitimate reasons of Member States for diverging national regulations; the lack of emphasis in a centralized EU system of criminal law protecting intrinsic EU interests deprives the EU of legitimate resources of law enforcement.

To be sure, the current system is at the same time too federal and not federal enough. It is too federal because certain institutions such as the EAW do not provide the necessary space for national diversity so that the national idiosyncrasy cannot be taken into account in such "intimate" fields as murder. It is not federal enough because the EU cannot by itself protect its own financial interests; Member States' law enforcement authorities are supposed to provide that service. To the same extent that national authorities feel threatened by Brussels in traditional fields of criminal law, the EU feels threatened by the lack of enforcement by national authorities. Would not it be more reasonable for each of them to "take care of their own business"?

As the pages of this book were being written, the European Union was experiencing an age of turbulence. The turmoil caused by the financial crisis and the European debt crisis has questioned the true nature of the EU. In the face of a potential disintegration of the eurozone, a tendency towards integration and sovereignty transfer to Brussels can be observed. This has not gone unnoticed or unquestioned. The EU is currently resorting to criminal law with the aim of protecting its financial interests. A Directive imposing criminal sanctions for market abuse or a Regulation establishing the European Public Prosecutor's Office are concepts that, prior to the crisis, seemed a distant future. In a way, the time has come for a substantial change in the area of European criminal law.

Additionally, the strong opposition of the UK to the Commission's newly appointed Jean-Claude Juncker on the grounds of the latter being an "arch-federalist" also shows that the federal debate is becoming more and more palatable in the political EU scene. The sheer fact of Prime Minister Cameron warning that if Juncker was elected the UK would opt out of the EU shows the nature of the controversy. It seems reasonable to conclude that under Juncker, the federal dimension of the EU will grow stronger. And this should have a notable impact on the conformation of European federal criminal law.

It might come as a surprise that the former European Commissioner in charge of Justice, Consumers and Gender Equality, Viviane Reding, relied on federal terms to justify the Proposal for establishing the European Public Prosecutor's Office in 2013: she noted that "A federal budget needs *federal protection*". The newly appointed European Commissioner for the same area, Věra Jourov, clearly signaled that she would continue the path initiated by Reding: "My main priorities are the European Public Prosecutor's Office (EPPO) and EU data protection". Though the debate is far from over, a tendency towards acknowledging the importance of federalism in the criminal law debate seems to be consolidating.

This book has two different goals: first, to convince the reader of the existence of certain federalizing elements in the current system of European criminal law; second, to provide certain guidelines for future action that, while acknowledging these federal elements, try to avoid the mistakes of the past. To achieve both aims, a comparative law approach is deployed. The US system of federal criminal law is one of the longest-standing and most effective systems in world. At the same time, it is polluted with unfairness and contradictions that ultimately lead to overcriminalization. The EU is clearly at risk of making the same mistakes and producing an inconsistent and unfair system of federalized criminal law like the American one. The longer it takes to recognize these federalizing elements, the greater the danger.

The book does not exhaustively review the various institutions of EU criminal law. Nor does it contain a detailed explanation of the institutions present in US federal criminal law. The learned reader will be rapidly aware of the deficiencies of this work from a purely European or American criminal law approach. A compromise has been reached in order to signal the core argument: the federalizing elements in certain institutions of EU criminal law. To be sure, the easy response is to deny that the EU is a federal state and that there is no such thing as European federal criminal law. But if the underlying rationale behind certain EU institutions of criminal law resemble their American counterparts, would not it be more reasonable to finally acknowledge that the EU is slowly but steadily federalizing criminal law and that the grave dangers of over-expansive criminal law federalization should be taken into account?

ACKNOWLEDGEMENTS

This book is the result of over a decade of valuable discussions with many individuals. Coinciding with the debate over the "Constitution for Europe" I published my first paper in Spanish on European federal criminal law in 2004, many academics were reluctant to acknowledge any value to the comparison with the US system of federal criminal law. However, I would like to express my gratitude to some of the first people in Spain that took the comparison seriously into account – even if it was in the form of harsh criticism: Manuel Cancio Meliá, Jesús-María Silva Sánchez, Miguel Bajo Fernández and Adán Nieto Martín.

My stay at Columbia University brought me the opportunity to discuss much of the key findings of this book with one of the major experts in US federal criminal law: Daniel C. Richman. Noting the resemblances and divergences between the two systems provided a considerable amount of value to the overall goal. Also, having a close account of how the US system works thanks to conversations and discussions with Hon. Judge Jed. S. Rakoff proved to be extremely enriching. My subsequent practice in federal litigation certainly added some interesting perspectives.

This book would have never seen the light without the great efforts and assistance of Nathan S. Wilson. Not only did he review and edit much of the content, but he also introduced much more than what can be expected from a research assistant. His keen sense of legal reasoning and his outstanding research skills made is possible to navigate through the tangled mess of comparative law.

Last but not least, I wish to express my sincere gratitude to Intersentia for accepting this book in their prestigious series. Though the initial version of this work dates from 2013, the (then) imminent approval of new European legislation that could impact its content cautioned some delay.

Madrid, 1 April 2015

CONTENTS

Preface vii
Acknowledgements xi
Findings xix

Introduction 1

1. Why the Comparison with the US System of Federal Criminal Law? 5
2. Some Notes on American Federalism 8
3. Structure of this Book 10

Chapter 1.
The EU Criminal Law Situation Prior to the Lisbon Treaty 13

1. Introduction 13
2. Preliminary Issues 15
   2.1. Vertical and Horizontal Federalism in Both Unions 15
   2.2. EU Criminal Law, Europeanized Criminal Law and European Criminal Law: *ante portas* or *intra muros*? 18
   2.3. Conclusion 19
4. Crime Policy 19
   4.1. Introduction 19
   4.2. European Criminal Policy 20
   4.3. Federal Crime Policy in the US System 23
   4.4. Conclusion 26
5. Criminal Law Scholarship 26
   5.1. EU Criminal Law Scholarship 26
   5.2. US Federal Criminal Law Scholarship 30
   5.3. Conclusion 34
6. The Fundamentals of European Horizontal Federal Criminal Law: The Principle of Mutual Recognition 34
   6.1. Introduction 34
   6.2. The Application of the Principle of Mutual Recognition to the Field of Criminal Law 35
      6.2.1. Introduction 35

6.2.2. Criticisms Generated by the Transplantation of the Principle of Mutual Recognition to the Criminal Law Field . . . 38
6.2.3. Responses to the Critics . . . 42
6.2.4. It Had It Coming: The Ruling of the German Constitutional Court on 18 July 2005 . . . 44
6.2.5. The Timid ECJ Response: *Advocaten voor der Wereld* (2007) . . . 46
6.3. The Full Faith and Credit Clause in the US System: A Valid Comparison? . . . 47
6.3.1. Introduction . . . 47
6.3.2. The Rules and the Exceptions to Full Faith and Credit . . . 48
6.3.3. Full Faith and Credit in Criminal Matters? . . . 51
6.3.4. Conclusion . . . 53

Chapter 2.
The Federal Criminal Law Dimension in the Lisbon Treaty . . . 55

1. Introduction . . . 55
2. Preliminary Issues . . . 60
2.1. How Many Different Sources of Criminal Powers Are There in Both Unions? . . . 60
2.2. Federal Courts in Both Unions . . . 64
3. The First Federal Dimension of the Unions' Criminal Law: Crimes Affecting the Unions' Interests . . . 74
3.1. Introduction . . . 74
3.2. The Protection of the EU's Financial Interests (Article 325 TFEU) . . . 76
3.3. The Protection of Direct Federal Interests in the US Constitution (Article I Section 8) . . . 85
4. The Second Federal Dimension of the Unions' Criminal Law: Interstate Criminality and the Enforcement of the Unions' Policies . . . 90
4.1. Introduction . . . 90
4.2. Criteria for Federalizing Crimes in the EU (Horizontally) and in the US (Vertically) . . . 91
4.2.1. Introduction . . . 91
4.2.2. Criteria for the Inclusion of Matters within the Area of Liberty, Security and Justice of the EU . . . 93
4.2.3. The Federalization of Crime in the US . . . 96
4.3. Interstate Criminality . . . 100
4.3.1. Introduction . . . 100
4.3.2. EU's Serious Cross-Border Criminality (Article 83(1) TFEU) . . . 101

4.3.2.1. Catalog of (Vertical) Federal Crimes Specified in Article 83(1) TFEU (EU) 101
4.3.2.2. The Open-Ended Nature of the Catalog (Article 83(1) TFEU *in fine*) 105
4.3.3. US's Criminality Affecting Interstate Commerce......... 108
4.3.3.1. Catalog of (Horizontal) Federal Crimes Specified in Title 18 of the U.S.C. (US) 108
4.3.3.2. The Open-Ended Nature of the Catalog: the Commerce Clause and Federal Criminal Law 109
4.4. Enforcement of Unions' Policies................................ 115
4.4.1. Introduction 115
4.4.2. Effective Implementation of an EU Policy (Article 83(2) TFEU).. 116
4.4.3. The Necessary and Proper Clause in the US Constitution 121
5. The Enforcement Federal Dimension in the Unions' Criminal Law.... 128
5.1. Introduction.. 128
5.2. European Public Prosecutor's Office (Article 86 TFEU): From Horizontal to Vertical Federalism?...................... 129
5.3. Federal Prosecutors in the US: The Raw Discretionary Power.... 132

Chapter 3.
Testing the Alleged Lack of Federalism 137

1. Introduction 137
2. Interstate Extradition.. 138
2.1. Introduction.. 138
2.2. European Arrest Warrant (EU) 139
2.3. Interstate Rendition (US) 144
2.4. Comparison 148
3. Double Jeopardy 149
3.1. Introduction.. 149
3.2. Article 54 Schengen Agreement and *ne bis in idem* (EU) 150
3.3. Double Jeopardy and the Dual Sovereignty Doctrine (US)....... 155
3.4. Comparison 160
4. Criminal Law Harmonization.................................... 161
4.1. Introduction.. 161
4.2. Mandatory Harmonization (EU): European Directives 162
4.3. Voluntary Harmonization (US): Interstate Compacts and Uniform State Law 165
4.4. Comparison 172

Chapter 4.
The Federal Dimension of Fundamental Rights 175

1. Introduction 175
2. The Bill of Rights and the Incorporation Debate (US) 177
   2.1. Introduction 177
   2.2. Background Concepts 177
   2.3. The Evolution of Incorporation 179
3. The Growth of European Due Process 182
   3.1. Due Process from the ECJ and the ECHR 182
   3.2. Specific European Due Process Rights 187
4. Comparing Systems 190
   4.1. Evolving Standards and Judicial Activism 190
   4.2. Federal/"Federal" Relationships 192
   4.3. Greater European Federalism: Maximum Standards 196
5. Other Criminal Procedure Harmonization 197
   5.1. Introduction 197
   5.2. The EU Roadmap on Procedural Rights 197
   5.3. The (Lack of) Sub-Constitutional Criminal Procedure in the US 198
6. Conclusion 199
7. Case Study: European Due Process in Action: The Case of Spanish Secrecy Court Proceedings 202
   7.1. Introduction 202
   7.2. Spanish Secrecy Proceedings 203
   7.3. European Due Process and Secrecy Proceedings 204
   7.4. The Right to Information in Article 6(3)(a) ECHR 206
      7.4.1. Information for the Preparation of Defense 207
      7.4.2. Article 6(3)(a) ECHR in the Context of Secrecy Proceedings 208
   7.5. Trial within a Reasonable Time in Article 6 ECHR 210
      7.5.1. Length of Proceedings: the Law 211
         7.5.1.1. Beginning of the "Reasonable Time" Measure 211
         7.5.1.2. Factors Considered by the Court 212
      7.5.2. Length of Proceedings in the Context of Secrecy Proceedings 213
   7.6. Conclusion 214

Chapter 5.
The Sovereign Debt Crisis and the Future of EU Criminal Law 217

1. Introduction 217
2. United States versus Europe: Different Approaches to the Same Problem? 218
   2.1. The Financial Markets' Pressure 220
   2.2. The European Approach 222
   2.3. The American Approach 223
   2.4. The Future Ahead 224
3. Recent Developments in the EU Approach 225
   3.1. Safeguarding Taxpayers' Money? 225
   3.2. The So-Called Anti-Fraud Strategy 226
   3.3. Towards an EU Criminal Policy 228
   3.4. Will this Well-Intended Language Suffice? 229
4. The First Benchmark: The Directive on Criminal Sanctions for Insider Dealing and Market Manipulation – Financial Markets and the Stability of the EU 231
5. The Second Benchmark: The Proposal for a Directive to Protect European Financial Interests through Criminal Law – Genuine EU Interests 234
6. The Third Benchmark: The European Prosecutor Office – "Blue Helmets" in the War against Crime? 236
7. The ESMA Case: A Prequel in Terms of Questioning Enforcement Powers? 241
8. Law Enforcement and Investors Rationality: Some Lessons from the Law and Finance Debate 245
9. The Current Greek Crisis: Would it Look Different with an Independent EPPO Effectively Enforcing the Protection of the EU Financial Interests? 248
10. A Proposed System of EU Criminal Law: The Balance between Vertical and Horizontal Federalism 249
    10.1. Introduction 249
    10.2. Enhancing the Vertical Federalism Dimension 250
        10.2.1. Rethinking the Model: Towards an EU Competition Law Model with the Necessary Checks and Balances 250
        10.2.2. Regulation Protecting EU Financial Interests through Criminal Law 252
        10.2.3. Regulation Introducing European Rules of Criminal Procedure 253
        10.2.4. EPPO: Single-Hat Prosecutors 253
        10.2.5. Eurojust: Coordination between EPPO and National Enforcement Authorities 254

10.2.6. The Role of National Prosecutors: Assisting the EPPO.... 254
10.2.7. OLAF: The European FBI 254
10.2.8. The Role of National Courts: Creating Specialized Courts to Authorize Measures Affecting Fundamental Rights and to Try EPPO Cases.......................... 255
10.2.9. Judicial Review before the ECJ: Article 257 TFEU to Review the Decision to Proceed to Trial and to Review the Convictions 255

FINDINGS

Time is a scarce resource. It pays to outline for the quick reader some of the findings resulting from the comparative law analysis conducted in this book:

1. The EU is not a federal state, yet it has the same problems as if it were. The federal nature of the EU is heavily debated, but, at least from a criminal law perspective, the EU is dealing with the problems associate with criminal law in a similar fashion as most federal states.

2. These common problems could be synthesized as follows: (i) how to protect the Unions' genuine interests; (ii) how to address serious interstate criminality; (iii) how to enforce the Unions' policies; and (iv) how to ensure equal protection of fundamental rights. In order to address this common problem, the US has resorted to vertical federalism, while the EU has resorted to horizontal federalism.

3. As a consequence, the US system of criminal justice shows a high degree of vertical federalism and lower degree of horizontal federalism. The EU system of criminal justice shows a high degree of horizontal federalism and a low degree of vertical federalism.

4. There is a power struggle between the Unions' government and state sovereignty. In the US case, this debate has been shaped by the Tenth Amendment of the US Constitution (the anti-commandeering clause) which resembles Article 4(2) TFEU.

5. Interstate commerce has fostered US vertical federal criminal law through the commerce clause of the US Constitution. The internal market has fostered EU horizontal federal criminal law through the principle of mutual recognition.

6. The technical equivalent of the EU principle of mutual recognition is the US Full and Faith and Credit Clause. The US concept has little impact in the field of criminal law while the EU counterpart has triggered an array of EU criminal legislation. This is probably due to the fact that the EU principle of mutual recognition has its origin in the internal market, while the US Full Faith and Credit Clause has no connection to interstate commerce.

7. Both Unions have a tendency to address matters concerning interstate criminality through federal criminal law (vertically in the US and horizontally in the EU). The greatest dangers of overfederalization are located at this level.

8. The list of criminal matters in which the EU has expressly conferred (horizontal) powers, i.e. Article 83(1) first paragraph TFEU, are all addressed by US (vertical) federal criminal law. The criterion for enriching that list, i.e. serious cross-border criminality, has triggered abundant criminal legislation in US federal criminal law. The expansive nature of this criteria forecasts more future EU criminal legislative action in those areas.

9. The US Necessary and Proper Clause has its EU counterpart in criminal matters in Article 83(2) TFEU. Experience shows that when the conferred powers in criminal law matters are not evident, the Unions resort to this clause to legitimate (vertical/horizontal) federal action.

10. The first proposed federal criminal laws in both Unions are related to protecting the Unions' financial interests: the Revenue Fraud Act of 1789 in the US and the proposed Directives to protect the financial interests of the EU. Though the US proposal was quickly adopted, the EU proposal was not enacted and it has recently been readdressed.

11. The debt crises triggered in both Unions an acute awareness of the need to use federal criminal law to protect the interests of the Unions. The protection of taxpayers' monies raises awareness at the federal level in both Unions.

12. The greater degree of horizontal criminal law federalism in the EU allows less national diversity in criminal matters compared to the uniform law mechanisms of the US system of criminal justice.

13. The greater degree of horizontal criminal law federalism in the EU provides fewer opportunities for individuals to question the extent of (horizontal) federal legislation in the EU. Direct access to the federal jurisdiction in the US enables citizens to question the degree of criminal law federalization.

14. The greater degree of horizontal criminal law federalism in the EU has created the mechanism of the European Arrest Warrant which is more federal than the US mechanism of interstate rendition.

15. The greater degree of horizontal criminal law federalism in the EU provides greater protection in cross-border cases than in the US. Article 54 of the Schengen Treaty establishes a prohibition on double jeopardy in cases that the US may prosecute under the dual sovereignty exception.

16. The greater degree of horizontal criminal law federalism in the EU forces EU Member States to reform their national legislation, while the US equivalent, i.e. uniform law and interstate compacts, is voluntary rather than mandatory.

17. The federalization of fundamental rights has taken place in the EU through similar mechanisms as the ones deployed in the US: incorporation of rights through the case law of the ECtHR and ECJ. Future development of this tendency will greatly depend upon the terms of the EU accession to the ECHR.

18. The current development of EU criminal law concerning fundamental rights, though, shows a horizontal federalism mechanism which has little resemblance in its US counterpart: directives harmonizing fundamental rights. Some of them are already in place and some are currently under discussion.

19. The sovereign debt crisis has stressed the importance of EU criminal law in protecting the financial interests of the EU. Since the beginning of the crisis, the EU has been keenly aware of the need to set up a system that effectively protects taxpayers' monies.

20. The European Public Prosecutor's Office will constitute the landmark institution in the protection of EU financial interests. The current debate among EU institutions and Member States shows a reluctance to fully deploy the mechanism available in the Lisbon Treaty.

21. There is a perceived need to foster the vertical federalism approach to ensure effective enforcement of EU legislation protecting the EU financial interests. As the crisis wanes, the current tendencies support horizontal federalism solutions in which Member States retain considerable control over the enforcement of such legislation.

INTRODUCTION

"A federal budget needs federal protection"
Viviane Reding

In a notorious speech to justify the creation of a European Public Prosecutor's Office, the Justice Commissioner, *Viviane Reding*, clearly stated "A federal budget needs federal protection". In her view the EU budget "is a federal budget. If we don't protect it, nobody else will do it for us".[1] Probably no other EU official has articulated such an obvious relationship between the EU budget and the enactment of a European federal criminal law. Not surprisingly, this speech was given the same day that the Commission laid out its proposal for the establishment of the European Public Prosecutor's Office[2] – another federalizing moment. Although federalism may be "[t]he Dreaded 'F Word'"[3] – not to mention federal criminal law – the current EU approach towards criminal law would surely benefit from a federal perspective. At a minimum, this could mean stepping outside of what is "politically correct" and acknowledging that, *although not a federal state, the EU has the same problems as if it were one.*[4] Federalism has many faces,[5] and so does federal criminal law.

To be sure, the term "European federal criminal law" evokes the existence of a European criminal code, enforced by European institutions and ruled by

1 SPEECH/13/644.

2 COM (2013) 534 final.

3 Philippe C. Schmitter, *Democracy in Europe and Europe's democratization*, Journal of Democracy 14 (2003) at 74. For an interesting wordplay see the theme of the Brussels Think Tank annual summit on 22 April 2013: "State of the Union 2013 – Federalism or Fragmentation: spelling out Europe's F-Word". At the time, the now former President of the European Commission José Manuel Barroso contained that "function federalism" was needed to counter emerging threats to European unity.

4 There is a conspicuous tendency to consider the European Union as a Federation of States (see Robert Schütze, *From Dual to Cooperative Federalism: The Changing Structure of European Law*, 2009); Jenia Iontcheva Turner, *The Expressive Dimension of EU Criminal Law*, American Journal of Comparative Law 60 (2012) at 555 has summarized a palatable sentiment: the European Union's identity is evolving from "an organization devoted primarily to economic integration to a political union that increasingly resembles a federal state."

5 Koen Lenaerts, *Constitutionalism and the Many Faces of Federalism*, American Journal of Comparative Law 38 (1990) at 205; Frank B. Cross and Emerson H. Tiller, *The Three Faces of Federalism: An Empirical Assessment of Supreme Court Federalism Jurisprudence*, Southern California Law Review 73 (2000) at 741.

European courts.[6] However, that conception of European federal criminal law is based on a certain "face" of federalism, i.e. vertical federalism, and dismisses, without further reference, another equally important federal perspective, i.e. horizontal federalism.[7] The way in which the EU is forcing cooperation among the Member States without creating an independent supranational structure precisely highlights the latter aspect. As we shall explore, the current most obvious federal dimension of EU criminal law[8] is horizontal federalism.

Nevertheless, vertical federal criminal law has timidly surfaced throughout EU history. For decades, countries in Europe and the EU itself have played with the idea of developing a strong system of European criminal law – with some vertical dimension.[9] Interest in this matter waxed and waned, but the idea neither disappeared nor came to fruition. It will probably take a dramatic event to provide a catalyst for the emergence of a European (federal) structure in matters concerning criminal law. In this sense, the 2010 sovereign debt crisis and its progeny have certainly reinforced the horizontal federal dimension of EU criminal law and some vertical federal elements have surfaced.

The situation during the crisis was extremely dramatic: entire nations were on the brink of default; large parts of EU population underwent major radical cuts to social welfare; a number of new EU agencies with new powers were created; and Member States transferred sovereignty in areas previously regarded as sacred. It would be hard to conceive that all these dramatic events would not affect the development of EU criminal law. And they certainly did provide a catalyzing effect.

At the least, it is probably fair to say that as a consequence of the crisis the EU has paid increasing attention to a set of circumstances closely related to criminal law.[10] Moreover, the very nature of the sovereign debt crisis has triggered certain

6 As Mills puts it: "In the European Union, references to 'federalism' are often associated with centralizing movements toward greater concentration of power in E.U. institutions. By contrast, in the United States, references to 'federalism' are usually associated with decentralizing movements, which emphasize state rather than federal powers" (see ALEX MILLS, *Federalism in the European Union and the United States: Subsidiarity, Private Law and the Conflict of Laws*, UNIVERSITY OF PENNSYLVANIA JOURNAL OF INTERNATIONAL LAW 32 (2010), fn. 4).

7 On vertical and horizontal federalism see below Chapter 1, section 2.1.

8 For a general overview on EU criminal law see ANDRE KLIP, *European Criminal Law: An Integrative Approach*, 2nd ed. 2012; HELMUT SATZGER, *International and European Criminal Law*, 2012; ESTER HERLIN-KARNELL, *The Constitutional Dimension of European Criminal Law*, 2012; VALSAMIS MITSILEGAS, *EU Criminal Law*, 2009; SAMULI MIETTINEN, *Criminal Law and Policy in the European Union*, 2011.

9 Probably the peak of such proposal was reached in the late 20th century with the so-called *Corpus Iuris*, M. DELMAS-MARTY et al., *Corpus Juris, introducing provisions for the purpose of the financial interests of the European Union*, 1997. The *corpus iuris*, which contained a small European criminal code, advocated for the creation of a European Prosecutor Office to act before a European Court. See also the analysis prior to the sovereign debt crisis of MARGHERITA CERIZZA and GIUSEPPE MARTINICO, *Supranationalism in EU Criminal Justice: Another Incoming Tide?*, CIVITAS EUROPA 25 (2010) (available at http://papers.ssrn.com/sol3/papers.cfm?abstract_id=1645804).

10 See below Chapter 5, section 3.

reactions from EU institutions that reinforce a federal dimension that should not go unnoticed. The words of the Justice Commissioner are a clear example. Speaking about a European federal budget that needs European federal protection precisely when proposing legislation creating a European Prosecutor Office to prosecute crimes against the financial interests of the EU includes a federal element that should not go to waste.

This should not come a surprise. To a greater or lesser extent, the EU institutions have increasingly acknowledged that the protection mechanisms currently in place have failed and the need for reform has become increasingly acute. The first reforms have primarily targeted national legislation in an attempt to force similar levels of protection through horizontal federal criminal law. Yet they have failed to address the underlying structural deficit of supranational power or the vertical structure. Probably the first serious attempt to avert such structural deficit is the introduction of a European Prosecutor's Office. This vertical approach sets the EU on the path towards enacting and enforcing an autonomous system of EU criminal justice.[11]

As mentioned previously, the catalyzing effect of existence-threatening events is not unknown to Europe. The history of the EU itself and the establishment of the foundational EEC Treaty can be explained as a reaction to a Europe-threatening crisis: the dramatic experience of World War II. At the time, a European Union – as Churchill[12] and Eisenhower[13] worded it, a "United States of Europe" – seemed the only way to avert a future crisis of that caliber. The current crisis, which has been termed – maybe too dramatically – World War III (the Currency War),[14] seems to point to a similar solution: more Europe, not less.[15] True, some critics of the EU propose disintegration as a better solution than unification.[16]

---

11 This recent development could imply a change on the general perception that was succinctly described by Maria Fletcher, Robin Lööf and Bill Gilmore, *EU Criminal Law and Justice*, 2008, at 108: "the underpinning concept remains one of coordinating the various systems of criminal justice of the Member States rather than the development of an autonomous EU system of criminal justice per se".

12 Winston Churchill, Speech at the University of Zurich, 19 September 1946 (available at: www.churchill-society-london.org.uk/astonish.html).

13 Dwight David Eisenhower, Speech at the English Speaking Union Dinner at Grosvenor House, London, 3 July 1951 (available at: www.eisenhowermemorial.org/stories/english-speaking-union-speech.htm).

14 James Richard, *Currency Wars. The Making of the Next Global Crisis*, 2011.

15 See also Elke Cloots, Geert De Baere and Stefan Sottiaux, eds., *Federalism in the European Union*, 2012, Preface ("At the time of writing, the tide is running quite strongly in favour of the idea that – now that we really have our backs against the financial wall – what is needed in 'more Europe' not less"). Certainly, 2012 was a decisive year with important EU bail-outs of Member States.

16 This includes the "more modest Europe" solution committing itself to "unity in diversity" proposed by Christian Joerges, *Europe's Economic Constitution in Crisis*, Zentra Working Papers in Transnational Studies No. 06/2012. Although acknowledging that "Europe is in bad shape" (at 3) he proposes a "conflicts law" based on requiring EU Member States to "take their neighbors' concerns seriously" and to "structure cooperative solutions to problems in specific areas" (at 25). This approach, again, does not address the underlying problem and will

However, the economic rationale (not to mention political and cultural European achievements) indicate otherwise.

The result has been a highly questioned, but more consolidated EU. And in order to achieve that European reassurance, the European stance on criminal law has played a particular role. A quick look at the period 2011–2013 shows that the communications of EU institutions regarding criminal law have a distinctive expressive function. In a way, the current approach of the EU institutions to criminal law has reaffirmed the political identity of the EU itself.[17] To put it differently, the fact that the existence of the EU has been questioned has resulted in a reassuring message from the EU institutions.

With all this in mind, it is time now to unfold some of the basic propositions of this book. For years, the federal dimension of EU criminal law has been neglected. This was probably due to the natural rejection of federalism in the EU and to the conceptual association of "European federal criminal law" with the establishment of European courts with European prosecutors enforcing a European penal code.[18] Denial of such a "European federal criminal law" has prevented the recognition of the existence of a well-established horizontal federalism in the area of EU criminal law. Moreover, horizontal federalism in the EU system of criminal justice by far exceeds the degree of horizontal federalism in the US system of criminal justice. In short, European (horizontal) federal criminal law is a reality today.

The sovereign debt crisis has reinforced the federal dimension (both vertical and horizontal) of EU criminal law. The relevance of distinct federal, i.e. European, interests, e.g. the EU budget, has become self-evident. So has the need for the EU to provide as much *direct* protection as possible and not rely on the *indirect* protection dispensed by Member States[19] – even if such protection is harmonized throughout the EU. As the crisis momentum wanes, the possibility of establishing a supranational structure of criminal law diminishes. Yet in order

---

probably not restore the confidence of the financial markets. A strong determination towards unification seems the only way to clearly signal that the EU is a "safe bet" for investors.

17 Some authors, prior to the sovereign debt crisis, already argued that the "European Union has used its powers to criminalize not only to address practical needs, but also to reaffirm its core values and strengthen its political identity" (see Jenia Iontcheva Turner, *The Expressive Dimension of EU Criminal Law*, American Journal of Comparative Law 60 (2012) at 555 noting that "one must look to the expressive value of criminal law to fully understand the EU's motivation to act").

18 This was possibly the idea behind the position of Mr Abbot at the Meeting on 25 September 2002 within the working group "Freedom, Security and Justice" at the European Convention: he "preferred mutual recognition (accompanied by harmonisation in procedures) as the right way forward and was not convinced by the need to set up a 'European Federal criminal law'" (CONV 313/02).

19 "The present situation, in which the prosecution of offences against the Union's financial interests is exclusively in the hands of the authorities of the Member States is not satisfactory and does not sufficiently achieve the objective of fighting effectively against offences affecting the Union Budget": Proposal for a Council Regulation on the establishment of the European Public Prosecutor's Office COM (2013) 534 final at 4.

to avert some of the daunting problems experienced by the EU and the Member States in the field of criminal law, greater vertical federalism (in reduced areas) with less horizontal federalism (in many areas) should be seriously considered – and for this we advocate.

The tension between vertical and horizontal federalism through the sovereign debt crisis has been marvelously described by one of the greatest philosophers of our time: *Jürgen Habermas*. In his well-known essay *The Crisis of the European Union: A response* he clearly stated: "The European Union must decide between transnational democracy and post-democratic executive federalism".[20] In his comparison with the constitutional federalizing moment in the United States of America, *Habermas* notes that "the European unification, unlike the American, does not find itself at the beginning of experimentation with forms of federation under conditions of the modern system states".[21] The same statement holds true for European federal criminal law. The EU has already developed a system for protecting the Union's financial interests and handling serious cross-border criminality, so it cannot address these issues from scratch. Yet, as a consequence of the crisis, it is time reconsider the approach taken so far, and contemplate the possibility of enabling greater national diversity in some areas while affirming the Union's sovereignty in directly protecting its own interests.

1. WHY THE COMPARISON WITH THE US SYSTEM OF FEDERAL CRIMINAL LAW?

Servata distantia the US system of federal criminal law could shed some light on the best approach to the problems faced currently by the EU.[22] This book is filled with references to the discussion and background of American federal criminal law.[23] There are essentially two reasons for this comparison with the US system of federal criminal law, and not with other federal systems. First, because, as some authors have correctly noted, "the United States has long been a source

---

20 Jürgen Habermas, *The Crisis of the European Union: A response*, 2012, at 12–53.

21 Ibid.

22 For a previous approach see Carlos Gómez-Jara Díez, *Constitución Europea y Derecho penal: ¿Hacia un Derecho penal federal europeo?*, in Silvina Bacigalupo Sagesse and Manuel Cancio Meliá, *Derecho Penal y Política Transnacional*, 2005, at 153; Carlos Gómez-Jara Díez, *Y a-t-il du fédéralisme juridique pénal dans la Constitution européenne?*, in Nieto Martín, Arroyo Zapatero and Muñoz de Morales Romero, *European Criminal Law: An Overview*, 2010, at 81; Carlos Gómez-Jara Díez, *Models for a European System of Criminal Law*, New Journal of European Criminal Law (2010) at 385; Carlos Gómez-Jara Díez, *European Federal Criminal Law: What Can Europe Learn from the US System of federal criminal law to solve its debt crisis*, European Criminal Law Review 3 (2013) at 170.

23 A similar approach, limited to Europol, in Alexandra De Moor and Geert Vermeulen, *Shaping the Competence of Europol*, Topical Issues in EU and International Crime Control (2010) at 63; Jenia Iontcheva Turner, *Interstate Conflict and Cooperation in Criminal Cases: An American Perspective*, European Criminal Law Review 3 (2014) at 114.

of influence and inspiration to the developing federal system in the European Union."[24] Second, because the EU institutions are paying increasing attention to the US system of criminal law when shaping the European policy on criminal law.[25]

This approach serves, again, two purposes. First, it may prevent in Europe the same mistakes that were (and are) made in the US system. At the same time, it may encourage adoption of the institutions and structure that have proven beneficial for the American system. The similarities between the problems faced by the US and the EU in the field of criminal law are worth noting. Both systems must determine how to protect the Unions' budget and how to combat cross-border criminal activity among the states. It is also worth highlighting the similar historical contexts leading both Unions to become aware of these problems. Just as the US Attorney General's Office and the first federal criminal law provisions were adopted in the aftermath of a existence threatening economic crisis in the late 18th century, the European Public Prosecutor's Office and the first criminal provisions protecting the EU budget are being proposed in the aftermath of the EU sovereign debt crisis.

Many academics may believe that the US system of federal criminal law has remained stable for centuries and that there has been no collision between state sovereignty and the Union's government. This is certainly not the case. Federal government's interference with state matters has been constant and power struggles between the Union and the states in the concrete area of criminal law have been abundant. While the tension did not emerge through the 19th century it certainly became palpable in the 20th century. The US Supreme Court provided some important limits to crime federalization, but in the turn of the 21st century it went back to business as usual.

Looking at history in the wake of financial crises both in the US and the EU, the US experience in the late 18th century provides a vivid parallel to the current European experience. After the American war for independence was over, the states were heavily indebted and the lack of a strong national central government threatened to disintegrate the fragile union.[26] The states (not the Union)

---

24 Alex Mills, *Federalism in the European Union and the United States: Subsidiarity, Private Law and the Conflict of Laws*, University of Pennsylvania Journal of International Law 32 (2010) at 369; For general US/EU comparison in terms of federalism see Anand Menon and Martin Schain, eds., *Comparative Federalism: The European Union and the United States in Comparative Perspective*, 2006; Elke Cloots, Geert De Baere and Stefan Sottiaux, eds., *Federalism in the European Union*, 2012.

25 See the Directorate General for International Policies Report, *Harmonization of criminal law in the EU: A special focus on the US judicial system*, 2010 (available at: www.europarl.europa.eu/committees/en/studiesdownload.html?languageDocument=EN&file=30499).

26 Federal Reserve Bank of Philadelphia, *The First Bank of the United States. A Chapter in the History of Central Banking*, 2009, at 1. The new nation's leaders had their work cut out for them: re-establishing commerce and industry, repaying war debt, restoring the value of the currency, and lowering inflation.

collectively owed about US$25 million. Alexander Hamilton suggested that the federal government assume the states' war debts. He felt that this consolidation of state and federal debt would give investors who held that debt a reason to support the federal government.[27] This led to the creation of the First National Bank of the United States, funded by US$10 million through an IPO directed primarily at private investors.

In the current European situation, the European Central Bank is already in place. Although it is funded by the EU Member States,[28] and the Eurobond solution[29] issued by the ECB itself does not seem to be a clear option right now, the crux of the matter from a criminal law perspective is the perceived need to provide EU protection for the Union's budget. Again, the historical resemblance should give pause to rethink a better approach. The US legislation that accompanied the national bank solution was the trigger for the early development of (vertical) federal criminal law. In 1798,[30] Congress passed the first penal legislation designed to protect the financial interests of the Union's Bank.

If the EU is to take similar measures regarding a fiscal Union with an interest in preserving Europe's financial health, then it follows that similar criminal legislation should be enacted to protect EU financial interests. Surely, the EU may continue to insist in its horizontal federalism approach forcing Member States to protect the EU's financial interests as if they were their own. But the EU could also start building the necessary European institutions to provide effective EU direct protection of such interests. The proposal for establishing a European Public Prosecutor's Office is a step forward that should be accompanied by other measures with an emphasis on the vertical not the horizontal dimension.

In this sense, in 2010 the Directorate General for Internal Policies at the European Parliament published an interesting study: "Harmonization of criminal law in the EU: A special focus on the US judicial system".[31] When addressing the

---

27 It goes without saying that many prominent figures of the American democracy were against Hamilton's solution. Thomas Jefferson, for one, was afraid that a fiscal union would create a financial monopoly that would undermine state banks, and that the solution was unconstitutional. James Madison was also against it noting that it was an affront to states' rights and would make the states too subservient to the new federal government, Federal Reserve Bank of Philadelphia, *The First Bank of the United States. A Chapter in the History of Central Banking*, 2009, at 3.

28 See the interesting analysis of Paul De Grauwe, *The European Central Bank: Lender of Last Resort in the Government Bond Markets?*, CESifo Working Paper No. 3569 (2011).

29 See Kenneth Matziorinis, *Is the 'Euro Bond' the Answer to the Euro Sovereign Debt Crisis? What Outcome can Investors Expect out of Europe?*, 2011 (available at: http://ssrn.com/abstract=1999518) suggesting that pooling fiscal risks, creating an EU Treasury and issuing jointly-backed Eurobonds is an optimal solution and the inevitable conclusion of the economic integration project in Europe.

30 Act of 27 June 1798, 1 Stat. 573. Chap. LXI. An Act to punish frauds committed on the Bank of the United States. The first federal criminal statute was signed into law on 30 April 1790.

31 Available at: www.europarl.europa.eu/committees/en/studiesdownload.html?languageDocument=EN&file=30499.

question of whether the US federal system could inspire the EU, the study arrived at the following conclusions:[32]

- Setting aside the fundamental difference in political nature of the USA and the EU, the question of common criminal rules and a common judicial process exists in both Unions.
- Some criteria could be proposed at an EU level to determine the moment when harmonization could occur. The question of a definition of serious crime might be difficult to solve but should not, in any case, be limited to the list proposed by Article 83 of the Lisbon Treaty.
- Under certain conditions, some criteria could also be set to limit the increasing number of conflicts of jurisdiction.
- In order to enhance implementation of EU criminal law, first instance and appellate national jurisdiction should be evaluated and strengthened. Another possibility could be to create European Regional Courts of Appeal.

This book shares some of those key findings, but, perhaps more importantly, it inquires further into some key institutions for both systems. By avoiding the federal dimension of EU criminal law, nothing but political correctness is achieved. The importance of being conscious of the federalizing elements in the current EU system of criminal justice cannot be stressed enough. Such awareness would enable a broader discussion: given that federalism is already present in the basic structure of the EU, should greater emphasis be placed on vertical or horizontal federalism? Should the EU alleviate the pressure exerted through horizontal federalism (enabling national diversity) and establish in exchange a vertical system of European criminal law for the protection of the Union's financial interests?

2. SOME NOTES ON AMERICAN FEDERALISM

As noted before, there are many studies comparing US federalism with EU federalism.[33] It would certainly go beyond the scope of this book to review the fundamental principles of US federalism and to analyze the current structure of the EU. For the purposes of what will be argued throughout the following pages, it suffices to note that the American federal system basically consists of four

[32] Ibid. at 24.

[33] For relevant comparisons between US federalism and EU federalism see Robert Schütze, *From Dual to Cooperative Federalism: The Changing Structure of European Law*, 2009 with further references; Anand Menon and Martin Schain, eds., *Comparative Federalism: The European Union and the United States in Comparative Perspective*, 2007; Alex Mills, *Federalism in the European Union and the United States: Subsidiarity, Private Law and the Conflict of Laws*, University of Pennsylvania Journal of International Law 32 (2010) at 369.

components: (1) state sovereignty and constitutional limitations on state power; (2) federal powers; (3) the relationship between the federal government and the states; and (4) the relationship between the states. In order to better understand the basic functioning of the American federal system, we may synthesize three basic propositions underlying the system. It goes without saying that it would be impossible to condense the richness and idiosyncrasy of such a long-standing system. But for the purposes of this book, it is worth articulating some basic tenets that will provide the necessary perspective when addressing some of the later issues.

First is the matter of state sovereignty. The American federal system grew out of the states, and thus state sovereignty is a given in the American constitutional system. The states do not depend on the federal Constitution as a source of sovereignty. The states exercise full sovereignty over domestic matters to the extent that such exercise is not prohibited or restricted by the Constitution. In terms of allocation of power, the Constitution restricts state sovereignty over domestic matters in three ways. First, it provides that certain powers, very few in number, are exclusively federal powers and cannot be exercised by the states or can only be exercised by the states with the consent of Congress. Second, under the Supremacy Clause there is federal supremacy in the event of a conflict between federal and state power, thus giving Congress the power to preempt state regulation over particular issues or areas of activity. Third, the US Supreme Court has held that the affirmative grant of the commerce power to Congress has a negative or dormant implication, prohibiting certain state actions affecting interstate commerce. Subject only to these limitations, the American states have plenary power over all activity within their jurisdiction.

The second proposition of American federalism deals with concurrent power in domestic matters. Although American constitutional theory holds that the powers of the federal government are limited to those enumerated in the Constitution, the supposedly "limited" powers have been construed very broadly by the Supreme Court – particularly the power of Congress over interstate and foreign commerce. The effect is that, with few exceptions, virtually any activity is subject to congressional regulation. The expansive interpretation of federal power combined with state sovereignty results in a system where both the states and Congress have enormous regulatory power and can usually regulate the same activity. Thus, it seems that the dominant feature of the American federal system as regards domestic matters is concurrent power.

The third proposition is that the states form a national union. The provisions of Article IV, Section 1 of the American Constitution, dealing with full faith and credit to judgments and public acts of sister states, and Article IV, Section 2, dealing with privileges and immunities of the citizens of sister states and interstate rendition, are specifically directed toward the end of constituting the citizens of the United States as one people. Here the role of horizontal federalism becomes paramount.

As an interesting final note, the Tenth Amendment to the Constitution (passed in 1791), was intended to limit the powers granted Congress in Article I[34] and therefore to limit the legislative authority of the federal government in favor of the states.[35] In other words, the Tenth Amendment means that Congress cannot force a state to pass any regulations or legislation. This has been the consistent interpretation of the US Supreme Court.[36] The so-called anti-commandeering doctrine implies that federal statutes cannot compel state legislatures or executives "to enact or enforce a federal regulatory program".[37] Of course, Congress may use lots of incentives[38] which in effect leave states with little choice, but US Supreme Court cases seem to indicate that the Court would actually prohibit Congress from acting as forcefully as the EU is able to in coercing states to enact laws.

3. STRUCTURE OF THIS BOOK

Chapter 1 initially reviews the situation prior to the Lisbon Treaty. It begins with a well-known distinction in the field of EU criminal law: European versus Europeanized (Euro-harmonized) criminal law. "European law" describes what would be a genuine system of European federal criminal law. Europeanized or Euro-harmonized law refers to the effects that EU law (in a broad sense) has over the national criminal laws of the EU Member States. From a law enforcement point of view, there is no European criminal law, i.e. offenses in EU legislation prosecuted by EU institution before EU courts. However, from an academic and policy perspective it appears the EU is adopting criminal law policies that are more federal in nature. The academic world is also increasingly specialized in developing concepts of criminal law institutions that spill over national jurisdictions. The

[34] "Powers not delegated to the United States by the Constitution, nor prohibited by it to the States, are reserved to the States respectively, or to the people".

[35] For a thorough reconstruction of the Tenth Amendment see Kurt T. Lash, *James Madison's Celebrated Report of 1800: The Transformation of the Tenth Amendment*, George Washington Law Review 74 (2006) at 165 (supporting that "Founders like James Madison viewed the Ninth Amendment, not the Tenth, as a rule limiting the construction of federal power" (at 168)).

[36] See the relevant cases *NY v. US*, 505 U.S. 144 (1992), *Printz v. US*, 521 U.S. 898 (1997). A summary of both in the following lines: "We held in *New York* that Congress cannot compel the States to enact or enforce a federal regulatory program. Today we hold that Congress cannot circumvent that prohibition by conscripting the State's officers directly. The Federal Government may neither issue directives requiring the States to address particular problems, nor command the States' officers, or those of their political subdivisions, to administer or enforce a federal regulatory program" (*Printz*, 521 U.S. 898 (1997) at 935).

[37] *Printz v. United States*, 521 U.S. 898, 935 (1997). For an early discussion following this case see Evan H. Caminker, *State Sovereignty and the Limits of Formalism*, Supreme Court Review (1997) at 199; Evan H. Caminker, *State Sovereignty and Subordinacy: May Congress Commandeer State Officers to Implement Federal Law?*, Columbia Law Review 95 (1995) at 1001, 1023; Vicki C. Jackson, *Federalism and the Uses and Limits of Law: Printz and Principle*, Harvard Law Review 111 (1997) at 2180.

[38] See a clear example in Joseph F. Zimmerman, *Congress and Crime: The Impact of Federalization of State Criminal Laws*, 2013, at 73.

similarities in this regard with the federal criminal law discussion in the US system are noted. Finally, the chapter analyzes the principle that has guided the development of EU criminal law: the principle of mutual recognition. This principle, resembling the principle of "full faith and credit" in the US system, has been heavily criticized in the academic world and has triggered violent reactions by constitutional courts throughout the EU Member States.

The second chapter provides an in-depth analysis of the provisions of the Lisbon Treaty relating to the concept of European criminal law. The main authority to produce EU criminal legislation, Article 83 TFEU, is dealt with first. The concept of "serious cross-border criminality" as the basis for enacting EU legislation is compared to the Commerce Clause debate in the US system. The underlying forces in both cases have resulted in an overcriminalization of these systems in the same areas. Addressed next is the traditional area of federal criminal law: protection of truly federal interests. Worth noting is the fact that protection of EU funds and US funds is addressed in a separate provision of the founding legal structure of both Unions. Finally, the focus is shifted to an institution that plays (or could play) a decisive role in the federal criminal law of both systems: the federal prosecutor. Although not yet established as this book is written, the European Public Prosecutor's Office characterizes the federalization of European criminal law.

The third chapter addresses the question of how federal the current EU system is. While the impulse is to deny the federal nature of EU criminal law, the truth is that some EU institutions are more federal that their American counterparts. Beginning with the European Arrest Warrant and the double jeopardy provisions in the Schengen Treaty, Chapter 4 reviews the method of harmonization in the EU and the US. While harmonization in the EU through Directives is mandatory, harmonization in the US has been achieved voluntarily through the Model Penal Code. The EU rejection of a clear body of European federal criminal law results in a mandatory harmonization of national legislation that preempts Member States from introducing their national idiosyncrasies.

The fourth chapter focuses on the evolution of fundamental rights in both Unions. Interestingly, the concept of due process has served as an instrument to incorporate certain fundamental rights through the case law of top courts in the EU and the US. Also, the distinction between vertical and horizontal federalism plays a great role, as the approach of both Unions differs in certain key areas. The use of horizontal federalism instruments is becoming an active measure of the EU, while the US rarely resorts to such instruments for the same purposes.

Finally, the fifth chapter addresses the impact of the sovereign debt crisis on the federalization of EU criminal law. First comparing the different approaches by the EU and the US to the financial crisis, a quick review is made of the communications by the EU. Trust in the current system, where EU Member States protect EU funds, is no longer taken as given. The sovereign debt crisis has provoked a rapid succession of events that ultimately led to EU legislation proposing the establishment a European Public Prosecutor's Office to prosecute crimes against EU financial interests. The goal of such a blunt move seems to be to restore investor confidence in the EU. Finally, as the Proposal of a Regulation establishing the EPPO is heavily discussed throughout EU institutions and academic, some guidelines for the future are noted. The core argument is to potentiate vertical federal criminal law in the EU through the tools available in the Lisbon Treaty.

CHAPTER 1
THE EU CRIMINAL LAW SITUATION PRIOR TO THE LISBON TREATY

"We must re-create the European family in a regional structure called, it may be, the United States of Europe."
Winston Churchill, 1946

1. INTRODUCTION

The lack of a United States of Europe (*Winston Churchill*'s comment notwithstanding) has always made so much harder the task of conceptualizing a European criminal law. The current European model does not entail European criminal legislation enacted by a European Congress, enforced by European Agencies and applied by the European judiciary. The "European way" of criminal law has been much more complicated. A fear of losing too much sovereignty in an area that has traditionally been regarded as inherent to states' sovereignty always impeded proposals for establishing a genuine European criminal law. Also important, the repeatedly cited democratic deficit of EU institutions, especially Parliament/Congress, has posed additional constraints in the criminal law field which is in constant need of valid justification. Furthermore, the unwillingness of the Member States to support the construction of a European jurisdiction, even for areas that are traditionally closer to EU interests, raises concerns whenever a proposal is put forward.

Notwithstanding the strong resistance to a system of European criminal law, the relentless development of EU law in general has exerted an increasing influence over criminal law. As noted below, from a law-in-action perspective there is, so far, no genuine European criminal law but rather a harmonizing effect over the national criminal legislation and jurisprudence of the EU Member States. However, the aftermath of the sovereign debt crisis of 2010 instigated EU institutions to adopt a harsher approach to enforcement. The proposal of a Directive on the fight against fraud to the Union's financial interests by means of criminal law[1] and the Proposal for a Council Regulation on the establishment of the European Public Prosecutor's Office[2] are clear examples of the new approach.

From an academic and policy perspective, there are some key areas that respond better to the logic of European criminal law. The establishment of the principle of mutual recognition as the pillar of judicial cooperation in criminal matters has been a key development in this field. Nevertheless, as it will also be elaborated, there is a new tendency to go beyond mutual recognition, propelled by the dramatic events of the EU sovereign debt crisis and increased need to protect the EU's financial interests.

This chapter reflects on the policy and academic dimensions of European criminal law. As to the first, a comparison with the US federal system demonstrates a similar message in the communications and legislation of the EU and the US in criminal law matters. It is not by chance that the terms of "tough on crime" and "fight against criminality" are commonly used by both Unions. It is no further coincidence that both Unions' power to enact legislation in criminal matters has been questioned. In the academic field, a separate body of scholarship has similarly developed around the concept of the Unions' criminal law, with discussions in this field bearing strong resemblances. The overcriminalization debate around federal legislation is strikingly similar. The need for consistent concepts of the General Part of criminal law is commonly advocated on both sides of the Atlantic.

Finally, the chapter reviews the basic force fueling EU criminal law: the principle of mutual recognition. This principle triggered an array of EU legislation in the early 21st century and provoked strong antagonism by constitutional courts throughout the EU Member States. As the first attempts to produce a consistent body of European criminal law in the late 20th century failed, the strategy of the EU dramatically changed. From protecting truly EU interests, the focus shifted to cooperation in criminal matters. As detailed in later chapters, the sovereign debt crisis has refocused the goals of the EU, and a movement back to the earlier focus on truly European law can be clearly perceived. The proposed European Public Prosecutor's Office with enforcement power over crimes against the EU financial interests clearly signals that the EU is determined to protect itself against conduct that harms its own interests.

---

1. Proposal for a Directive of the European Parliament and of the Council on the fight against fraud to the Union's financial interests by means of criminal law, COM (2012) 363 final.
2. Proposal for a Council Regulation on the establishment of the European Public Prosecutor's Office COM (2013) 534 final.

2. PRELIMINARY ISSUES

2.1. VERTICAL AND HORIZONTAL FEDERALISM IN BOTH UNIONS

Although the natural reluctance to acknowledge the federal dimension of the EU is fading over time,[3] there is still a strong opposition, especially on the political side, to consider that we are anywhere near a "United States of Europe".[4] Yet even the strongest opponents of a federal Europe will agree that both the EU and US are a Union of states. Therefore, throughout this book we will repeatedly use the undisputed term "Union", i.e. European *Union* and *United* States of America, to refer to the political entity producing and enforcing criminal legislation.

When discussing the federal dimension of EU criminal law, the first concept that comes to mind a European criminal code, enforced by European authorities according to certain European federal rules of criminal procedure before a European court. Of course, this is not the current situation in the EU. As powerful as it seems, even this perspective would fail to address the full federal dimension of criminal law. In this sense it is worth distinguishing between vertical[5] and horizontal federalism.[6] Many federal systems allocate sovereign power between governments along two dimensions:[7] a vertical plane that establishes a hierarchy and boundaries between federal and state authority and a horizontal plane that attempts to coordinate coequal states that must peaceably coexist. Both vertical and horizontal federalism are fundamental elements of the system. As *Erbsen* words it for the US discussion: "The Supremacy Clause makes federal/state interactions hierarchical – and thus in a sense 'vertical' – while state/state interactions are between entities on an equal plane of constitutional status, and are thus 'horizontal'. This taxonomy of vertical and horizontal federalism does not exist in Supreme Court decisions, and has only recently started to appear prominently in legal scholarship. Nevertheless, the distinction provides a helpful framework for conceptualizing recurring constitutional dilemmas"[8] – we might

---

3 See below Chapter 2.

4 See below Chapter 2.

5 For examples of the many broad approaches to vertical federalism, see Erwin Chemerinsky, *Enhancing Government: Federalism for the 21st Century*, 2008; David L. Shapiro, *Federalism: A Dialogue*, 1995; Akhil Reed Amar, *Of Sovereignty and Federalism*, Yale L.J. 96 (1987) at 1425.

6 See Joseph F. Zimmerman, *Horizontal Federalism. Interstate Relations*, 2011.

7 As Daniel Halberstam, *Comparative Federalism and the Role of the Judiciary*, in Keith Whittington, Daniel Kelemen and Gregory Caldeira, eds., *The Oxford Handbook of Law and Politics*, 2008: "Federalism means the co-existence within a single polity of multiple levels of government each with constitutionally grounded claims to some degree of organizational autonomy and jurisdictional authority".

8 Allan Erbsen, *Horizontal Federalism*, Minnesota L. Rev. 93 (2008) at 493, 501–502 with further references to the US Supreme Court decisions and academic literature.

add: and a helpful framework for conceptualizing recurring EU criminal law dilemmas.

Against this conceptual framework, the notion of European authorities enforcing a European criminal code before European courts refers only to vertical federalism, failing to address horizontal federalism. However, this other dimension of federalism, i.e. horizontal federalism, seems to be equally significant.[9] As some prominent US scholars have recently noted,[10] the literature focusing on the politics of interstate relations is sparse and typically old in the American discussion. As for the EU, the longstanding reluctance to use the word "federal" in the European discussion has resulted in academic neglect per se of the existence of federalizing elements in the EU configuration. It is rarely acknowledged that some aspects of the EU bear strong resemblances to their US counterparts.

Yet if we examine some salient features of what is termed horizontal federalism in the US discussion, similarities become apparent. Notably, dual sovereignty is a central characteristic of the US federal system and involves powers exercisable by Congress and state legislatures. The latter may use these concurrent powers and other reserved powers to cooperate with each other or to regulate national problems. The division of political power in a federal system between the national government and the states automatically produces relations between the latter. As *Zimmerman* puts it, "these relations may be cooperative as manifested by interstate compacts, uniform state laws or reciprocity statutes".[11]

A quick review of certain basic principles of horizontal federalism in the US shows that institutions such as the Full Faith and Credit Clause,[12] Interstate Rendition[13] and Uniform State Law[14] mirror the rationale of the Principle of Mutual Recognition, European Arrest Warrant and harmonization of criminal law. Moreover, as shown later, the development of horizontal federalism in the EU has increased exponentially in the past years. EU horizontal federalism in criminal law largely stems from the existence of a supranational authority forcing Member States of the Union to implement the Union's legislation in their national criminal codes and acknowledging other Member States rulings as binding in

---

9 Allan Erbsen, *Horizontal Federalism*, Minnesota L. Rev. 93 (2008) at 493; Gillian E. Metzger, *Congress, Article IV, and Interstate Relations*, Harvard L. Rev. 120 (2007) at 1468.

10 Joseph F. Zimmerman, *Horizontal Federalism. Interstate Relations*, 2011, at ix; Joseph F. Zimmerman, *Interstate Relations. The Neglected Dimension of Federalism*, 2006, at vii.

11 Joseph F. Zimmermann, *Horizontal Federalism. Interstate Relations*, 2011, at 1. See also below Chapter 3, section 4.3.

12 Ibid. at 63–87. See also below Chapter 1, section 6.3.

13 Ibid. at 103–117. See also below Chapter 3, section 2.3.

14 As Joseph F. Zimmermann, ibid. at ix notes: "The lack of uniform states statutes and administrative rules and regulations on a wide variety of subjects creates serious problems for citizens travelling to sister states and for multistate and multinational corporations. Organized state efforts have been made since 1892 to harmonize diverse state regulatory laws in the form of uniform state laws". This statement seems perfectly valid for the EU a hundred years later.

their national systems. In its most forceful application, horizontal federalism deals with the power of the Union to force interstate cooperation.

At this point it is worth advancing one of the fundamental theses of this book: in our view, the EU has a low level of vertical federal criminal law, but has achieved a high level of horizontal criminal law, even higher than in the US system of criminal justice. The EU exerts greater influence over the national authorities (legislative, executive and judiciary) than its US counterpart. On the other hand, the US exerts greater influence over its citizens than the EU. Our proposal, reiterated throughout this book, is to soften some of the pressure by the EU over the Member States by allowing direct regulation of EU citizens. This in turn will actually enable national diversity while still granting the EU the power to protect its own interests.

Regardless of the level of acceptance that such statements may have, some minimal agreement may be reached over the following. The federal dimension of the EU has been gaining momentum over the past decade. The number of studies noting federal elements in the nature of the EU has been increasingly significantly. At least some attention should be paid to the consequences of such federalizing findings for the area of criminal law. As *Schütze* put it recently: "European constitutionalism is gradually unlocking itself from [the] dead end. The 'renaissance' of the federal principle and the idea of a "Federation of States", allows us to analyze the European Union in federal terms and, finally, to ask what sort of federation the European Union is".[15] The conclusion seems clear: there is "dual government, dual sovereignty, and also dual citizenship".[16] In the collective work *Federalism in the European Union*, the editors explain: "The EU is sometimes qualified as a federal system".[17] The essays contained in that volume provide a fair assessment of the situation so far.[18]

Following *Schütze*'s contention, it pays to paraphrase his words and note that the renaissance of the federal principle allows us to analyze EU criminal law in federal terms and ask what sort of European federal criminal law is already in place. The result -already noted – is that the EU has a functioning system of horizontal federal criminal law. And moreover, that the degree of horizontal federalism achieve in the area of criminal in the EU is greater than the degree of horizontal federalism in the US. To be sure, the greater level of horizontal federalism in the EU than in the US, at least in the criminal law field, can be seen

15 Robert Schütze, *From Dual to Cooperative Federalism: The Changing Structure of European Law*, 2009, at 4.

16 Ibid. at 29.

17 Elke Cloots, Geert De Baere and Stefan Sottiaux, *Federalism in the European Union*, 2012.

18 On a more political note it is not a matter of providence that the "European federalist party" – which advocates for further integration of the European Union through the establishment of a democratic and federal Europe – was launched in Paris on 6 November 2011. Although they failed to secure a seat in the European Parliament election of 2014 it certainly provides an interesting movement towards clear federalization of the EU.

in a number of areas. Advancing some of the results of our investigation, here are some examples. The ability of the EU to force Member States to acknowledge other EU Member States' criminal law rulings as binding with their full force and to force Member States to harmonize their penal national legislation according to EU legislation are clear examples EU power over national governments. And this federal dimension has increased as a consequence of the 2010 sovereign debt financial crisis.

2.2. EU CRIMINAL LAW, EUROPEANIZED CRIMINAL LAW AND EUROPEAN CRIMINAL LAW: *ANTE PORTAS* OR *INTRA MUROS*?

A quick look at the EU discussion concerning criminal law – especially in the German influenced area – reveals that the terms EU criminal law, Europeanized criminal law and European criminal law have distinct meanings. First, using a distinction coined by *Satzger*,[19] "Europeanized criminal law" refers to the influence of common European Union law on the national criminal law of each Member State.[20] On the other hand, "European criminal law" normally refers to those elements of criminal law that are part of the common European Union law and which have a direct impact and application on the Member States. Against this backdrop, "EU criminal law" would serve as a concept encompassing both Europeanized criminal law and European criminal law.

The opposing terms – *ante portas* versus *intra muros* – have been used to characterize the debate around whether the *Europeanization* of criminal law and the creation of a truly *European* criminal law are phenomena that are about to happen (*ante portas*) or already exist (*intra muros*).[21] With respect to the Europeanization of criminal law, the perspective *intra muros* generally prevails among scholars over *ante portas*. However, with regard to the existence of a true European criminal law, the situation seems to be the opposite.[22] We use the term

---

19 See Helmut Satzger, *Die Europäisierung des Strafrechts*, 2001, at 8, 57–67. See also Prittwitz, ZStW 113 (2001) at 788–789; Nelles, ZStW 109 (1997) at 739; Ulrich Sieber, *Europäische Einigung und Europäisches Strafrecht*, 1993, at 12; Zabel, *Die Bedeutung der freiheitsgesetzlichen Prämissen rechtlicher Konfliktbewältigung für die Konzeption eines Strafrechts in Europa*, KritV (2003) at 363.

20 This is therefore a clear example of the so-called "interlegality". This concept has been applied mainly in the field of private law. See among many Robert Wai, *The Interlegality of Transnational Private Law*, Law and Contemporary Problems 71 (2008) at 107, but it should be equally applicable to the field of public (criminal) law.

21 See generally Bernd Schünemann, *Ein Gespent geht um Europa – Brüsseler "Strafrechtspflege" intra muros*, Goltdammer's Archiv (2002) at 510; Lorenz Schulz, *Europäisches Strafrecht ante portas – Tagungsbericht*, Strafverteidiger 11 (2001) at 85.

22 See Helmut Deutscher, *Die Kompetenz der Europäischen Gemeinschaften zur originären Strafgesetzgebung*, 2000, at 345–350; Bernd Hecker, *Strafbare Produktwerbung im Licht des Gemeinschaftsrechts*, 2001, at 2; Thomas Weigend, *Spricht Europa mit zwei Zungen?*, Strafverteidiger (2001) at 63.

"seems", because recent developments suggest that the establishment of a truly European criminal law may already be underway.

In any event, the dichotomy between *ante portas* and *intra muros* is largely based on a formal, regulatory viewpoint that refers to the current law on the books.[23] If from this perspective Europeanized criminal law is seen as an already consolidated and growing reality while European criminal law is still a future phenomenon, other perspectives, such as a policy or academic viewpoint, may view both as *intra muros* phenomena. Of course, the addition of the purely legislative perspective to the other two would strengthen this conclusion. As a consequence, it is worth paying attention to these two perspectives – the European criminal policy and the European scholarship – to better understand the current state of affairs. Here we can initially observe to what degree European criminal law has developed and, what legal trends can be seen in the Lisbon Treaty text and in recent developments.

2.3. CONCLUSION

The distinction between Europeanized criminal law and European criminal law coined by German academics nicely dovetails with the distinction between vertical and horizontal federalism. While the degree of horizontal federalism, i.e. Europeanized criminal law, is extremely acute in the EU, there is a deficit of vertical federalism, i.e. European criminal law. From a federal perspective, vertical federalism would be *ante portas* and horizontal federalism would be *intra muros*. Yet, as the discussion regarding crime policy and criminal law scholarship will reveal, certain aspects of EU horizontal federalism are common to the US vertical federalism discussion.

4. CRIME POLICY

4.1. INTRODUCTION

The purpose of this section is to show the strong resemblance between some elements of the so-called European criminal policy and corresponding elements of US federal criminal policy. Two main features are present in the approach of

---

23 From a technical point of view, harmonization is meant to be a reduction of the more serious differences between national provisions. But, contrary to unification, it does not set real common rules. See MIREILLE DELMAS-MARTY, *Introduction*, in MIREILLE DELMAS-MARTY and JOHN VERVALE, eds., *The Implementation of the Corpus Juris in the Member States: Penal Provisions for the Protection of the European Finances*, Vol. I, 2000, at 29. The harmonization process is imbedded in the Lisbon Treaty when reference is made to "minimum rules" in Articles 82(2) and 83(1) and (2). These minimum rules contain a description of the punishable conduct and the basic sanctioning range that should be applied in the Member States.

both Unions to criminal law. First, the mantra of "tough of crime" and the use of military terminology, like a "fight" or "war" against criminality, can be found in both systems. Second, the expansive nature of the Unions' legislation, criticized as overcriminalization, is apparent. The more time passes, the more both Unions see themselves fit to regulate criminal offenses, regardless of state considerations.

Admittedly, both of these features may be seen in modern criminal policy around the world. However, there is a distinct commonality in the way the EU and the US fall into this current trend. The cross-border dimension, be it transnational or interstate, of today's criminality paves the way for both Unions to expand the realm of matters appropriate for federal legislation. Put otherwise, regardless of toughness of state enforcement, the Unions perceive a missing link that goes unattended: the cross-border dimension. Given the lack of authority of the national states to regulate such dimension, the Unions see fit to intervene.

4.2. EUROPEAN CRIMINAL POLICY

As *Vogel* noted, "a European crime policy has been in place for many years".[24] This should not come as a complete surprise, given the fact that more transnational[25] – in this case, more European – crime creates a greater need to confront crime in a transnational – or European – way. Three basic EU criminal policies were identified by *Vogel*. The first is *judicial cooperation* and coordination, mainly conducted through the office of Eurojust.[26] Second is *police cooperation*, achieved through and leading to the strengthening of Europol.[27]

24 Joachim Vogel, *Europäische Kriminalpolitik – europäische Strafrechtsdogmatik*, Goltdammer's Archiv (2002) at 517.

25 On transnational or cross-border criminality see Petrus C. van Duyne, Vincenzo Ruggiero, Miroslav Scheinost and Wim Valkenburg, *Cross-border Crime in a Changing Europe*, 2001; Frank Zieschang, Eric Hilgendorf and Klaus Laubenthal, *Strafrecht und Kriminalität in Europa*, 2003; Petrus C. van Duyne, Georgios A. Antonopoulos, Almir Maljevic, Jackie Harvey, Tom Vander Beken and Klaus von Lamp, *Cross-border crime inroads on integrity in Europe*, 2010.

26 Regarding Eurojust see the Council Decision setting up Eurojust with a view to reinforcing the fight against serious crime, 2002/187/JHA (amended by Council Decision 2003/659/JHA and Council Decision 2009/426/JHA). For a general overview see Madalina Busuioc and Martijn Groenleer, *Beyond design: the evolution of Europol and Eurojust*, Perspectives on European Politics and Society 14 (2013) at 285–304. For harsh criticism see Peter Alexis Albrecht and Stephan Braum, *Deficiencies in the development of European Criminal Law*, European L.J. 5 (1999) at 293–310; Bernd Schünemann, *Grundzüge eines Alternativ-Entwurfs zur europäischen Strafverfolgung*, ZStW 116 (2004) at 387–390; Thomas Weigend, *Der Entwurf einer Europäischen Verfassung und das Strafrecht*, ZStW 116 (2004) at 298. In the area of environmental crime see the recent Council of the European Union's *Report of the Strategic Meeting towards an enhanced coordination of environmental crime prosecutions across the EU: The role of Eurojust*, Brussels, 24 March 2014, 8101/14.

27 See generally Council Decision establishing the European Police Office (Europol), 6 April 2009, 2009/371/JHA; Madalina Busuioc and Martijn Groenleer, *Beyond design: the evolution of Europol and Eurojust*, Perspectives on European Politics and Society 14 (2013) at 285–304 (noting that "Europol has been a highly controversial body from the very beginning, for

Third, there is *legislative cooperation*, operated through the harmonization of criminal law, both substantive and procedural. Interestingly, it should be noted that although the first two criminal policies have been part of what was termed the Third Pillar (cooperation among states) of the EU, the latter touched upon certain elements belonging to the First Pillar (EU powers). Nevertheless, in the current configuration of the Lisbon Treaty, the three Pillars are grouped under the common umbrella of the *Area of Freedom, Security and Justice.*

From a crime policy perspective, *Vogel* has pointed out three fundamental problems faced by future EU criminal law.[28] First, the well-known problem revolving around the democratic legitimacy of a potential European criminal law. The second issue deals with the constitutional and legal control of such European criminal law. Thirdly, there is the question of the limits of European criminal law. Although these are far from the only issues in European criminal policy, it is worth taking a moment to elaborate on these three under the influence of the Lisbon Treaty.

The democratic legitimacy question has been a constant problem in the creation of a European criminal law. As referred to throughout this book, the criminal law traditions of the Member States closely link criminal law to national parliaments, and hence to their Member States' sovereignty.[29] Given the scant participation of the European Parliament in the legislative process of the European Union and the impossibility of considering the European Union as a European state, the legitimacy of proposed European criminal law was harder to accept. However, the fact that the Lisbon Treaty establishes a representative and participative democracy that has the European Parliament actively participate in the ordinary legislative procedure softens, to some extent, part of the criticism.[30] As was noted before, while the European Union is not a federal state in a traditional

instance labelled as an 'unaccountable European FBI'"); FLORIN COMAN-KUND, *EU Agencies as Global Actors: A Legal Assessment of Europol's International Dimension*, Maastricht Faculty of Law Working Paper No. 2014/6 (available at: http://ssrn.com/abstract=2506568) arguing that "under the principle of institutional balance and the present-day Meroni requirements there is room for Europol and EU agencies in general to develop an international dimension". For general background see MARIA FLETCHER, ROBIN LÖÖF and BILL GILMORE, *EU Criminal Law and Justice*, 2008, at 77–80 and the contributions contained in SABINE GLESS, RAINER GROTE and GÜNTER HEINE, *Justizielle Einbindung und Kontrolle von Europol*, 2001.

28 JOACHIM VOGEL, *Europäische Kriminalpolitik - europäische Strafrechtsdogmatik*, GOLTDAMMER'S ARCHIV 517 (2002) at 525.

29 On the problematic issue of sovereignty see NINA PERSAK, ed., *Legitimacy and Trust in Criminal Law, Policy and Justice: Norms, Procedures, Outcomes*, 2014, for further references.

30 As CHRISTIAN CALLIESS, *Die neue Europäische Union nach dem Vertrag von Lissabon*, 2010, at 71 notes the Lisbon Treaty currently in effect supports the thesis that sovereignty is "shared" between the citizens and the states (coinciding JÜRGEN HABERMAS, *The Crisis of the European Union: A response*, 2012 at 34–35). But see the opposing view of KAIAFA-GBANDI, *Europäisches Strafrecht - Die Perspektive des Grundrechtsschutzes nach dem Verfassungsentwurf für Europa*, 14 KRITV (2004) at 19 (considering that such participation is not enough to amend the democratic deficit). See also BERND SCHÜNEMANN, *Grundzüge eines Alternativ-Entwurfs zur europäischen Strafverfolgung*, ZSTW 116 (2004) at 391-393; LÜDERSSEN, 116 ZSTW, at 448–449 (2004) (holding that the problem is not solved due to the voting inequality with the EU).

sense, it is beginning to acquire the features of a federation of states endowed with federal sovereignty.[31]

Regarding constitutional and judicial control of EU criminal law, the crucial link between criminal law and fundamental rights creates a need for some European control as to the scope and content of the fundamental rights contained in the Charter.[32] This constitutional style control is reinforced by the binding nature of the Charter in the interpretation of the fundamental rights of EU citizens.[33] Still, the current approach, again, resorts to horizontal federalism instead of vertical federalism. The violation of these fundamental rights cannot be invoked directly by individuals before a strictly European court. At most, there is indirect control by the Court of Justice of the European Union through preliminary ruling petitions of national courts pursuant to Article 267 TFEU. In a horizontal federalism fashion, the EU is producing various Directives concerning certain procedural rights of the defendants that should be correctly implemented by the Member States' legislatures.

Finally, one of the biggest problems faced by European criminal policy is determining the scope of EU criminal law. This is a two-sided problem. On the one hand lies the same question that countries deal with in respect of their own criminal policies: what matters should be criminalized? It must be determined what social matters should fall within the penal system and what should be left out of the criminal justice system. The second problem is deciding which matters should be regulated indirectly by the European Union. And here it is easy to see the expansive nature of horizontal federalism in the EU. The EU increasingly forces Member States to introduce or reshape their national penal legislation concerning certain offenses. Instead of adopting a vertical federalism approach regarding offenses that affect genuine European interests and enabling national diversity with respect to many others affecting primarily national interests, the EU spreads its influence over many areas of national criminal legislation.

---

31 See Robert Schütze, *The European Union as a Federation of States*, in *From Dual to Cooperative Federalism: The Changing Structure of European Law*, 2009. In this sense, the problem of distinguishing between the powers of the states and the power of the federation does not belong exclusively to the EU, but, to the contrary, is present in many federal states such as the United States. See Ernest A. Young, *State Sovereign Immunity and the Future of Federalism*, Supreme Court Review 1 (1999); Roderick M. Hills, *The Political Economy of Cooperative Federalism: Why State Autonomy Makes Sense and Dual Sovereignty Doesn't*, 96 Michigan L. Rev. 813 (1998).

32 There have been important developments in this arena involving the European Union Charter of Fundamental Rights and the jurisprudence from the European Court of Human Rights. See below Chapter 4.

33 Filippo Fontanelli, *The European Union's Charter of Fundamental Rights two years later*, Perspectives on Federalism 3 (2011). Sybe de Vries, Ulf Bernitz and Stephen Weatherill, *The Protection of Fundamental Rights in the EU after Lisbon*, 2013; Sionaidh Douglas-Scott, *The European Union and Human Rights after the Treaty of Lisbon*, Human Rights L. Rev. 11 (2011) at 645–682.

Not surprisingly, many of these issues have been addressed by the so-called European Criminal Policy Initiative (ECPI).[34] By way of a Manifesto,[35] fourteen scholars from ten Member States enumerated certain principles embedded in European law that should serve as guidelines for the development of substantial criminal law in the EU. In 2013 a second Manifesto authored by sixteen scholars was published,[36] focusing on the procedural aspects of EU criminal law. To a certain extent, some of the findings of the ECPI were followed in the EU Communication "Towards an EU Criminal Policy: Ensuring the effective implementation of EU policies through criminal law".[37] But it is fair to note that, as a general assessment, many problems are still unresolved, and there is a lack of consistency in the general approach.

4.3. FEDERAL CRIME POLICY IN THE US SYSTEM

Having reviewed the basic elements of the European discussion, it is worth looking at the evolution of US federal criminal law. Federal law *enforcement* in the US can be traced back to 1789, when the Office of the Attorney General of the US was created and when the first federal police agency was established to help prevent smuggling. Although the first federal penal provisions were shortly passed (1790), initially there was still little activity related to federal criminal law. It took the US attorneys and the courts *more than a century* to become notably active in the field of criminal law. It was not until the 1970s that the enforcement of federal criminal laws became visible. Although most of the instruments of enforcement had probably been available since the 1930s, active enforcement on all fronts came some decades after.[38]

Returning to the three distinct features that *Vogel* outlined in reference to EU criminal policy, it is interesting to address their American counterparts. To the extent that the US has dealt with the same problems as the EU now faces, it is beneficial to learn from the US experience. It will also become clear that some of the policies that the EU is now pursuing were explored long ago by the US. Others have no resemblance in the American discussion given the substantial differences in the political structure of the two entities.

---

34 www.crimpol.eu.

35 EuCLR 1 (2011) at 86–103.

36 ZIS (2013) at 412–446.

37 Communication from the Commission to the European Parliament, the Council, the European Economic and Social Committee and the Committee of the Regions: *Towards an EU Criminal Policy: Ensuring the effective implementation of EU policies through criminal law*, COM (2011) 573 final, Brussels, 20 September 2011. See also below Chapter 5.

38 For an interesting recapitulation see Kenneth M. Murchinson, *Federal Criminal Law Doctrines. The Forgotten Influence of National Prohibition*, 1994, at 178. See also Daniel Richman, *The Past, Present, and Future of Violent Crime Federalism*, CRIME & JUST 34 (2006) at 377–385 focusing in the specific area of violent crime, but with a broader perspective of the evolution of federal criminal law in general.

The first issue that troubles the Europeans, the democratic deficit of the Parliament/Congress, is probably not of notable concern for the Americans. The strong position of Congress and the even stronger democratic process in the US leave little or no room to question whether Congress has the authority and the legitimacy to enact federal crimes. Still, even accepting the power of Congress to produce criminal statutes, there is still a question of the extent of such legislation, especially when it deals with matters traditionally regulated by the states. To put it differently, there is a very distinct US problem that is increasing within the EU, though it has not been as heavily discussed in Europe as concerning criminal law: to what extent does certain federal legislation "threaten" the states' sovereignty[39] and intrude upon the life of regular citizens?

Even minimal research will reveal an explosion of literature pursuant the Supreme Court decisions in *Lopez*[40] and *Morrison*,[41] which struck down federal statutes for exceeding the powers afforded to Congress in federal law-making.[42] The tension between the ever-reaching federal congress and state sovereignty became obvious. Congress possesses broad powers to regulate under the Commerce Clause, as we will discuss later. However, when Congress interferes in areas that traditionally have been reserved to the states, the states are displeased.[43] One way to reduce controversy is to have, as is most often the case, overlapping statutes[44] with no preemption, preserving the sovereignty of both federal and

39 This issue becomes specially pressing in the context of the dual state sovereignty and the features of the so-called cooperative federalism. See among many *National League of Cities v. Usery* (1976) arguing with precedents of the Supreme Court that although Congress possesses broad power to regulate under the Commerce Clause the Tenth Amendment protection of state sovereignty acts as an external limit to that power. The Supreme Court in that case stated that although Congress may otherwise possess the legislative authority to do so, it may not invade certain attributes fundamental to the sovereignty of state governments and essential to their functioning.

40 514 U.S. 549 (1995).

41 529 U.S. 848 (2000).

42 See one of the many contributions at the time George D. Brown, *Constitutionalizing the Federal Criminal Law Debate: Morrison, Jones and the ABA*, Uni. Ill. L. Rev. (2001) at 983. As will be noted below, after the *Lopez* revolution, the Supreme Court returned in *Raich* (*Gonzalez v. Raich*, 545 U.S. 1 (2005)) to the business-as-usual policy of deferring to congressional power and upholding the acts. As Norman Abrams, Sara Beale and Susan Klein, *Federal Criminal Law and its Enforcement,* 5th ed., 2010, at 39, the *Lopez* revolution was somewhat appeased.

43 An interesting area in violent crimes, natural turf for state legislation and prosecution. For the evolution of this sector and the mutual cooperation between federal and state level see Daniel Richman, *The Past, Present, and Future of Violent Crime Federalism*, CRIME & JUST 34 (2006) at 377–397.

44 A consequence of this overlapping is the troubling position of the double jeopardy clause. In order to soften the confrontation, an exception to the double jeopardy protection has been developed on the basis of the so-called "dual sovereignty". This way both sovereignties remain intact – at the expense, of course, of the defendants' rights. The erosion of civil liberties is not always easy to justify, and therefore it comes to no surprise the petite policy of the US Attorneys concerning prior prosecution at the state level of felonies that could also be subject to criminal proceedings at the federal level. The unequal treatment of defendants in federal and state proceedings for the same type of offense has been well argued by Steven D. Clymer, *Unequal Justice: The Federalization of Criminal Law*, S. Cal. L. Rev. 70 (1997) at 643.

state government. It is when different levels of regulation differ substantially that the confrontation between federal and state interests arises.

Although the federal and state crime policy share many common concerns, there are certain issues that pertain traditionally to the federal criminal law debate. Probably the first topic is the broader federalism discussion. It is necessary to note at this stage that policy concerns regarding what to criminalize federally and on what grounds is an ongoing topic among the legislature, the judiciary and academia. Not surprisingly, the last three major decisions of the US Supreme Court on federalism, whether striking down statutes or upholding their constitutionality, dealt with issues closely related to criminal law: the Gun Free School Act in *Lopez*,[45] the Violence Against Women Act in *Morrison*,[46] and the Compassionate (Marijuana) Use Act in *Raich*.[47]

This increasing breadth and number of federal criminal statutes has raised red flags for some.[48] In this sense the debate about overcriminalization that has been ongoing for some time in the US is closely linked to the federal system of criminal law. Although criticism is also raised against overcriminalizing policies in most states, the main core of the heated debate is directed towards federal criminal law. Congress not only steps into areas of criminal law traditionally reserved for the states (federalism debate),[49] but it also criminalizes conduct that was before considered only unethical or at most civilly reprehensible.

Moving beyond federalism and overcriminalization issues, there seems to be a common policy stance present in almost every federal criminal law statute: the goal of combating "evil" and being "tough on crime".[50] The vocabulary of war is applied regularly to US Department of Justice policies and to the related legislation, as apparent in the "war on drugs", the "war on terror", etc. In some sense, federal criminal law seems to be engaged in a moral crusade against evilness, and when questions are raised about the scope or the penalties of federal crimes, Congress and the courts are quick to claim an ethical obligation to combat the worst forms of evil present in our society.

---

45 514 U.S. 549 (1995).

46 529 U.S. 848 (2000).

47 125 U.S. 2195 (2005).

48 By the count of John S. Baker, Jr., *Revisiting the Explosive Growth of Federal Crimes*, Heritage Foundation L. Memo No. 26 (2008) there are more than 4,450 federal criminal statutes. Not surprisingly this author argues against the enhanced role of federal authority in the criminal law as an affront to the paramount role of the states in criminal law matters.

49 See however Tom Stacy and Kim Dayton, *The Underfederalization of Crime*, Cornell J.L. and Public Pol'y 6 (1997) at 247 ("The image of a runaway national government increasingly taking away the enforcement of the criminal law from the States is essentially false. The available evidence indicates that the national government's share in the enforcement of criminal law has been actually diminishing for more than the last half century").

50 A handy definition is provided by Julie R. O'Sullivan, *The Federal Criminal "Code" is a Disgrace: Obstruction to Justice as a Case Study*, J. Crim. L. and Criminology 96 (2006) at 643 ("New crimes are often enacted in patchwork response to newsworthy events, rather than as part of a cohesive code developed in response to an identifiable federal need").

4.4. CONCLUSION

As a general statement, it may be concluded that both Unions use a "tough on crime" approach regarding their legislation in criminal matters. Both the US vertical federal criminal law and the EU horizontal federal criminal law distinctively label their legislation with terms such as "fighting criminality". It seems to be a common thread that the federal approach to criminal law – whether vertical or horizontal – implies a belligerent attitude from the Unions.

Both Unions have developed a strategy for protecting their federal interests through the judiciary and the police. While the US has created independent vertical bodies, i.e. the federal courts and the FBI, the EU has resorted to horizontal coordination institutions such as Eurojust and Europol. Yet there seems to be a common federal thread in the fact that these institutions operate in cases of serious cross-border criminality. As we shall explore at a later stage, the concept of matters affecting "interstate commerce" or "serious cross-border criminality" is a constant in federal criminal law discussions in both Unions.

As to the legislative dimension, there is a constant questioning of the federal intervention – whether vertical or horizontal – of both Unions. Given the unquestioned legitimacy of US Congress, the American discussion is focused on the power of the federal government to intervene on certain areas. The EU discussion mainly deals with the preliminary issue of the democratic deficit of the EU parliament to legislative in areas pertaining to criminal law. In both cases the power to legislate in certain areas of criminal law is heavily questioned.

As final interesting remark should be acknowledged. While US citizens may challenge before the courts whether a piece of legislation should be federalized, EU citizens cannot challenge that a particular provision has been subject to EU influence. This is important as the federalism discussion in the US shows that some of the most important decisions concerning the scope of federal criminal law have been provoked by citizens questioning whether the federal government can produce legislation over a certain matter. This way of civil society having direct control over the breath of federal legislation is preempted in the EU given the horizontal federalism strategy in place in the EU.

5. CRIMINAL LAW SCHOLARSHIP

5.1. EU CRIMINAL LAW SCHOLARSHIP

The gradual increase of EU criminal legislation and its enforcement by EU Member States has created an augmented awareness in the scholarly community.

Although there is currently no unified criminal law theory across the EU,[51] European academics are creating a distinctive European criminal law doctrine, which targets issues raised by the specific nature of EU criminal law.[52] In fact, since there is no consolidated European penal code, European scholarship has focused on problems common to all EU jurisdictions that deal with the implementation of European legislation.[53] With the proliferation of the practice experience that followed the implementation of the principle of mutual recognition in criminal law, the number of academic contributions in this field has subsequently increased.

It should also be noted that the possibility of observing a *common scientific language* beyond national borders has always been of interest to those dealing with the "science" of criminal law, not only in Europe but also internationally. Moreover, the search for a *universal grammar*[54] of criminal law, or perhaps even a *proto* criminal law,[55] has reoccurred over time. If shared social values may be added to this convergent scholarly tradition, the possibility of establishing a common ground for discussing transnational criminal law is increased. This perspective has been reinforced by considering that criminal law is a product of society and, in the EU case, there is a notable European tradition of shared values.[56]

In short, throughout the second half of the 20th century and increasing in the first decade of the 21st century, academic interest has not disregarded the process

---

51 See among others Joachim Vogel, *Europäische Kriminalpolitik – europäische Strafrechtsdogmatik*, Goltdammer's Archiv (2002) at 519–523, 529–535.

52 See Kristian Kühl, *Der Beitrag der Strafrechtswissenschaft zur Europäisierung des Strafrechts*, in *Festschrift für Söllner* (Hellen ed., 2000) at 617. But see Vogel's opinion who without distinguishing between those levels he nevertheless acknowledges some effect of the academic work over the law-as-applied.

53 See Kristian Kühl, *Europäiserung der Strafrechtswissenschaft*, ZStW 109 (1997) at 777. Precisely Kühl has coined the term "European discourse on criminal law" (europäischen Strafrechtsdiskurs) (ibid. at 787); Kristian Kühl, *Der Beitrag der Strafrechtswissenschaft zur Europäisierung des Strafrechts*, in *Festschrift für Söllner* (Hellen ed., 2000) at 621. This terminology has been welcomed by other commentators such as Joachim Vogel, *Europäische Kriminalpolitik – europäische Strafrechtsdogmatik*, Goltdammer's Archiv (2002) at 519.

54 George P. Fletcher, *The Grammar of Criminal Law: American, Comparative, International*, 2007; see Kai Ambos, *Towards a Universal System of Crime: Comments on George Fletcher's Grammar of Criminal Law*, Cardozo L. Rev. 29 (2007) at 2648.

55 O. Höffe, *Proto-Strafrecht: Programm und Anfragen eines Philosphen*, in Albin Eser, Winfried Hassemer and Björn Burkhardt, eds., *Die Deutsche Strafrechtswissenschaft vor der Jahrtausendwende*, 2000, at 309.

56 For an interesting take on Europe as community of shared values see Veith Mehde, *Die europäische Wertegemeinschaft, Grundrechte und die irische Abtreibungsdebatte*, KritV (2002) at 438. For thoughtful considerations see Ester Herlin-Karnell, *The EU as a Promoter of Values and the European Global Project*, Germ. L.J. 13 (2012) at 1226. For a criminal law perspective see the insights of the professor and former Justice of the German constitutional court Winfried Hassemer, *Ein Strafrecht für Europea*, in Frank Zieschang, Eric Hilgendorf and Klaus Laubenthal, eds., *Strafrecht und Kriminalität in Europa*, 2003, at 14. The European shared values were a "trending topic" in the Constitution for Europe debate. See the always interesting thoughts of Armin von Bogdandy, *The European Constitution and European Identity. Text and subtext of the Treaty establishing a Constitution for Europe*, Int. J. Const. L. 3 (2005) at 295–315. See also Ulrich Haltern, *On Finality*, in Armin Bogdandy and Jürgen Blast, *Principles of European Constitutional Law*, 2nd ed., 2009, at 227.

of European unification.[57] Specifically, since the 1990s there has been a notable increase in the concerns about the European unification process.[58] The number of publications dedicated to these issues has increased significantly, demonstrating the high level of interest in criminal law and the European Union.[59] This may stem from an increased involvement of European Union law on national criminal law since the 1980s, not only with respect to interpreting statutes but also in developing criminal legislation. This has been especially true since the turn of the century, as the European harmonization trend has gained momentum. Additionally, the growing scholarship may reflect an increased need for comparative law studies not only to understand how to harmonize European penal law but also to establish common criteria that would permit the development of European criminal law. The existence of different criminal law traditions in the European Union – in addition to the classical opposition between the continental system and common law – and an acute need to move forward with such harmonization makes the analysis of comparative law[60] and the discussion around which perspective should be adopted more relevant than ever before.

Precisely because of the coexistence in the European Union of different criminal law traditions, German academics have been debating which legal tradition should dominate,[61] if any. One camp favors a systematic approach based on categories, which is typical of German criminal law thinking; the other adopts a functional, problem-solving approach.[62] The confrontation between both camps may be personified by the position of *Schünemann* on the one hand and *Vogel* on the other.[63] The former argues that German criminal law theories, due to their unique capability of dealing with categories, is better situated to address the fundamental

---

57 See in general Kristian Kühl, *Der Beitrag der Strafrechtswissenschaft zur Europäisierung des Strafrechts*, in *Festschrift für Söllner* (Hellen ed., 2000) at 617.

58 Agreeing with such a statement see Frank Zieschang, *Chancen und Risiken der Europäisierung des Strafrechts*, ZStW 113 (2001) at 255; Heike Jung, *Konturen und Perspektiven des europäischen Strafrechts*, JuS 10 (2000) at 417.

59 Probably, a fair indicator of this evolution is the number of congresses, symposia and workshops discussing these topics. It is impossible now to provide even a brief overview given the relentless rhythm of events surrounding EU criminal law.

60 See for instance Kristian Kühl, *Der Beitrag der Strafrechtswissenschaft zur Europäisierung des Strafrechts*, in *Festschrift für Söllner* (Hellen ed., 2000) at 616–620; Ulrich Sieber, *Einheitliches europäisches Strafgesetzbuch als Ziel der Strafrechtsvergleichung*, in Gunnar Duttge, ed., *Gedachtnisschrift für Ellen Schlüchter*, 2002, at 107.

61 In this sense it must be noted that Article 82(2) TFEU states that such minimum rules "shall take into account the differences between the legal traditions and systems of the Member States".

62 See Joachim Vogel, *Europäische Kriminalpolitik – europäische Strafrechtsdogmatik*, Goltdammer's Archiv 517 (2002) at 523.

63 To be sure, in both of them there is a clear reluctance against following the Americanization of criminal law (see Joachim Vogel, *Europäische Kriminalpolitik – europäische Strafrechtsdogmatik*, Goltdammer's Archiv (2002) at 517; Bernd Schünemann, *Das Strafrecht in Zeichen der Globalisierung*, in Goltdammer's Archiv (2003) at 204).

issues of Europeanization.[64] *Schünemann* appeals to the "supremacy" of German thinking and proposes the establishment of a European penal law based out of German theories.[65] In stark contrast to this position, *Vogel* believes that the German approach is "questionable and faces a lack of understanding in Europe".[66] Following the generally prevailing strategy in comparative law,[67] *Vogel* supports methodological openness[68] and prevalence of the problem-solving, functional approach over the systematic-categorical one.[69] As a consequence, he points out that it is incorrect from a regulatory and functional perspective[70] to propose the adoption of the German theories, or any other doctrine in the European criminal law, without further consideration. From a normative perspective all national criminal laws should be recognized as equal before the European Union and European Union law should be recognized as autonomous even from a methodological perspective. From a functional perspective it follows that the task of the European penal doctrine is to convey a comprehensive message across Europe. Given the notable differences between criminal law systems within the European Union,[71] *Vogel's* proposal is to crystallize certain "concepts in order to resolve problems" (*Problemlösungskonzepte*), which should result in consistent reasoning to avoid the arbitrary resolution of cases.[72]

---

64 Bernd Schünemann, *Gespent geht um Europa - Brüsseler "Strafrechtspflege" intra muros*, in Goltdammer's Archiv (2002) at 511. But see Walter Perron, *Hat die deutsche Straftatsystematik eine europäische Zukunft?*, in Albin Eser, ed., *Festschrift für Theodor Lenckner*, 1998, at 228 ("In any event, national arrogance would be inadequate from a scientific point of view").

65 See the clear words used by Bernd Schünemann, *Strafrechtsdogmatik als Wissenschaft*, in *Festschrift für Claus Roxin*, 2001, at 11: "The analytic level achieved ... in Germany should be also demanded from Europe, in order to put a strong defense against all those less evolved systems such as the French or the British ... which are linked to outdated ideologies of the 18th and 19th Century". For Bernd Schünemann, *Ein Gespent geht um Europa - Brüsseler "Strafrechtspflege" intra muros*, in Goltdammer's Archiv (2002) at 511, both French and the common law are excluded of the "core values of European criminal law". Yet immediately thereafter he acknowledges that in the discussion held in Brussels there was a strong preference for the common law model in substantive criminal law and for the French model in criminal procedure (at 514).

66 Joachim Vogel, *Europäische Kriminalpolitik - europäische Strafrechtsdogmatik*, Goltdammer's Archiv (2002) at 523.

67 Walter Perron, *Hat die deutsche Straftatsystematik eine europäische Zukunft?*, in Albin Eser, ed., *Festschrift für Theodor Lenckner*, 1998, at 289.

68 Joachim Vogel, *Europäische Kriminalpolitik - europäische Strafrechtsdogmatik*, Goltdammer's Archiv (2002) at 523, underlining the fact that to have an open methodology does not by any means imply introducing discretionary judgments.

69 See Joachim Vogel, *Europäische Kriminalpolitik - europäische Strafrechtsdogmatik*, Goltdammer's Archiv (2002) at 522.

70 Bernd Schünemann has opposed such views that this is the only way for "taking rights seriously" in the EU (Bernd Schünemann, *Bürgerrechte ernst nehmen bei der Europäisierung des Strafverfahrens!*, Strafverteidiger (2003) at 120 with footnote 32).

71 See Joachim Vogel, *Europäische Kriminalpolitik - europäische Strafrechtsdogmatik*, Goltdammer's Archiv (2002) at 524.

72 Ibid. at 525.

Yet what happens if two European legal traditions propose opposite solutions to the same problem? Here, *Vogel* relies on the Discourse Theory as an appropriate instrument to resolve conflicts that may arise among the diverse legal traditions. In his opinion, the opposition should be resolved by resorting to the strength of the "best argument". The Discourse Theory is not a legal method, but a methodological and theoretical framework that can be fruitful for Europe.[73] *Vogel*'s proposal resembles the approach of the ECtHR which, for many years, has been developing a system of jurisprudence that is considered the cornerstone of the European Union's legal tradition. It can be argued that there is a need to develop a minimum common standard, respected in all cases and responsive to the evolution of fundamental rights, as already exists in the ECtHR case law.[74]

5.2. US FEDERAL CRIMINAL LAW SCHOLARSHIP

A first interesting note that could shed some light into certain European discussions is that, although the United States is considered to be a common law jurisdiction, federal criminal law is completely statutory. In other words, it is codified law, and the existence of any form of federal common law is expressly forbidden.[75] Therefore, the US is a clear example of how a traditionally common law country may perfectly deal with statutory principles of civil law jurisdictions. Those suggesting that it is impossible to unify principles of common law and civil law jurisdiction should bear in mind that experience shows, at least in the area of federal criminal law, that common law countries may handle with normality statutory criminal law.

Now, it seems reasonable that scholars focusing on an in-depth analysis of criminal law would subsequently research the area of federal criminal law; however, this is not the case. As a matter of fact, the scholars focused in "traditional" criminal law do not pay much attention to the key issues in the federal criminal law debate. An interesting exception came in the late 20th century when some prominent criminal law scholars discussed a very civil law type of

---

73 Ibid. at 523.

74 Among many, see the analysis of Jeremy McBride, *Human rights and criminal procedure: The case law of the European Court of Human Rights*, 2009, published by the Council of Europe (available at: www.coe.int/t/dgi/hr-natimplement/Source/documentation/Echr_and_crim_procedure.pdf).

75 We cannot pursue at this stage a comparison between the common law and civil law jurisdictions. But it is worth noting that, apparently, there is no "federal criminal common-law" (see *United States v. Hudson & Goodwin*, 11 U.S. (7 Branch) 32 (1812)). The use of the term "apparently" is due to the fact that even though some decisions clearly revert to this prohibition of federal criminal common law, in practice the Supreme Court not only searches the common law foundations of certain criminal law institutions, but also conducts itself as a common law maker (although not explicitly).

movement: codification. Contributions from such scholars as *Paul Robinson*[76] added heavy criminal law weight to the discussions. Still, it is fair to say that such contributions were more focused on the pros and cons surrounding codification than on the concerns of federal criminal law.

As a result, the basic scholarly literature in federal criminal law is produced by specialized academics. Probably the most consulted work in the field is the outstanding *Federal Criminal Law and its Enforcement*, by *Norman Abrams, Sara Sun Beale* and *Susan Riva Klein*.[77] However, it is also worth noting some specialized monographs of recent years, such as the one provided by *Julie Rose O'Sullivan: Federal White Collar Crime*.[78] A recent overall and in-depth work has been produced by *William Stunz* and *Daniel Richman: Defining Federal Crimes*.[79]

The discussion regarding federal criminal law also has a very distinctive flavor. Some of the most common topics are the following: overcriminalization,[80] federalization,[81] the structure of the US Attorney's Office,[82] and the *mens rea* requirement in federal statutes.[83] Regarding the Special Part, there are often discussions about the mail and wire fraud statute, RICO, drug law enforcement, or terrorism issues. Also, when addressing potential statutory reforms, there is

---

76 Paul H. Robinson, *Reforming the Federal Criminal Code. A Top Ten List*, Buff. Crim. L. Rev. 1 (1997) at 225 suggesting five innovations pioneered by the Model Penal Code drafters that are of central importance in a new federal criminal code and five reforms that should be considered by the drafters of any Model Pedal Code (federal or state).

77 Norman Abrams, Sara Beale and Susan Klein, *Federal Criminal Law and its Enforcement*, 5th ed., 2010. See also Peter W. Low and Joseph L. Hoffmann, *Federal Criminal Law*, 1997.

78 *O'Sullivan's Federal White Collar Crime*, 3rd ed., 2007.

79 Daniel C. Richman, Kate Stich and William J. Stunz, *Defining Federal Crimes*, 2014.

80 Classic work by Stuart P. Green, *Why It's a Crime to Tear the Tag Off a Mattress: Overcriminalization and the Moral Content of Regulatory Offenses*, Emory L.J. 36 (1997) at 1533; Ellen S. Podger, *Overcriminalization: The Politics of Crime*, Am. U. L. Rev. 54 (2005) at 541; Erik Luna, *The Overcriminalization Phenomenon*, Am. U. L. Rev. 54 (2005) at 703, 716. A brilliant political analysis in William Stuntz, *The Pathological Politics of Criminal Law*, Mich. L. Rev. 100 (2001) 505, 519–20, 531. More recently, the House has held two hearings on the report and its recommendations. See *Reining in Overcriminalization: Assessing the Problems, Proposing Solutions, Before the Subcomm. on Crime, Terrorism, and Homeland Sec. of the H. Comm. on the Judiciary*, 111th Cong. 2 (2010); Over-Criminalization of Conduct and Over-Federalization of Criminal Law, Before the Subcomm. on Crime, Terrorism, and Homeland Sec. of the H. Comm. on the Judiciary, 11th Cong. 1 (2009).

81 Among many, a clear example is provided by Richard W. Garnett, *The New Federalism, The Spending Power, and Federal Criminal Law*, Cornell L. Rev. 89 (2003) at 1 (concluding that the expansion of federal criminal jurisdiction through spending is inconsistent with the structures explicitly created and reasonably implied by the US Constitution, with the values these structures were designed to advance, and with the liberties they were intended to protect).

82 A classic piece Daniel C. Richman, *Federal Criminal Law, Congressional Delegation, and Enforcement Discretion*, UCLA L. Rev. 46 (1999) at 757 (showing the extent to which Congress balances concern with enforcer accountability against suspicion of presidential power).

83 Geraldine Scott Mohr, *Playing with the Rules: An Effort to Strengthen the Mens Rea Standards of Federal Criminal Law*, J.L. Econ. & Pol'y 7 (2011) at 685 (assessing the recommendations of recent proposals to reform the mens rea standard in federal criminal law).

some rejection of the Model Penal Code discussion that is regularly cited in the state criminal law debate.[84]

The hesitance expressed towards the Model Penal Code provides an opportunity to note an interesting phenomenon: the growing concern about the need for a proper federal criminal code. As a common law country, the United States should be comfortable with a federal criminal law that is judge-made. Yet, since the first decisions of the Supreme Court, it has been clearly established that there is no "federal common law of crimes".[85] From this assertion, it seems logical to expect a somewhat organized and uniform federal criminal code. To be sure, this is not the case.[86] Title 18 U.S.C. is "a host of internally-disorganized statutes containing fragmentary coverage into a series of chapters laid out in … alphabetical order".[87]

It is not surprising then that the US Supreme Court faces important challenges when interpreting such basic concepts of criminal law as the *mens rea* doctrine. For one, the need for a certain mental state has been the landmark of criminal law and, accordingly, one feature that differs from civil law. At the same time, certain provisions in Title 18 U.S.C. do not mention any type of *mens rea* standard. Leaving aside regulatory offenses (for which strict liability is valid), the Supreme Court had to incorporate, beyond the express will of Congress, a *mens rea* element, resorting in the process to basic tenets of common law. Perhaps this interpretation stems from the rule of lenity, or *pro reo* nature of American law, allowing the court more leeway when interpreting laws in favor of the defendant. However, this is not clear. In any event, there is currently a strong movement towards requiring a *mens rea* element in every federal criminal law statute.[88]

---

84 This could be considered a bit surprising given that federal criminal in the US is a system that is self-purported as non-common-law-based and therefore statute-based. It would seem logical that the federal legislature paid attention to the wording of the statutes in the carefully crafted Model Penal Code. This is clearly not the case. The federal reform proposals do not take into account how the Model Penal Code addresses the same problems they are trying to solve.

85 *United States v. Hudson and Goodwin*, 11 U.S. 32 (1812) which decided that federal courts had no jurisdiction to define new common law crimes, and that there must always be a (constitutional) statute defining the offense and the penalty for it. Another famous quote: federal crimes "are solely creatures of statute." *Liparota v. United States*, 471 U.S. 419, 424 (1985).

86 Julie Rose O'Sullivan, *The Federal Criminal "Code" is a Disgrace: Obstruction Statutes as Case Study*, J. Crim. L. & Criminology 96 (2006) at 643–726 ("There actually is no federal criminal 'code' worthy of the name … my use of the term 'federal criminal code' within this Article is simply a shorthand for an 'incomprehensible,' random and incoherent, 'duplicative, ambiguous, incomplete, and organizationally nonsensical' mass of federal legislation that carries criminal penalties").

87 Ronald L. Gainer, *Federal Criminal Code Reform: Past and Future*, Buff. Crim. L. Rev. 45(2) (1998) at 93.

88 Geraldine Scott Mohr, *Playing with the Rules: An Effort to Strengthen the Mens Rea Standards of Federal Criminal. Laws*, J. L., Econ. & Pol'y 7 (2011) at 685; Darryl K. Brown, *Federal Mens Rea Interpretation and the Limits of Culpability's Relevance*, Law and Contemporary Problems, Spring 2012; Brian W. Wals and Tiffany M. Joslyn, *Without Intent. How Congress Is Eroding the Criminal Intent Requirement in Federal Criminal Law*, 2012.

The lack of consistency and coherence in substantive US federal criminal law is in contrast to the specificity and care with which procedural federal criminal law has been legislated. The federal rules of criminal procedure, although not perfect, are at least a coherent body of rules capable of systematic interpretation. The logic of these rules enable reasoned conclusions that, with some caveats, provide one the most precious gems in a legal system: foreseeability.[89] The argument by critics of American law is quite simple: just as there is a federal code of criminal procedure, Congress should enact a federal code of criminal law.

It seems likely, however, that such a code would face strong resistance from federal prosecutors. The flexibility that federal prosecutors enjoy in the interpretation of Title 18 U.S.C. would certainly be curtailed if their theories were confronted with a structured and coherent federal penal code. In other words, the same limitations on novel theories which already exist in the realm of federal criminal procedure would apply to substantive criminal law. Especially in a system so dependent on prosecutorial discretion, there must be some room for interpretation no matter how meticulously codified the criminal law were to become. However, the heyday of exotic unforeseeable theories in substantive federal criminal law would be over. In this sense, US attorneys would face limitations similar to those of their continental counterparts. Given the affirmative bar against a federal common law of crimes, this proposition should not be that strange.

Now, in the US there is no competing "national" theory of the offense as the federal criminal law has its own roots when it comes to the General Part.[90] This shows how futile the discussion in the EU is as to which theory of the offense should be taken as the basis of EU criminal law. This is due, in part, to the preponderance of categories in the German criminal law tradition that – as the discussion referring to international criminal law and the Rome Statute has shown – is not shared worldwide. Were EU instruments not mandatory for the Member States, the hesitation from some European scholars would not be so great. Moreover, if an independent vertical system of European criminal law based on the case law of the ECtHR and the ECJ were to be developed, the reluctance against such a system would be probably greatly diminished.

89 In the US discussion this is basically addressed under the "fair notice" problematic. See among many Ronald L. Gainer, *Federal Criminal Code Reform: Past and Future*, Buff. Crim. L. Rev. 45(2) (1998) at 93; Julie Rose O'Sullivan, *The Federal Criminal "Code" is a Disgrace: Obstruction Statutes as Case Study*, J. Crim. L. & Criminology 96 (2006) 643–726 (exemplifying with § 1346 Honest Service Fraud Statute).

90 Although not a discussion per se, the most obvious challenge between theories in the US is the question as to whether the federal system should follow the states system of a Model Penal Code. The difference is that most academics agree on the need for such a code. The power preventing the enactment of this code comes from the Executive (DOJ would not have as much freedom as it enjoys in playing around with statutes) and Congress (they would not be able to enact laws as comfortably to show their tough of crime policy when electorally favorable).

5.3. CONCLUSION

Academics in both Unions deal with a similar set of problems posed by the federalization of criminal law: whether the Union has the power to intervene in certain matters concerning criminal law, and, if so, how that power should be exercised. Yet the discussion is again tainted by the distinction between vertical and horizontal federalism. US scholars are focused on the breadth of US federal criminal legislation and the lack of a coherent system of federal criminal law. The provisions in the US code do not amount to a rational lay-out such as the one present in the states' penal codes. EU scholars are dealing with the increasing influence of the EU and, at least in Germany, the search for a leading national "theory of the crime" that should guide future action.

In any event, the academic literature concerning the Unions' federalization of criminal law has become quite distinctive. There seems to be a specific academic interest in the task of distinguishing the very special nature of federalizing (vertically or horizontally) certain areas of criminal law.

6. THE FUNDAMENTALS OF EUROPEAN HORIZONTAL FEDERAL CRIMINAL LAW: THE PRINCIPLE OF MUTUAL RECOGNITION

6.1. INTRODUCTION

It is time now to turn our attention to the guiding principle of horizontal European federal criminal law: the principle of mutual recognition.[91] It is commonplace to say that the principle of mutual recognition is born out of the creation of a single European market.[92] The European Commission found it difficult to harmonize different national regulations in order to guarantee the actual free movement of goods between states. In addressing these difficulties, the Commission decided to implement this principle as a new strategy of harmonization at the *economic* level. Instead of negotiating procedures and regulations to create more uniformity, the

[91] Much of discussion reflected in the following pages deals with German scholarship. The main reason for this is the fact that this scholarship greatly influenced the terms of the debate and the final decision by the German Constitutional Court on 18 July 2005. This was probably the first decision by a Constitutional Court addressing some of the concerns revolving around the principle of mutual recognition in criminal law matters. For an overview see SIMONE MÖLDERS, *Case Note – The European Arrest Warrant in the German Federal Constitutional Court*, GERM. L.J. 7 (2006) at 45–58.

[92] See BERND SCHÜNEMANN, *Das Strafrecht in Zeichen der Globalisierung*, GOLTDAMMER'S ARCHIV (2003) at 202; BERND SCHÜNEMANN, *Bürgerrechte ernst nehmen bei der Europäisierung des Strafverfahrens!*, STRAFVERTEIDIGER (2003) at 119.

Commission chose to recognize each state's regulations as equal to those of the other Member States.[93]

Consequently, the cornerstone of the "new" idea was to recognize *prima facie* the reasonableness of each Member States' economic regulation.[94] The strategy has clearly been successful in creating a single market. However, when this rationale is applied to the field of criminal justice, some inconsistencies quickly materialize. It is surprising that a key principle in liberalizing the free movement of *goods* between structurally similar markets has become the ruling principle in criminal law cooperation. Essentially, the EU has liberalized the trade of legal decisions in criminal matters. The grounds noted in the European Arrest Warrant (EAW) Framework Decision phrase it as follows: "It is necessary to replace the traditional cooperation relations that used to prevail among member states for a system of *free movement of legal decisions for criminal matters.*"[95]

Clearly, there is a question about whether a guiding principle of free movement of goods can also serve as the guiding principle of judicial cooperation. Are goods and legal decisions so comparable that principles governing the free movement of one apply to the other? As will be shown, a large group of German legal scholars answer this question in the negative. However, before further examining these critics, it is necessary to briefly review the evolution of the principle of mutual recognition in the criminal law context. A few words on how the principle of *economic liberalization* has turned into a principle of *judicial liberalization* are needed.[96]

6.2. THE APPLICATION OF THE PRINCIPLE OF MUTUAL RECOGNITION TO THE FIELD OF CRIMINAL LAW

6.2.1. Introduction

Much has been written on the topic of mutual recognition as applied to criminal cooperation.[97] It is not our intent to provide an in-depth analysis of the origins

93 See WOLFGANG KAHL, *Art. 14 EGV*, in CHRISTIAN CALLIES and MATTHIAS RUFFERT, eds., *Kommentar zu EU-Vertrag und EG-Vertrag*, 2010, at 14; RUDOLF STREINZ, *Europarecht*, 2008, at 955, 973.

94 See HELMUT SATZGER, *Gefahren für eine effektive Verteidigung im geplanten europäischen Verfahrensrecht*, STRAFVERTEIDIGER 13 (2003) at 141. This is quite clear in the findings of the European Arrest Warrant Framework Decision.

95 See Official Journal of the EU L 190, 18 July 2002, at 1.

96 For an excellent discussion of the problems arising from such conception see VALSAMIS MITSILEGAS, *EU Criminal Law*, 2009, at 117–121 (explaining that "the extent to which one can successfully 'borrow' the mutual recognition principle from its internal market framework and transplant it to the criminal law sphere is a contested issue", and concluding that "EU intervention in criminal matters must not be equated with intervention regarding the internal market" at 118).

97 For a recent account see ANNIKA SUOMINEN, *The Principle of Mutual Recognition in Cooperation in Criminal Matters. A study of the principle in four framework decisions and*

and evolution of this principle, but only to signal some key moments and features. At the institutional level, this principle first surfaced in the criminal law area in 1998 in a Council meeting in Cardiff.[98] At an academic level, it had been used a couple of years previously in the *Corpus Juris on the Protection of Financial Interests of the European Community*, drafted by a group of experts in 1996 at the request of the European Commission.[99] Given this context, it did not take long for the principle of mutual recognition to emerge as a driving force in EU criminal law. In conclusions 33, 35 and 36 of the Tampere Summit in 1999, the foundations of the principle of mutual recognition in the criminal law field were established:

> "33. Enhanced mutual recognition of judicial decisions and judgments and the necessary approximation of legislation would facilitate co-operation between authorities and the judicial protection of individual rights. The European Council therefore endorses the principle of mutual recognition which, in its view, should become the cornerstone of judicial co-operation in both civil and criminal matters within the Union. The principle should apply both to judgments and to other decisions of judicial authorities. ...
>
> 35. With respect to criminal matters, the European Council urges Member States to speedily ratify the 1995 and 1996 EU Conventions on extradition. It considers that the formal extradition procedure should be abolished among the Member States as far as persons are concerned who are fleeing from justice after having been finally sentenced, and replaced by a simple transfer of such persons, in compliance with Article 6 TEU. Consideration should also be given to fast track extradition procedures, without prejudice to the principle of fair trial. The European Council invites the Commission to make proposals on this matter in the light of the Schengen Implementing Agreement.
>
> 36. The principle of mutual recognition should also apply to pre-trial orders, in particular to those which would enable competent authorities quickly to secure

---

in the implementation legislation in the Nordic Member States, 2011, at 26, 43, 60. For an overview see André Klip, *European Criminal Law*, 2nd ed., 2012, at 362–395; Maria Feltcher, Robin Lööf and Bill Gilmore, *EU Criminal law and Justice*, 2008, at 108–125; Guillemine Taupiac-Nouvel, *The Principle of Mutual Recognition in Criminal Matters: A New Model of Judicial Cooperation Within the European Union*, European Crim. L. Rev. 3 (2012) at 236–251 (supporting that mutual recognition should be viewed both as a new legal principle and, in a broader sense, a new system of European criminal cooperation). For the impact of the case law of the ECJ in the principle of mutual recognition see Matthias J. Borgers, *Mutual Recognition and the European Court of Justice: The Meaning of Consistent Interpretation and Autonomous and Uniform Interpretation of Union Law for the Development of the Principle of Mutual Recognition in Criminal Matters*, European Journal of Crime, Criminal Law and Criminal Justice 18 (2010) at 99–114 (concluding that national courts will have to take increasingly more account of the meaning of that principle in the interpretation of national rules having their origin in European law in the area of cooperation in criminal matters).

98 For a comprehensive review of the milestones of the principle of mutual recognition see Green Paper on the approximation, mutual recognition and enforcement of criminal sanctions in the European Union (COM (2004) 334 final at 13).

99 The wording of Article 24 I b of the *Corpus Iuris* read: "Warrants for arrest and decisions relating to the offenses defined above made by the courts of any of the Member States are valid across the whole territory of the Union, as are judgments."

> evidence and to seize assets which are easily movable; evidence lawfully gathered by one Member State's authorities should be admissible before the courts of other Member States, taking into account the standards that apply there."

In the years following its introduction into the area of criminal law, the implementation of the principle of mutual recognition was spectacular.[100] Beginning with the Framework Decision on the European Arrest Warrant, many European legal instruments of the early 21st century were substantially based on this principle. The Framework Decision of 22 July 2003 on the Implementation of the European Union Orders Freezing Property or Protecting Evidence[101] and the Framework Decision on the Commission on the Warrant for Obtaining Objects, Documents and Data for Use in Criminal Proceedings[102] both recognize the principle of mutual recognition as a guiding principle on European legislation in criminal matters.[103] This trend was then confirmed by the Lisbon Treaty, particularly in section 1 of Article 82 TFEU.[104]

Those who had disapproved of the principle of mutual recognition as embedded in previous Treaties obviously extended their criticism now to the Lisbon Treaty. In fact, when the Constitution for Europe was being discussed in 2004/2005, critics expressly stated that if the principle of mutual recognition were to be adopted in its current form, the Constitution should not be approved.[105] Despite their efforts, the Lisbon Treaty was ultimately ratified with such a principle, although, not surprisingly, those same detractors persevered in their criticism in the years following ratification.

The wording of the Lisbon Treaty, Article 82 in particular, relates to the developments of criminal law in Europe in the last decade and exerts a certain influence over the issues covered in this section. The heaviest emphasis in the treaty is placed on the criminal area of the Area of Freedom, Security and Justice – Articles 82 and subsequent articles. The significant commitment to what had been the Third Pillar – intergovernmental cooperation – follows the trend by

---

100 Bernd Schünemann, *Das Strafrecht in Zeichen der Globalisierung*, Goltdammer's Archiv (2003) at 202 considers that the principle of mutual recognition is a speeding-up principle (*Turboprinzip*).

101 Official Journal of the EU L 196, 2 August 2003.

102 COM (2003) 688 final.

103 See the recitals of the Framework Decision and points 1.2 and 2.2, among others, of the *Green Paper on the Approximation, Mutual Recognition and Enforcement of Criminal Sanctions in the European Union* (COM (2004) 334 final).

104 Judicial cooperation in criminal matters in the Union shall be based on the principle of mutual recognition of judgments and judicial decisions and shall include the approximation of the laws and regulations of the Member States in the areas referred to in paragraph 2 and in Article 83.

105 See Bernd Schünemann, *Das Strafrecht in Zeichen der Globalisierung*, Goltdammer's Archiv (2003) at 203.

European institutions since the 1990s of shifting criminal law focus from the First to the Third Pillar.[106]

In the early discussion on whether to harmonize criminal law in Europe, the European Commission looked mainly within the First Pillar competencies, those related to the single European market and the criminal law jurisprudence of the European Court of Justice.[107] Proceeding accordingly, the EU Commission used the Directive as its primary legislative instrument. Perhaps because this strategy proved unsuccessful, the EU changed its approach in following years and began to carry out the harmonization of criminal law through the Third Pillar. In other words, it began to use intergovernmental cooperation rather than directives as a way to achieve harmonization. This strategy gave the Council a dominant position and used Framework Decisions and the Conventions as the appropriate legal instruments.[108] In this way criminal law harmonization began to appear in the so-called Area of Freedom, Security and Justice, and until very recently, most initiatives have taken place within this sphere.

Still, the harmonization process has not been fully organized and this poses a significant problem. Mutual recognition has commenced in some areas without a plan for full harmonization in all the different penal areas. The impact of piecemeal harmonization can already be felt even in areas where there is still no agreement as to whether it is appropriate. In other words, there are currently harmonizing penal trends in the European Union,[109] but not a consolidated and defined harmonization. In order to understand the importance of this situation, it pays to examine certain viewpoints, particularly those criticisms that point to the consequences of such action.

6.2.2. Criticisms Generated by the Transplantation of the Principle of Mutual Recognition to the Criminal Law Field

While in some Member States there has been little criticism of the principle of mutual recognition, in Germany[110] it has been called a "wolf in sheep's clothing" or a "Trojan horse".[111] Behind these words a real movement opposing the implementation of the principle in the criminal law field has been growing

---

106 On this shift see among many Joachim Vogel, *Europäische Kriminalpolitik - europäische Strafrechtsdogmatik*, Goltdammer's Archiv 517 (2002) at 521.

107 See in more detail Joachim Vogel, *Europäische Kriminalpolitik - europäische Strafrechtsdogmatik*, Goltdammer's Archiv 517 (2002) at 522.

108 Ibid. at 524.

109 See Joachim Vogel, *Harmonisierung des Strafrechts in der Europäischen Union*, Goltdammers Archiv 103 (2003) at 320–325.

110 As Joachim Vogel, *Cooperation in Criminal Matters in the European Union: Five Major Tendencies - Five Proposals for Future Action*, 2003 (on file with the author): "The mutual recognition principle is, at the moment, in the center of a critical academic discussion in Germany".

111 See Bernd Schünemann, *Das Strafrecht in Zeichen der Globalisierung*, Goltdammer's Archiv (2003) at 202.

for some time. This opposition may be clearly seen in the ruling of the German Constitutional Court concerning the implementation of the EAW Framework decision in German national law. Moreover, *Schünemann*, a significant German scholar, claims that the adoption of the European legislation in the German legal system would make the German parliament a "lackey of Brussels".[112] In fact, he explicitly states that the European Arrest Warrant in Germany violates the rule of law principle contained in Articles 16.I.2, 20 and 79.3 of the German Constitution.[113] Looking to the first and second thesis of a well-known set of proposals signed by no less than 123 German law professors one may grasp the magnitude of the opposition.

> "1st – With good reason, the fight against transnational crime has been carried out in the third pillar of the European Union Treaty, and corresponds to the joint approach of the member states. However, Liberty of Space and Justice, as defined by the European Union, should be pursued by means that respect the rights of citizens. The 'Principle of Mutual Recognition' within penal decisions, which is currently implemented through a Council framework decision, and which is covered in the first draft of the Constitution, violates this consideration discussed above.
>
> 2nd – The Principle of Mutual Recognition has its origin and justification in the area of free movement of goods. Its transplantation to the area of criminal prosecution leads to more punitive behavior by the governments throughout Europe and disturbs the balance that has been achieved in some national legal systems between the power of the state prosecution and the guarantees of freedom for its citizens. Its most extreme manifestation, the European Arrest Warrant, means that delivery of an individual to a foreign country, including nationals of their own country – which is partly vaguely defined – in which a determination as to whether there is double jeopardy has not been made, constitutes a violation of the rights of citizens."[114]

This criticism points to at least three key, interrelated areas. First, the authors object to an amplified punitive legal framework with a lower degree of fundamental rights guarantees within the principle of mutual recognition. Their second complaint rests on the unjustified violation of the principle of non-surrender of nationals and other similar, traditional principles of national criminal law. Third, the critics cite a lack of democratic legitimacy in the EU approach. An in-depth analysis of each of these issues would exceed the scope of this book; however, a brief discussion of each of these key areas is appropriate.

---

112 Bernd Schünemann, *Ein Gespent geht um Europa – Brüsseler "Strafrechtspflege" intra muros,* Goltdammer's Archiv (2002) at 531–532.

113 Ibid. at 507.

114 Additional thesis can be reviewed in the Manifesto of the European Criminal Policy Initiative (www.crimpol.eu/).

As *Schünemann* words the first complaint, the principle of mutual recognition "leads to the accumulation of the lowest threshold with the least possible level of precaution and the most extensive penal law which, in general, causes the most punitive legal framework to expand its reach within all of Europe. In other words, this leads to the permanent and sly expansion of European criminal law."[115] This statement refers generally to the catalogue of crimes found in the EU legal instruments based on the principle of mutual recognition, but the idea may be extended to the consequences of the strong presence of the principle of mutual recognition in the Lisbon Treaty.[116] Thus, those most punitive systems among the Member States – those sanctioning EAW offenses with more than three years of incarceration or those including in their national legislation the highest number of EAW crimes – will request the European warrants in such a way that expands their punitive nature beyond their borders and throughout the European territory. For example, if in the field of computer crimes (itself highly contested) "hacking" in one Member State is punishable by more than three years, such legislation extends, in some way,[117] to the other European Union countries, even though they may not consider this practice a crime at all, much less one punishable by a prison sentence.

Two considerations come into play in this area. The first refers to the types of crimes. One of the biggest problems in the application of the principle of mutual recognition is that, in some cases, it defines the matters it covers in such a generic way that different Member States will treat the same issue very differently. The computer crimes example is a good illustration of this problem. Yet where there is general agreement around the issue in question, there is less criticism. Matters such as terrorism, for example, are more uniformly thought of throughout the Union, in terms of how to approach the problem and the need to punish individuals involved.[118]

The problem more commonly arises when dealing with, *inter alia*, organized crime, computer crimes, environmental crimes, etc. Even those academics favoring the principle of mutual recognition acknowledge that, while some of these catalogued crimes are harmonized, the vast majority are not. Moreover, the elements of each of these crimes can be interpreted very differently between Member States. Ultimately, a point made throughout this book, if Europe is to continue down this path, the reasonable approach would have criminal law harmonization precede and foster the principle of mutual recognition, not vice versa. Nevertheless, the situation today is actually the opposite: the principle of

115 Bernd Schünemann, *Das Strafrecht in Zeichen der Globalisierung*, Goltdammer's Archiv (2003) at 204.

116 Ibid. at 203.

117 Bernd Schünemann, *Europäische Haftbefehl und EU-Verfassungsentwurf auf schiefer Ebene*, Zeitschrift für Rechtspolitik (2003) at 187.

118 See Bernd Schünemann, *Bürgerrechte ernst nehmen bei der Europäisierung des Strafverfahrens!*, Strafverteidiger (2003) at 120.

mutual recognition is currently operating without a defined and consolidated harmonization.

The second consideration raised by an expanded punitive system is the decrease in procedural guarantees that accompanies recognition without harmonization. The principle of mutual recognition disrupts both the rights of the defendant and the intra-procedural balance. Take, for example, a system where the right against self-incrimination is heavily limited and wiretaps and search and seizures are easily allowed. If the consequences of this national regulation must be recognized throughout the EU without further questioning, the rights of individuals in other Member States, including witnesses and third parties, can be severely affected, especially given the possibility of investigation methods being used beyond national borders. In short, there is the possibility of maximum punishment with minimum safeguards. Critics describe a Europe that is creating "Freedom of Insecurity and Deprivation of Liberty".[119]

Against this criticism, the generic reference contained in the Framework Decision to Article 6 the former European Union Treaty, i.e. the due process requirement, does not seem to sufficiently safeguard the uniform procedural and intra-procedural rights throughout the European Union. Therefore, until there is real and consolidated harmonization of criminal law in the European Union, both of content and form, there remains a potential for greater punishment with a minimum safeguards.

The second complaint voiced by the German scholars above, dealing with the traditional non-surrender of nationals, has been primarily aimed at the first legal instrument based on the principle of mutual recognition: the EAW. Critics claim that the EAW violates a principle rooted in the 19th century[120] and the origin of modern European states: the principle of no extradition of national citizens. In their view, although this principle has been weakened over the years, as can be seen in the Convention on Extradition between Member States adopted in 1996, it remains a valid precept in European law. Subsequent limitations of this principle codified in the Rome Statute in relation to the International Criminal Court can be justified as they are limited to fighting crimes against humanity.[121] The bottom line is that Article 16.II of the German Constitution serves as a general principle with exceptions to be made only contingent upon the protection of the fundamental principles of a rule-of-law-abiding state. Accordingly, these German authors consider that the extradition of a national pursuant to an EAW would constitute a violation of the constitutional provision, since it violates an essential principle of rule of law: the democratic principle that an individual shall be subject only to those laws in which he has had the opportunity to participate. This

---

119 Bernd Schünemann, *Europäische Haftbefehl und EU-Verfassungsentwurf auf schiefer Ebene*, Zeitschrift für Rechtspolitik (2003) at 188.

120 Ibid. at 187.

121 So stated by Bernd Schünemann, *Ein Gespent geht um Europa – Brüsseler "Strafrechtspflege" intra muros*, Goltdammer's Archiv (2002) at 532.

links to the final sphere of criticism, the perceived lack of democratic legitimacy in European institutions and legislation.

German criminal law scholars argue that the power to enact criminal laws "should be assumed by the most legitimate democratic body – Parliament – and not transferred to the executive", asserting this principle as one of the cornerstones of democratic thought.[122] This raises one of the most intense discussions penal scholars have entertained over recent years around European criminal law: whether the European Union has any type of *ius puniendi*.[123] We will revisit this topic in the following chapter,[124] but for now it is important to note that if European Union powers are exercised through legal instruments in which the European Parliament participates, i.e. through the ordinary legislative procedure, the democratic legitimacy is fairly high (another issue is the strict democratic formality of the Parliament). However, the Framework Decisions were passed by the Council, a governmental body without parliamentary review. Thus the signal of legitimacy was substantially reduced at the time.

6.2.3. Responses to the Critics

Some authors have attempted to provide convincing answers to these criticisms. The main area of discussion has been, again, the EAW, which remains the first and most notable European legal instrument based on the principle of mutual recognition. *Lagodny* considers that the extradition principle of dual criminality should be abandoned in the interest of effective prosecution of the crime.[125] In a similar vein, certain authors have discussed the potential of removing this requirement as a real advancement. It is common to appeal to the greatest degree of flexibility and efficiency provided for by the European Arrest Warrant. *Vogel* argues that, on one hand, the executing state does not carry on its own criminal prosecution but rather only participates in that of another state.[126] On the other hand, the fact that the principle of mutual recognition implies respect for acquittals of other courts in the EU may also be beneficial to the affected party based on the *ne bis in idem* principle.[127]

These responses have in turn generated criticisms of their own. The efficiency argument is criticized as highly misleading. Some note that, in reality, "when we deal with a behavior that in the state where it took place is not

---

122 Bernd Schünemann, *Bürgerrechte ernst nehmen bei der Europäisierung des Strafverfahrens!*, Strafverteidiger (2003) at 120.

123 See the different positions in Helmut Satzger, *International and European Criminal Law*, 2002 at 58–75.

124 See below Chapter 2.

125 Christian Lagodny, *§ 3 IRG*, in Lagodny and Schomburg, eds., *Internationale Rechtshilfe in Strafsachen*, 1998, reference number 2.

126 See Joachim Vogel, *The European Integrated Criminal Justice System and Its Constitutional Framework*, 12 Maastricht J. European and Comparative Law 125 (2005).

127 Ibid. at 127.

punishable – meaning, it is part of the citizen's freedom of action, – and the state where the behavior took place still extradites this national, then such state is not taking part in the prosecution of a crime as it is understood in its own set of values, but in the prosecution of innocent citizens -and hence, in a form of state terrorism."[128]

Critics also argue that *Vogel*'s first argument ignores the principles of rule of law and democracy. Surrendering a national should still be subject to the principle that the citizen can only be treated as a criminal suspect under the state's power based on its own legal system promulgated by its own parliament. Thus extradition without these protections would not meet the requirement of Article 16.II of the German Constitution.[129] Regarding the second argument, the logic of the principle *ne bis in idem* can only operate when the conduct is punishable in both states, i.e. when the principle of double incrimination is verified, which, as we have discussed, is not always the case.[130] Therefore, in the problem cases where the EAW is issued for a national who has not committed a crime under his own country's law, there would be no benefit from this principle.

In light of such responses, *Vogel* has unsurprisingly tempered his position on the principle of mutual recognition, leading to a set of conclusions discussed in the following chapter. Although he continues to defend the principle of mutual recognition, he points out that limitations regarding the European "public order" should be established. This European public order would be contained in the European Declaration of Human Rights and the Charter of Fundamental Rights of the European Union.[131] The goal seems to be set to minimum guarantees in all Member States to provide protection against criminal inequalities, especially in the procedural area. Moreover, and probably the most important issue within this entire discussion, *Vogel* recognizes that mutual trust (which is integral to this principle) requires the existence of minimum standards that must be accepted by all Member States and should be effectively implemented in all cases. Therefore, he concludes, "[m]utual recognition is not an alternative but a complement to harmonization."[132]

Conflicts become even clearer when dealing with some offenses that are traditionally considered as belonging to the core of national legislation. For example, as *Fuchs* noted, in Austria assisted suicide is punishable as a killing done

128 Bernd Schünemann, *Das Strafrecht in Zeichen der Globalisierung*, Goltdammer's Archiv (2003) at 203.

129 Ibid. at 204.

130 Ibid. at 204.

131 Joachim Vogel, *Cooperation in Criminal Matters in the European Union: Five Major Tendencies – Five Proposals for Future Action*, 2003 at 5.

132 Joachim Vogel, *Cooperation in Criminal Matters in the European Union: Five Major Tendencies – Five Proposals for Future Action*, 2003 at 5. As noted before, this approach is now reflected in the wording of Article 82 TFEU when it explicitly acknowledges at the principle of mutual recognition "shall include the approximation of the law and regulations of the member states".

by request, whereas in Germany it is not.[133] The famous debate over euthanasia, which is capable of being treated as homicide or innocent conduct, provides an example of the problems that arise in such basic areas of criminal law. These problems are not theoretical but very practical in nature.

In conclusion, the matters contained in the EU instruments based on the principle of mutual recognition are still not effectively harmonized across all European criminal legal systems. Furthermore, given the lack of effective appellate review by the European courts – there is only the preliminary ruling procedure at the request of the often-reluctant national courts – there is not even the possibility of a harmonized interpretation of these statutes. In short, the trend towards harmonization does not mean that full harmonization has been achieved. Even if this were true in the "European Fifteen" it would be even more complicated amongst the "European Twenty-Eight".

6.2.4. *It Had It Coming: The Ruling of the German Constitutional Court on 18 July 2005*

Two years after the above discussion took place, the German Constitutional Court (*Bundesverfassungsgericht* or *BVerfG*) ruled, on 18 July 2005, that the German Act of 2004 implementing the European Framework Decision regarding the European Arrest Warrant (EAW) was unconstitutional on its face and therefore void. The judgment demonstrates the remarkable influence of the criticisms posed by the vast majority of German academics.[134] However, the reasons given by the court reflect only part of these criticisms. A brief examination of the ruling shows that the legal (constitutional) basis for the unconstitutionality of the act was Article 16.II.2 of the German Constitution.[135] As noted before, this constitutional provision requires any exceptions to the principle of non-surrender of national (German) citizens to still recognize basic and founding principles of the state of law (*Rechtsstaat*). In the opinion of the German Constitutional Court, these principles were not sufficiently acknowledged in the German Act implementing the European Framework Decision. Consequently, it declared the whole Act unconstitutional and ordered the German legislature to pass a new regulation which would properly include these principles.

Reactions to the German ruling have been mostly critical. First among such critics were, of course, the dissenting justices, *Broß*, *Lübbe-Wolf* and *Gerhardt*. Most relevant to this discussion were the dissenting opinions of *Lübbe-Wolf* and

---

133 Helmut Fuchs, *Europäische Haftbefehl in Staatensoveranität*, Juristische Blätter (2003) at 408.

134 It should be noted that one of the Justices was also a renowned Professor of Criminal Law (Winfried Hassemer) and that a specialist in EU criminal law, Prof. Dr Martin Böse, was consulted regarding the allegations (see BVerfG, Ruling, §§ 30–58). Other important academics participated in the oral hearing as well (see BVerfG, Ruling, § 59).

135 BVerfG, Ruling, § 60.

Gerhardt. While agreeing with some parts of the ruling, *Lübbe-Wolf* nevertheless expresses clear disagreement with other legal reasoning and, most of all, with final decision to invalidate the German Act.[136] *Gerhardt* goes even further, stating that the petition should have been dismissed, as it was not compatible with the jurisprudence of the ECJ.[137]

As for German academia, it should be noted that criticism came from Euro-enthusiasts and Euro-skeptics in equal measure. Generally, the former criticized the result, finding that the legal reasoning of the Court implied, at most, partial unconstitutionality.[138] The latter disapproved of the court's failure to rule on basic questions regarding the European proceedings in criminal law matters,[139] resembling the attitude of the court in *Solange III*. These critics felt the act should be declared unconstitutional in its entirety because it violated Article 103.II GG, the regulation containing the well-known legality principle, as it lacked sufficient democratic legitimacy.[140]

The Spanish court which had issued the European Arrest Warrant against the German citizen, i.e. the *Audiencia Nacional*, took further issue with the decision. On 21 July 2005, the Spanish court decided to continue normal procedures based on the European Arrest Warrant until an official notification from the German Constitutional Court was received by the court. On 20 September 2005, with no official communications from the German court, the *Audiencia Nacional* concluded that Germany had decided not to cooperate with the Framework Decision on the European Arrest Warrant. Therefore, based on the reciprocity principle of international law, the Spanish court decided to deny European Arrest Warrants coming from German authorities and treat them instead as traditional extradition petitions.[141]

---

136 Ibid. at § 154.

137 Ibid. at § 184.

138 Joachim Vogel, *Europäischer Haftbefehl und deutsches Verfassungsrecht*, Juristische Zeitung (2005) at 801; Jürgen Jekewitz, *Der Europäische Haftbefehl vor dem Bundesverfassungsgericht*, Goltdammer's Archiv (2005) at 625; Lothar Knopp, *Bundesverfassungsgericht contra EU-Haftbefehl- Zum Urteil des Bundesverfassungsgericht von 18 Juli 2005*, Juristische Rundschau (2005) at 448, 452–453 (considers whether the dispute only affects the BVerfG and the German legislator, and he hopes that the latter are successful next time); Tomuschat, *Inconsistencies – The German Federal Constitutional Court on the European Arrest Warrant*, European Constitutional Law Review 2 (2006) at 209–226; (argues that the court should have focused more on the actual case); Hufeld, *Der Europäische Haftbefehl vor dem BVerf*, Juristische Schülung (2005) at 865 (takes into account a time-perspective that was omitted by the court).

139 Bernd Schünemann, *Die Entscheidung des Bundesverfassungsgerichts zum europäischen Haftbefehl: markiges Ergebnis, enttäuschende Begründung*, Strafverteidiger (2005) at 681; Ranft, *Die Verfassungswidrigkeit des (deutschen) Europäischen Haftbefehlsgesetzes*, Zeitschrift für Wirtschafts- und Steuerstrafrecht (2005) at 361.

140 Bernd Schünemann, *Die Entscheidung des Bundesverfassungsgerichts zum europäischen Haftbefehl: markiges Ergebnis, enttäuschende Begründung*, Strafverteidiger (2005) at 683.

141 See also the dissenting vote of Justices Rodríguez Zapata and García-Calvo, to the ruling of the Spanish Constitutional Court on 18 July, 2005 (ATC 314/2005), in which the court ordered

The issue was eventually resolved when Germany enacted legislation implementing the EAW Framework Decision. Since then, cooperation between both countries has been reestablished. However, the broader question remains: to what extent can the principle of mutual recognition force cooperation between EU Member States in criminal matters where no harmonization has been achieved? The further implementation of EU legislation on evidence gathering will surely prompt violent reactions among Member States. It is just a matter of time.

6.2.5. *The Timid ECJ Response: Advocaten voor der Wereld (2007)*

Given the "insurrection" of several constitutional courts of various Member States the ruling of the ECJ in the case of *Advocaten voor der Wereld*[142] has received considerable attention. It was probably the first case in which there was a direct questioning of the foundation and consequences of the principle of mutual recognition. The ECJ had to address certain key issues of criminal law and how the increasingly used EAW, i.e. the flagship instrument of mutual recognition in criminal matters, affected those areas. In this regard, the ECJ expressed its views regarding the principle of legality of criminal offenses[143] and penalties as well as the principle of equality and discrimination.[144]

The bulk of the ECJ's response was to defer those questions to the Member States.[145] Concerning the principle of legality, the ECJ affirmed that it was up to the Member States to properly define the offenses and the penalties under the principle of mutual recognition.[146] As the principle of equality and discrimination goes, the ECJ noted that the goal of the principle of mutual recognition is not to harmonize national legislation.[147]

---

the suspension of the General Agreement of the Audiencia Nacional accepting an EAW issued by French authorities.

142 3 May 2007, Case C-303/05 *Advocaten voor der Wereld VZW v. Leden van der Ministerraad* (2007).

143 Ibid. at § 48–54.

144 Ibid. at § 55–60.

145 For comments on this case see F. Geyer, *Judgment of 3 May 2007, Case C-303/05, Advocaten voor de Wereld VZW v. Leden van de Ministerraad*, European Constitutional Law Review 4 (2008) at 149–161; Ester Herlin-Karnell, *In the wake of Pupino: Advocaten voor der Wereld and Dell'Orto*, German L.J. 8 (2007) at 1153. A further development in Ester Herlin-Karnell, *European Arrest Warrant Cases and the Principles of Non-discrimination and EU Citizenship*, Modern L. Rev. 73 (2010) at 824–835.

146 3 May 2007, Case C-303/05 *Advocaten voor der Wereld VZW v. Leden van der Ministerraad* (2007) § 53. They "continue to be matters determined by the law of the issuing Member State, which ... must respect fundamental rights and fundamental legal principles as enshrined in Article 6 EU, and, consequently, the principle of the legality of criminal offences and penalties".

147 3 May 2007, Case C-303/05 *Advocaten voor der Wereld VZW v. Leden van der Ministerraad* (2007) § 53 it suffices "to point out that it is not the objective of the Framework Decision to harmonise the substantive criminal law of the Member States and that nothing in Title VI of the EU Treaty, Articles 34 and 31 of which were indicated as forming the legal basis of the Framework Decision, makes the application of the European arrest warrant conditional on

The response was mild in the sense that it could have addressed one of the major concerns of the principle of mutual recognition: the fact that the categories of criminality listed in the instruments of the principle of mutual recognition are not defined offenses. Instead of acknowledging that the lack of definition in those categories at least questioned the principle of legality, the ECJ decided to leave up to the Member States the definition of those offenses and the corresponding penalties in accordance with the principle of legality – as if such definitions had nothing to do with EU criminal law.

In the background, the same issue arises with the questioning of the principle of equality and non-discrimination. To what extent must the definition of offenses and penalties be previously harmonized throughout the EU in order for the principle of mutual recognition to work properly? Denying that the principle of mutual recognition does not aim at harmonizing criminal law in the Member States only begs questions.

Not surprisingly, the Lisbon Treaty reversed course and current Article 82 TFEU clearly states that: "Judicial cooperation in criminal matters in the Union shall be based on the principle of mutual recognition of judgments and judicial decisions *and shall include the approximation of the laws and regulations of the Member States* in the areas referred to in paragraph 2 and in Article 83". Once the definitions of offenses and penalties are harmonized throughout the EU, the concerns raised by the principle of legality and the principle of equality and non-discrimination basically disappear. It is noteworthy that the European legal instruments are currently referring to a greater extent to the definitions of offenses and penalties contained in EU legislation and not providing broad categories of criminality.

6.3. THE FULL FAITH AND CREDIT CLAUSE IN THE US SYSTEM: A VALID COMPARISON?

6.3.1. Introduction

Having reviewed the heavy criticism of the principle of mutual recognition in the EU, it is worth exploring any similar principles in the US. The situation is a bit more complicated than what might initially be expected. The Full Faith and Credit Clause of the US Constitution is similar to the principle of mutual recognition,[148] but its influence is radically different. This probably comes from the difference between vertical and horizontal federalism noted at the beginning

harmonisation of the criminal laws of the Member States within the area of the offences in question".

148 As a leading commentator of international criminal law also very familiar with the US system of criminal law justice refers to the most fundamental instrument of the principle of mutual recognition, i.e. the EAW: "This is similar to the Full Faith and Credit Clause of the

of this chapter. As stated before, the US is more active in vertical federalism, while the EU, lacking clear criminal law powers, has focused more on horizontal federalism. Because the EU principle of mutual recognition is a consequence of horizontal federalism, the extent to which is used in the EU does not resemble its American counterpart, the Full Faith and Credit Clause.

6.3.2. The Rules and the Exceptions to Full Faith and Credit

Article IV, Section 1 of the US Constitution provides that "Full Faith and Credit shall be given in each State to the public Acts, Records and judicial Proceedings of every other State. And the Congress may by general Laws prescribe the Manner in which such Acts, Records and Proceedings shall be proved, and the Effect thereof."[149] The original congressional intent is not very clear.[150] But in any event, the difference between the first 1790 Full Faith and Credit Statute and the second Congressional Act of 1804 shows some expansion of the clause's scope.[151] Noteworthy for our discussion is the fact that in 1790 the first legislation on federal criminal was passed and the first statute developing full faith and credit was adopted.

As early as the 19th century, the US Supreme Court awarded this clause a similar effect so as to foster free movement of judicial decisions through the Union – which resembles the principle of mutual recognition. "[T]he judgment of a state Court carries with it into every state all its original attributes, energies, and incidents; that it goes forth armed with the powers of the Court that pronounced it, and clothed with the authority of the laws under which it was pronounced; *that it is at home whithersoever it goes, through the whole length and breadth of the Union*; that, in relation to judicial proceedings, the states are not foreign to each other".[152]

By the mid-20th century, the US Supreme Court had conferred this clause a unifying power. "These results flow from the *unifying purpose of the full faith and credit clause* to give nationwide effect to rights judicially established in any part

US Constitution Article IV, Section 1" (CHERIF BASSIOUNI, *International Extradition: United States Law and Practice*, 2014, at 28 fn. 158).

149 U.S. Const. art. IV, § 1.

150 WILLIAM L. REYNOLDS and WILLIAM M. RICHMAN, *The Full Faith and Credit Clause. A reference guide to the United States Constitution*, 2006: "The origins of the Full Faith and Credit Clause are somewhat murky". For a thorough account of the debate see ibid. at 6–36. For a summarized exposition see JOSEPH ZIMMERMAN, *Horizontal Federalism. Interstate Relations*, 2011, at 64–65.

151 The full faith and credit statute, 28 U.S.C. § 1738, passed by the first Congress, simply provided that "[t]he records and judicial proceedings of any … State, Territory or Possession … shall have the same full faith and credit in every court within the United States and its Territories and Possessions as they have by law or usage in the courts of such State, Territory or Possession from which they are taken."

152 *McElmoyle v. Cohen*, 38 U.S. 312 (1839) (emphasis added).

of the nation".[153] Moreover, the US Supreme Court went so far as to establish that "the very purpose of the purpose of the full faith and credit clause *was to alter the status of the several states as independent foreign sovereignties*, each free to ignore obligations created under the laws or by the judicial proceedings of the others, *and to make them integral parts of a single national* throughout which a remedy upon a just obligation might be demanded as of right, irrespective of the state of its origin".[154]

Clearly, the primary historical purpose of the Full Faith and Credit Clause was to ensure that judgments rendered by one state court be recognized by another state court. In light of that historical purpose, the Supreme Court held that the Full Faith and Credit Clause requires maximum *recognition* of Union state judgments.[155] As a consequence of the Clause, Union state judgments must be recognized even in circumstances where principles of private international law would not require recognition of foreign court judgments. Thus, an American state court cannot refuse recognition of another American state judgment on the ground that recognition of the judgment would offend its "public policy",[156] or that it has an interest in refusing to recognize the judgment.[157] Also important is the fact that, although neither the constitutional or statutory provision refers to federal court judgments, it has long been established that they are entitled to recognition in the same manner as judgments rendered by a state court.[158] Also, under the corresponding statute, federal courts must recognize state court judgments as well.

In short, under the Full Faith and Credit Clause, a final judgment on the merits[159] rendered by a state court or a federal court must be recognized by another state court or federal court, subject only to the *following exceptions*.

First, the judgment may not be recognized if the exercise of jurisdiction by the rendering court *violated due process*, provided that the party challenging

153 *Magnolia Petroleum Co. v. Hunt*, 320 U.S. 430 (1943) at 439 (emphasis added).
154 *Milwaukee County v. M. E. White Co.*, 296 U.S. 268 (1935) (emphasis added).
155 *Hughes v. Fetter*, 341 U.S. 609, 611 (1951).
156 See *Fauntleloy v. Lum*, 210 U.S. 230 (1908).
157 See *Yarborough v. Yarborough*, 290 U.S. 202 (1933).
158 See *Stoll v. Gottleib*, 305 U.S. 165, 170 (1938).
159 It should be noted that a judgment dismissing a suit on procedural grounds, such that suit is barred by the statute of limitations or on grounds of public policy, is not a judgment on the merits (see Restatement of Judgments § 49 cmt. A (2009) and the case law in *Angel v. Bulington*, 330 U.S. 183, 189-90 (1947)). Also, a custody decree is not a final judgment for full faith and credit purposes because it is subject to modification by the court that has rendered it in light of changed conditions (see *Kovacs v. Brewer*, 356 U.S. 604, 607–08 (1958)). Therefore, it is worth noting that in an effort to prevent endless relitigation of custody questions by courts of different states, Congress in 1980 enacted the federal Parental Kidnapping Prevention Act, 28 U.S.C. § 1738A, which generally requires that Union state custody decrees be recognized and enforced by other Union states in accordance with their terms, and that proceedings to modify the custody decree be brought before the court that rendered the original decree, 28 U.S.C.A. § 1738A(a).

it did not appear in the original proceeding.[160] To the contrary, where both parties participated in the original proceeding, the court's determination of its jurisdiction is binding on the parties and may not be challenged in a subsequent proceeding.[161]

Second, the judgment is subject to collateral attack in the executing state on grounds such as *fraud or lack of subject matter jurisdiction*.[162] Since the judgment is subject to collateral attack in the executing state, *another state may permit the collateral attack in accordance with the law of the executing state*, thereby giving the judgment the same "credit" it has in the state of rendition.[163]

Third, enforcement of the judgment is barred by the nondiscriminatory *statute of limitations* applicable to judgments in the state where enforcement of the judgment is sought.[164]

Fourth, the judgment is a limited effect judgment.

The US Supreme Court has not used the Full Faith and Credit Clause to limit the power of state courts to apply their own law over the law of another state. As a general rule, the constitutional test for the permissible application of a state's law under both due process and the Full Faith and Credit Clause are co-extensive,[165] so when the application of a state's law is valid as a matter of due process, the state will not be required by full faith and credit to apply the law of another state.[166] The US Supreme Court has specifically rejected the contention that a state is required to recognize the sovereign immunity of out-of-state agencies involved in accidents or other controversies with residents of that state.[167] However, under the Full Faith and Credit Clause, a state may not discriminate against claims existing under the law of a Union state.[168] So, for example, if a state allows an action for wrongful death under its own law, it may not refuse to entertain an action for wrongful death brought under the law of another state.[169]

160 *Richards v. Jefferson County*, 517 U.S. 793, 797 n. 4 (1996).
161 See *Durfee v. Duke*, 375 U.S. 106 (1963).
162 See, e.g., *Thompson v. Whitman*, 85 U.S. 457, 469–70 (1873).
163 Ibid.
164 *Watkins v. Conway*, 385 U.S. 188, 190 (1966).
165 A state may constitutionally apply its own law whenever it has a "significant contact or significant aggregation of contacts, creating state interests, such that choice of its law is neither arbitrary nor fundamentally unfair." *Allstate Ins. Co. v. Hague*, 449 U.S. 302, 313 (1981). This test imposes very few limitations on a state's application of its own law, since it will be rare when a state's decision to apply its own law will be arbitrary or fundamentally unfair.
166 See *Pac. Employers Ins. Co. v. Indus. Accident Comm'n of Cal.*, 306 U.S. 493 (1939).
167 See *Nevada v. Hall*, 440 U.S. 410 (1979); *Franchise Tax Bd. of Cal. v. Hyatt*, 538 U.S. 488 (2003).
168 *Pac. Employers Ins.*, 306 U.S. 493, 501–502 (1939).
169 *Hughes*, 341 U.S. 609, 612–613 (1951). Yet it may also apply its non-discriminatory statute of limitations for wrongful death to bar a wrongful death action brought under the law of a Union state. For this see *Wells v. Simonds Abrasive Co.*, 345 U.S. 514, 518–19 (1953).

6.3.3. *Full Faith and Credit in Criminal Matters?*

With all this in mind, it would seem that the Full Faith and Credit Clause would provide a fair term of comparison with the principle of mutual recognition. The response turns out to be a bit more complicated than expected in the area of criminal law. This is the case as the main area of the Full Faith and Credit Clause is civil, not criminal law. The hot topics in the Full Faith and Credit Clause discussions have been, for instance, same-sex marriage,[170] divorce or child support.[171] Moreover, as we shall explore later in the book, in the area of criminal law, the dual sovereignty doctrine implies that a conviction or acquittal in one of the states does not preempt further prosecution in the sister states.[172]

This being said, there are certain aspects of criminal law that have been introduced in the Full Faith and Credit Clause discussion, and that actually deal with the distinction between vertical and horizontal federalism. Interesting examples are the child support cases. As noted, child support has been a traditional area of Full Faith and Credit.[173] Given the anti-commandeering doctrine already noted, i.e. Congress may not force states to pass laws, the only way to achieve uniform enforcement throughout the Union was through the so-called uniform laws,[174] which are proposed by the National Conference of Commissioners on Uniform State laws (Uniform Law Commission). The Commission drafted the Uniform Reciprocal Enforcement of Support Act in 1950, which was amended in 1952, 1958 and 1968.[175] The uniform law, although devoted principally to civil procedures, authorizes an enforcement procedure, similar to interstate rendition,[176] for an individual charged with the crime of nonsupport.[177] That is, a person who is in a state different to the one in which he/she is obliged to provide child support may be subject to interstate rendition. Probably due to the lack of real enforcement power of such interstate rendition provision, federal Congress

---

170 Joseph F. Zimmerman, *Horizontal Federalism. Interstate Relations*, 2011, at 67–68. For a basic overview Steve Sanders, *Is the Full Faith and Credit Clause Still "Irrelevant" to Same-Sex Marriage? Toward a Reconsideration of the Conventional Wisdom*, Indiana L.J. 89 (2014) at 95 with further references.

171 Joseph F. Zimmerman, *Horizontal Federalism. Interstate Relations*, 2011, at 71–76.

172 See below Chapter 3, section 3.3.

173 See the Full Faith and Credit for Child Support Act of 1994 addressed state agencies administering child support enforcement plans under Title IV-D of the social security act and other interested individuals. The law requires states to enforce child support orders made by other states, and prohibits states from modifying other states' child support orders unless certain jurisdictional requirements are met.

174 For a more in-depth analysis see below Chapter 3, section 4.3.

175 All states, except New York, enacted one version of the act. In 1981 and 1987 various amendments to the New York law brought it into nearly total conformity with the uniform law (Joseph F. Zimmerman, *Horizontal Federalism. Interstate Relations*, 2011, at 71–77).

176 For a thorough analysis of this form of intra-state extradition (similar to the European Arrest Warrant) see below Chapter 3, section 2.3.

177 Uniform Reciprocal Enforcement of Support Act, §§ 12, 18.

decided to intervene.[178] The Child Support Recovery Act of 1992 made it a federal felony for an obligor residing in a state other than the one in which the oblige resides willfully to refuse to pay a past due support obligation which is defined as one "that has remained unpaid for a period longer than one year, or is greater than $5,000".[179] The basis for this federal legislation was the interstate commerce clause. The provision was challenged both under the interstate commerce clause and the Tenth Amendment, but both challenges were rejected.[180]

As *Lind* put it at the time: "Traditionally, states have had primary authority in collecting child support. Because states have failed to adequately resolve the child support problem, some are advocating for more federal involvement".[181] To put it differently, given that the uniform law already adopted by all states of the Union and the interstate rendition system did not provide the service, i.e. the federal government had to deploy billions of dollars because parents were failing to provide child support, the federal government decided to criminalize such a conduct. The financial interests of the Union were at stake and the states were not providing adequate protection of those funds, so the federal government decided to intervene. Probably the most controversial issue was that that federal intervention was founded on the power to regulate interstate commerce,[182] i.e. the Commerce Clause.

This is probably a clear example of how the relationship between horizontal and vertical federalism works in the area of criminal law. In areas basically

178 On top of ethical considerations, the cost to the federal funds may have played a decisive role. See Eric S. Lind, *Interstate Collection of Child Support and Federalism: Why the States Have Authority and What They Need to Do to Keep it*, B.Y.U. J. Public Law 11 (1996) at 103: "Failure to collect child support has become a nation-wide problem and costs taxpayers billions in federal welfare funding".

179 Child Support Recovery Act of 1992, 106, Stat. 3403, 18 U.S.C. § 228(a)(d)(1)(A).

180 Case law referred in Joseph F. Zimmerman, *Horizontal Federalism. Interstate Relations*, 2011 at 71–76. Basically the decisions in *United States v. Crawford,* 522 U.S. 934, 118 S.Ct. 258 (1997) and *United States v. Johnson,* 522 117 S Ct. 228 (1997) (certs. denied) and *United States v. Sage,* 519 U.S. 1099, 117 S.Ct. 784 (1997).

181 Eric S. Lind, *Interstate Collection of Child Support and Federalism: Why the States Have Authority and What They Need to Do to Keep it*, B.Y.U. J. Public Law 11 (1996) at 103. See also Kathleen A. Burdette, *Making Parents Pay: Interstate Child Support Enforcement after United States v. Lopez*, Uni. Penn. L. Rev. 114 (1996) at 1469.

182 In the case *United States v. Schroeder,* 894 F. Supp. 360 (D. Ariz. 1995) the federal court struck down the Child Support Recovery Act as unconstitutional on the grounds that criminalization of child support does not "substantially affect interstate commerce" and that it constituted a violation of the tenth amendment as the powers granted to the federal government are few and defined while those that remain with state governments are numerous and indefinite (ibid. at 368 referring to Madison's Federalist No. 45). Similarly *United States v. Kerley,* 544 F. 3d. 172 (2nd Cir. 2008). The US Supreme court is yet to decide on this issue. During 1996–1997 it refused to hear appeals from courts that have upheld the CSRA. For a discussion of the implications of the then recently held case *United States v. Lopez* (1995) see Kathleen A. Burdette, *Making Parents Pay: Interstate Child Support Enforcement after United States v. Lopez*, Uni. Penn. L. Rev. 114 (1996) at 1469; Ronald S. Kornreich, *The Constitutionality of Punishing Deadbeat Parents: The Child Support Recovery Act of 1992 After United States v. Lopez*, Fordham L. Rev. 64 (1995) at 1989.

belonging to civil law, e.g. child support, the Full Faith and Credit Clause gives sister states' orders the same enforcing power as orders of the state of execution. Given the lack of uniformity among sister states, the Uniform Law Commission drafts a legislative text that can – not shall – be incorporated into state law. This legislation contains provisions to facilitate interstate rendition in cases where some states have criminalized not providing child support. If all this lax horizontal federalism technique does not work, then vertical federalism kicks in. The federal government criminalizes not providing child support when the obligor resides in another state on the grounds of interstate commerce.

6.3.4. *Conclusion*

The Full Faith and Credit Clause and the principle of mutual recognition are both horizontal federalism mechanisms. Their common goal is to serve (in European terms) the free movement of judicial decisions throughout the unions, or (in American terms) that the ruling of a state "is at home whithersoever it goes, through the whole length and breadth of the Union". Yet, as the previous discussion shows, it is fair to conclude that the Full Faith and Credit Clause does not basically refer to the area of criminal law and certainly does not include the power to unify state laws. In short, the Full Faith and Credit Clause is not used to criminalize certain conducts through all the states that comprise the United States of America.

Translating these two key findings into European terms, applying the Full Faith and Credit Clause to the EU would imply that the principle of mutual recognition would not basically refer to criminal law and would not include the harmonization of Member States' legislation. At this stage there is a discrepancy with current EU law. As noted, Article 83(2) specifically addresses both issues: "Judicial cooperation in *criminal matters* in the Union shall be based on the principle of mutual recognition of judgments and judicial decisions and *shall include the approximation of the laws and regulations of the Member States*".

If this brief assessment holds true, then the consequence is not hard to derive. At least in criminal law matters, the EU has reached, through the principle of mutual recognition, a substantially higher degree of horizontal federalism than the US.[183] The principle of mutual recognition in criminal matters includes federalizing elements which are unknown to the Full Faith and Credit Clause. Now, academics and legislators may criticize these findings by stating that nowhere in the European Treaties does the term "federal" refer to the principle

[183] As Cherif Bassiouni, *International Extradition. United States Law and Practice*, 2014, footnote 105 at 25 notes, the Full Faith and Credit Clause required that one state obtain a judgment that recognized the judgment of the other state, where as the principle of mutual recognition goes directly to the implementing judge in any EU country. Also, a challenge based on a violation of due process rights is available in the US system while not specifically accounted for in the EU system.

of mutual recognition. Yet if the Full Faith and Credit Clause and the principle of mutual recognition are so extremely similar in their goal and the Full Faith and Credit Clause is considered a clear example of horizontal federalism, it does not seem unreasonable to conclude that the principle of mutual recognition is also a notorious example of horizontal federalism.

For the next chapter a broader interesting question is worth noting: what happens when state action is not effective, when interstate cooperation does not work? Both Unions resort to their federal powers (vertical in the US, horizontal in the EU) to address the problem. The US uses the Interstate Commerce Clause to (vertically) federalize certain criminal conduct. The EU resorts to serious cross-border criminality to (horizontally) federalize certain criminal conduct. Probably the key difference here is that the origin of the Full Faith and Credit Clause had nothing to do with interstate commerce. On the other hand, the origin of the principle of mutual recognition was closely linked with the EU internal market. Both Unions followed different paths: interstate commerce has been used as a means to foster vertical federalism in the US; the internal market has been used as a means to foster horizontal federalism in the EU. But the federalizing force of interstate commerce/the internal market remains.

CHAPTER 2

THE FEDERAL CRIMINAL LAW DIMENSION IN THE LISBON TREATY

1. INTRODUCTION

So far, this book has noted certain horizontal federalism trends in EU criminal law. It has also conducted a more in-depth analysis of the principle propelling the development of EU criminal law for over a decade: the principle of mutual recognition. Finally a brief comparison between this and its US counterpart, the Full Faith and Credit Clause, has been drawn, with the interesting result that, in this area, the EU system of criminal justice exhibits greater horizontal federalism than the US system. The probable cause of this result is that the pressures fostering horizontal federalism in the EU are channeled through vertical federalism in the US.

From this point forward, the book will focus on those aspects of the Lisbon Treaty that provide a legal basis for federalization trends, while noting the resemblances between these provisions and US provisions addressing similar matters. Clearly, the Lisbon Treaty contains numerous matters relating to the criminal law, but only a limited number of them will be addressed here in the interests of space. The purpose of this work, rather, is to focus on certain aspects of the Lisbon Treaty that have a horizontal federalism character and to note how the US has dealt with similar issues through a vertical federalism approach. The end result confirms our previous findings: the problems posed by criminal law in the EU are addressed with horizontal federalism. The same problematic is addressed in the US through vertical federalism.

To be sure, the ratification of the Treaty of Lisbon[1] was a historical milestone[2] in the evolution of the European unification. What started in 1957 as an agreement

---

1 On the Constitution for Europe see PHILLIPPE SCHMITTER, *Democracy in Europe and Europe's Democratization*, 14 JOURNAL OF DEMOCRACY (2003) at 74. But also see THOMAS OPPERMANN, *Vom Nizza-Vertrag 2001 zum Europäischen Verfassungskonvent 2002/2003*, 101 DVBl (2003) at 1.

2 Valéry Giscard d'Estaing, President of the European Convention on the Future of Europe referred to the Convention that established the basis of the Lisbon Treaty – then referred as the Treaty establishing a Constitution for Europe CONV 820/03 – as "our Philadelphia", which supports the adequacy of comparing the EU and US systems. This has wide implications as

between a few sovereign nations over certain basic economic principles has led to a debate over a possible European Constitution that ultimately culminated in the Lisbon Treaty and its substantial impact on Europe.[3] This evolution will continue and it is certainly fair to think that the Lisbon Treaty will have a profound, transformative effect on Europe going forward.[4] Historically, the draft of the Lisbon Treaty was passed amid concern over an issue that has been polemical among Member States: the expansion of the European Union. The initial fifteen Member States of the European Union became twenty-five Member States under the Lisbon Treaty, bringing significant change to the Union. To a certain extent, this situation reflected the intense process of *globalization*[5] that was taking place worldwide. However, this reflection had its own connotations in the European context; in other words, the process of "Europeanization" contains distinct characteristics due to the idiosyncrasies of "Old Europe".

For the purposes of this book, it is worth looking at the potential relevance of this European development for criminal law.[6] It is readily apparent that the adoption of the Lisbon Treaty has had a critical impact for EU criminal law: there are certain powers expressly conferred to the EU in criminal law matters.[7] As noted previously, the Treaty of Lisbon reopened the debate over the creation of a European federation, a so-called United States of Europe.[8] Over time, the

---

PHILLIPE SCHMITTER, *Democracy in Europe and Europe's Democratization*, 14 JOURNAL OF DEMOCRACY (2003) at 73.

3 On the issue of whether Europe needed a constitution see DIETER GRIMM, *Does Europe needs a Constitution?*, 1 EUROPEAN LAW JOURNAL (1995) at 282 for one perspective and JÜRGEN HABERMAS, *The Inclusion of the Other: Studies in Political Theory* (ed. Ciaran Cronin and Pablo De Greiff), 2000 at 185 for the opposing view. For a more recent approach see JÜRGEN HABERMAS, *The Crisis of the European Union. A response*, 2012 at 1–71.

4 For an introduction see ESTER HERLIN-KARNELL, *The Lisbon Treaty and the Area of Criminal Law And Justice*, EUROPEAN POLICY ANALYSIS 3 (2008) at 1; ALEXANDRA HORVATHOVA, *EU Criminal Law and the Treaty of Lisbon – Where Shall We Go Now?*, November 30, 2010 (available at: http://ssrn.com/abstract=1836754); CLEMENS LADENBURGER, *Police and Criminal Law in the Treaty of Lisbon: A New Dimension for the Community Method*, EUROPEAN CONSTITUTIONAL LAW REVIEW 4 (2008) at 20–40.

5 Globalization has been mainly considered as an economic process, which has implications for democratic forms of government; see ARMIN VON BOGDANDY, *Demokratie, Globalisierung, Zukunft des Völkerrechts – eine Bestandsaufnahme*, ZAÖRV 63 (2003) at 854.

6 See THOMAS WEIGEND, *Der Entwurf einer Europäischen Verfassung und das Strafrecht*, ZEITSCHRIFT FÜR DIE GESAMTE STRAFRECHTSWISSENSCHAFT 116 (2004) at 275 warning of the possible spillover effects that the Lisbon Treaty could have over the systems of criminal law of the Member States.

7 See ESTER HERLIN-KARNELL, *The Constitutional Dimension of European Criminal Law*, 2012 at 64: "The Lisbon Treaty opened up a new chapter in the development and creation of EU criminal law by explicitly listing it as a supranational competence".

8 That was the intention of the EU "Founding Fathers", says MICHAEL BURGESS, *Federalism and European Union: The Building of Europe, 1950–2000*, 2000 at 55–64. STEFAN OETER, *Federalism and Democracy*, in A. VON BOGDANDY and J. BAST, eds., *Principles of European Constitutional Law*, 2011 at 63 considers that the Fathers were, to this extent, extremely federalist. But see DAHRENDORF, *The Challenge of Democracy*, JOURNAL OF DEMOCRACY 14 (2003) at 101 denying that there will ever be a United States of Europe.

European Union has taken a form that increasingly resembles a federation,[9] as repeatedly pointed out by a number of scholars.[10] The Lisbon Treaty seems to represent a milestone in the final consolidation of a trend where clear hints of federalism, or federalism as in the German concept of *Föderalität*,[11] are apparent. Clear examples of this may be found in the independent, legal personhood of the European Union (Article 7[12]) and the merging of the original pillars that comprised the European Union.

This evolution was heavily debated at the time that the Constitution for Europe, i.e. the precursor to the Lisbon Treaty, was at stake. One of the greatest philosophers of our time, *Habermas*, described the tendency as follows: "The 'Euro-federalists' aspire to undertake a process that will transform the current international treaties into a political constitution for Europe, and this as a way to widen the legal reach of the decisions by the European Commission, the Council of the European Union and the European Union Court of Justice."[13] In conclusion, *Habermas* considered that "the expansion of political action has to go hand in hand with increased legitimacy",[14] which undoubtedly has had an impact on the criminal law field. More recently, at the height of the sovereign debt crisis, *Habermas* further stated that Europe is "now more than ever a constitutional project",[15] though warning that the type of federalism in the Lisbon Treaty is a post-democratic executive federalism that should be reinforced with transnational democracy.[16]

---

9 See, prior to the Lisbon Treaty, K. Nicolaïdis and R. Howse, eds., *The Federal Vision: Legitimacy and Levels of Governance in the United States and the European Union*, 2001. Recently, Alexander H. Trechsel, ed., *Towards a Federal Europe?*, 2013.

10 See Alexander H. Trechsel, *How to Federalize the European Union ... and why bother*, in Alexander H. Trechsel, ed., *Towards a Federal Europe?*, 2013 at 1: "While there is little doubt that the majority of contemporary observers ascribe to the EU certain federal qualities, detecting processes of federalization here and there scholars of comparative politics increasingly include the EU among their cases when investigating the impact of federalism on, for instance, policy making", with further references at 2. See also Stefan Oeter, *Federalism and Democracy*, in A. von Bogdandy and J. Bast, eds., *Principles of European Constitutional Law*, 2011 at 71.

11 See Helmut Willke, *Heterotopia. Studien zur Krisis der Ordnung moderner Gesellschaften*, 2003 at 15–16. See the more recent considerations in Helmut Willke and Gerhard Willke, *Political Governance of Capitalism. A Reassessment Beyond the Global Crisis*, 2012 at 109–110.

12 Treaty of Lisbon amending the Treaty on European Union and the Treaty establishing the European Community, 13 December 2007, Official Journal of the European Union, 2007, C 306/01. Noteworthy is the fact that Declaration No 24 states: "The conference confirms that the fact that the European Union has a legal personality will not in any way authorize the Union to legislate or to act beyond the competences conferred upon it by the Member States in the Treaties".

13 Jürgen Habermas, *Towards a Cosmopolitan Europe*, 14 Journal of Democracy (2003) at 96.

14 Ibid. at 97.

15 Jürgen Habermas, *The Crisis of the European Union: A response*, 2012, at 1.

16 Ibid. at 12–53, concluding that the only viable alternative to address the asymmetry between the democratic participation of the peoples in what their governments obtain for them on the far-off Brussels stage and the indifference, even apathy, of the EU citizens regarding the decision of their Parliament in Strasbourg (at 48).

As a result of this process, there is a consolidated tendency to describe the European Union as a federation of states.[17] To put it bluntly, the European Union has evolved from a mere grouping of states (*Staatenverbund*) to an entity with greater federal character.[18] As we have noted previously, there is a clear reluctance in Europe to acknowledge the increasing federalized nature of the EU. But such rejection, based primarily on historical preconceptions, should not preclude the benefits of addressing some of the current problems of the EU, e.g. criminal law, from a federal perspective. In other words, there are certain federalizing tendencies in the Lisbon Treaty that significantly affect the development of EU criminal law.

For instance, from a constitutional perspective, the Charter of Fundamental Right of the European Union signed on 7 December 2000 in Nice,[19] now binding pursuant to Article 6 of the Lisbon Treaty,[20] illustrates the significant impact that the development of federalizing elements of the EU has on criminal law. Important principles emerge from the Charter that can be compared to those derived from some federal constitutions. Concerning the fundamental rights of the defendant, various provisions contained in Title VI may be considered the so-called "criminal constitution", which are crucial to modern criminal law:[21] Article 47, the right to effective remedy and a fair trial; Article 48, presumption of innocence and right of defense; and Article 49, principles of legality and proportionality of criminal offenses and penalties.

Most notably, the Lisbon Treaty amends Article 6 TEU to include an important provision relevant to this discussion. The third paragraph of Article 6 reads as follows: "Fundamental rights, as guaranteed by the European Convention for the Protection of Human Rights and Fundamental Freedoms and as they result from the constitutional traditions common to the Member States, shall constitute general principles of the Union's law". This implies that the abundant criminal case law of the ECtHR should have a decisive impact on the interpretation of criminal statutes throughout the EU. Although the EU itself has not yet acceded

---

17 Robert Schütze, *From Dual to Cooperative Federalism: The Changing Structure of European Law*, 2009 at 4 with further references. See also Jürgen Habermas, *The Crisis of the European Union: A response*, 2012 at 36: "federative political community beyond the nation state".

18 Highly illustrative is the title of Joschka Fischer, 23 Integration (2000) at 149: "*Von Staatenverbund zum Föderation – Gedanken über die Finalität der europäischen Integration*".

19 See Official Journal of the EU, C 364, December 18, 2000.

20 On the European Charter of Fundamental Rights see Kühling, *Fundamental Rights*, in A. von Bogdandy and J. Bast, eds., *Principles of European Constitutional Law*, 2006 at 479; Meyer, *Kommentar zur Charta der Grundrechte der Europäischen Union*, 2003.

21 The so-called Frankfurt School considers that the development of European criminal law should be based on the European Charter of Fundamental Rights. Moreover, the legitimacy of EU criminal law lies precisely in securing the effective enforcement of those rights throughout the EU (see the contributions in Albrecht et al, KritV 2001).

to the ECHR,[22] through this provision it will be bound to a greater extent by the interpretation of the ECHR produced by the ECtHR.

Moving beyond this constitutional dimension, this chapter focuses on the treaty provisions that empower the EU to enact criminal legislation and provide for criminal enforcement. This book contends that the Lisbon Treaty entails two different potential sources of power to enact EU criminal law legislation. First, the Area of Freedom, Security and Justice, starting at Article 81, has a significant importance for criminal law, particularly in Section 4 relating to judicial cooperation in criminal matters (Articles 82 et seq).[23] Additionally, under the heading of "Combatting Fraud", Article 325 TFEU grants the EU power to adopt "the necessary measures in the fields of the prevention of and fight against fraud affecting the financial interests of the Union".[24]

It will be argued that the clearest source of a genuine European criminal law lies in the second power, as it deals with truly EU (federal) interests. Here the legitimacy of the EU protecting its own interests can hardly be questioned. The deficient protection of these interests that the Member States have provided so far adds a necessity factor that strengthens the case for European-level protection. The interesting issue arises when, looking at the Lisbon Treaty, the first black-letter law provisions conferring powers to the EU to legislate in criminal law matters lies in the judicial cooperation within the Area of Freedom, Security and Justice. As noted before, the principle fostering this dimension of the Lisbon Treaty is the principle of mutual recognition, derived from the internal market approach. Here, a common theme surfaces between the underlying principles of the free movement of goods in the EU and of interstate commerce regulation in the US. Similarly, the criticism raised against the proliferating use of such powers in both Unions is also comparable. The difference as it relates to federalism is that, while interstate commerce has fostered vertical federalism, the free movement of goods – through the principle of mutual recognition – has propelled horizontal federalism.

---

22 Official talks on the European Union's accession to the European Convention of Human Rights started on July 7, 2010, launched by Thorbjørn Jagland, the Secretary General of the Council of Europe, and Viviane Reding, Vice-President of the European Commission. Discussed since the late 1970s, the accession became a legal obligation under Article 6 of the Treaty of Lisbon. Negotiators of the 47 Council of Europe Member States and the European Union finalized the draft accession agreement of the European Union to the European Convention on Human Rights. Yet the ruling of the ECJ on December 18, 2014 concluded that the draft agreement on the accession of the European Union to the ECHR was not compatible with EU law for a number of reasons (see Press Release No 180/14 of the ECJ). For a general analysis see Steve Peers, *The CJEU and the EU's accession to the ECHR: a clear and present danger to human rights protection* (available at: http://eulawanalysis.blogspot.com.es/2014/12/the-cjeu-and-eus-accession-to-echr.html).

23 See below Chapter 2, section 4.3.2. The AFSJ was heavily discussed during the negotiations of the Lisbon Treaty. See David Phinnemore, *The Treaty of Lisbon. Origins and Negotiation*, 2012 at 164–168.

24 See below Chapter 2, section 3.2.

Finally, the chapter ends with a thorough review of the institution with the most potential significance so far in the EU system of criminal justice: the recently proposed European Public Prosecutor's Office (EPPO). It has taken five years and a dramatic crisis affecting the EU financial interests for the EU to establish a European prosecutor to prosecute crimes against EU financial interests, pursuant to Article 86 TFEU. As detailed below, the EU system of double-hat prosecutors does not coincide with the US system of federal US attorneys. The lack of independence of the prosecutor in the European proposal, necessary for effective protection of EU interests, is a clear deficit that should be amended rapidly. In addition, the potential of Article 86 TFEU to regulate the admissibility of evidence when the EPPO is performing its task should be put to use. In this sense, the exhaustive regulation of the Federal Rules of Evidence in the US could provide a useful guideline.

2. PRELIMINARY ISSUES

2.1. HOW MANY DIFFERENT SOURCES OF CRIMINAL POWERS ARE THERE IN BOTH UNIONS?

The most obvious source of EU criminal powers is contained in the provisions establishing the Judicial Cooperation in Criminal Matters within the Area of Freedom, Security and Justice (Title II of the TFEU). Though it will be addressed in greater detail at a later stage, for now it is worth noting that Article 83(1) TFEU confers criminal powers to the EU in matters concerning serious cross-border criminality; Article 83(2) TFEU confers equal powers when criminal law is needed for the effective implementation of EU policies; and last but not least, Article 325 TFEU, the "combatting fraud" provision, is located in Title VI, which deals with the financial provisions of the European Union. We include this last reference due to the fact that, historically, the discussions regarding a true and genuine European criminal law have been ongoing regarding this latter provision – and the former Article 280 ToA.[25]

As to US federal criminal law, the US Constitution vests Congress with explicit authority to enact criminal laws relating to counterfeiting, piracy, crimes on the high seas, offenses against the law of nations, and treason. The US Constitution also grants Congress other broad powers, such as the power to regulate interstate commerce. Finally, the Constitution's Necessary and Proper Clause allows Congress to enact criminal laws when reasonably related to the regulation of commerce or to one of the other constitutionally enumerated powers. Last but not least, the so-called Spending Clause establishes that "Congress shall have Power

[25] See below Chapter 2, section 3.2.

to lay and collect Taxes ... to provide ... for the general Welfare of the United States".

With just this brief outlay, some similarities between the federal approach of both Unions regarding criminal law – horizontal in the EU and vertical in the US – start to become clear. First the Necessary and Proper Clause is not far from the need to effectively implement Unions' policies. The Unions' funding seems to enable a similar approach in the Spending Clause (US) and Title VI (EU). Finally, the rationale behind criminal provisions pursuant to the interstate commerce powers of the US seem to fall along the lines of combating serious cross-border criminality. All these similarities will be explored later on.

But for now it is interesting to look a little closer into the potential relationship between Articles 325 and 83(2) TFEU or, in US terms, between the Spending Clause and the Necessary and Proper Clause. A number of scholars consider that EU *criminal* powers to combat fraud would not be contained in Article 325, but in Article 83(2) TFEU.[26] Yet, an alternative federalizing interpretation would be that Article 83(2) TFEU *supplements* Article 325, a result suggested by the experience of US federal criminal law. US federal powers in combatting fraud are contained in Article I Section 8 of the US Constitution and the Necessary and Proper Clause contained in Article I Section 8 Clause 18 supplements those powers. To the same extent, EU powers in combatting fraud contained in Article 325 TFEU could be supplemented by Article 83(2) TFEU.

This discussion is not a mere theoretical exercise, but has recently acquired a practical connotation. In the EU Commission's Proposal for a Directive on the fight against fraud to the Union's financial interests by means of criminal law,[27] there was absolutely no reference to Article 83(2) TFEU. On the contrary, it specifically referred to Article 325 TFEU as its legal basis.[28] This was significant, as other legal instruments entertaining the possibility of imposing criminal sanctions to protect EU policies, e.g. the Directive on market manipulation,[29] do cite Article 83(2) TFEU[30] as their legal basis.

In the legislative procedure 2012/0193/COD,[31] the European Parliament reassessed the legal basis for the enactment of the Directive. The first amendment

---

26 See Bernd Hecker, *Europäisches Strafrecht*, 4th ed., 2012 at 278 with further references.

27 Proposal for a Directive of the European Parliament and of the Council on the fight against fraud to the Union's financial interests by means of criminal law, COM (2012) 363 final.

28 COM (2012) 363 final, at 7.

29 Directive 2014/57/EU of the European Parliament and of the Council of 16 April 2014 on criminal sanctions for market abuse (Market Abuse Directive) (OJ L 173, 12 June 2014, p. 179–189).

30 To be sure, the Directive Proposal on the fight against fraud (COM (2012) 363 final) also cites Article 83(1) TFEU to signal that crimes committed by EU officials are included among the offenses listed in Article 83(1) TFEU: corruption, etc. But it is clearly not considered the legal basis for legislative action.

31 http://eur-lex.europa.eu/procedure/EN/201814?qid=1416076099748&rid=1.

introduced by the European Parliament[32] was to change the proposed wording "Having regard to the Treaty on the Functioning of the European Union, and in particular Article *325(4)* thereof" to "Having regard to the Treaty on the Functioning of the European Union, and in particular Article *83(2)* thereof,". Put differently, the European Parliament specifically rejected the idea of holding Article 325(4) of the TFEU as the legal basis for enacting EU criminal legislation and therefore resorted to Article 83(2) TFEU.

Against this backdrop it is interesting to note the debate concerning the Spending Clause and its relationship to the Necessary and Proper Clause in the area of criminal law. The basic criminal legislation concerning the protection of US federal funds, Section 666 U.S.C., i.e. the federal bribery statute, "was adopted pursuant to Congress' spending power, Art. I, § 8, cl. 1."[33] Section 666 was designed "to augment the ability of the United States to vindicate significant acts of theft, fraud, and bribery involving Federal monies", even though no federal officials are involved, and thereby "to protect the integrity of the vast sums of money distributed through federal programs".[34]

Some courts and commentators argued that Section 666, and any other criminal statutes whose purported jurisdictional hook is the flow of federal dollars in pursuit of the general welfare, are constitutional, not because they are contractual conditions attached to money grants to state and local governments, but because they are "Laws … necessary and proper for carrying into Execution" another of Congress's Article I powers, namely the spending power itself.[35] That is, to uphold the constitutionality of this federal statute, a combination of the Spending Clause and the Necessary and Proper Clause is needed. To put it another way, the Spending Clause alone would not provide the necessary basis for the enactment of such statute.

It seems that this was the path chosen by the US Supreme Court in *Sabri v. United States* (2004).[36] The Court established the following: "Congress has authority under the Spending Clause to appropriate federal monies to promote the general welfare, Art. I, § 8, cl. 1, and it has corresponding authority under the Necessary and Proper Clause, Art. I, § 8, cl. 18, to see to it that taxpayer dollars appropriated under that power are in fact spent for the general welfare, and not frittered away in graft or on projects undermined when funds are siphoned off or corrupt public officers are derelict about demanding value for dollars".[37]

32 See document TA/2014/427/P7 at www.europarl.europa.eu/sides/getDoc.do?pubRef=-//EP//TEXT%20TA%20P7-TA-2014-0427%200%20DOC%20XML%20V0//en.

33 *Fischer v. United States*, 529 U.S. 667, 689 n. 3 (2000).

34 See S. REP. No. 98-225, at 369–70; see also, *Salinas v. United States*, 522 U.S. 52 (1997) at 57–58 (noting legislative history and statute's stated purpose).

35 See *United States v. Lipscomb*, 299 F.3d 303, 318 (5th Cir. 2002). See also Richard W. Garnett, *The New Federalism, The Spending Power, and Federal Criminal Law*, 89 Cornell L. Rev. 1 (2003) at 67 with further references.

36 *Sabri v. United States*, 541 U.S. 600 (2004).

37 Ibid.

Expressly resorting to the link between the criminal dimension of the statute and the Necessary and Proper Clause, the court further noted:

> "For those of us who accept help from legislative history, it is worth noting that the legislative record confirms that § 666(a)(2) is an instance of necessary and proper legislation. The design was generally to 'protect the integrity of the vast sums of money distributed through Federal programs from theft, fraud, and undue influence by bribery', see S. Rep. No. 98 No. 225, p. 370 (1983), in contrast to prior federal law affording only two limited opportunities to prosecute such threats to the federal interest: 18 U. S. C. § 641, the federal theft statute, and § 201, the federal bribery law."[38]

Quite interestingly for the EU discussion, the US Supreme Court, when addressing the link between the original power, i.e. the Spending Clause, and the implicit power, i.e. the Necessary and Proper Clause,[39] focused on certain issues that are relevant to the discussion over the logic of Article 83(2) TFEU: "Congress's decision to enact § 666 only after other legislation had failed to protect federal interests is further indication that it was acting within the ambit of the Necessary and Proper Clause."[40] The common rationale for both Unions in this area would be the following: in order to trigger the powers of these clauses, Article 83(2) TFEU and the Necessary and Proper Clause, previous measures adopted by the Union must "have proven inadequate to the task"[41] of protecting the Unions' interests. This would be the interpretation of the Article 83(2) TFEU when it enables EU criminal legislation when it "proves essential to ensure the effective implementation of a Union policy in an area which has been subject to harmonisation measures".

As we shall see below, the fact of whether the explicit power enables criminal legislation or whether the implicit power is needed is not such an issue in the US, but it may very well be a delicate matter in the EU. The specific form of legislation pursuant to the original power, i.e. Article 325 TFEU, may be the Regulation, which has more unifying effect than the Directive. The implicit power, i.e. Article 83(2) TFEU, only enables the use of the Directive, with a more harmonizing, less unifying, character. The current Proposal for a Directive on the fight against fraud to the Union's financial interests by means of criminal law[42]

---

38 *Sabri v. United States*, 541 U.S. 604–605 (2004).

39 The necessary and proper by itself would not provide sufficient grounds. As the US Supreme Court pointed out, for the claim of unconstitutionality to prevail, the plaintiffs would have to show that the federal statute "had nothing to do with the congressional spending power" (*Sabri v. United States*, 541 U.S. 606 (2004)).

40 *Sabri v. United States*, 541 U.S. 605 (2004).

41 Ibid.

42 Proposal for a Directive of the European Parliament and of the Council on the fight against fraud to the Union's financial interests by means of criminal law, COM (2012) 363 final.

relies on the Directive, and therefore the discussion, for now, is more theoretical than practical.

It is interesting to note the opinion adopted by the Legal Affairs Committee of the European Parliament regarding the use of Article 83(2) as a legal basis.[43] On its own initiative, the Committee decided to review the appropriate nature of the legal basis chosen by the Commission and the possibility of replacing Article 325(4) TFEU with Article 83(2) TFEU. On 14 December 2012 the Committee issued its opinion deciding to "recommend that the appropriate legal basis for the proposal … should be Article 83(2) TFEU".[44] The grounds for such a decision lie in the fact that, according to the Committee, "the choice of legal basis for a Community measure must rest on objective factors amenable to judicial review, including in particular the aim and the content of the measure".[45] In the Committee's opinion the main goals of the Directive are to strengthen and the harmonize criminal law provisions of the Member States. All in all, the Committee considers that Article 83(2) represents a *lex specialis* compared to Article 325(4) "as regards the conferral of competence for substantive criminal law".

According to the Committee's view, Article 83(2) contains specific requirements and limits the content of the rules that can be based on this provision, providing for the specific mechanism of an emergency-brake provision contained in Article 83(3). From an overall perspective, the Committee concludes, "it would be surprising if these limitations could be circumvented by recourse to another substantive legal base. To allow recourse to different potential legal bases on substantive policies would also hamper the coherent development of future legislation in the area of criminal law harmonisation. This could not have been intended under the Treaty of Lisbon".[46]

2.2. FEDERAL COURTS IN BOTH UNIONS

If we were to pick a specific dimension of federalism that highlights the differences between the EU and the US in criminal law, it would be the operation of the federal courts. As this chapter will note, there has been substantial EU improvement in the areas of codification and enforcement, yet the lack of a European jurisdiction over criminal matters clearly differentiates the EU system from the US system.[47] Although the Lisbon Treaty provides some advances in

43 European Parliament, Opinion on the legal basis for the proposal for a Directive of the European Parliament and of the Council on the fight against fraud to the Union's financial interests by means of criminal law (COM (2012) 363 – C7-0192/2012).

44 Ibid. at 6.

45 Ibid. at 3.

46 Ibid. at 5.

47 See generally Daniel Halberstam, *Comparative Federalism and the Role of the Judiciary*, in K. Whittington, D. Keleman and G. Caldeira, eds., *The Oxford Handbook of Law and Politics*, 2008 at 142–64.

the potential future establishment of a European specialized court in criminal matters under Article 257 TFEU, there is remarkable difference when compared with the federal courts in US system. Basically, in the EU system, there is no direct access of individual defendants to a European jurisdiction and there is no European court to impose direct criminal sanctions over individual citizens. In short, EU citizens are tried before national (not federal) courts and they can only appeal to national (not federal) courts.

Unlike the EU system, however, the US Constitution goes on to grant an expansive congressional power to establish inferior courts within the federal system.[48] Moreover, the law enacted to create the federal court system on 24 September 1789, i.e. the Judiciary Act, also established some of the most important institutions of federal criminal law: the US attorneys[49] and the US marshalls.[50] Yet, most importantly, the federal courts in the United States are empowered to hear a broad array of cases, with no limits on procedural posture.[51] While there is a modern presumption that most cases fall under the concurrent jurisdiction of both state and federal courts,[52] Congress has the power to provide the federal courts with *exclusive* jurisdiction over matters under federal law.[53] Significantly, Congress has chosen to exercise the power and granted exclusive federal jurisdiction over federal criminal laws.[54] This stands in contrast to the EU system,

---

48 U.S. Const. art III, § 1 ("such inferior Courts as the Congress may from time to time ordain and establish").

49 The Judiciary Act of 1789, ch. 20, 1 Stat. 92 (1789): The United States Attorney was "to prosecute in (each) district all delinquents for crimes and offenses cognizable under the authority of the United States, and all civil actions in which the United States shall be concerned." Within a few days of the passage of the Judiciary Act, President George Washington appointed thirteen distinguished people to fill the offices of United States Attorneys in the newly created federal judicial districts.

50 Section 27 of the Judiciary Act reads: "be it further enacted, That a marshal shall be appointed in and for each district for a term of four years, but shall be removable from office at pleasure, whose duty it shall be to attend the district and circuit courts when sitting therein, and also the Supreme Court in the district in which that court shall sit. And to execute throughout the district, all lawful precepts directed to him, and issued under the authority of the United States, and he shall have the power to command all necessary assistance in the execution of his duty, and to appoint as shall be occasion, one or more deputies".

51 U.S. Const. art III, § 2 ("The judicial Power shall extend to all Cases, in Law and Equity, arising under this Constitution, the Laws of the United States, and Treaties made, or which shall be made, under their Authority; – to all Cases affecting Ambassadors, other public Ministers and Consuls; – to all Cases of admiralty and maritime Jurisdiction; – to Controversies to which the United States shall be a Party; – to Controversies between two or more States; – between a State and Citizens of another State; – between Citizens of different States; – between Citizens of the same State claiming Lands under Grants of different States, and between a State, or the Citizens thereof, and foreign States, Citizens or Subjects.").

52 *Charles Dowd Box Co. v. Courtney*, 368 U.S. 502, 507–08 (1962) ("nothing in the concept of our federal system prevents state courts from enforcing rights created by federal law. … [E]xclusive federal court jurisdiction over cases arising under federal law has been the exception rather than the rule.").

53 § 3527 Exclusive Federal Court Jurisdiction, 13 Fed. Prac. & Proc. Juris. § 3527 (3d ed.).

54 18 U.S.C. § 3231 (2006) ("The district courts of the United States shall have original jurisdiction, exclusive of the courts of the States, of all offenses against the laws of the United States."). For a quick outline of the American court system, see Federal Judicial Center,

as discussed below.[55] Theoretically, the bulk of potential jurisdiction remains vested in the states (everything not listed in Article III of the Constitution), although with the expansion of federal law in the US[56] a creative prosecutor could arguably take her pick of factual scenarios to pursue in the federal courts.[57]

The history of federal courts in the United States has been one of ever-expanding reach, not necessarily in function, but rather in tandem with a growing body of federal law. Based on the initial constitutional grant, Congress provided for federal trial court jurisdiction over "all crimes and offences that shall be cognizable under the authority of the United States."[58] Thus, with the expansion of criminal laws passed at a national level, the amount of federal prosecutions increased.[59] By the 20th century, prosecutions at a federal level had grown, highlighted by the Volstead Act[60] and the American experiment with Prohibition, where "massive numbers of prohibition prosecutions forced federal courts 'to perform the function of petty police courts.'"[61] Prosecutions were so numerous that the federal government had to enlist the aid of state law-enforcement officials in implementing the ban.[62] Even since the end of Prohibition, federal courts have continued to hear more criminal cases, particularly "as Congress expanded its authority under the Commerce Clause to establish federal penalties for what

The U.S. Legal System: A Short Description, www.fjc.gov/public/pdf.nsf/lookup/U.S._Legal_System_English07.pdf/$file/U.S._Legal_System_English07.pdf. On the specific topic of federal criminal jurisdiction, see Federal Judicial Center, *Criminal Jurisdiction in Federal Courts*, www.fjc.gov/history/home.nsf/page/jurisdiction_criminal.html.

55 It is especially notable at this point that the TFEU states that: "Save where jurisdiction is conferred on the Court of Justice of the European Union by the Treaties, disputes to which the Union is a party shall not on that ground be excluded from the jurisdiction of the courts or tribunals of the Member States" (Article 274 TFEU) and even the proposed European prosecutor is required to operate "in the competent courts of the Member States" (Article 86(2) TFEU).

56 See below Chapter 2, section 4.3.2.

57 Sara Sun Beale, *Too Many and Yet Too Few: New Principles to Define the Proper Limits for Federal Criminal Jurisdiction*, Hastings L. J. 45 (1995) at 979, 997 ("Dual federal-state criminal jurisdiction is now the rule rather than the exception"). See also *Perez v. United States*, 402 U.S. 146 (1971) (upholding a federal conviction under a loan sharking law, regardless of the local nature); Harry Litman and Mark D. Greenberg, *Dual Prosecutions: A Model for Concurrent Federal Jurisdiction*, Annals Am. Acad. Pol & Sci. 543 (1996) at 72–83 (noting that the Hobbs Act, criminalizing threats or violence interfering with interstate commerce, could allow prosecution of convenient store robberies); Craig M. Bradley, *Racketeering and the Federalization of Crime*, 22 Am. Crim. L. Rev. 213 (1984) at 258 (noting that under the RICO Act, a person who sold small quantities of marijuana to two people could be federally prosecuted).

58 Judiciary Act of 1789, ch. 20, 1 Stat. 73 (1789).

59 See below Chapter 2, section 4.2.3.

60 The Volstead Act, ch. 85, 41 Stat. 307 (1919).

61 Robert Post, *Federalism, Positive Law, and the Emergence of the American Administrative State: Prohibition in the Taft Court Era*, Wm. & Mary L. Rev. 48 (2006) at 1–27 (quoting from *Prohibition and Federal Judges*, N.Y. Times, 29 May 1926 at 16).

62 Ibid. at 24.

traditionally had been subject of local and state law enforcement" in the second half of the 20th century.[63]

This expansion of federal criminal law heard by federal criminal courts has been accompanied by the creation of the federal prosecutor, a position which as yet has no equivalent in the European system. As noted before, although not envisioned anywhere in the Constitution, the federal prosecutor was introduced by the same law which established the first federal courts,[64] and continues to pursue federal crimes today. As with the courts, the federal prosecutor has seen an increase in power consequent with the increase in federal criminal legislation, and has become a legal actor of virtually unreviewable power.[65] The expansion of federal laws as well as the power of federal prosecutors will be discussed later in this chapter, but to frame the comparison between the US and EU systems, it is important to emphasize that this nexus of federal power which is found in the US federal courts – criminal legislation, trial jurisdiction, and federal enforcement – has no real parallel in Europe.

Without a thorough examination of judicial power in the EU, it is fair to say that the EU system lacks European judges that impose criminal sanctions based on EU legal provisions. Rather, national judges impose sanctions that are contained in national legislation. When national legislation is adapted to European standards – both substantial and procedural – through EU legislation, a certain type of European jurisdiction is exercised. However, this is far removed from a US system that has a distinct – though deficient – federal "criminal code" enforced by federal prosecutors and heard by federal courts. Therefore, enforcement of EU law is traditionally based on indirect enforcement;[66] that is, for the achievement of policy goals, the EU relies on the institutional and procedural design in the jurisdictions of the Member States.

Against this backdrop, any comparison in the area of federal criminal jurisdiction would seem doomed to failure. This, however, would be a shortsighted conclusion. There are *at least* two issues that are worth exploring a little closer: first, the similarity between the ECJ and the US Supreme Court; and second, the possibility of establishing a special court in criminal matters within the ECJ, similar to the already existing Civil Service Tribunal. In a way, the first issue deals

---

63 Federal Judicial Center, *Criminal Jurisdiction in Federal Courts*, www.fjc.gov/history/home.nsf/page/jurisdiction_criminal.html.

64 Judiciary Act of 1789, ch. 20, 1 Stat. 73, 92–93 (1789).

65 Angela J. Davis, *The American Prosecutor: Independence, Power, and the Threat of Tyranny*, Iowa L. Rev. 86 (2001) at 393; James Vorenberg, *Decent Restraint of Prosecutorial Power*, Harv. L. Rev. 94 (1981) at 1521 ("Prosecutors exercise essentially unchecked power in making decisions about charging and plea bargaining").

66 See generally, Koen Lenaerts, Ignace Maselis and Kathleen Gutman, *EU Procedural Law*, 2014 at 159–253 noting that there are basically two avenues of enforcement of EU law: the action for infringement of Union law by a Member State and the Preliminary Ruling on the interpretation of Union law.

with what has been achieved so far; the second with what could be achieved in the near future.

As the reader is probably already aware, the comparisons between the "highest courts of the land" in both Unions are abundant.[67] In a few words, both the ECJ and the US Supreme Court have the authority to determine how the Unions' legislation is to be interpreted.[68] A prominent scholar, *Martin Shapiro*, considers that both the ECJ and the US Supreme Court "are courts of general jurisdiction of federal systems".[69] In a similar fashion, *Koen Lenaerts*, renowned professor and Vice-President of the European Court of Justice, recently noted that "[t]he Court of Justice is not a human rights court; it is the Supreme Court of the European Union."[70]

On top of many functional similarities,[71] the ECJ and the US Supreme Court have helped to define the fundamental rights of criminal defendants throughout the territory of both Unions. Certainly this role of the ECJ has increased since the entry into force of the Lisbon Treaty[72] and will likely continue to increase given the now binding nature of the Charter of Fundamental Rights of the EU.[73] Especially interesting is the resemblance from an operational point of view concerning the cases in which state law and the Unions' constitutional law is at stake. In this sense, the US Supreme Court need not, and frequently does not, reach a final decision

---

67 See among many Michel Rosenfeld, *Comparing Constitutional Review by the European Court of Justice and the U.S. Supreme Court*, International Journal of Constitutional Law 4 (2006) at 618–651; Mark Höreth, *The European Court of Justice and the US Supreme Court: Comparable Institutions?*, in Michael Gehler, Günter Bischof, Ludger Kürhnhardt and Rolf Steininger, eds., *Towards a European Constitution: A Historical and Political Comparison with the United States*, 2005 at 143–160, both with further references.

68 See generally Koen Lenaerts, *Federalism and the Rule of Law: Perspectives from the European Court of Justice*, Fordham International Law Journal 33 (2010) at 1338–1387.

69 Martin Shapiro, *The US Supreme Court and the European Court of Justice Compared*, in Anand Menon and Martin A. Schain, eds., *Comparative Federalism. The European Union and the United States in Comparative Perspective*, 2006 at 195. Yet he acknowledges that the EU "would remain less 'federal' than the US in the sense that the broader governments' laws largely would continue to be implemented not by its own bureaucracy and judiciary but by those of its member-states" (at 209).

70 See www.verfassungsblog.de/ecj-european-supreme-court-setting-aside-citizens-rights-eu-law-supremacy/#.VG-R7kvnmTM.

71 Just to review some of them see Mark Höreth, *The European Court of Justice and the US Supreme Court: Comparable Institutions?*, in Michael Gehler, Günter Bischof, Ludger Kürhnhardt and Rolf Steininger, eds., *Towards a European Constitution: A Historical and Political Comparison with the United States*, 2005 at 150–154.

72 For a historical perspective see Ditlev Tamm, *The History of the Court of Justice of the European Union Since its Origin*, in *The Court of Justice and the Construction of Europe: Analyses and Perspectives on Sixty Years of Case-Law*, 2013 at 9–37.

73 Koen Lenaerts, *The Contribution of the European Court of Justice to the Area of Freedom, Security and Justice*, The International and Comparative Law Quarterly 59 (2010) at 255–30 (arguing that the ECJ's contribution to the Area of Freedom, Security and Justice is largely grounded in the protection of fundamental rights); Koen Lenaerts, *The Court of Justice of the European Union and the Protection of Fundamental Rights*, Polish Yearbook of International Law XXXI (2011) at 79–106; Koen Lenaerts, *Exploring the Limits of the EU Charter of Fundamental Rights*, European Constitutional Law Review 8 (2012) at 375–403.

in appeals cases that flow to it from the states. In cases that mix issues of state law and US constitutional law, the Supreme Court normally remands the proceedings to the state court from whence it came for final disposition.[74] Therefore, at least in this area, the contrast between the ECJ reference procedure, i.e. national courts requesting a preliminary ruling from the EU, and the US Supreme Court is not that obvious.[75]

To be sure, the EU system poses great risk to a uniform interpretation of Union's law and, for that matter, to the rights contained in the Charter of Fundamental Rights of the EU. The potential control through the so-called preliminary ruling proceeding of Article 267 TFEU[76] has been sparse. As is well known, in theory, when national judges have doubts about how to interpret certain national provisions in accordance with European legal principals, they should request a preliminary ruling from the ECJ to ensure a correct European interpretation. Yet, in most instances, national courts are reluctant to resort to the preliminary ruling proceedings. When confronted directly by the defendants with issues of EU law, they normally refer to the *acte clair* doctrine, i.e. the correct application of Union law is so obvious as to leave no scope for any reasonable doubt, and therefore there is no need to refer a preliminary ruling to the ECJ.[77]

Now, two recent developments will probably foster the national courts resort to the preliminary rulings proceedings. The first has to do with what should be considered as "a court or tribunal of a Member State against whose decisions there is no judicial remedy under national law". The second deals with the consequences faced by national courts if they do not resort to the preliminary ruling proceedings of the ECJ and do not provide the grounds of their decision not to pursue that avenue. This latter deals with the true enforcement of the obligation to request a preliminary ruling.

---

74 Martin Shapiro, *The US Supreme Court and the European Court of Justice Compared*, in Anand Menon and Martin A. Schain, eds., *Comparative Federalism. The European Union and the United States in Comparative Perspective*, 2006 at 196.

75 Generally see J.C. Cohen, *The European Preliminary Reference and the U.S. Court Review of State Court Judgments: A Study in Comparative Judicial Federalism*, American Journal of Comparative Law 44 (1996) at 421–438.

76 For a general overview see Koen Lenaerts, Ignace Maselis and Kathleen Gutman, *Procedural Law EU*, 2014 at 48–107, 215–253 with further references.

77 The general *acte clair* doctrine was established in the *CILFIT* case (ECJ, Case 283/81 CILFIT, para. 16). On the doctrine itself see generally Paul Craig and Gráinne De Búrca, *EU Law - Texts, Cases and Materials*, 5th ed., 2011; Koen Lenaerts, Ignace Maselis and Kathleen Gutman, *EU Procedural Law*, 2014 at 100–102. This has been especially controversial in the area of tax law (see generally the contributions in Ana Paulo Dorado and Ricardo Da Palma Borges, *The Acte Clair Doctrine in EC Direct Tax Law*, 2008). For an overview and critical assessment of the criteria of the *acte clair* doctrine see Ilija Vukčević, *CILFIT Criteria for the Acte Clair/Acte Éclairé Doctrine in Direct Tax Cases of the CJEU*, Intertax 40 (2012) at 654–665. Some leading commentators have noted that many courts "at one time abused the *acte clair* doctrine" (Koen Lenaerts, Ignace Maselis and Kathleen Gutman, *EU Procedural Law*, 2014 at 101). Already in 1989 Anthony Arnull, *The Use and Abuse of Article 177 EEC*, Mod. L. Rev. (1989) at 622–639 noted English courts' cases abusing the *acte clair* doctrine.

The fact that the preliminary ruling procedure should be mandatory when a court of last resort is faced with questions of interpretation of EU law concerning defendants' rights has meant that, in jurisdictions with national supreme courts and constitutional courts, the national supreme court argued that the court of last resort to review such claims would be the national constitutional court, i.e. therefore the former not being bound by Article 267 TFEU. In its decision on the *Krizan* case (C-416/2010) dated 15 January 2013, the ECJ ruled to the contrary, establishing the following:

> "72. Finally, as a supreme court, the Najvyšší súd Slovenskej republiky is even required to submit a request for a preliminary ruling to the Court of Justice when it finds that the substance of the dispute concerns a question to be resolved which comes within the scope of the first paragraph of Article 267 TFEU. The possibility of bringing, before the constitutional court of the Member State concerned, an action against the decisions of a national court, limited to an examination of a potential infringement of the rights and freedoms guaranteed by the national constitution or by an international agreement, cannot allow the view to be taken that that national court cannot be classified as a court against whose decisions there is no judicial remedy under national law within the meaning of the third paragraph of Article 267 TFEU.
>
> 73. In the light of the foregoing, the answer to the first question is that Article 267 TFEU must be interpreted as meaning that a national court, such as the referring court, is obliged to make, of its own motion, a request for a preliminary ruling to the Court of Justice even though it is ruling on a referral back to it after its first decision was set aside by the constitutional court of the Member State concerned and even though a national rule obliges it to resolve the dispute by following the legal opinion of that latter court."

Certainly it would be far more effective if private parties could request a preliminary ruling of the ECJ. But the fact that this traditional escape route of the Supreme Court of Member States has been cut short, should foster preliminary ruling procedures, especially involving defense rights.[78]

The second development has been advanced not by the ECJ, but by the ECtHR.[79] In *Dhahbi v. Italy* (App. No. 17120/09, judgment of 8 April 2014) the

---

[78] In any event, there has been a conspicuous increase in the number of preliminary ruling procedures since the enactment of the EAW Frame-work decision. Just to name a few over the past four years: C-398/12 *Procura della Repubblica v. M.*, Judgment of 5 June 2014; C-129/14 *Zoran Spasic*, Judgment of 27 May 2014; C-60/12 *Marián Baláž*, Judgment of 14 November 2013; C-168/13 *Jeremy F. v. Premier Ministre*, Judgment of 30 May 2013; C-399/11 *Stefano Melloni*, Judgment of 26 February 2013; C-396/11, *Ciprian Vasile Radu*, Judgment of 29 January 2013; C-42/11 *Joao Pedro Lopes Da Silva Jorge*, Judgment of 5 September 2012; C-79/11 *Maurizio Giovanardi*, Judgment of 12 July 2012; C-192/12 PPU *Melvin West*, Judgment of 28 June 2012; C-83/12 PPU *Minh Khoa Vo*, Judgment of 10 April 2012; C-261/09 *Mantello*, Judgment of 16 November 2010.

[79] On the relationship between both courts see Tobias Lock, *The ECJ and the ECtHR: The Future Relationship between the Two European Courts*, The Law and Practice of International

ECtHR established, for the first time, a violation of Article 6 owing to the failure to provide any reasons for refusing to request a preliminary ruling by the ECJ. To be sure, the case did not involve defendants' rights in criminal proceedings, but the prohibition against discrimination. Yet the fact that defense rights in criminal proceedings are considered paramount should only emphasize the findings of the court.

In *Dhahbi*, the Court reiterated that from the angle of Article 6 ECHR, national courts whose decisions were not open to appeal under domestic law were required to give reasons, based on the applicable law and the exceptions laid down in ECJ case law, for their refusal to refer a preliminary question on the interpretation of EU law. They should set out their reasons for considering that the question was not relevant, that the provision had already been interpreted by the CJEU (*acte éclairé*), or that the correct application of EU law was so obvious as to leave no scope for reasonable doubt (*acte clair*).[80] Here, two major issues arise: one related to the enforcement side; one related to the reasonableness of the refusal to pursue preliminary rulings proceedings.

Certainly, if there are no legal consequences for the Member State that has not referred the case to the ECJ, then the enforcement side certainly weakens.[81] Unfortunately, that seems to be the case. The ECJ held in *Köbler*[82] that the infringement of the obligation to make a reference for a preliminary ruling is one of the most important criteria in assessing whether a state has to pay damages for the loss suffered by an individual;[83] but it also considered that the infringement itself is not sufficient to make a state liable under EU law. Therefore, the ECJ's current position is that although references for preliminary ruling are mandatory in certain cases, the infringement of such obligation does not amount to Member

---

Courts and Tribunals 8 (2009) at 375–398. On the relationship between the ECtHR and the Charter see Koen Lenaerts, *The Court of Justice of the European Union and the Protection of fundamental Rights*, Polish Yearbook of International Law XXXI (2011) at 98–104.

80 The ECJ based its decision of the previous findings in *Vergauwen v. Belgique et autres* (déc.), no 4832/04, §§ 89–90, 10 April 2012. These are traditional limits placed on the duty to request a preliminary (see Koen Lenaerts, Ignace Maselis and Kathleen Gutman, *EU Procedural Law*, 2014 at 98–102).

81 For the enforcement of the obligation to request a preliminary see Koen Lenaerts, Ignace Maselis and Kathleen Gutman, *EU Procedural Law*, 2014 at 98–102, which basically consists in that the Commission or a Member State may seek a declaration from the Court of Justice pursuant to Articles 258 or 259 TFEU that, through its national court's refusal to seek a ruling, the Member State in question has infringed the third paragraph of Article 267 TFEU. To this extent, courts and tribunals are in fact "institutions of the Member State concerned".

82 Case C-224/01, *Gerhard Köbler v. Republik Österreich* [2003] ECR I-10239. See also Case C-495/03 *Intermodal Transports* [2005] ECR I-8151, para. 37; Case C-173/03 *Traghetti del Mediterraneo* [2006] ECR I-5177, paras. 30–46.

83 Union law requires Member States to recognize the possibility of a claim in damages against public authorities where an infringement by a court of last resort of its obligation to make a reference for a preliminary ruling demonstrably thwarts a right conferred on individuals by Union law (see Koen Lenaerts, Ignace Maselis and Kathleen Gutman, *EU Procedural Law*, 2014 at 3.58).

State liability. Put differently, there is a potential national remedy, i.e. claim in damages, but not a real European remedy, i.e. infringement action.[84]

In a similar fashion, the national court may consider that the EU law interpretation is self-evident and provide an absolutely unreasonable interpretation the Union's law.[85] Judges may certainly err and, if they do so with the interpretation of EU law, they seem nevertheless to meet the criteria in *Dhabhi*. The main finding in *Dhabhi* is that the national court must provide reasons for not referring the case, not that the reasons are reasonable. Probably, in the near future, the ECtHR or the ECJ will further pursue this issue and establish that the grounds for refusal must provide a reasonable interpretation of EU law. In any event, as noted before, it would be far more desirable if the defendants could challenge before the ECJ the reasonableness of the grounds provided by the national court not to refer the proceedings to the ECJ. This will possibly take place through the court to which defendants have direct access: the ECtHR.[86]

Finally, the second issue to explore is the existence of anything in the EU similar to federal jurisdiction in terms of a European court adjudicating cases directly. Though not criminal, this would be the so-called Civil Service Tribunal (CST), a specialized court.[87] This type of specialized court with limited jurisdiction is now foreseen in Article 257 TFEU: "The European Parliament and the Council, acting in accordance with the ordinary legislative procedure, may establish specialised courts attached to the General Court to hear and determine at first instance certain classes of action or proceeding brought in specific areas". After the entry into force of the Lisbon Treaty, the power contained in Article 257 TFEU has not been used to create any other type of European court – the CST actually being a relic from the past.

---

84 "The conclusion is that, in practice, the obligation to seek a preliminary ruling cannot be enforced directly" (see Koen Lenaerts, Ignace Maselis and Kathleen Gutman, *EU Procedural Law*, 2014 at 3.57). Certainly, in Case C-129/ 00, *Commission v Italy* [2003] ECR I-14637, the Commission did not hesitate file infringement proceedings regarding the failure to amend rules of evidence that were constructed by its judiciary and therefore it is fair to conclude that the Commission acknowledges a duty to oversee the way in which national courts subject to the obligation to seek preliminary rulings make use of the *acte clair* doctrine footed in CILFIT (see the reasoned opinion of the commission concerning the failure of the Swedish Supreme Court to comply with the duty to refer under Article 267 TFEU (2003/ 2161, C(2004) 3899, 13 October 2004)).

85 As we noted before, this is an abuse of the *acte clair* doctrine.

86 As Koen Lenaerts, Ignace Maselis and Kathleen Gutman, *EU Procedural Law*, 2014 at 3.56 note: "there is no remedy available from the Court of Justice to parties to the main proceedings against a refusal of a court of last resort to make a preliminary reference".

87 Hannes Kraemer, *The European Union Civil Service Tribunal: A New Community Court Examined After Four Years of Operation*, Common Market Law Review 46 (2009) at 1873–1913; Paul Mahoney, *The European Union Civil Service Tribunal: A Specialised Tribunal or a Special Tribunal?*, in Aline De Walsche and Laura Levi, eds., *Mélanges en hommage à Georges Vandersanden: promenades au sein du droit européen*, 2008 at 955–970; Waltraud Kahenberg, *The European Union Civil Service Tribunal: A Three-tier Structure*, in Elias Olufemi, ed., *The Development and Effectiveness of International Administrative Law*, 2012 at 251–265.

First established in 2004[88] the CST is composed of seven judges. Basically, it has jurisdiction to adjudicate in disputes between the European Union and its civil servants.[89] Until 2005 such jurisdiction was exercised by the General Court, i.e. not by a separate specialized court. Procedurally, its decisions are subject to appeal on questions of law only to the General Court and, in exceptional cases, to review by the European Court of Justice. These disputes concern not only issues of working relations in the strict sense (pay, career progress, recruitment, disciplinary measures, etc.), but also the social security system (sickness, old age, invalidity, accidents at work, family allowances, etc.). The court also has jurisdiction in cases concerning certain employees, particularly those of Eurojust, Europol, the European Central Bank, and the Office for Harmonisation in the Internal Market (OHIM).

In light of the existence of the CST, the question is whether it should become a precedent for the establishment of specialized judicial panels in other fields of EU law fields.[90] If the limited subject matter jurisdiction of the CST is to provide any guidance, then the first specialized criminal court in the ECJ that comes into mind would a Tribunal dealing with EU fraud perpetrated by EU civil servants. Moreover, in order not to alter the current structure, it could be argued that the CST should expand its jurisdiction to foresee EU fraud perpetrated by EU civil servants.[91] If it is widely acknowledged that the CST resolves disputes between the European Administration and its officials, then it would seem consistent that when those disputes are criminal in nature (the European officials have embezzled EU monies), the competent court for deal with this matter would be the CST.

In any event, the need to establish a specialized court in criminal matters has become more pressing with the debate around the European Public Prosecutor's Office and the judicial control of its actions. In the so-called Model Rules for the Procedure of the EPPO,[92] the experts participating in the research were convinced

---

88 Council Decision of 2 November 2004 establishing the European Union Civil Service Tribunal (2004/752/EC, Euratom). This type of jurisdiction, i.e. involving disputes with the European Union civil service were previously been exercised by the Court of Justice and then, following its creation in 1989, by the Court of First Instance (now the General Court).

89 The court hears 150 cases a year for approximately 40,000 members of staff of the institutions, bodies, offices and agencies of the European Union.

90 For a discussion of such option in competition law (especially mergers) or intellectual property, see Hannes Kraemer, *The European Union Civil Service Tribunal: A New Community Court Examined After Four Years of Operation*, Common Market Law Review 46 (2009) at 1873–1913.

91 This would certainly require passing new European legislation that would replace the now standing Council Decision of 2 November 2004, and replacing the reference in article 1 of the annex i.e., "shall exercise at first instance jurisdiction in disputes between the Communities and their servants referred to in Article 236 of the EC Treaty and Article 152 of the EAEC Treaty, with shall exercise at first instance jurisdiction in disputes between the Communities and their servants referred to in … and Article 325 TFEU".

92 On the EPPO see below Chapter 2, section 5.2 and Chapter 5, section 6, and generally Martijn Zwiers, *The European Public Prosecutor's Office. Analysis of a Multilevel Criminal Justice System*, 2011; Katalin Ligeti, *Toward a Prosecutor for the European Union Volume 1. A Comparative Analysis*, 2013; Leendert H. Erkelens, Arjen W.H. Meij and Marta Pawlik,

that in order to guarantee the equivalent and effective enforcement of the Rules, judicial review *ex post* should not be left to the courts of the individual Member States. To that extent, they proposed the creation of a "European court".[93] In their view, in accordance with Article 257 TFEU a European court should be competent for this kind of subsequent review of the decisions made by the EPPO.

Yet none of these proposals will see the light shortly. First, Article 86(2) TFEU mandates that the European prosecutor "shall exercise the functions of prosecutor in the competent courts of the Member States in relation to such offences". Therefore, it would seem that this precludes the European Prosecutor from acting before a competent court of the European Union, i.e. the specialized court in criminal matters. By the same token, Article 36 of the proposed Regulation[94] establishes that "the European Public Prosecutor's Office shall be considered as a national authority for the purpose of judicial review." The intention is clear: for now, the European prosecutor will not try cases before a European court.

3. THE FIRST FEDERAL DIMENSION OF THE UNIONS' CRIMINAL LAW: CRIMES AFFECTING THE UNIONS' INTERESTS

3.1. INTRODUCTION

The emergence of a federal Union – whether a federal state, a federal community of states or equivalent concepts[95] – rapidly creates certain federal interests that are key to the survival of the Union. From the standpoint of the vertical/horizontal federalism discussion, the two basic avenues that are readily available to protect those interests can be synthesized as follows: the Union itself can provide such protection (vertical federalism) or the Union can force the states to provide such protection (horizontal federalism). Yet, in both cases, the Union acts to provide either way the necessary protection, ultimately including criminal law protection.

As will be described below, the first initiatives in both Unions to use (vertically or horizontally) their conferred powers to provide criminal law protection have been related to the Union's financial interests. This is not surprising. The income and expenditure of the Union is a pre-condition for the existence of the Union itself. The attitude of both Unions (EU and US) has been similar: they have

The European Public Prosecutor's Office: An extended arm or a two-headed dragon?, 2015. For this issue see Đurđević, *Judicial Control in Pre-Trial Criminal Procedure Conducted by the European Public Prosecutor's Office*, in K. Ligeti, ed., *Toward a Prosecutor for the European Union. Vol. 1. A Comparative Analysis*, 2013 at 986.

93 Rule 7: "To the extent indicated in these Rules, decisions of the EPPO affecting individual rights are subject to review by the European court".

94 Council Regulation on the establishment of the European Public Prosecutor's Office of 2013, COM (2013) 534 final – 2013/0255.

95 See above Chapter 1, section 2.1.

trusted the states to provide the protection, and after blatant disappointments, they have both decided to take action on this matter. The clearer conferral of federal criminal law powers in certain areas in the US case enabled an earlier approach to these issues. But the problems posed by the mismanagement of the Unions' funds ultimately triggered intervention in both Unions.

To be sure, probably the first act of the US Congress containing criminal provisions was the *Revenue Fraud Act* of 1789.[96] The Crimes Act of 1790, formally titled *An Act for the Punishment of Certain Crimes Against the United States*,[97] defined some of the first federal crimes in the United States and expanded on the criminal procedure provisions of the Judiciary Act of 1789. The punishment of treason, piracy, counterfeiting, crimes committed on the high seas or against the law of nations followed from relatively explicit constitutional authority.[98] Yet shortly after, in 1798, the first provisions to punish fraud against the Bank of the United States were enacted.[99] The federal nature of such provisions was not questioned as the connection with the interests of the Union and the explicit powers conferred in the US constitution was evident.

As we shall see, the EU has been concerned for a long time with the criminal law protection of its financial interests. However, only recently the federal nature of such approach was clearly recognized. On top of Commissioner *Viviane Reding*'s speech when presenting the Commission's proposal to establish the European Public Prosecutor's Office, the comments provided in a Law Review editorial by the Commissioner herself and the EU Commissioner responsible for Taxation and Customs Union *Algirdas Semeta* are noteworthy: "EU money must not be pocketed by criminal. We have a federal budget – with money coming from

---

96 Revenue Fraud Act of 1789, 1 Stat. 29 at 46 (1789). See Joseph F. Zimmerman, *Congress and Crime: The Impact of Federalization of State Criminal Laws*, 2014 at Chapter 2.

97 Crimes Act of 1790, ch. 9, 1 Stat. 112.

98 As noted before, those are matters explicitly referred to in the US Constitution.

99 Act of June 27, 1798, 1 Stat. 573. Chap. LXI. – *An Act to punish frauds committed on the Bank of the United States.* "If any person shall falsely make, alter, forge or counterfeit, or cause or procure to be falsely made, altered, forged or counterfeited, or willingly aid or assist in falsely making, altering, forging or counterfeiting any bill or note issued by order of the president, directors and company of the Bank of the United States, and signed by the president, and countersigned by the cashier thereof, or any order or check on the said cashier or corporation, for the payment of money, with intention to defraud the said corporation, or any other body politic or person, or shall utter or publish, as true, any false, altered, forged or counterfeited bill or note issued by order of the president, directors and company of the Bank of the United States, and signed by the president, and countersigned by the cashier thereof, or any order or check on the said cashier or corporation, for the payment of money, with intention to defraud the said corporation, or any other body politic or person, knowing the same to be falsely altered, forged or counterfeited, every such person shall be deemed and adjudged guilty of felony, and being thereof convicted, according to the due course of law, shall be sentenced to be imprisoned and kept at hard labour for a period not less than three years, nor more than ten years, or shall be imprisoned not exceeding ten years, and fined not exceeding five thousand dollars: *Provided*, that nothing herein contained shall be construed to deprive the courts of the individual states of a jurisdiction under the laws of the several states over the offences declared punishable by this act."

the 28 EU Member States – and as a consequence, we also need federal laws to protect this budget".[100]

The following pages explore how both Unions dealt with the criminal law protection of their "direct" or inherent federal interests. The initial approach of both Unions mimics the overall vertical/horizontal federalism underlying rationale. The US has used its conferred powers and the Necessary and Proper Clause to establish a direct federal protection of such interests. The EU has resorted to forcing the Member States to provide the adequate criminal law protection of the Union's financial interest, although attempting to add a vertical feature through the European prosecutor. The future developments of this European approach will probably stress the vertical dimension due to the inherent lack of interest by state officials to effectively protect the EU's financial interests.

3.2. THE PROTECTION OF THE EU'S FINANCIAL INTERESTS (ARTICLE 325 TFEU)

A quick review of the decade-long discussion on EU criminal law shows that the protection of the EU's financial interest has been a key issue in the development of EU criminal law.[101] It is fair to say that providing EU financial interests with an adequate level of criminal law protection has been a primary concern of EU institutions for decades.[102] The first attempts to introduce EU legislation specifically addressing criminal law were related to EU fraud. After an interim in which EU institutions seemed more focused on the principle of mutual recognition,[103] the sovereign debt crisis has again positioned EU fraud at the forefront of the EU's criminal law agenda.[104] A brief explanation on both issues is due.

The *gravitas* of the EU's financial interest in the area of criminal law may be perceived not only in the first academic proposals establishing a system of EU

---

100 Eucrim, The European Criminal Law Association's Forum, 2013/04 at 109.

101 In this sense, when the financial contributions of the Member States were substituted by the resources of the then-named Economic European Community in the 1970s, the need for inherently European criminal protection seemed to be self-evident (see the first proposals dated back in 1976: COM (1976) 418, Official Journal 222, 22 September 1976). This need was highlighted during the 1990s, due to the fraud figures (see the figures in Green Paper on criminal-law protection of the financial interests of the Community and the establishment of a European Prosecutor, COM (2001) 715 final at 8) in the European Union, among other reasons. Also, the demonstrated deficiencies of granting jurisdiction to the Member States in the prosecution of such fraud played a significant role. Some academics have also raised bigger concerns with the expansion of the EU to new territories/states in the East. See SCHÜNEMANN, ZSTW 116 (2004) at 387.

102 See VALSAMIS MITSILEGAS, *EU Criminal Law*, 2009 at 67: "A key focus of the Commission has been the fight against fraud relating to the Community Budget, which was perceived as a quintessential 'Community' interest necessitating criminal law harmonization in the first pillar".

103 See above Chapter 1, section 6.

104 See below Chapter 5, section 3.

criminal law, i.e. the 1996 and 2000 so-called *Corpus Iuris*, but also in the first EU proposal on a Directive in criminal matters i.e., the Proposal for a Directive of the European Parliament and of the Council on the criminal law protection of the Community's financial interests in 2001.[105] Though this has been discussed at length,[106] "*Corpus Juris*: introducing penal provisions for the purpose of the financial interests of the European Union" was a study written by eight academic lawyers from EU Member States and published first in 1997,[107] and then amended in 2000.[108] This study led to considerable discussion in the EU over whether and how criminal powers should be exercised by the EU.[109]

Yet, as just noted, with the drive of the principle of mutual recognition in the early 21st century and the rapid implementation of legal instruments based on it, the interest in the connection between criminal law and the EU's financial interests seemed to fade. The sovereign debt crisis propelled the criminal law protection of the EU's financial interests to the center stage. After a number of communications addressing the relevance of this issue to EU taxpayers and EU institutions,[110] the EU decided to take action and proposed two legal instruments addressing this issue: the Directive on the fight against fraud to the Union's financial interests by means of criminal law[111] and the European Regulation establishing a European Public Prosecutor's Office[112] with jurisdiction over offenses related to the Union's financial interests are the result of those concerns. Put simply, the sovereign debt crisis has propelled concern over EU financial interests into the spotlight, and the

105 COM (2001) 272. Additionally, in 2001 the Commission published the Green Paper on criminal-law protection of the financial interests of the Community and the establishment of a European Prosecutor, COM (2001) 715 final. Prior to the Proposal of the Directive, in 1995 a Convention drawn up on the basis of Article K.3 of the Treaty on European Union, on the protection of the European Communities' financial interests was agreed (Official Journal C 316, 27 November 1995). The convention entered into force on 17 October 2002, along with its first protocol and the protocol on its interpretation by the Court of Justice. The second protocol entered into force on 19 May 2009. For an extensive review of the progress made by the 27 EU countries in ratifying and implementing the instruments for protecting the European Communities' financial interests (highlighting the problems arising from the frequent delays in ratification and cases of incorrect implementation) see the EU Commission's, Second Report from the Commission – Implementation of the Convention on the Protection of the European Communities' financial interests and its protocols, COM (2008) 77 final.

106 See Carlos Gómez Jara-Diez, *Models for a European System of Criminal Law*, New Journal of European Criminal Law (2010) at 385.

107 Mireille Delmas-Marty, *Corpus Juris: Introducing Penal Provisions for the Purpose of the Financial Interests of the European Union*, 1997.

108 John Vervaele and Mireille Delmas-Marty, *The Implementation of the Corpus Juris in the Member States I and II*, 2000.

109 See Carlos Gómez Jara-Diez, *Models for a European System of Criminal Law*, New Journal of European Criminal Law (2010) at 385.

110 See below Chapter 5, section 3.

111 Proposal for a Directive of the European Parliament and of the Council on the fight against fraud to the Union's financial interests by means of criminal law, COM (2012) 363 final.

112 Proposal for a Council Regulation on the establishment of the European Public Prosecutor's Office, COM (2013) 534 final.

question of criminal law protection has regained its salient position after almost a decade of dormancy.

With this in mind a closer analysis of the statutory basis for EU power at this level should be conducted. First we will review the language of Article 325(4) TFEU and address some of the traditional criminal law discussions related to the change in wording compared with former Article 280 ToA. Second we will address the key issue of whether Article 325(4) TFEU contains an explicit power in criminal law matters or whether it must be supplemented with Article 83(2) TFEU – with consequences for both approaches. Finally, we will insist on the fact that the approach so far has been based on the classic European horizontal federalism technique; however, some vertical federalism tendencies are present. Although maybe too early to tell, it seems that time will reinforce the vertical federalism dimension in the future.

As is well known, the explicit referral to the protection of the EU financial interests is contained under the heading of "Combatting Fraud", Article 325(4).[113] Though not containing a specific criminal law provision, the language reads as follows:

> "Art. 325
> 4. The European Parliament and the Council, acting in accordance with the ordinary legislative procedure, after consulting the Court of Auditors, shall adopt the necessary measures in the fields of the prevention of and fight against fraud affecting the financial interests of the Union with a view to affording effective and equivalent protection in the Member States and in all the Union's institutions, bodies, offices and agencies."

Certainly, it is difficult to interpret Article 325(4) TFEU without taking into consideration the discussion regarding its predecessor, Article 280 ToA:

> "4. The Council, acting in accordance with the procedure referred to in Article 251, after consulting the Court of Auditors, shall adopt the necessary measures in the fields of the prevention of and fight against fraud affecting the financial interests of the Community with a view to affording effective and equivalent protection in the Member States. *These measures shall not concern the application of national criminal law or the national administration of justice.*"

To be sure, the discussion on the possibility of enacting criminal law provisions to protect the EU financial interests, may be found as early as the debate regarding

---

113 For a summary of the current stand see Commission Staff Working Paper, Implementation of Article 325 by the Member States in 2012, Accompanying the document, Report from the Commission to the European Parliament and the Council, Protection for the European Union's financial interests – Fight against fraud Annual Report 2012, SWD (2013) 283 final.

Article 209 of the Maastricht Treaty.[114] Yet it is fair to say that it received a major boost in 1995 with the drafting of Article 280 ToA – specifically paragraph 4. There were proposals for reform in this area on the basis of that article,[115] but what probably matters the most is whether the new wording of this clause – contained in Article 325 TFEU – is substantively different from Article 280 ToA and what impact, if any, may have the new wording.

With respect to Article 280 ToA, there were two opposing camps: those who saw the provision as a legal basis for the granting the EU powers to enact criminal provisions,[116] and those who considered the article's contents to be insufficient, particularly due to the special considerations surrounding criminal law.[117] The strongest argument for reading former Article 280 ToA as a grant of criminal law powers to the European Union was probably that provided by *Tiedemann*,[118] a leading scholar in European criminal law. We will now briefly explore the core of his argument to see whether the situation has changed in favor of recognizing such power, given the changes to Article 325 TFEU.

Tiedemann's argument analyzed the ToA under an objective, goal-oriented approach which is common in the case law of the ECJ.[119] The main focus from his viewpoint was the principle of supremacy of EU law over state law.[120] From this standpoint, he believed that the key issue was to determine how EU institutions could provide effective protection of their financial interests that was equivalent to the protection that Member States provide for their own financial interests.

---

114 See John Vervaele, *Towards an Independent European Agency to Fight Fraud and Corruption in the EU?*, in Hans-Jörg Albrecht and André Klip, eds., *Crime, Criminal Law and Criminal Justice in Europe*, 2013 at 543.

115 See Proposal for a Directive of the European Parliament and of the Council on the criminal-law protection of the Community's financial interests, COM (2001) 272 final. After a long legislative procedure (European Parliament, Report on the proposal for a Directive on the criminal-law protection of the Community's financial interests, COM (2001) 272-C50225/2001-2001/115(COD)), the Directive was never enacted. See generally Patrycja Szarek-Mason, *The European Union's Fight Against Corruption: The Evolving Policy Towards Member States and Candidate Countries*, 2010 at 49 (noting that the 2001 proposed Directive was a reaction to the lack of ratification of the Convention). Although the draft directive was not accepted by the Council, the Member States were then eager to ratify the Convention, which entered into force in 2002.

116 See Klaus Tiedemann, *Legal Basis for the Implementation*, in John Vervaele and Mireille Delmas-Marty, eds., *The Implementation of the Corpus Juris in the Member States I and II*, 2000 at 385–387; Wolffgang & Ulrich, EuR (1998) at 616, 644; Zieschang, ZStW 113 (2001) at 260; doubtful Dannecker, *Handbuch des Wirtschafts- und Steuerstrafrechts* (Wabnitz and Janovsky, 2nd ed., 2004) § 3 n.m. 72.

117 See Stephan Braum, *Europäische Strafgesetzlichkeit*, 2003, at 413, 416, 419; Kaifa-Gbandi, KritV (2001) at 291; Köhler, KritV (2001) at 307; Musil, NStZ (2000) at 69, 70; Helmut Satzger, *International and European Criminal Law*, 2010 at 437; Schmitz, ZStW 115 (2003) at 516; Schröder, *Europäische Richtlinien* at 145; Schünemann, *Strafverteidiger*, 2003 at 116; Schünemann, Goltdammer's Archiv (2002) at 501, 505.

118 We will now refer to the position of Klaus Tiedemann, *EG und EU als Rechtsquellen des Strafrechts*, in Festschrift für Claus Roxin, 2001 at 1401–1412.

119 Ibid. at 1408.

120 Ibid. at 1408.

To do so, he considered that criminal legislation by EU institutions in criminal matters could not be excluded for two basic reasons. First, criminal sanctions have proven to be exactly the sort of "necessary measures" referred to in former Article 280 ToA (current Article 325 TFEU). Second, Article 29 of the former EU Treaty – concerned with the principle of mutual recognition – specifically allowed for the harmonization of criminal provisions of the Member States with EU law.[121] In a way, he was advocating for a relationship between the provisions regarding the protection of the EU financial interests and the principle of mutual recognition – in current legislative terms, for a connection between Article 325 TFEU and Article 83 TFEU.[122]

Now, the most interesting issue dealt with the last sentence in former Article 280 ToA: "These measures shall not concern the application of national criminal law or the national administration of justice".[123] Many scholars argued that this sentence was prohibitive of EU power in criminal matters,[124] although there were others who disagreed.[125] Against this backdrop, Article 325 TFEU thus introduces an important novelty: it suppresses the aforementioned sentence to avoid any type of misinterpretation. Therefore, the question is whether suppressing such a controversial sentence in Article 280 ToA reinforces or weakens the possibility of EU intervention in such matters through criminal law.[126]

It could be argued that the fact that such wording was suppressed indicates that the EU has no criminal powers to protect its financial interests, i.e. there is absolutely no reference to criminal law in the current Article 325 TFEU's wording. Conversely, such suppression of a sentence that stated that it "shall not concern" state criminal law could indicate otherwise, i.e. that it reaffirms EU powers for

---

121 Ibid. at 1408, noting that it would be wrong to interpret former article 280 as a clear intention to strike out EU criminal law.

122 As noted in Chapter 2, sections 3 and 4.4.3, the tendency resembles the path undertaken by the Necessary and Proper Clause discussion in the US concerning the Spending Clause.

123 Klaus Tiedemann, *EG und EU als Rechtsquellen des Strafrechts*, in Festschrift für Claus Roxin, 2001 at 1409–1411 proposes various interpretations of that sentence that are consistent with the original intent of the Treaty drafters and with its position in the text.

124 Maria Kaifa-Gbandi, KritV (2001) at 291; Küdlich, JA (1999) at 526; Dannecker, *Handbuch des Wirtschafts- und Steuerstrafrechts* (Wabnitz and Janovsky, 2nd ed., 2004) § 3 n.m. 72; G.F.M. Corsten, *Criminal law in the first pillar?*, European Journal of Crime, Criminal law and Criminal Justice 11 (2003) at 142–143; W. van Werven, *Constitutional Conditions for a Public Prosecutor's Office at the European Level*, European Journal of Crime, Criminal law and Criminal Justice 8 (2000) at 306–307; John Spencer, *Legal Basis for the Implementation*, in John Vervaele and Mireille Delmas-Marty, eds., *The Implementation of the Corpus Juris in the Member States I and II*, 2000 at 380.

125 There were many commentators that refused to interpret that phrasing as a mandatory exclusion of EU powers in criminal matters: Helmut Deutscher, *Die Kompetenz der Europaïschen Gemeinschaften zur originären Strafgesetzbuch*, 2000 at 344–345; Zuccalá, *GS Ellen Schlüchter*, at 123; Hefendehl, *FS Klaus Lüderssen*, 2002 at 414.

126 For a review of the discussion of the suppression of this sentence at the time the European Constitution was to be adopted see Tonio Walter, *Inwieweit erlaubt die Europäische Verfassung ein europäisches Strafgesetz*, Zeitschrift für die gesamte Strafrechtswissenschaft 117 (2005) at 917–918.

the necessary criminal law protection to its financial interests. The major position today is that one of the reasons arguing against an EU *ius puniendi*, i.e. the last sentence in former Article 280 ToA, has completely disappeared with the removal of this controversial sentence by the Lisbon Treaty.[127]

In the face of such developments, it is probably fair to say that the question today is not whether the EU has criminal powers to protect its own financial interests, but whether such powers derive exclusively from Article 325 TFEU or if they must be supplemented with Article 83(2) TFEU.[128] As we noted before, the path of connecting an explicitly conferred power with the Necessary and Proper Clause is a well-known strategy in the US system.[129] The question is whether there is a need to establish such connection or whether Article 325 TFEU is a standalone clause in criminal matters.

The reason for paying attention to this discussion basically lies in the fact that there are some relevant consequences to the standalone interpretation. First and foremost, if criminal law protection regarding the EU financial interests is established as an independent source of EU powers, i.e. not related to Article 83(2) TFEU, then the EU can legislate through Regulations pursuant to Article 289 TFEU. If, on the contrary, the protection of the financial interests of the EU financial interests is considered yet another policy of the EU that pertains to the Area of Freedom, Security and Justice, then the only legal instrument available to

---

127 Thomas Weigend, *Der Entwurf einer Europäischen Verfassung und das Strafrecht*, Zeitschrift für die gesamte Strafrechtswissenschaft 116 (2004) at 288. Valsamis Mitsilegas, *EU Criminal Law*, 2009 at 109. See also Andre Klip, *European Criminal Law. An Integrative Approach*, 2nd ed., 2012 at 172 directly states "Article 325 TFEU (formerly article 280 TEC) makes reference to *one specific crime*: 'fraud and any other illegal activities affecting the financial interests of the Union'" (at 172, emphasis added). He also notes that "the area that leads to most vertical co-operation is European Union Fraud" (at 359). Helmut Satzger and Frank Zimmermann, *The Protection of EC Financial Interests by Means of Penal Law*, in M. Cherif Bassiouni, Vincenzo Militello and Helmut Satzger, eds., *European cooperation in penal matters*, 2008 at 182. See also the contributions is Francesca Galli and Anne Weyembergh, *Approximation of substantive criminal law in the EU: The way forward*, 2013; Peter Asp, *The Substantive Criminal law competence of the EU*, 2012 at 142–143; Rosaria Sicurella, *Some Reflections on the need for a General Theory of the Competence of the European Union in Criminal Law*, in Andre Klip, ed., *Substantive Criminal Law of the European Union*, 2011 at 236; Valsamis Mitsilegas, *EU Criminal Law Competence after Lisbon: From Securitised to Functional Criminalisation*, in Diego Acosta Arcarazo and Cian C. Murphy, eds., *EU Security and Justice Law*, 2014 at 119.

128 Valsamis Mitsilegas, *EU Criminal Law*, 2009 at 109. "It is not clear whether the 325(4) wording here ... signifies that the Union has competence under article 325 TFEU to adopt criminal laws on fraud without the need to have recourse to article 83(2) TFEU".

129 See below Chapter 2, section 4.4.3.

the EU is the Directive.[130] Needless to say, legislating through Regulations versus Directives has a distinct impact.[131]

To be sure, the possibility of using Regulation as a legal instrument in this area pursuant to Article 325(4) TFEU may be derived from at least two factors. *On the one hand*, in the Proposal of the Directive on the fight against fraud to the Union's financial interests by means of criminal law, the Commission explicitly referred that it was "choosing" between legal instruments.[132] If there was a *choice*, then it is reasonable to conclude that the Regulation was also available. *On the other hand*, in the Convention establishing a Constitution for Europe i.e., the basis of the Lisbon Treaty, both legal instruments were foreseen in Article III-415.[133]

Of the various arguments supporting an autonomous source of criminal law in Article 325(4) TFEU,[134] we mention the following. *First*, the rationale behind "Combatting Fraud" does not seem to be increasing judicial cooperation in a certain area, i.e. the rationale of Title II containing Article 83.2 TFEU, but to provide criminal law protection to very specific Union interests.[135] *Second*,

130 See generally Anne Weyembergh and Serge de Biolley, *Approximation of substantive criminal law: The new institutional and decision-making framework and new types of interaction between EU actors*, in Francesca Galli and Anne Weyembergh, *Approximation of substantive criminal law in the EU: The way forward*, 2013 at 19, stating that "It is to be noted that if Article 325 TFEU is considered as entailing independent criminal law competence, then the possibility to use regulations opens the way not only to an approximation or harmonisation of criminal law but to a real unified supranational EU criminal law". Valsamis Mitsilegas, *EU Criminal Law Competence after Lisbon: From Securitised to Functional Criminalisation*, in Diego Acosta Arcarazo and Cian C. Murphy, eds., *EU Security and Justice Law*, 2014 at 118: "Using a legal basis other than Article 83(1) and 83(2) TFEU has significant constitutional consequences: it may enable the adoption of EU substantive criminal law measures in the form of Regulations".

131 See Helmut Satzger, *International and European Criminal Law*, 2012 at 46–47 noting the difference between "European Law-Making" and "Harmonisation of Laws".

132 Proposal for a Directive of the European Parliament and of the Council on the fight against fraud to the Union's financial interests by means of criminal law, COM (2012) 363 final, at 8: "3.3 Choice of instruments. In order to set out harmonised criminal law provisions in the field of the protection of the Union's financial interests, while allowing Member States a certain degree of flexibility as regards how to impose more stringent provisions, a Directive is the appropriate instrument."

133 III-415: "4. European laws or framework laws shall lay down the necessary measures in the fields of the prevention of and fight against fraud affecting the Union's financial interests with a view to affording effective and equivalent protection in the Member States and in all the Union's institutions, bodies, offices and agencies. They shall be adopted after consultation of the Court of Auditors."

134 Rosaria Sicurella, *Some reflections on the need for a General Theory of the Competence of the European Union in Criminal Law*, in Andre Klip, ed., *Substantive Criminal Law of the European Union*, 2011 at 236–237 further contends that Article 325(4) contains a stronger obligation to legislate in comparison with Article 83, i.e. difference between "shall" and "may", and that Article 325(4) calls for the adoption of "necessary measures" and not only "minimum rules".

135 In a similar fashion, certain academics have argued that EU powers in this area would not result from the cross-border dimension of the criminal behavior or its particular seriousness, but mainly because of a relationship to inherently European interests – whether or not there are serious or interstate concerns (see Bernd Schünemann, *The Foundation of Transnational Criminal Proceedings*, in Bernd Schünemann, ed., *A Programme for European Criminal*

the independent legal personhood of the EU affirmed in Article 47 TEU[136] is consistent with considering the Union's interests as different from those of the Member States.[137] Third, given that pursuant to Article 86 TFEU the European Prosecutor is mandatorily established by means of a Regulation, and given that it is specifically provided in Article 86 TFEU that the European Prosecutor will have jurisdiction to prosecute "offenses against the Union's financial interests", it seems reasonable to conclude that such offenses should be contained, to the same extent, in a Regulation and not in a Directive.[138]

This approach indicates that when dealing with inherently or genuine Union interests, EU criminal law powers are derived from a different source than judicial cooperation in criminal matters. In this sense, at least since the introduction of the so-called Alternative Project for a European criminal law,[139] a discussion has been ongoing over what exactly "inherently European interests" are. For the drafters of the Alternative Project, EU criminal law can only legitimately protect "inherently European interests" and not interests related to interstate/cross-border criminality.[140] Moreover, to that first group belong almost exclusively the offenses of EU public officials.[141] As we will see,[142] at least from an academic perspective, US scholars also differentiate between the criminal law protection of "direct federal interests" and interstate criminality. In any event, the current structure of the Lisbon Treaty seems to support the existence of a special level of federal protection[143] that, at least potentially, could enable the EU to claim

Justice, 2006 at 349–350, distinguishing between the protection of EU interests and the enforcement of interstate/cross border criminality).

136 Article 47 TFEU: "The Union shall have legal personality".

137 This is explicitly referred in the Proposal for a Directive of the European Parliament and of the Council on the fight against fraud to the Union's financial interests by means of criminal law, COM (2012) 363 final, at 6: "The protection of Union public money is a solidarity interest at Union level *which is different from the sum of the Member States' national financial interests*" (emphasis added).

138 See a similar argument in Valsamis Mitsilegas, *EU Criminal Law Competence after Lisbon: From Securitised to Functional Criminalisation*, in Diego Acosta Arcarazo and Cian C. Murphy, eds., *EU Security and Justice Law*, 2014 at 120.

139 See Bernd Schünemann, *A Programme for European Criminal Justice*, 2006.

140 See Bernd Schünemann, *Grundzüge eines Alternativ-Entwurfs zur europäischen Strafverfolgung*, Zeitschrift für die gesamte Strafrechtswissenschaft 116 (2004) at 377. For this scholar, the key issue is to determine which areas of criminal law and which institutions of law enforcement are "indispensable".

141 See Roland Hefendehl, *European Criminal Law: How Far and No Further?* in Bernd Schünemann, *A Programme for European Criminal Justice*, 2006 at 450–466.

142 See below Chapter 2, section 3.3.

143 The distinction between Member States' interests and Union's interests seems to be consistent with the logic of applying European criminal law only to those areas where "inherently European interests" are at stake. To put it differently, it is reasonable to argue that when the Union's interests are threatened, the legal basis for Union action is contained in provisions that are not related to judicial cooperation. As we will see, this is certainly the case in the US; the wording of the TFEU contains, at least, a systematic logic that enables similar arguments for the EU.

criminal powers by virtue of the direct federal, i.e. the Union's, interest at stake and not because there is a common goal to cooperate judicially.[144]

This logic seems to be behind the Commission's Proposal for a Directive on the fight against fraud to the Union's financial interests by means of criminal law.[145] The legal basis specifically noted in the Commission's proposal was not Article 83(2) TFEU, but solely Article 325(4) TFEU. Yet the EU Parliament's amendment clearly indicates that they are not willing to consider, for now, that Article 325(4) TFEU provides an autonomous source of criminal law powers to the EU.[146] In the end, the probable outcome is that this piece of legislation will be approved with a connection between Article 325(4) TFEU and Article 83(2) TFEU, which parallels the connection between the Spending Clause and the Necessary and Proper Clause in the US debate.

That is why we have used the term "potentially", because, as equally noted before, the discussion is currently more theoretical than practical given that the Commission chose to submit a proposal for a Directive and not for a Regulation. The reasons for this approach have probably more to do with the political correctness of avoiding the confrontation with Member States that would surely arise if the Commission proposed a Regulation in this area. Also, the fact that the proposed legal text included corruption, forgery and misappropriation offenses, i.e. ancillary offenses, not specifically listed in Article 325(4) TFEU added pressure to the final decision of choosing between the Regulation and the Directive.

Be that as it may, the EU approach has so far resorted to the comfortable area of horizontal federalism i.e., the Directive, with a certain vertical federalism "touch", i.e. the establishment of a European Public Prosecutor's Office. We refer to only a "touch" of vertical federalism, as the system envisioned in the Proposal establishing the EPPO is primarily based on national prosecutors "wearing" a so-called "double hat", i.e. they are national prosecutors and European prosecutors at the same time. This system of prosecutorial "blue helmets" probably lacks the necessary independence to provide an effective criminal law protection of the EU financial interests.[147]

From a federalism perspective, though the EU had the opportunity to really test the limits of the vertical federal dimension of EU criminal law by proposing a Regulation protecting the financial interests of the EU and a Regulation

144 The question of whether there is a legislative power to enact criminal legislation in the EU treaties pursuant to the protection of those genuine Union's interests is separate from the question of is whether the exercise of such power can be considered to be legitimate (see for instance Müsil, NStZ (2000) at 70). On the basis of the *ultima ratio principle*, harsh criticism against EU criminal law even in this area has been expressed (see among many Maria Kaifa-Gbandi, *The Importance of Core Principles of Substantive Criminal Law for a European Criminal Policy respecting Fundamental Rights and the Rule of Law*, EuCLR (2011), at 7-34).

145 Proposal for a Directive of the European Parliament and of the Council on the fight against fraud to the Union's financial interests by means of criminal law, COM (2012) 363 final.

146 See above Chapter 2, section 3.2.

147 See below Chapter 2, section 5.3.

establishing a European Public Prosecutor's Office with fully independent European prosecutors not connected to the Member States, it eventually chose the horizontal federalism approach, i.e. a Directive protecting the financial interests and a Regulation basically using national prosecutors, to ensure that, in the end, the EU financial interests are better protected than how they are protected today. Depending on the effectiveness of the current approach over time, the EU will have to reconsider its position.

3.3. THE PROTECTION OF DIRECT FEDERAL INTERESTS IN THE US CONSTITUTION (ARTICLE I SECTION 8)

As just noted, the Lisbon Treaty seems to differentiate between cooperation over general common interests in criminal matters among the Member States, and direct European interests that should be protected (maybe through criminal law). The question becomes whether this reading of the Lisbon Treaty is consistent with other federal systems. Interestingly enough, a similar distinction can be found in US federal criminal law. At least some scholars have differentiated between those powers which involve the protection of direct federal interests and those which do not. As Professors *Abrams, Beale,* and *Klein* put it: "direct federal interests can be defined as those that involve the protection of federally-owned property, persons employed by the federal government, federal programs or the federal purse".[148] According to these scholars, Congress's authority to enact criminal statutes aimed at protecting the direct interests of the federal government is derived from certain of the enumerated powers set forth in Article I Section 8 of the Constitution. In addition to the direct grants of power, congressional authority is *supplemented* by the Necessary and Proper Clause included at the last paragraph of Section 8,[149] which follows the logic of Article 83(2) TFEU, with different consequences, as equally noted before.

It seems quite interesting that the first criminal law provisions of the incipient federal system were closely related to the financial interests of the Union. In 1789 the US Congress passed the *Revenue Fraud Act,*[150] i.e. closely related to the financial interests of the Union, containing certain provisions dealing with the crime of *smuggling*[151] and with fraudulent declarations of the *value of goods and*

---

148 Norman Abrams, Sara Sun Beale and Susan R. Klein, *Federal criminal law and its enforcement*, 5th ed., 2010 at 18.

149 Ibid. at 18.

150 Revenue Fraud Act of 1789, 1 Stat. 29 at 46 (1789).

151 Act of July 31, 1789, ch. 5, § 12, 1 Stat. 29, 39. It provided for a $400 fine, forfeiture of the contraband, and publication of the names of the criminals in the local newspaper. The same statute authorized customs officers to obtain a warrant to search for contraband which was believed to be stored in warehouses (§ 24, at 43).

bribing a customs officer.[152] Also in the first comprehensive piece of legislation establishing federal crimes, i.e. the Crimes Act of 1790,[153] the Union's financial interests occupied a relevant position – this law introduced the federal crimes of treason, piracy, counterfeiting, crimes committed on the high seas or against the law of nations. As it has been noted, the 1789 Judiciary Act created the basic structure of the system of federal criminal law (district courts, US attorneys, etc.) but the definition of crimes and the establishment of punishments remained a missing link of the criminal system.[154] The Crimes Act of 1790 provided that connection.

Though it is not clear whether the authority to pass such legislation was based exclusively on the expressly conferred powers of the US Constitution or whether the authority was supplemented by the Necessary and Proper Clause,[155] the lack of referral in the legal text to the rationale of the latter and the black-letter law of Article I Section 8 of the US Constitution, seem to support that it was an act of Congress supported in the expressly conferred powers. In this sense, Article I, Section 8, the US Constitution establishes that Congress shall have power:

> "To provide for the punishment of counterfeiting the securities and current coin of the United States;
>
> To define and punish piracies and felonies committed on the high seas, and offenses against the law of nations ..."

Out of the 1790 list, the only offense not contained in Article I Section 8 was the crime of treason. Yet Article III Section 3 of the US Constitution itself defines the crime of treason and empowers Congress to set its punishment: "The Congress shall have Power to declare the Punishment of Treason, but no Attainder of Treason shall work Corruption of Blood, or Forfeiture except during the Life of the Person attainted".

In any event, it is fair to say that for the remainder of the so-called federalist presidencies,[156] the provisions establishing federal crimes were closely connected to the language of the Constitution. The financial interests or interests related to

---

152 Act of July 31, 1789, ch. 5, § 22, at 42; § 35, at 46. (See David P. Currie, *Constitution in Congress: Substantive Issues in the First Congress, 1789–1791*, U. Chi. L. Rev. 61 (1994) at 775, 833).

153 Crimes Act of 1790, ch. 9, 1 Stat. 112. Formally titled *An Act for the Punishment of Certain Crimes Against the United States.* For a thorough account of the historical evolution of US criminal law see Lawrence Friedman, *Crime and Punishment in American History*, 1993.

154 Dwight Henderson, *Congress, Courts, and Criminals: The Development of Federal Criminal Law*, 1801–1829, 1985, at 7.

155 David P. Currie, *Constitution in Congress: Substantive Issues in the First Congress, 1789–1791*, U. Chi. L. Rev. 61 (1994) at 832: "Whether Congress thought authority over such places included within the ostensibly narrower term 'high Seas,' necessary and proper to the regulation of commerce or to the exercise of admiralty jurisdiction, or implicit in a central government responsible for external affairs is not clear."

156 John Murrin, Paul Johnson, James McPherson, Alice Fahs and Gary Gerstle, *Liberty, Equality, Power: A History of the American People*, Volume I: To 1877, 2013 at 161.

the finances of the Union were gradually deserving criminal law protection. It is clear that not only the Union's budget, but also some genuine federal interests, were subject to criminal law protection. Some of these acts created criminal offenses for interfering with the postal service,[157] or failure to comply with the laws governing the importing of goods and other revenue laws.[158]

The politically opposing views of the so-called Jeffersonians did not trigger a different approach as to the type of criminal law passed during the presidency of Thomas Jefferson. On top of a small number of Acts concerning various federal interests, new criminal laws consisted of enforcement provisions of legislation regulating trade and imposing taxes,[159] punishing government corruption,[160] and counterfeiting and other fraud on the government.[161] It seems evident that in the early stages of the development of the US federal criminal law system certain federal interests – including those of financial nature – needed and deserved criminal law protection. And the US Congress had the authority to provide for this.[162]

After almost a century of dealing with federal crimes, a codification of federal law was completed in 1873 listing most criminal provisions in Title 70.[163] This title contained 128 sections in nine chapters. Six of these chapters defined the core of the major categories of federal offenses: (1) crimes against the existence of the government; (2) crimes arising within the maritime and territorial jurisdiction of the United States; (3) crimes against justice; (4) crimes against the operation of the government (including counterfeiting, fraud, and postal offenses); (5) official misconduct; and (6) crimes against the elective franchise and civil rights.[164]

Against this backdrop, it is worth noting certain differences between the EU and the US conferred powers related to specific crimes. The protection of the euro against counterfeiting is not treated as a truly direct interest, but as an example of interstate serious criminality,[165] while it is one of the only US congressional powers

157 Act of February 20, 1792, ch. 7, §§ 5, 11, 14, 16, 1 Stat. 232, 234, 235, 236; Act of May 8, 1794, ch. 23, §§ 5, 14, 16, 20, 1 Stat. 354,358, 360, 362.

158 Act of August 4, 1790, ch. 35, 1 Stat. 145; Act of March 3, 1791, ch. 15, 1 Stat. 199; Act of December 31, 1792, ch. 1, 1 Stat. 287; Act of July 6, 1797, ch. 11, §§ 12, 13, 14, 17, 1 Stat. 527, 530, 531, 532.

159 Act of March 30, 1802, ch. 12, 2 Stat. 138; Act of March 3, 1804, ch. 20, § 2, 2 Stat. 262; Act of February 28, 1806, ch. 9, 2 Stat. 351; Act of April 18, 1806, ch. 29, §§ 2, 3, 4, 5, 2 Stat. 379, 380; Act of January 9, 1808, ch. 8, § 3, 2 Stat. 453; Act of January 9, 1809, ch. 5, 2 Stat. 506; Act of March 1, 1809, ch. 24, 2 Stat. 528.

160 Act of February 28, 1803, ch. 9, §§ 7, 8, 2 Stat. 203, 204, 205; Act of April 21, 1806, ch. 48, § 6, 2 Stat. 402, 403.

161 Act of March 2, 1803, ch. 18, 2 Stat. 209; Act of April 21, 1806, ch. 49, 2 Stat. 404; Act of February 24, 1807, ch. 20, 2 Stat. 423.

162 See William Baude, *Rethinking the Federal Eminent Domain Power*, Yale L.J. 122 (2013) at 1738 (noting that "there were a few early constitutional objections to an implied criminalization power") providing further references.

163 Revised Statutes of the U.S. of 1873, at 1037–1081.

164 Revised Statutes of the U.S. of 1873, at 1037–1081.

165 Article 83(1) TFEU (listing "counterfeiting of means of payment" among the specifically identified areas of "particularly serious crime with a cross-border dimension").

which specifically provides for federal criminal sanctions.[166] In addition, the US Constitution seems to provide for a particularly federal power over foreign policy, including a power "to define and punish … offenses against the law of nations", another clear grant of criminal law competence.[167] This differs from the European Union, where foreign policy is a more nuanced issue, "subject to specific rules and procedures".[168] The historical context of the two Unions probably explains this difference,[169] but the growing role of the EU in foreign policy, superseding national policies of Member States, further emphasizes the increasingly federal nature of the Union, like its American counterpart.[170]

Yet, and here probably lies one of the most important differences in federal criminal law terms with the EU structure, among the powers contained in Article I Section 8 of the US Constitution, i.e. the legislative powers granted herein shall be vested in a Congress of the United States, the Necessary and Proper Clause is included in the last paragraph. That is, the Necessary and Proper Clause is not devised as a mechanism to foster judicial cooperation among the States, but as a direct source of the Union's power to legislate (including criminal legislation). As we shall explore further, when federal intervention has been questioned in a particular area, the US Supreme Court has regularly turned to this clause for justification. When protecting direct interests, the power of the US government to regulate and even criminalize private behavior is relatively unquestioned. It is when the federal government begins to encroach on those traditional state prerogatives without a federal stake that the debate heats up. "Direct interests" are not listed in the Constitution, but may be found through interpretation of the

[166] U.S. Const. art. I, § 8, cl. 6 (listing an enumerated power "to provide for the Punishment of counterfeiting the Securities and current Coin of the United States").

[167] U.S. Const. art. I, § 8, cl. 10. In the American context, foreign policy is an especially clear federal power, as the framers of the Constitution were particularly concerned.

[168] Article 24(1) TEU.

[169] In the American context, foreign policy is an especially clear federal power, as the framers of the Constitution were concerned with the perceived failure of the Articles of Confederation, predecessor to the Constitution, to provide clear federal exclusivity in foreign affairs. See John C. Yoo, *Globalism and the Constitution: Treaties, Non-Self-Execution, and the Original Understanding*, Colum. L. Rev. 99 (2013) at 1955 (generally providing a historical account of federal foreign policy power, and specifically noting that "enforcement of treaties became one of the key problems that led to the movement for a new constitution"); Michael Schaefer, *Constraints on State-Level Foreign Policy: (Re)Justifying, Refining, and Distinguishing the Dormant Foreign Affairs Doctrine*, Seton Hall L. Rev. 41 (2011) at 201, 221–227. It is no surprise that the Member States of the European Union, comprised of established nation states rather than recently independent colonies, would be more hesitant to cede foreign policy powers to another institution.

[170] See e.g. Article 24(3) TEU ("The Member States shall support the Union's external and security policy actively and unreservedly in a spirit of loyalty and mutual solidarity and shall comply with the Union's action in this area" – notably, the Treaty of Lisbon added the phrase, "shall comply with the Union's action"); Article 32 TEU ("Member States shall ensure, through the convergence of their actions, that the Union is able to assert its interests and values on the international scene").

enumerated congressional powers of Article I Section 8 via the expanding lens of the Necessary and Proper Clause.

The powers to tax and spend,[171] to borrow on US credit,[172] to coin money,[173] and to punish counterfeiting[174] all deal with a federal prerogative which gives federal enforcement preference over state enforcement. Thus there are currently US criminal laws punishing fraud against the United States[175] and criminal activity against federal agents, or those receiving federal funds.[176] Statutes like these which protect direct federal interests are "easy to justify on both a constitutional and a pragmatic level. The government has a legitimate interest in protecting itself from individuals who are trying to cheat it. Furthermore, the federal government is best able to determine the seriousness of the threat presented by a particular scheme to defraud it."[177]

Of course, the United States has expanded the reach of its criminal law far beyond those actions which have a direct effect on federal money and concerns. As will be discussed below, the Commerce Clause in particular has been a vehicle to extend federal regulation to areas which are perceived as important, but lack the direct connection to the federal government, and thus, some would argue, are equally able to be controlled by the states.[178] Later in this chapter, the expansion of US federal law into areas of non-direct interest will be discussed, as well as the many complaints against what is perceived as an encroachment by a supposedly limited federal government into state prerogatives. The important lesson to be drawn at the moment is that even in the US system, where direct federal authority is much more established than in the EU, there is still a distinction to be drawn between those laws which are directly related to federal interests (like in Article 325 TFEU) and those which are merely indirect interests based on importance and cross border concerns (like in Article 83(1) TFEU). Thus, by limiting itself to criminal legislation over those things which truly "need federal protection",[179] the European Union may focus on federal prerogatives and perhaps avoid the quagmire of theoretical and practical problems that the US has encountered by overly expanding its criminal law.

---

171 U.S. Const. art. I, § 8, cl. 1.

172 U.S. Const. art. I, § 8, cl. 2.

173 U.S. Const. art. I, § 8, cl. 5.

174 U.S. Const. art. I, § 8, cl. 6.

175 e.g. 18 U.S.C. §§ 286–89 (2012) (false claims against United States); 18 U.S.C. § 371 (2012) (conspiracy to defraud United States); 18 U.S.C. § 641 (1994) (embezzlement of United States property); 18 U.S.C. § 1031 (2012) (major fraud against the United States).

176 e.g. 18 U.S.C. § 245(b) (1) (B & E) (2012) (act of violence against those participating in any program run by or receiving funds from the United States); 18 U.S.C. §§ 656–57 (2012) (embezzlement from federally-insured financial institutions); 18 U.S.C. § 1344 (2012) (bank fraud); 18 U.S.C. § 2155 (2012) (destruction of national defense property).

177 Terrence M. Messonier, *Neo-Federalism, Popular Sovereignty, and the Criminal Law*, 29 Akron L. Rev. (1996) at 549, 577.

178 Chapter 2, sections 4.2.3 and 4.3.3.

179 Viviane Reding, SPEECH/13/644.

4. THE SECOND FEDERAL DIMENSION OF THE UNIONS' CRIMINAL LAW: INTERSTATE CRIMINALITY AND THE ENFORCEMENT OF THE UNIONS' POLICIES

4.1. INTRODUCTION

In the previous section we noted how both Unions began their federal criminal law career focusing on the protection of certain direct federal interests. In the case of the EU this basically comprised the financial interests; in the US case, a wider range of interests specified in the enumerated powers listed in the US Constitution. The following section deals with the expansion of federal criminal law in both Unions – again: vertical in the US and horizontal in the EU. And, again, the resemblances are noteworthy. Both Unions are concerned with the problem of interstate criminality and ensuring the effectiveness of their policies. They want to eliminate safe harbors for criminality and effectively implement the Unions' policies. The tendency in both cases has been to expand the Unions' reach as much as possible. This creates a sense of overcriminalization that is consistent with the perceived federal intrusion into local matters. *A key difference, though, is that, while the US federalizes certain offenses but allows local regulation of the same matter, the EU forces national authorities to adapt their own legislation to Union parameters.* Which approach threatens state sovereignty to a greater extent is hard to say. Yet from an efficiency perspective, the US approach seems to be more effective.

In general terms, concern over the impact of certain conducts on interstate commerce (US) / internal market (EU) has triggered a myriad of legislation in criminal matters in both Unions. Under this flag, the ships of criminal law have sailed through the murky waters of cross-border criminality. However, as noted previously, the institutional framework differs between the two Unions. While the US has seen vertical federalism in the form of federal offenses that are subject to federal jurisdiction (enforced by federal agencies and adjudicated by federal courts), the EU has been utilizing horizontal federalism to require states to implement certain EU legislation in criminal matters, which is then enforced and adjudicated by national authorities. In this section we will examine the intricacies of both approaches but focus on the EU approach.

4.2. CRITERIA FOR FEDERALIZING CRIMES IN THE EU (HORIZONTALLY) AND IN THE US (VERTICALLY)

4.2.1. Introduction

This section will review some tendencies in both Unions concerning the exercise of criminal law powers. As we shall see, there is a common denominator in the fact that the problems experienced by the Unions could not be properly addressed with the enumerated powers. Both Unions have resorted to a broad interpretation of certain powers to implicitly include powers in certain areas. Needless to say, this has been a slow process. The broader experience of the US system in this area seems obvious as it has dealt with these issues for over two hundred years – though real enforcement came in the 20th century. But the young and relatively smaller experience of the EU shows a similar approach to the problems raised.

In this sense, it is worth noting that prior to the Lisbon Treaty there was a tendency towards shifting the criminal policies from the First to the Third Pillar,[180] i.e. from considering the EU as a possible source of criminal law, to a potential coordinator of Member States' criminal law. For instance, in the initial approaches to harmonizing criminal law in Europe, the European Commission mainly looked for criminal law powers in certain areas in the First Pillar, which focuses on the creation and functioning of a European single market.[181] In doing so, it mainly used the Directive as the appropriate legislative instrument. However, perhaps due to the lack of success of this strategy, an attempt to carry out this harmonization through the Third Pillar, i.e. through intergovernmental

[180] The discussion on such a movement can be found in Andre Klip, *European Criminal Law*, 2nd ed., 2012 at 52–59; Valsamis Mitsilegas, *EU Criminal Law*, 2009 at 69–70; Valsamis Mitsilegas, *The third wave of third pillar law: which direction for EU criminal justice?*, European Law Review 34 (2009) at 523; Ester Herlin-Karnell, *Commission v. Council: Some Reflections on Criminal Law in the First Pillar*, European Public Law 15 (2007) at 69; Steve Peers, *EU Justice and Home Affairs*, 2011 at 656–664; Stephan Braum, *Europäische Strafgesetzlichkeit*, 2003 at 410–430; Thomas Weigend, *Mindestanforderungen an ein europaweit geltendes harmonisiertes Strafrecht*, in Frank Zieschang, Eric Hilgendorf and Klaus Laubenthal, eds., *Strafrecht und Kriminalität in Europa*, 2003 at 60–75. The discussion has become obsolete since the entry into force of the Lisbon Treaty, where the traditional division of Pillars has been erased. But the rationale behind the approaches remains. The difference between both approaches was clarified by the ECJ judgment of 13 September 2005 (Case C-176/03 *Commission v. Council*). For an explanation of the EU institutions pursuant to this ECJ landmark decision see Communication from the Commission to the European Parliament and the Council on the implications of the Court's judgment of 13 September 2005 (Case C-176/03 *Commission v. Council*) (COM (2005) 583 final). For a general enforcement perspective on this issue see Michael Dougan, *From the Velvet Glove to the Iron Fist: Criminal Sanctions for the Enforcement of EU Law*, in Marise Cremona, ed., *Compliance and the Enforcement of EU Law*, 2012 at 94–95.

[181] See Joachim Vogel, *Europäische Kriminalpolitik – europäische Strafrechtsdogmatik*, Goltdammer's Archiv 517 (2002) at 522.

cooperation, was made. This strategy gave the Council a predominant position and used mostly framework decisions and agreements.[182]

The result in the Lisbon Treaty was a sort of a compromise. The enumerated powers of the EU in criminal law are contained in the area of judicial cooperation in criminal matters.[183] Yet the underlying principle to foster such cooperation is the principle of mutual recognition, which derives from the strategies to consolidate a European single market.[184] The enumerated criminal law powers are now to be exercised through Directives so the direct effects of the Directives and the enforcement incentives through the infringement proceedings are now present in all criminal law legislation passed by the EU institutions.[185]

Looking at the history of US federal criminal law,[186] a departure from the few enumerated powers in criminal law prescribed in the US Constitution seems to be fair statement. Interstate commerce and the Necessary and Proper Clause have provided much of the grounding for federal criminal legislation in the 20th century.

---

182 See JOACHIM VOGEL, *Europäische Kriminalpolitik – europäische Strafrechtsdogmatik*, GOLTDAMMER'S ARCHIV 517 (2002) at 523. See also ELSPETH GUILD and SERGIO CARRERA, *The European Unions' Area of Freedom, Security and Justice Ten Years on*, in ELSPETH GUILD, SERGIO CARRERA and ALEJANDRO EGGENSWEILER, eds., *The Area of Freedom, Security and Justice Ten Years on. Successes and Future Challenges under the Stockholm Programme*, 2010 at 9–12. Framework decisions increasingly became the most frequently used instrument by the EU; more than Conventions. Framework decisions, however, implied numerous difficulties that in the end seriously affect their effectiveness: first there was no need for the Parliament to intervene in their adoption; second, in case of a serious breach of the duties included in the Convention, no cause of action before the ECJ was generated; third, the "direct effect" in the national legal systems of the member states was missing until the landmark *Pupino* case (2007). For a general overview of the differences between Directives and Framework decision in the area of criminal law see MARTA MIGLIETTI, *The New EU Criminal Law in Action: The Proposal for a Directive on Criminal Sanctions for Insider Dealing and Market Manipulation*, IES Working Paper 5 (2013) at 10–11 (available at: www.ies.be/files/Working%20Paper%20 Miglietti.pdf).

183 The relevance of the now expressly stated conferred powers in the area of criminal law can be seen in the Explanatory Statement supporting the European Parliament resolution of 22 May 2012 on an EU approach to criminal law: "With the entry into force of the Lisbon Treaty, the pillar structure was abandoned and the basis was created for the development of criminal law as part of EU Community law. Considering that in the past criminal law had long been regarded as the exclusive competence of Member States, and only with the Treaty of Maastricht in 1992 a first opening towards the development of EU criminal was created, this can be considered as a major decision".

184 See above Chapter 1, section 6.

185 In any event, as CHRISTINA ECKES, *A European Area of Freedom, Security and Justice. A long way ahead?*, UPPSALA FACULTY OF LAW WORKING PAPER No. 6a (2011) (available at: http://ssrn.com/abstract=2098952) notes: "The area has grown out of the originally rather week cooperation between national activities, first within TREVI and later within the Union's Third pillar. It does not have the strong supranational Community roots. This has remained the approach: a political preference prevails for cooperation between national systems rather than forcing harmonization through. Leaving national systems unchanged."

186 For an overview of the history of US federal criminal law see SUSAN A. EHRLICH, *The Increasing Federalization of Crime*, ARIZONA STATE LAW JOURNAL 32 (2000) at 827–836; SUSAN R. KLEIN and INGRID B. GROBEY, *Debunking Claims of Over-Federalization of Criminal Law*, EMORY LAW JOURNAL 62 (2012) at 11–16.

And the undeniable tendency has been to expand, on the grounds of such provisions, the scope of federal criminal law. A report by the Task Force on the Federalization of Criminal Law, created by the American Bar Association, found that there were around 3,000 criminal law provisions in the federal code in 1996, and that around forty per cent of these had been passed since 1970.[187] There is no indication that this trend has changed in the almost two decades since, with more recent estimates putting the number over 4,000.[188]

Both Unions have significantly expanded their criminal legislation. Both Unions have resorted to interstate criminality and to the need to resort to criminal law to effectively implement the Unions' regulatory policies as means to produce criminal legislation. In the European case, the TFEU has specifically addressed the use of criminal law in both areas. In the American case, the US Supreme Court jurisprudence found that criminal law was an adequate means to address interstate criminality and enforce federal regulatory policies.

4.2.2. *Criteria for the Inclusion of Matters within the Area of Liberty, Security and Justice of the EU*

Regarding the EU, it is important to note that in Article 3 of the Lisbon Treaty, which sets the objectives of the European Union, the second stated objective is to offer "to the citizens an area of freedom, security and justice", *even before* providing them with a "single market where competition is free and unrestrained". This illustrates the spirit that currently prevails in Europe, where the guarantees of a single market are placed, at least from a systematic perspective, after the creation of the aforementioned area.[189] As is well known, the Area of Freedom, Security and Justice was established by the Maastricht Treaty[190] and has since played a significant role in the Europeanization of criminal law. The Lisbon Treaty confirms the critical importance of this area, which will thus have the responsibility of advancing and developing EU criminal law. It is precisely in this Area where reference is made to key issues such as "legal standards" and the creation of a European prosecutor.

---

187 See James A. Strazzella, A.B.A. Crim. Just. Sec., *The Federalization of Criminal Law*, 1998.

188 Sara Sun Beale, *The Many Faces of Overcriminalization: From Morals and Mattress Tags to Overfederalization*, Am. U. L. Rev. 54 (2005) at 747, 753.

189 For a brilliant introduction see Ester Herlin-Karnell, *The Lisbon Treaty and the Area of Criminal Law And Justice*, European Policy Analysis 3 (2008) at 1.

190 This Area was formerly based in Articles 29 and 31(c) of the European Treaties. For a comprehensive approach see Kraus-Vonjahr, *Der Aufbau eines Raums der Freiheit, der Sicherheit und des Rechts in Europa*, 2002. For a recent comprenhensive approach see Christina Eckes and Theodore Konstadinides, *Crime within the Area of Freedom, Security and Justice. A European Public Order,* 2011, addressing the "Europeanisation" of the fight against crime. For an overview of the justice and home affairs area since its inception, Steve Peers, *EU Justice and Home Affairs Law*, 3rd ed., 2011.

Some authors have noted an "incrementalist" approach by the EU Council concerning this area.[191] This is a (politically correct) way of addressing the ever-expanding approach of the EU in this subject. This tendency will not be easily put to rest, as the criteria for (horizontally) federalizing crime contained in Article 83 TFEU are inherently expansive: interstate criminality – Article 83(1) TFEU – and effective enforcement of EU policies – Article 83(2) TFEU.[192] Not surprisingly this part of the Area of Freedom, Security and Justice is propelled by the principle of mutual recognition – Article 82 TFEU – and, as has been outlined above,[193] has a natural tendency to grow.

It is true, as some savvy commentators have pointed out,[194] that there is a chance for decriminalization based on two general provisions contained in the first article governing the Area of Freedom, Security and Justice: Article 67 TFEU. On the one hand, approximation of national legislation should only be exercised when it is *necessary* (Article 67(3) TFEU); on the other hand, it shall respect national diversity, i.e. the "different legal systems and traditions of the Member States" (Article 67(1) TFEU).

Precisely this respect for national, i.e. state, sovereignty was highlighted by the German Constitutional Court (*Bundesverfassungsgericht*) in its well-publicized decision of June 2009 concerning the Lisbon Treaty.[195] The *Bundesverfassungsgericht* listed five particularly sensitive policy areas where European competence must be exceptionally well justified.[196] Remarkably, the

---

191 Theodore Konstadinides and Noree O'Meara, *Fundamental Rights and Judicial Protection*, in Diego Acosta Arcarazo and Cian C. Murphy, eds., *EU Security and Justice Law*, 2014 at 77–92; in Diego Acosta Arcarazo and Cian C. Murphy, *Rethinking Europe's Freedom, Security & Justice*, in Diego Acosta Arcarazo and Cian C. Murphy, eds., *EU Security and Justice Law*, 2014 at 2–16.

192 Some commentators have distinguished both criminalizing powers as follows: "EU competence to criminalise can be justified in a twofold manner: Upon the need for the Union to address security threats (securitised criminalisation); and upon the need for the Union to use criminal law in order to ensure the effectiveness of Union law (functional criminalization)" (see Valsamis Mitsilegas, *EU Criminal Law Competence after Lisbon: From Securitised to Functional Criminalisation*, in Diego Acosta Arcarazo and Cian C. Murphy, eds., *EU Security and Justice Law*, 2014 at 100).

193 See above Chapter 1, section 6.

194 Valsamis Mitsilegas, *EU Criminal Law Competence after Lisbon: From Securitised to Functional Criminalisation*, in Diego Acosta Arcarazo and Cian C. Murphy, eds., *EU Security and Justice Law*, 2014 at 121–124.

195 German Constitutional Court, *Lisbon* decision, judgment of the Second Senate of 30 June 2009 (2 BvE 2/08; 2 BvE 5/08; 2 BvR 1010/08; 2 BvR 1022/08). For a thorough account of this decision see the *Special Section: The Federal Constitutional Court's Lisbon Case*, German Law Journal 10 (2009) at 1201–1308. See also Ester Herlin-Karnell, *The Constitutional Dimension of European Criminal Law*, 2012 at 139–142; Christina Eckes, *A European Area of Freedom, Security and Justice. A long way ahead?*, Uppsala Faculty of Law Working Paper No. 6a (2011) (available at: http://ssrn.com/abstract=2098952).

196 German Constitutional Court, *Lisbon* decision, paras. 248–260: (1) substantive and formal criminal law; (2) the disposition of the police monopoly on the use of force towards the interior and of the military monopoly on the use of force towards the exterior; (3) the fundamental fiscal decisions on public revenue and public expenditure; (4) the shaping of circumstances of

list included substantive and formal criminal law as the *first point*. The German court noted that certain elements of criminal law are central to the constitutional identity of Germany.[197] It emphasized that the Member States have the police monopoly on the use of force towards the interior and that the requirement of democratic self-determination substantially limits what can be determined at the EU level.

Yet the current approach undertaken by the Council in the so-called Stockholm Programme[198] seems to be to move in the opposite direction. In both areas, i.e. interstate criminality and effective enforcement of Union policies, the Council noted that they "should become the object of common definitions of criminal offences and common minimum levels of maximum sanctions and that these are the serious criminal offenses referred to in article 83(1) TFEU".[199] True, the Council noted that "criminal law provisions should be introduced only when they are considered essential in order for the interests to be protected and, as a rule be used only as a last resort".[200] But as the specific assessment of the Council shows regarding most of the matters contained in Article 83(1) TFEU,[201] the approach is expansive, not restrictive.

All in all, the national identity flag waved by the German Constitutional Court and contained in Article 4(2) TFEU could provide a relative safeguard against excessive horizontal federalization of criminal law in Europe.[202] To be sure, Article 4 TFEU contains a similar wording to the so-called anti-commandeering clause of the US Constitution.[203] Where Article 4 notes that "competences not conferred upon the Union in the Treaties remain with the Member States", the Tenth Amendment reads, "[t]he powers not delegated to the United States by the Constitution, nor prohibited by it to the States, are reserved to the States respectively, or to the people". Moreover, Article 4(2) details to a greater extent

life in a social state; and (5) culture, for instance as regards family law, the school and education system and dealing with religious communities.

197 German Constitutional Court, *Lisbon* decision, judgment of the Second Senate of 30 June 2009 (2 BvE 2/08; 2 BvE 5/08; 2 BvR 1010/08; 2 BvR 1022/08), para. 253 (these elements are criminal liability, concepts of fair and appropriate trial, and the administration of criminal law).

198 The Stockholm Programme – An Open and Secure Europe Serving and Protecting Citizens, OJ 2010, C115/01. See generally Elspeth Guild, Sergio Carrera and Alejandro Eggensweiler, eds., *The Area of Freedom, Security and Justice Ten Years on. Successes and Future Challenges under the Stockholm Programme*, 2010.

199 The Stockholm Programme – An Open and Secure Europe Serving and Protecting Citizens, OJ 2010, C115/15 ("In the face of cross-border crime, more efforts should be made to make judicial cooperation more efficient" at 12).

200 The Stockholm Programme – An Open and Secure Europe Serving and Protecting Citizens, OJ 2010, C115/15.

201 Protection against serious and organised crime, Trafficking in human beings, Sexual exploitation of children and child pornography, Cybercrime, Economic crime and corruption, Drugs and Terrorism (The Stockholm Programme – An Open and Secure Europe Serving and Protecting Citizens, OJ 2010, C115/21-25).

202 See Ester Herlin-Karnell, *The Constitutional Dimension of European Criminal Law*, 2012 at 116 questioning whether national identity can be considered as the new "safeguard clause".

203 See above Introduction.

the meaning of this clause,[204] in a similar fashion to the articles of confederation prior to the US Constitution.[205]

To the same extent that the Tenth Amendment has provided in some instances an effective safeguard against forcing the states to pass any regulations or legislation,[206] the national identity clause of Article 4(2) TFEU could be used in a similar fashion.[207] To be sure, the Tenth Amendment has not served as an effective tool against vertical federalism, but as a relative limit to horizontal federalism.[208] This reinforces the thesis of this book: the EU should exercise greater vertical federalism in specific (few) areas of criminal law, and lesser horizontal federalism in a number of criminal law areas related to national identity. In simple terms: horizontal federalism (in many areas) is a greater threat to national diversity than vertical federalism (in few areas).

4.2.3. The Federalization of Crime in the US

Earlier in this chapter, the distinction between direct and indirect federal interests was noted, with protection of direct interests (like federal funds) proving to be a relatively uncontroversial source of federal criminal power. Even in those areas, however, the Constitution makes little specific mention of a criminal power, but simply delineates areas over which Congress has any power whatsoever. Despite this lack of reference to criminal law, which may be surprising to some, the federal government's role in criminal law has exploded since the early conception of the federal power. This explosion has generated a great deal of concern among scholars and practitioners and ultimately resulted in what could be termed the federalization of crime debate.[209] Not intending to reproduce in the following

---

204 "The Union shall respect the equality of Member States before the Treaties as well as their national identities, inherent in their fundamental structures, political and constitutional, inclusive of regional and local self-government. It shall respect their essential State functions, including ensuring the territorial integrity of the State, maintaining law and or- der and safeguarding national security. In particular, national security remains the sole responsibility of each Member State".

205 Articles of Confederation, March 1, 1781, II: "Each state retains its sovereignty, freedom, and independence, and every power, jurisdiction, and right, which is not by this Confederation expressly delegated to the United States, in Congress assembled".

206 See the relevant cases *NY v. US*, 505 U.S. 144 (1992), *Printz v. US*, 521 U.S. 898 (1997).

207 For an account of the tenth amendment as a limit to crime federalization see Keith R. Fischer, *Toward a basal Tenth Amendment: a riposte to national bank preemption of state consumer protection laws*, Harvard Journal of Law & Public Policy 29 (2006) at 981. Erin Ryan, *Federalism and the Tug of War Within*, 2011.

208 See above the discussion above in Chapter 1, section 6.3 (full faith and credit).

209 Kathleen Brickey, *Criminal Mischief: The Federalization of American Criminal Law*, Hastings Law Journal 46 (1995) at 1135; Sara Sun Beale, *Federalizing Crime: Assessing the Impact on the Federal Courts*, Annals American Academy of Politics & Social Sciences 543 (1996) at 39; Edwin Meese III, *Big Brother on the Beat: The Expanding Federalization of Crime*, Tex. Rev. L. & Pol. 1 (1997) at 1; Steven D. Clymer, *Unequal Justice: The Federalization of Criminal Law*, Southern California Law Review 70 (1997) at 647; American Bar Association, Criminal Justice Section, Task Force on the Federalization of

pages this complex and intense debate, a brief overview of certain key points should suffice for now.

In an early Supreme Court case (1812), it was established that there was no criminal common law at a federal level.[210] In the United States as in the European Union, the constituent states had been operating for years with their own laws and courts, and thus by the time of the revolution they had their own bodies of criminal law. From the understanding of the US as a government of limited powers, the court found that "the powers of the general Government are made up of concessions from the several states – whatever is not expressly given to the former, the latter expressly reserve."[211] This sentiment, mirroring the wording of the Tenth Amendment to the US Constitution,[212] reflects a broader idea that criminal law is precisely one of those traditional state realms of authority where federal power should be limited.[213]

The early history of the US illustrates this concept.[214] Although even the first US Congress did not hold itself limited to the very few specific grants of federal

Criminal Law, *The Federalization of Criminal Law*, 1998 (for an overview of the discussion up to the turn of the century see pages 50–78); Susan A. Ehrlich, *The Increasing Federalization of Crime*, Arizona State Law Journal 32 (2000) at 837; Federalist Society for Law & Pub. Policy Studies, *Measuring the Explosive Growth of Federal Crime Legislation* (John S. Baker & Dale E. Bennett, 2004); Stephen E. Smith, *Proportionality and Federalization*, Virginia Law Review 91 (2005) at 880; Sara Sun Beale, *The Many Faces of Overcriminalization: From Morals and Mattress Tags to Overfederalization*, Am. U. L. Rev. 54 (2005) at 744; J. Richard Broughton, *Congressional Inquiry and the Federal Criminal Law*, U. Rich. L. Rev. 46 (2012) at 457; for an opposing view see Tom Stacy and Kim Dayton, *The Underfederalization of Crime*, Cornell Journal of Law & Public Policy 6 (1997) at 247; Susan R. Klein and Ingrid B. Grobey, *Debunking Claims of Over-Federalization of Criminal Law*, Emory Law Journal 62 (2012) at 1 (probably providing the more in-depth statistical analysis so far); Susan R. Klein and Ingrid B. Grobey, *Overfederalization of Criminal Law? It's a Myth*, Criminal Justice 28 (2013) at 23 (see a response in Julie Rose O'Sullivan, *The Federal Criminal "Code": Return of Overfederalization*, Harv. J.L. & Pub. Pol'y 37 (2014) at 57–67). For a recent broad perspective see Joseph F. Zimmerman, *Congress and Crime: The Impact of Federalization of State Criminal Laws*, 2014. According to Zimmermann the first concern "with the impact of such federalization was expressed for the first time by prominent individuals commencing in 1922".

210 *United States v. Hudson*, 11 U.S. (7 Branch) 32 (1812).

211 Ibid. at 33.

212 "The powers not delegated to the United States by the Constitution, nor prohibited to it by the States, are reserved to the States respectively, or to the people." U.S. Const. amend. X.

213 Lawrence M. Friedman, *Crime and Punishment in American History*, 1993 at 261–62. Although this is a widely touted idea among modern proponents of federalism limits, others suggest that even the founders were not so limited in their conception of federal power. See Adam H. Kurland, *First Principles of American Federalism and the Nature of Federal Criminal Jurisdiction*, 45 Emory L.J. 1, 25–61 (1996) (outlining the Constitutional bases for federal criminal law, and pointing out that even early American legislation went beyond these grants).

214 Susan A. Ehrlich, *The Increasing Federalization of Crime*, Arizona State Law Journal 32 (2000) at 827–836; American Bar Association, Criminal Justice Section, Task Force on the federalization of Criminal Law, *The Federalization of Criminal Law*, 1998 at 5–7.

criminal power,[215] federal criminal legislation was very limited and tended to remain close to explicit constitutional grants of power. For instance, early laws criminalized theft of mail.[216] This is not exactly the same as "establish[ing] Post Offices and post roads",[217] but it is clearly related to an express federal power, expanded through the Necessary and Proper Clause. Similarly, the bulk of the criminal legislation emerging from the early federalist and Jeffersonian presidencies was closely connected to the text of the Constitution.[218] This trend would change radically in the modern era.

As the US entered the 20th century, the role of the federal government in general was on the rise. The Civil War Amendments,[219] passed from 1865–1870, are often described as creating a "shift in the federal-state balance", resulting in a "diminution of state sovereignty ... intended by the Framers".[220] From a policy perspective, which perhaps has played a more important role than theoretical federalism concerns, an increasingly mobile society led to a greater need for regulation which went beyond state borders.[221] Naturally, the interstate commerce clause began to play an increased role in justifying federal criminal laws combatting interstate crime where the individual states were limited by jurisdictional restrictions.[222] As a result, the Commerce Clause has become a dominant source of federal authority over crime control.[223] As in the EU model, there seems to be a fundamental, or at least practical, understanding of interstate criminality as a federal concern. However, in the US system, the "interstate" element of crimes became simply "a facile (and seductive) route to federalized crime ... [and] the nexus between commerce and the criminal conduct

215 Adam H. Kurland, *First Principles of American Federalism and the Nature of Federal Criminal Jurisdiction*, 45 Emory L.J. 1, 25–61 (1996) at 56 (noting that the first criminal provisions enacted by the federal government were passed under the Necessary and Proper Clause).

216 1 Stat. 237 (1792).

217 U.S. Const. art. 1, § 8, cl. 7.

218 Terrence M. Messonier, *Neo-Federalism, Popular Sovereignty, and the Criminal Law*, Akron L. Rev. 29 (1996) at 549, 577 (noting that "criminal laws passed during the Federalist presidencies were closely connected to the language of the Constitution," and that "Despite the different political philosophies of the Federalists and the Jeffersonians, there was not a significant difference in the type of criminal law passed").

219 U. S. Const. amends. XIII, XIV, & XV.

220 *Fitzpatrick v. Bitzer*, 427 U. S. 445, 455 (1976).

221 See Alfred C. Aman Jr., *Federalism Through a Global Lends: A Call for Deferential Judicial Review*, Ind. J. Global Legal Stud. 11 (2004) at 109, 109–110 (referring to the increasingly national economy and consequent expansion of congressional power); Kathleen F. Brickley, *The Commerce Clause and Federalized Crime: A Tale of Two Thieves*, Annals Am. Acad. Pol. & Sci. 543 (1996) at 27, 28 ("The primary force behind the transformation of 'crime' into 'federal crime' was the emergence of a culture of mobility").

222 Kathleen Brickey, *Criminal Mischief: The Federalization of American Criminal Law*, Hastings Law Journal 46 (1995) at 29–30 (referencing the Dyer Act of 1919, which made interstate car theft a federal crime, responding to a sharp increase in car theft which crossed state borders, which hindered state police efforts).

223 Sara Sun Beale, *Federalizing Crime: Assessing the Impact on the Federal Courts*, Annals Am. Acad. Pol. & Soc. Sci. 543 (1996) at 39, 42–44.

diminished to the point of being tenuous at best."[224] Thus, while the connection between the US Constitution's interstate Commerce Clause and Article 83 TFEU illustrates link between federalization in the EU and the US, the US experience with rampant overfederalization argues for a considered approach in Europe.

We have already noted the expansion of US federal criminal in the wake of the "tough on crime policy",[225] and the narrow use of the conferred powers to federalize criminal law in the early beginnings. The interesting issue here is that this expansion in federal criminal law has taken place on the grounds of two justifications contained in the Lisbon Treaty: interstate criminality and enforcement of the Union's policies. As some academics at the time noted, "the increasing federalization of crime has the potential to cause an unplanned but nonetheless fundamental change in the relationship between the federal government and the states".[226] This seems to be of equal concern in the current status of the relationships between the EU and the Member States in matters relating to criminal law.

A final note at the institutional level.[227] The Judicial Conference of the United States in 1991 expressed its strong opposition to congressional federalization of state crimes.[228] In 1995 it noted that Congress should not federalize a state crime unless the federal government has a distinctive interest in the crime.[229] It is worth

---

224 Kathleen Brickey, *Criminal Mischief: The Federalization of American Criminal Law*, Hastings Law Journal 46 (1995) at 30.

225 See above Chapter 1, section 4.3. As the American Bar Association, Criminal Justice Section, Task Force on the federalization of Criminal Law, *The Federalization of Criminal Law*, 1998 at 2 notes: "new federal laws are not passed because federal prosecution is necessary, but because federal crime legislation in general is thought to be politically popular". See also Thomas M. Mengler, *The Sad Refrain of Tough on Crime: Some Thoughts on Saving the Federal Judiciary from the Federalization of State Crime*, Kansas Law Review 43 (1995) at 509; John S. Backer, *Jurisdictional and Separation of Powers Strategies to limit the Expansion of Federal Crimes*, American University Law Review 54 (2005) at 546.

226 Sara Sun Beale, *Report Reporter's Draft for the Working Group on Principles to Use When Considering the Federalization of Criminal Law*, Hastings Law Journal 46 (1995) at 1277. For an opposing view see Susan R. Klein and Ingrid B. Grobey, *Debunking Claims of Over-Federalization of Criminal Law*, Emory Law Journal 62 (2012) at 5: "we will demonstrate through empirical data that in spite of the large increase in the number of federal criminal statutes, this growth itself has caused almost no impact on federal resources, nor has it destabilized the traditional balance of power between state and federal courts."

227 Most of these considerations in the US are driven by the negative impact of federalization of state crimes on the US judicial system and the judicial systems of the states (see Joseph F. Zimmerman, *Congress and Crime: The Impact of Federalization of State Criminal Laws*, 2014).

228 Report of the Proceedings of the Judicial Conference of the United States (1991).

229 Judicial Conference of the United States, Long Range Plan for the Federal Courts (1995). The report urges Congress to establish a new criminal offense only if it (1) is against the United States government or its agents or Congress determines the need for nationally uniform control over the concerned activity, (2) involves multistate or international activities, (3) concerns complex commercial or institutional enterprises beyond the expertise and the resources of states, (4) undermines public confidence in the ability of local prosecutors to address serious state government corruption or local government corruption, or (5) generates sensitive issues in the concerned community leading to the perception federal prosecution would be more objective.

noting that in the US, calls have been made for stronger judicial cooperation between the Union and the states. The Federal Courts Study Committee, created in 1988, recommended the establishment of a national state judicial council by the chief justice of the United States Supreme Court and the chairman of the Conference of Chief Justices of the States.[230]

This shows that the increased federalization of crime has drawn considerable attention and criticism in the US. It should give pause to the current approach of the EU institutions towards the expansive use of horizontal federalism in achieving the same goals. There is broad consensus around the fact that where direct federal interests are at stake, the Union's actions are legitimate and necessary. But to extend the Unions' criminal law power beyond the borders of genuine federal interests is a questionable exercise in the US and in the EU. That is the reason we advocate for more vertical federalism in limited areas strictly connected to the EU's interests and allowing for national diversity in areas intrinsically connected to the states' sovereignty.

4.3. INTERSTATE CRIMINALITY

4.3.1. Introduction

Up to this point, it has been noted that both Unions – the US and the EU – are dealing with certain offenses at a supranational level in a similar fashion. The Lisbon Treaty clearly provides a basis for EU powers in criminal matters that would enable the EU to develop basic, agreed upon legislation across Europe, in other words a "minimum agreed upon European criminal law". As this book strives to expose a certain (horizontal) federal approach contained in the Lisbon Treaty, it has been shown that the guiding criteria of such jurisdiction – the cross-border/interstate dimension and seriousness of the crime, and effective enforcement of the Unions' policies – are fully consistent with elements of United States federal criminal law.[231] Thus, just as the Lisbon Treaty underlines the federal nature of the European Union, the criminal law contained in the Area of Freedom, Security and Justice follows the ruling principles of federal criminal law.

Two key points arise from the comparison which has been highlighted. First, when developing European (federal) criminal legislation, the potential problems of federalization must be taken into account. The reach and scope of federal criminal law must be considered in light of, *inter alia*, the issues of United States federal criminal law, perhaps the greatest of which is the inherently expansive, i.e.

The same conclusion was reached by the American Bar Association, Criminal Justice Section, Task Force on the federalization of Criminal Law, *The Federalization of Criminal Law*, 1998.

230 Report of the Federal Courts Study Committee (1990) at 17.

231 For a pre-Lisbon assessment see Brice Ruyver, Gert Vermeulen and Tom Beken, *Strategies of the EU and the US in Combating Transnational Organized Crime*, 2002.

overcriminalizing, nature of federal criminal law. The second point raised by our comparison is that the Lisbon Treaty ultimately forms a hybrid, i.e. horizontal, criminal law federalism, given that national not federal courts will apply such laws. Thus, this book argues that federalism in the Lisbon Treaty is not vertical federalism in the sense of a Union's federalism; therefore criminal legislation contained therein does not correlate to traditional notions of federal criminal law (federal crimes prosecuted in a federal court). Rather, the federalism of the European Union, including the federal criminal law elements, is supranational in nature.

As we shall now explore, the recurring tool used by the Unions to advance criminal legislation has been the fight against interstate/cross-border criminality. The grounds for the US approach are rooted in interstate commerce. The EU has resorted to a principle derived from the internal market experience: the principle of mutual recognition. A key to understand this development is that mutual recognition, though technically similar to the Full Faith and Credit Clause of the US Constitution,[232] has served a notably different purpose in the EU. The referred clause of the US Constitution has no connection with interstate commerce. Conversely, the principle of mutual recognition is based on the internal market tenets. The consequence is that the expansion of US (vertical) federal criminal law based on interstate commerce has its correspondence in the expansion of EU (horizontal) federal criminal law.

4.3.2. EU's Serious Cross-Border Criminality (Article 83(1) TFEU)

4.3.2.1. Catalog of (Vertical) Federal Crimes Specified in Article 83(1) TFEU (EU)

Before addressing the logic behind this (horizontal) federalization of crime, it is worth noting the list of matters that according to the Lisbon Treaty meet the criteria of serious interstate, i.e. cross-border, criminality: terrorism, trafficking in human beings and sexual exploitation of women and children, illicit drug trafficking, illicit arms trafficking, money laundering, corruption, counterfeiting of means of payment, computer crime and organized crime.[233] It should be noted first of all that *these crimes are all regulated in US federal criminal law.*[234] To be

232 See above Chapter 1, section 6.3.

233 For an overview of the legislation in place up to 2012 see André Klip, *European Criminal Law*, 2nd ed., 2012.

234 For an overview of the US federal criminal regulation addressing the same offenses see Norman Abrams, Sara Sun Beale and Susan R. Klein, *Federal criminal law and its enforcement*, 5th ed., 2010 at Chap. 7 and 8 (Public Corruption), Chap. 9 (Drug Trafficking), Chap. 10 (Currency Reporting Offenses and Money Laundering), Chap. 11 (Firearms Regulation); Chap. 14 (Anti-terrorism Enforcement), Chap. 13 and 15 (Organized Crime). Federal regulation of computer crime is basically contained in the Computer Fraud and Abuse Act, enacted in 1986 and amending 18 U.S.C. § 1030 (for a theory and practice perspective see

sure, before the Lisbon Treaty, all these issues had already been subject to some type of EU legislation. Yet there is a continuation of trends already underway. In this context, the future EU criminal law has a more expansive potential, consistent with the trend in US federal criminal law[235] and demonstrated by the fact that the catalog in Article 83(1) TFEU is not a *numerus clausus*, but open-ended.[236]

Consistent with pre-Lisbon EU legislation, all these crimes are subject (or will be imminently subject) to post-Lisbon criminal legislation.[237] Beginning with a traditional federalized crime, i.e. *currency counterfeiting*, a new Directive 2014/62/EU entered into force on 22 May 2014.[238] This Directive is meant to boost the protection of the euro against counterfeiting by criminal law measures.[239] Another crime traditionally listed in the area of federal criminal law, i.e. *money laundering*, has been subject to EU legislation for some time[240] and is currently subject to a Proposal for a Directive of the European Parliament and of the Council on the prevention of the use of the financial system for the purpose of money laundering and terrorist financing,[241] which was approved by the EU Parliament in March

the Manual produced by the Computer Crime and Intellectual Property Section, Criminal Division of the US Attorney's Office, Prosecuting Computer Crimes, 2011 (available at: www.justice.gov/criminal/cybercrime/docs/ccmanual.pdf)). Sexual exploitation of women and children is basically contained in Chapter 110 of Title 18 U.S.C. §§ 2251–2260A. Counterfeiting in Chapter 25 of Title 18 U.S.C. §§ 470–514.

235 See American Bar Association, Criminal Justice Section, Task Force on the Federalization of Criminal Law, The Federalization of Criminal Law, 1998 at 9-10.

236 See above Chapter 2, section 4.3.2.

237 For an overview up until 2013 see Samuli Miettinen, *Criminal Law and Policy in the European Union*, 2013 at 146–175 labelling these offenses as "Euro-crimes". For a thorough account of the sanctions (and practice) of the EU member states concerning part of the catalog contained in Article 83(1) TFEU see the 2014 report by the EU Commission: Study on criminal sanction legislation and practice in representative Member States Final Report (available at: http://ec.europa.eu/justice/criminal/document/files/sanctions_delivery_en.pdf) addressing Child Pornography, Drug Trafficking, Money Laundering, Frauds with no cash means of payment and illegal entry.

238 Directive 2014/62/EU of the European Parliament and of the Council of 15 May 2014 on the protection of the euro and other currencies against counterfeiting by criminal law, and replacing Council Framework Decision 2000/383/JHA (Official Journal of the European Union 21.5.2014, L 151/1). It is justification is noted: "As the single currency shared by the Member States of the euro area, the euro has become an important factor in the Union's economy and the everyday life of its citizens. However, since its introduction in 2002, as a currency continuously targeted by organised crime groups active in money counterfeiting, counterfeiting of the euro has caused financial damage of at least EUR 500 million. It is in the interests of the Union as a whole to oppose and pursue any activity that is likely to jeopardise the authenticity of the euro by counterfeiting", acknowledging the "pre-eminent role of the euro for the economy and society of the Union,"

239 The Directive replaced Framework Decision 2000/383/JHA (Framework Decision dated May 29, 2000 on the increased protection against counterfeiting through criminal legal penalties, Official Journal of the EU L140 14–06–2000) and the decision of the Council on May 28, 2001 on fighting fraud and counterfeiting of means of payment other than cash (Official Journal of the EU L153, 8 June 2001).

240 See the so-called Third Directive 2005/60/EC of the European Parliament and of the Council on the prevention of the use of the financial system for the purpose of money laundering and terrorist financing.

241 COM (2013) 45 final.

2014. Probably the only area pending post-Lisbon EU criminal legislation in the area of financial crime is associated with private corruption. The current legal text is Framework Decision of 22 July 2003,[242] though it will probably not take too long before legislation is proposed in this area.[243]

Leaving financial crime aside for now, another traditional area where federal criminal law is present, i.e. drug trafficking, was subject to EU legislation prior to the Lisbon Treaty[244] and is currently on the verge of being reviewed.[245] Continuing with "trafficking" offenses, a 2011 Directive addressed human trafficking and replaced pre-Lisbon legislation.[246] The same holds true for child exploitation and pornography[247] and, although not related to trafficking offenses, computer crime was also subject to pre- and post-Lisbon legislation in 2005 and 2013.[248]

Finally, it is time turn our attention to *organized crime*,[249] not because it has been subject to specific post-Lisbon legislation *per se* – which surprisingly it has not – but because it was present in the justifications for the adoption of the aforementioned legislation. To be sure, the common agreement adopted on 21 December 1998, relating to the punishment for participation in a criminal organization,[250] provided an initial approach to the subject. Then, the document published by the Council on 27 March 2000 on the Prevention and Fight Against

---

242 Council Framework Decision 2003/568/JHA of 22 July 2003 on combating corruption in the private sector.

243 In 2011 the EU Commission established a mechanism for periodic assessment of EU States' efforts in the fight against corruption (Commission Decision of 6 June 2011 Establishing an EU Anti-corruption reporting mechanism for periodic assessment ("EU Anti-corruption Report"), COM (2011) 3673 final.

244 Council Framework Decision 2004/757/JHA of 25 October 2004 laying down minimum provisions on the constituent elements of criminal acts and penalties in the field of illicit drug trafficking.

245 Proposal for a Directive of the European Parliament and of the Council mending Council Framework Decision 2004/757/JHA of 25 October 2004 laying down minimum provisions on the constituent elements of criminal acts and penalties in the field of illicit drug trafficking, as regards the definition of drug, COM (2013)0618.

246 Directive 2011/36/EU of the European Parliament and of the Council of 5 April 2011 on preventing and combating trafficking in human beings and protecting its victims, and replacing Council Framework Decision 2002/629/JHA.

247 Directive 2011/93/EU of the European Parliament and of the Council of 13 December 2011 on combating sexual abuse and sexual exploitation of children, and child pornography, replacing the Council Framework Decision 2004/68/JHA.

248 Directive 2013/40/EU of the European Parliament and of the Council of 12 August 2013 on attacks against information systems and replacing Council Framework Decision 2005/222/JHA; OJ L 218/8, 14 August 2013. the Directive retained prior crimes from the Framework Decision – namely the criminalization of illegal access, illegal system interference and illegal data interference – but added criminalization of certain tools for committing offenses, as well as the notion of "illegal interception". It is also noteworthy the creation of a European Cybercrime Centre (European Commission. 2012. Communication from the Commission to the Council and the European Parliament: Tackling Crime in our Digital Age: Establishing a European Cybercrime Centre: European Cybercrime Centre (EC3): https://www.europol.europa.eu/ec3).

249 For a general comparative overview see Liz Campbell, *Organised Crime and the Law: A Comparative Analysis*, 2013.

250 Official Journal of the EU L 351, 29 December 1998.

Organized Crime – A European Union Strategy for Beginning the Millennium[251] advanced the previous goals. A Council Framework Decision in 2008 laid out the basis of the EU strategy.[252] An interesting note is that the fight against organized crime has not only influenced substantive criminal legislation, but also procedural criminal legislation.[253] Something similar maybe be asserted concerning *terrorism*. On top of the Framework Decision of 13 June 2002,[254] much of the EU legislation concerning the issues aforementioned is embedded in the fight against terrorism.[255]

The Lisbon Treaty considers that these offenses satisfy the serious cross-border criminality requirement. Yet many of the offenses listed in the catalog *may* have a cross-border dimension, or *may not*. Just to pick an easily understandable example, money laundering can be just a local matter with no transnational dimension. Moreover, given the now unlimited scope of the predicate offenses, i.e. precedent illegal activity, many money laundering charges may have absolutely no connection to organized crime. Practice shows that national courts of the EU Member States regularly deal with money laundering charges not related neither to organized crime nor to transnational crime.[256] But it is now too late to reverse course: because in many instances serious cross-border criminality is related to money laundering, the EU has produced criminal legislation with the result that

---

251 Official Journal of the EU C 124, 3 May 2000. See Council Decision of 28 May 2001 setting up a European crime prevention network (Official Journal of the EU L 153, 8 June 2001).

252 Council Framework Decision 2008/841/JHA of 24 October 2008 on the fight against organised crime, OJ L 300, 11 November 2008, p. 42–45. See generally Francesco Calderoni, *Harmonization and Approximation of Criminal Law, National Legislations and the EU Framework Decision on the Fight Against Organized Crime*, 2010 with further references.

253 Directive 2014/42/EU of the European Parliament and of the Council of 3 April 2014 on the freezing and confiscation of instrumentalities and proceeds of crime in the European Union. The recitals are self-explanatory:
"(1) The main motive for cross-border *organised crime*, including mafia-type criminal organisation, is financial gain. As a consequence, competent authorities should be given the means to trace, freeze, manage and confiscate the proceeds of crime. However, the effective prevention of and fight against *organised crime* should be achieved by neutralising the proceeds of crime and should be extended, in certain cases, to any property deriving from activities of a criminal nature.
(2) *Organised criminal groups* operate without borders and increasingly acquire assets in Member States other than those in which they are based and in third countries. There is an increasing need for effective international cooperation on asset recovery and mutual legal assistance.
(3) Among the most effective means of combating *organised crime* is providing for severe legal consequences for committing such crime, as well as effective detection and the freezing and confiscation of the instrumentalities and proceeds of crime."

254 Official Journal of the EU L 164, 22 June 2002.

255 For a comprenhensive list see the Statewatch report authored by Ben Hayes and Chris Jones, *Report on the transposition of EU counter-terrorism measures,* 2013 (available at: www.statewatch.org/news/2013/nov/secile-report-on-the-transposition-of-eu-counter-terrorism-measures.pdf).

256 Probably, a good example of what has been said, is that there is an increase addition of money laundering charges in regular national tax crime proceedings in which the organized crime/transnational crime is completely absent.

nowadays the penal codes of all Member States contain the provisions determined by the EU – regardless of whether the case at hand involves serious cross-border criminality.

This is yet another example of the dangers of horizontal federalism. In a vertical federalism system there is the possibility (and danger) of concurrent criminal legislation:[257] federal and state. But this leaves the door open to non-federalized state criminal law enforcement when a case has no federal element, i.e. serious cross-border criminality.[258] This however does not seem to be possible in the EU system of criminal justice. Member States are obliged to transpose EU legislation, which ultimately implies that even local cases with no transnational dimension will be enforced according to the EU mandates. It is hard to deny that states' sovereignty is compromised to a greater extent in the EU case.

4.3.2.2. The Open-Ended Nature of the Catalog (Article 83(1) TFEU *in fine*)

We have noted on several occasions that the EU approach to criminal law shows a tendency towards expansion that resembles the expansion experienced by US federal criminal law. A clear example of this tendency is the open-ended nature[259] of the catalog we just reviewed in the previous section. The third paragraph of Article 83(1) TFEU states that "[o]n the basis of developments in crime, the Council may adopt a decision identifying other areas of crime that meet the criteria specified in this paragraph. It shall act unanimously after obtaining the consent of the European Parliament." The criteria, as noted before, are comprised of a two-prong test: first, it must be particularly serious, i.e. egregious, conduct; second, it must have a cross-border dimension.

The seriousness requirement seems to be aimed at preventing EU legislation regarding certain petty offenses. Yet, as the US experience shows, how serious an offense may be, depends on many political factors that vary over time. The lack of further references to determine when the seriousness criteria is met clearly locates the egregious conduct debate on the side of the political, and not on the technical. In any event, it would be fair to conclude that it does not provide too much of a safeguard against federalization.

---

257 See above Introduction.

258 It is true that this determination is mostly decided by federal prosecutors, who exercise this power with great discretion. This, in turn, makes the system vulnerable to selective prosecution (see Robert Heller, *Selective Prosecution and the Federalization of Criminal Law: The Need for the Meaningful Judicial Review of Prosecutorial Discretion*, University of Pennsylvania Law Review 145 (1997) at 1309–1358; Lisa L. Miller and James Eisenstein, *The Federal/State Criminal Prosecution Nexus: A Case Study in Cooperation and Discretion*, Law & Social Inquiry 33 (2005) at 248; Michael G. Collins and Jonathan R. Nash, *Prosecuting Federal Crimes in State Courts*, Virginia Law Review 97 (2011) at 251–278, 315).

259 The open-ended nature has been acknowledged by some leading commentators as Samuli Miettinen, *Criminal Law and Policy in the European Union*, 2013 at 145 notes, "The Treaty provides some open-ended provisions which in the future can be used as legal basis".

If with regards to gravity no further criteria are provided, the opposite happens with the cross-border dimension. This dimension is further limited by reference to the nature or impact of such offenses, or by a specific need to fight such infractions according to common criteria. Again, a broad approach is clearly perceived and is unlikely to provide appropriate caution against proliferation of EU legislation. This grant of power raises at least two important observations.

First, legislation pursuant to this part of Article 83 may establish minimum rules concerning the definition of criminal offenses and penalties. This largely involves defining the core of the criminal offenses that make up the Special Part.[260] A priori, the Member States could decide on the details of their implementing statutes and could also have discretion over the criteria for adjudication that belongs to the General Part.[261] This indicates that, as is typical of European criminal harmonization, Article 83 is targeted at the Special Part of criminal law, not at the General Part.[262] This approach has garnered much valid criticism from European scholars. It is rightly pointed out that the harmonization of the Special Part without a corresponding harmonization of the General Part is doomed to failure, and may also lead to arbitrary uses of the law.[263] To ensure consistency and justice, common criteria for the General Part are needed. Of course, the problem is finding a legal basis provided by the Lisbon Treaty to introduce common General Part provisions.[264]

---

260 See Andre Klip, *European Criminal Law*, 2nd ed., 2011 at 211–223; Rosaria Sicurella, *Some Reflections on the Need for a General Theory of the Competence of the European Union in Criminal Law*, in Andre Klip, ed., *Substantive Criminal Law of the European Union*, 2011 at 244–247 noting the distinction between General and Special Part of EU criminal law (advocating for a General Part of EU criminal law); Samuli Miettinen, *Criminal Law and Policy in the European Union*, 2013 at 122–123, 145; See Ester Herlin-Karnell, *The Constitutional Dimension of European Criminal Law*, 2012 at 226–227; Ester Herlin-Karnell, *Waiting for Lisbon ... Constitutional Reflections on the Embryonic General Part of EU Criminal Law*, European Journal of Criminal Law and Criminal Justice 17 (2009) at 227.

261 Nevertheless, the tendency in latter times is to harmonize key issues of the General Part (Ester Herlin-Karnell, *The Constitutional Dimension of European Criminal Law*, 2012 at 226). This can be certainly seen in the Green Paper on Approximation § 4.1.1.2 were "sentencing guidelines" – similar to their US counterparts – are introduced in an attempt to obtain some degree of uniformity.

262 This is not surprising, as the European harmonization has first affected the Special Part. See Vogel, Goltdammer's Archiv (2003) at 322.

263 See Thomas Weigend, *Der Entwurf einer Europäischen Verfassung und das Strafrecht*, Zeitschrift für die gesamte Strafrechtswissenschaft 116 (2004) at 287.

264 For Ester Herlin-Karnell (Ester Herlin-Karnell, *The Constitutional Dimension of European Criminal Law*, 2012 at 226; Ester Herlin-Karnell, *Waiting for Lisbon ... Constitutional Reflections on the Embryonic General Part of EU Criminal Law*, European Journal of Criminal Law and Criminal Justice 17 (2009) at 227) "is it possible to refer to Chapter 1 of Title V as the general part of EU criminal law". For a deeper of the minimum requirements in the General Part see Thomas Weigend, *Mindestanforderungen an ein europaweit geltendes harmonisiertes Strafrecht*, in Frank Zieschang, Eric Hilgendorf and Klaus Laubenthal, eds., *Strafrecht und Kriminalität in Europa*, 2003 at 59 referring the principle of legality, the principle of culpability, principle of proportionality, the distinction between intent and negligence, principal and accessories, inchoate crimes, duress and self-defense.

Second, it is alarming how much current national criminal law already meets the criteria contained in this rule.[265] It has been pointed out that the scope of Article 83(1) is broader than it appears at first sight. Not only is EU competence defined here on the basis of areas of crime, rather than on the basis of specific criminal offenses, but it has been recently used by the EU Commission to introduce certain type of sanctions and not only the definition of criminal offenses.[266] As a result, it seems fair to conclude that there is a clear risk of overfederalization, as is the case in the US system.[267] This issue becomes even more obvious, for instance, in the context of white-collar crime. Indeed, the increased globalization of the economy and the corresponding increase in the geographic range of individuals operating internationally will often satisfy the cross-border dimension required for EU action. As noted, seriousness does not seem to offer restrictive criteria to limit the considerable expansion possible under this provision.[268]

To conclude, we make two final remarks before addressing how interstate criminality is dealt with by the US system of federal criminal law. It is interesting to note that, as is currently happening in the EU, the development of US federal criminal law has taken place through provisions related to the Special Part, while a General Part is missing. This has been one among many criticisms of the current US status quo and one of the main reasons behind the proposal to produce a proper federal criminal code.[269] Second, as the discussion on the US system

---

265 But see SAMULI MIETTINEN, *Criminal Law and Policy in the European Union*, 2013 at 145 noting that "general offences against persons, offences against property such as theft, fraud, or criminal damage, and minor offences against the public order, are unlikely to be harmonized at EU level in the near future". Yet it is reasonable to conclude that as soon as there is an organized crime element, EU legislation will come into play. And it is easy to see that some of these offenses may entail such organized crime element. For a similar interpretation in the expansive reach of the organized crime provisions see VALSAMIS MITSILEGAS, *EU Criminal Law Competence after Lisbon: From Securitised to Functional Criminalisation*, in DIEGO ACOSTA ARCARAZO and CIAN C. MURPHY, eds., *EU Security and Justice Law*, 2014 at 116: "A clear example of the potential to overstretch EU criminal law competence under Article 83(1) TFEU involves the use of the concept of organised crime".

266 See VALSAMIS MITSILEGAS, *EU Criminal Law Competence after Lisbon: From Securitised to Functional Criminalisation*, in DIEGO ACOSTA ARCARAZO and CIAN C. MURPHY, eds., *EU Security and Justice Law*, 2014 at 116–117.

267 Certain commentators have noted the similarity between the current development of EU criminal law and the US system of federal criminal law. Moreover, *Schünemann* criticizes the approach of creating Eurocrimes on the basis of cross-border criminality precisely because of the result that such approach rendered in the US. See BERND SCHÜNEMANN, *Das Strafrecht in Zeichen der Globalisierung*, GOLTDAMMER'S ARCHIV (2003) at 194, 199; BERND SCHÜNEMANN, *The Foundation of Transnational Criminal Proceedings*, in BERND SCHÜNEMANN, ed., *A Programme for European Criminal Justice*, 2006 at 81 and KLAUS TIEDEMANN, *Wirtschaftsstrafrecht*, 2004 at 46.

268 See in a similar path THOMAS WEIGEND, *Der Entwurf einer Europäischen Verfassung und das Strafrecht*, ZEITSCHRIFT FÜR DIE GESAMTE STRAFRECHTSWISSENSCHAFT 116 (2004) at 283.

269 See above Chapter 1, section 5.2. For a summarized review of the deficits of the US federal criminal "code" see the sharp analysis of JULIE ROSE O'SULLIVAN, *The Federal Criminal "Code" is a Disgrace: Obstruction Statutes as Case Study*, J. CRIM. L. & CRIMINOLOGY 96 (2006) at 643–726; JULIE ROSE O'SULLIVAN, *The Federal Criminal "Code": Return of Overfederalization*, HARV. J.L. & PUB. POL'Y 37 (2014) at 57–67.

will show that, out of all the potential sources of federal criminal law, interstate criminality has been the most actively used.

4.3.3. *US's Criminality Affecting Interstate Commerce*

4.3.3.1. Catalog of (Horizontal) Federal Crimes Specified in Title 18 of the U.S.C. (US)

Something that regularly gives pause to those strong opponents of acknowledging any type of federal dimension in EU criminal is the fact that all the criminal matters listed in Article 83(1) TFEU are regulated as federal crimes in the United States Code. Certainly, it could be a mere coincidence. But it also could be – and it probably is – a result of the federalizing tendencies in both Unions. To be sure, the list of US federal crimes is larger than the listing contained in Article 83(1) TFEU. Also, all these US federal crimes are not based on serious interstate criminality, although a substantial part has some connection to the Commerce Clause that we will review in this section. For now, it pays to briefly note the US regulation of what is sometimes called the Euro-crimes list.[270]

- Counterfeiting: Chapter 25 of Title 18 U.S.C. §§ 470–514.
- Sexual exploitation of women and children: Chapter 110 of Title 18 U.S.C. §§ 2251–2260A.
- Computer crime: Computer Fraud and Abuse Act, enacted in 1986 and amending 18 U.S.C. § 1030.
- Terrorism: Chapter 113B of Title 18 U.S.C. §§.
- Public corruption; Chapter 11 of Title 18 U.S.C.
- Drug trafficking; Chapter 13 of Title 21 USC: §§ 841–865.
- Money laundering: Chapter 95 of Title 18 U.S.C. §§ 1956.
- Organized crime: Chapter 96 of Title 18 U.S.C. §§ 1961–1963.

[270] See the Communication from the Commission to the European Parliament, the Council, the European Economic and Social Committee and the Committee of the Regions. Towards an EU Criminal Policy: Ensuring the effective implementation of EU policies through criminal law, COM (2011) 573 final, at 5: "First of all, measures can be adopted under Article 83(1) TFEU concerning a list of explicitly listed ten offences (the so-called 'Euro crimes') which refers to terrorism, trafficking in human beings, sexual exploitation of women and children, illicit drug trafficking, illicit arms trafficking, money laundering, corruption, counterfeiting of means of payment, computer crime and organised crime". Samuli Miettinen, *Criminal Law and Policy in the European Union*, 2013 at 145–176.

4.3.3.2. The Open-Ended Nature of the Catalog: the Commerce Clause and Federal Criminal Law

The relationship between interstate commerce and federal criminal law is probably one of the most debated topics in the US system of criminal justice.[271] Not only does every single in-depth academic analysis of US federal criminal law probably contain a section devoted to such connection, but the US Supreme Court has also focused around the Commerce Clause much of its efforts to limit federal criminal law.[272] Moreover, a substantial part of the broader discussion around the scope of federalism has revolved around certain landmark decisions of the US Supreme Court concerning the use of interstate commerce as a legitimate power in the area of federal criminal law. Needless to say, the expansion of US federal criminal law has not taken place solely on the basis of the Commerce Clause. But it is fair to say that the relationship of this clause with federalism in general, and with federal criminal law in particular, has been especially intense.

As a recap of what has been noted previously, Congress's authority to enact criminal statutes not aimed at protecting direct federal interests has always been based in one of the enumerated powers. The three enumerated powers most frequently relied upon are the commerce power, the postal power and the taxing power. In modern times, the commerce power has been the dominant jurisdictional basis used to enact federal crimes.[273] Prior to 1970, it was actually the taxing power which was used for most federal drug enforcement laws, until a new federal drug statute based in the commerce power was substituted. In addition, the "true love" of federal prosecutors[274] – the mail and wire fraud statute in 18 U.S.C. § 1341 – is a heavily used statute in the area of white-collar crime which is based on the postal power.

In the current law, the most often used of the enumerated powers, i.e. the Commerce Clause, has provided three methods for granting federal jurisdiction over substantive areas of criminal law. First, statutes may cover activities that have an impact on interstate commerce; the perfect example would be the Hobbs Act criminalizing acts of robbery or extortion which affects interstate commerce.[275] Second, statutes may cover crimes where something is "in" or "engaged in"

---

271 For a brief introduction see BRANDON L. BIGELOW, *The Commerce Clause and Criminal Law*, BOSTON COLLEGE LAW REVIEW 41 (2000) at 913, written at a time were the US Supreme Court had begun to "set an outer limit to Congress commerce clause power to enact criminal law … and that the Court would police that limit".

272 For an introductory analysis see NORMAN ABRAMS, SARA SUN BEALE and SUSAN R. KLEIN, *Federal criminal law and its enforcement*, 5th ed., 2010 at Chap. 3.

273 For a recent broad overview see Charles Doyle, "Congressional Authority to Enact Criminal Law: An Examination of Selected Recent Cases", CRS REPORT FOR CONGRESS, 2013, addressing recent cases in the most commonly used sources of US federal criminal law: interstate commerce and the Necessary and Proper Clause.

274 JED S. RAKOFF, *The Federal Mail Fraud Statute (Part I)*, 18 DUQ. L. REV. 771 (1980).

275 NORMAN ABRAMS, SARA SUN BEALE and SUSAN R. KLEIN, *Federal criminal law and its enforcement*, 5th ed., 2010 at 22–23, 42–53 with further references to relevant case law.

commerce, such as RICO or the Arson Statutes.[276] Third, statutes may cover activities which include travel or use of the facilities of commerce, such as certain sexual and firearm offenses.[277] This approach to interstate commerce as a basis for federal criminal legislation is not far from the criteria set out in Article 83(1) TFEU: the nature or impact of such offenses or from a special need to combat them on a common basis.

Interestingly, the requirement of a jurisdiction hook lead the US legislature to define these statutes in a not-very-criminal way: focused on the cross-border dimension. The central element of the offense becomes the transportation in interstate commerce and not the egregious conduct itself. At some level, a question arises about why the mere involvement of interstate commerce transforms a non-federal interest into an appropriate topic for federal legislation.[278] Still, the jurisprudence of American courts has done little to curtail congressional use of the Commerce Clause on any grounds,[279] and it is no surprise that this has become the most used justification for the exercise of congressional power. This particular power over interstate markets is very similar to the origin of the European Union and the fundamental objective of creating a single market between Member States.

Additionally, while it is not spelled out in the Constitution, the seriousness of criminal activity is a key criterion of US criminal policy. Those actions that are more likely to shock the consciousness of the public are also most likely to be covered by federal laws, as legislators strive to distinguish themselves as "tough on crime".[280] Naturally, the crossing of interstate borders is still an important factor

---

276 Norman Abrams, Sara Sun Beale and Susan R. Klein, *Federal criminal law and its enforcement*, 5th ed., 2010 at 54–60 with further references to relevant case law.

277 Ibid. at 61–75 with further references to relevant case law.

278 As Judge Henry Friendly notably asked: "Why should the federal government care if a Manhattan businessman takes his mistress to sleep with him in Greenwich, Connecticut, although it would not if the lovenest is in Port Chester NY?" (Henry Friendly, *Federal Jurisdiction. An Overview*, 1973 at 58).

279 U.S. Const. Art. I, § 8, cl. 3. Yet as a highly illustrative example of the expanding nature of federal criminal law, it is worth noting the case *U.S. vs. Pascucci*, 943 F.2d 1032 (9th Cir. 1991). Here federal legislation was applied because of the fact that the victim was a representative of the Ford Company and the stress that the extortion caused on him affected his capacity to perform his commercial duties – thus affecting interstate commerce. On the expanding nature of the Commerce Clause applied to the criminal area see a Christy H. Dral and Jerry J. Phillips, *Commerce by another Name: The Impact of US v. Lopez and US. V. Morrison*, Tenn. L. Rev. 68 (2001) at 605; Kelly D. Miller, *Recent Development, The Hobbs Act, The Interstate Commerce Clause, and United States v. McFarland: The Irrational Aggregation of Independent Local Robberies to Sustain Federal Convictions*, Tul. L. Rev. 76 (2002) at 1761; Louis J. Virelli III and David Leibowitz, *Federalism Whether They Want It Or Not: The New Commerce Clause Doctrine and the Future of Federal Civil Rights Legislation After United States v. Morrison*, Pa. J. Const. L. 3 (2001) at 926.

280 Again, a perfect example of the current understanding of the use (and abuse) of federal legislation in the criminal context is how Sara Sun Beale describes the situation Sara Sun Beale, *What's Law Got to Do with It?: The Political, Social, Psychological and Other Non-Legal Factors Influencing the Development of (Federal) Criminal Law*, Buff. Crim. L. Rev. 1 (1997) at 29: "the epithet 'soft on crime' is the contemporary equivalent of 'soft on Communism'"

for asserting federal jurisdiction under appropriate federal laws.[281] Therefore, it is fair to conclude that both the interstate dimension and the seriousness elements have played a major role in the development – most academics would say overdevelopment – of US federal criminal law on the basis of the Commerce Clause.

Given the parallels between the US law in this regard and the EU situation – interstate/cross-border dimension and the seriousness elements – it is worth noting how the US Supreme Court reacted to the expansive nature of federal criminal law in this area. In order to recreate the stage leading to the landmark decisions of the US Supreme Court we must bear in mind that, particularly since the 1970s, there had been an unprecedented expansion of US federal criminal law.[282] This expansion consequently led to debate in the United States, both from a policy perspective where concerns of overcriminalization have been repeatedly noted, and in the Supreme Court's jurisprudence on federal power.

The first landmark case that curtailed criminal law powers on the basis of the Commerce Clause – and the underlying serious cross-border rationale – was *United States v. Lopez*.[283] Prior to *Lopez*, there had been many challenges to the enactment of federal criminal laws on the basis of the Commerce Clause, but to no avail. In what was at the time termed "New Federalism",[284] or a "Revolution",[285] the US Supreme Court established certain limits on the possibility of federalizing crime. The other side of the coin was, although not specifically noted by the

(providing the rationale behind the exponential increase behind the rapid enactment of multitude of federal crimes).

281 This to the extent that in certain cases *US v. Wills*, 234 F.3d 174 (4th Cir. 2000) nd 531 U.S. 911 (2001), the Circuits and the Supreme Court have ceased to follow existing case law that considered to be necessary – as a jurisdictional hook – that the perpetrator trespassed with the victim interstate boundaries (*US v. McInnis*, 601 F. 2d 1319 (5th Cir. 1979)), and established that is was enough for the federal system to act that the perpetrator induces the victim to cross such boundaries even if he does not.

282 As a matter of fact, the ABA considers that over 40% of the federal statutes passed since the Civil War, have been enacted since the 1970s. (See American Bar Association, Criminal Justice Section, Task Force on the federalization of Criminal Law, *The Federalization of Criminal Law*, 1998 at 7). In Norman Abrams, Sara Sun Beale and Susan R. Klein, *Federal criminal law and its enforcement*, 5th ed., 2010 at 64, this expounding feature of federal criminal law has played a decisive role in the modern debate on federal criminal law. On the various factors accounting for this expansion see Sara Sun Beale, *What's Law Got to Do with It?: The Political, Social, Psychological and Other Non-Legal Factors Influencing the Development of (Federal) Criminal Law*, Buff. Crim. L. Rev. 1 (1997) at 23.

283 *United States v. Lopez*, 514 U.S. 549 (1995). *Lopez* was a major revolution at the time, as it was the first decision in 60 years to strike down a federal statute on the ground that it violated the Commerce Clause. There was a strong reaction in the courts and in academic literature. Interestingly enough there were *Lopez* challenges in the lower courts virtually to every criminal statute founded on the comer cause (Norman Abrams, Sara Sun Beale and Susan R. Klein, *Federal criminal law and its enforcement*, 5th ed., 2010 at 39).

284 See also Richard W. Garnett, *The New Federalism, The Spending Power, and Federal Criminal Law*, Cornell L. Rev. 89 (2003) at 1.

285 Erwin Chemerinsky, *The Federalism Revolution*, N.M. L. Rev. 31 (2001) at 7, 30.

Court, the Tenth Amendment.[286] The Court identified three broad categories that Congress may regulate under its commerce power: (1) the use of channels of interstate commerce; (2) the instrumentalities of interstate commerce, as well as persons or things in interstate commerce; and (3) activities which have a substantial connection to interstate commerce.[287] Finding that possession of a gun in a school zone did not fall within either of the first two categories, the Court considered whether Congress could legitimately regulate gun possession as an activity which had a substantial relation to interstate commerce. Finally, the Court concluded that the Gun-Free School Zones Act was a criminal statute which had nothing to do with commerce, or any sort of economic enterprise, much less affecting interstate commerce.[288]

This first curtailment of congressional authority to produce criminal legislation on the grounds of the Commerce Clause triggered a series of challenges to federal criminal law legislation based on the Commerce Clause.[289] Yet for five years thereafter, lower courts routinely rebuffed *Lopez*-like challenges to a host of federal laws having little or no connection to interstate commerce. Although petitions for certiorari were filed in many of these cases, the Supreme Court routinely denied certiorari in them, leading many commentators to believe that *Lopez* had quickly become merely an anomaly.[290]

Many legal scholars were surprised, therefore, when five years after *Lopez* the Court chose *Morrison*,[291] i.e. a challenge to the Violence Against Women Act, to reiterate its commitment to *Lopez* and its principled adherence to the doctrine that the United States is a limited government of specifically enumerated powers.[292] Although not a criminal case *per se*,[293] the findings were closely related to criminal law.[294] In an adamant statement, the US Supreme Court declared that "under

286 Brandon L. Bigelow, *The Commerce Clause and Criminal Law*, Boston College Law Review 41 (2000) at 922–933. See also Keith R. Fischer, *Toward a basal Tenth Amendment: a riposte to national bank preemption of state consumer protection laws*, Harvard Journal of Law & Public Policy 29 (2006) at 988.

287 514 U.S. 549, at 558–59.

288 Ibid. at 561. It is fair to say that since the *Lopez* decision there has been an especially intense focus on the constitutional dimension of federal law enactment. See among many George D. Brown, *Constitutionalizing the Federal Criminal Law Debate: Morrison, Jones and the ABA*, 2001 U. Ill. L. Rev. (2011) at 983 and Roderick M. Hills, *The Political Economy of Cooperative Federalism: Why State Autonomy Makes Sense and 'Dual Sovereignty' Doesn't*, Mich. L. Rev. 96 (1998) at 813.

289 William Funk, *The Lopez Report*, Admin. & Reg. L. News 23 (1998) at 1 (noting over 400 *Lopez* challenges).

290 See e.g. Glenn H. Reynolds and Brannon P. Denning, *Lower Court Readings of Lopez, or What if the Supreme Court Held a Constitutional Revolution and Nobody Came?*, Wisc. L. Rev. (2000) at 369 (citing cases).

291 *United States v. Morrison*, 529 U.S. 598, 609 (2000).

292 Ibid. at 607–618.

293 The case dealt with the violation of 42 U.S.C. § 13981 which provides a federal civil remedy for the victims of gender-motivated violence.

294 This is clear, among other evidence, by the fact that the *Lopez* decision is referred to constantly in the *Morrison* decision.

our written Constitution, however, the limitation of congressional authority is not solely a matter of legislative grace". The Court rejected "the argument that Congress may regulate noneconomic, violent criminal conduct based solely on that conduct's aggregate effect on interstate commerce. The Constitution requires a distinction between what is truly national and what is truly local".[295]

Ten years after *Lopez*, the US Supreme Court delivered an opinion that, for many, put an end to this federalism revolution.[296] In *Raich*[297] the Court upheld the portion of the Controlled Substances Act (CSA) that prohibited the possession or cultivation of marijuana. The plaintiffs sought to prevent enforcement of the CSA's restrictions against their use of marijuana for medicinal purposes, which Californian law permitted. While the CSA contained no jurisdictional restriction or congressional findings dealing with marijuana use for medicinal purposes, the Court upheld its ban because allowing medicinal marijuana use could undercut the CSA's effectiveness.[298] The Court applied the aggregation principle of *Wickard v. Filburn*,[299] i.e. a landmark case from the New Deal era, finding that Congress could have rationally believed that the prohibition against medical marijuana *was an essential part of a larger regulation of economic activity.*[300]

Although the later impact of *Raich*[301] – which, as we just noted, defers substantially to congressional determination – can be seen as a retreat from the position in *Lopez*,[302] the general *Lopez* framework analysis stands. Under *Lopez*, the Court must perform a two-step inquiry when evaluating a law under the

---

295 529 U.S. 848 (2000) at 864. This was also affirmed in *Jones v. United States*, 529 U.S. 848, 854 (2000) (holding that the language "any activity affecting ... commerce" demonstrates Congress's intent to invoke its full authority under the Commerce Clause).

296 See Norman Abrams, Sara Sun Beale and Susan R. Klein, *Federal criminal law and its enforcement*, 5th ed., 2010 at 39, "The 'revolution' that wasn't"; "it was a brief revolution, and the end result in most cases (if not the reasoning) has reverted to the pre-*Lopez* affirmance of congressional authority to enact any federal criminal law prohibition it views as appropriate" (at 27).

297 *Gonzales v. Raich*, 545 U.S. 1, 5 (2005).

298 Ibid. at 26–27.

299 317 U.S. 111, 127–29 (1942).

300 *Raich*, 545 U.S. at 18–19.

301 See among many Randy E. Barnett, *Federalism After Gonzales v. Raich: Limiting Raich*, Lewis & Clark Law Review 9 (2005) at 743; Ernest A. Young, *Just Blowing Smoke? Politics, Doctrine and the Federalist Revival after Gonzales v. Raich*, Supreme Court Review 1 (2005); Ilya Soming, *Gonzales v. Raich: Federalism as a Casualty of the War on Drugs*, Cornell Journal of Law & Public Policy 15 (2006) at 507.

302 See e.g. Jonathan H. Adler, *Is* Morrison *Dead? Assessing a Supreme Drug (Law) Overdose*, Lewis & Clark L. Rev. 9 (2005) at 751 (regarding *Raich* as a repudiation of the doctrines espoused in *Lopez* and *Morrison*); Mollie Lee, Note, *Environmental Economics: A Market Failure Approach to the Commerce Clause*, Yale L.J. 116 (2006) at 456, 468 ("One way to understand *Raich* is as a retreat from the Court's new Commerce Clause jurisprudence, and thus reading *Lopez* and *Morrison* as mere aberrations."). But *cf.* Robert J. Pushaw, Jr., *The Medical Marijuana Case: A Commerce Clause Counter- Revolution?*, Lewis & Clark L. Rev. 9 (2005) at 879, 884 ("it is impossible to determine whether the majority or the dissent correctly applied the *Lopez* and *Morrison* standards, because they are so malleable as to justify either result").

substantial-effects test. First, the Court must determine whether the activity regulated is economic activity. If the activity regulated is economic, the Court will be highly deferential to Congress's determination that it substantially affects interstate commerce and will most likely uphold the regulation. If the Court determines that the activity regulated is not economic, the Court will be less deferential, considering three factors to determine whether the regulation is within congressional power: (1) whether the statute contains a jurisdictional element limiting its reach to activities affecting interstate commerce;[303] (2) whether Congress has offered any findings showing the regulated activity's effect on interstate commerce;[304] and (3) whether the statute is a necessary part of a larger regulation of economic activity.[305] In any event, these cases serve to illustrate the intense discussion over federalism currently ongoing in the United States, particularly in reference to criminal law and the limits of Congress to legislate on this matter.[306]

After *Raich*, a recent and well-known decision of the US Supreme Court, *National Federation of Independent Business v. Sebelius*,[307] concerning the Affordable Care Act, i.e. so-called Obamacare, confirms that the Supreme Court's federalism jurisprudence has shifted from its once-typical form of inquiry into the scope of Congress's commerce power, refracted through the Tenth Amendment, to become an inquiry into the transsubstantive reasons for allowing Congress to regulate at all.[308] Probably the most interesting feature for our discussion on federal criminal law is that *NFIB* brought the narrow post-*Lopez/Morrison* commerce power back into the doctrinal fray and made it an integral part of the necessary and proper power analysis.[309] In *NFIB*, Chief Justice Roberts recombined the two strands and declared that the individual mandate contained in the ACA is not a valid exercise of Congress's power under the Commerce Clause and the

303 *United States v. Lopez*, 514 U.S. 549, 561 (1995).

304 See *Morrison*, 529 U.S. at 614–15.

305 See *Gonzales v. Raich*, 545 U.S. 1, 23–25 (2005).

306 The literature on the topic is breathtaking. Among many see John S. Baker, Jr., *United States v. Morrison and Other Arguments Against Federal "Hate Crime" Legislation*, Boston University Law Review 80 (2000) at 1191, 1220–21; Craig Bradley, *Federalism and Federal Criminal Law*, Hastings Law Journal 55 (2004) at 573; George D. Brown, *Constitutionalizing the Federal Criminal Law Debate: Morrison, Jones, and the ABA*, U. Ill. L. Rev. (2001) at 983; George D. Brown, *New Federalism's Unanswered Question: Who Should Prosecute State and Local Officials for Political Corruption*, Wash. & Lee L. Rev. 60 (2003) at 419, 421; Richard W. Garnett, *The New Federalism, The Spending Power, and Federal Criminal Law*, Cornell L. Rev. 89 (2003) at 1; Daniel C. Richman, *Federal Criminal Law, Congressional Delegation, and Enforcement Discretion*, UCLA L. Rev. 46 (1999) at 757.

307 132 S. Ct. 2566 (2012) (upholding the individual mandate provision of the Patient Protection and Affordable Care Act but invalidating the Medicaid expansion provision).

308 Alison L. LaCroix, *The Shadow Powers of Article*, Yale L.J. 123 (2014) at 1626.

309 Alison L. LaCroix, *The Shadow Powers of Article*, Yale L.J. 123 (2014), at 1626; David A. Strauss, *Commerce Clause Revisionism and the Affordable Care Act*, Sup. Ct. Rev. (2013) at 1, 4.

Necessary and Proper Clause.[310] The court then resorted to the Taxing Clause in order to uphold the individual mandate.[311]

As a broad conclusion of this general discussion it is fair to note that while the US Supreme Court continues to repeat that "[t]he States possess primary authority for defining and enforcing the criminal law",[312] it is equally true that "it is hard to think of a crime under state law that cannot be prosecuted federally".[313] The expansive nature of the Commerce Clause led the US Supreme Court to establish certain boundaries (1995). These limitations did not prove to last long, and ten years after (2005) the US Supreme Court again adopted a deferral attitude towards the power of the Unions' Congress to regulate interstate commerce. Recently, the analysis of the limits of the Commerce Clause has been grouped with a review of the Necessary and Proper Clause extensions (2012). Given the historical and current importance of this Clause, it is time now to pay closer attention to its development and equivalence with Article 83(2) TFEU.

4.4. ENFORCEMENT OF UNIONS' POLICIES

4.4.1. Introduction

In the previous section we saw how concerns over interstate commerce/internal market have played a major role in the development of federal criminal law in both Unions. Yet throughout this volume we have also referred to the natural resort of the US and EU in certain instances to the need for Union legislation in order to enforce Union policies. Though present since the conception of US federal law, this source of federal legislation has gained significant relevance in certain periods of time. In a 200-year history of federal criminal law, references to the Necessary and Proper Clause are not as abundant as those to the Commerce Clause, but they are extremely significant.

In the case of EU criminal law history, the principle behind the Necessary and Proper Clause gained momentum in a landmark 2005 decision of the ECJ, and has ever since been considered a fundamental source of criminal law powers codified in Article 83(2) TFEU. Recently it passed the test as a basis for the Directive on criminal sanctions for market abuse[314] and there is some debate about whether it will serve as the legal basis for the proposal of a Directive on the fight against EU

---

310 132 S. Ct. 2582–2598 (2012).

311 132 S. Ct. 2601–2610 (2012) "the individual mandate may be upheld as within Congress's power under the Taxing Clause".

312 *United States v. Lopez*, 514 U.S. 549, 561 (1995).

313 Norman Abrams, Sara Sun Beale and Susan R. Klein, *Federal criminal law and its enforcement*, 5th ed., 2010 at 22–23, 64.

314 Directive 2014/57/EU of the European Parliament and of the Council of 16 April 2014 on criminal sanctions for market abuse (market abuse directive) (OJ L 173, 12 June 2014, p. 179–189).

fraud through criminal law.[315] Regardless of the final outcome of this debate, it is fair to say that Article 83(2) TFEU will play a major role in the future development of (horizontal) federal criminal law.

The comparison with the history of the Necessary and Proper Clause shows, again, that this criterion for crime federalization is expansive in nature. When even a broad interpretation of the enumerated powers does not suffice to confer criminal law powers to the Union, resorting to the Necessary and Proper Clause greatly helps the Unions' cause and the strongest objections are easily circumvented by the need to enforce the Unions' policies. We have seen a clear example in the development of the Directive on the fight against EU fraud through criminal law: if a broad interpretation of Article 325 TFEU is not sufficient, Article 83(2) TFEU will surely do the job.[316]

4.4.2. *Effective Implementation of an EU Policy (Article 83(2) TFEU)*

It seems impossible to fully understand the development of this TFEU provision without referring to the landmark case *Commission v. Council* (2005).[317] Further, the legal and political significance of this judgment can only be fairly grasped if we bear in mind the shifting of criminal powers from the first pillar to the third pillar that we noted previously. As a brief recap: though the Commission had been leading the way in terms of EU criminal law in the late 20th century (First Pillar), the Council initiated a "crusade" through framework decisions based on the principle of mutual recognition (Third Pillar). These trains collided when both institutions sought to regulate concomitantly the same criminal law matter. The fact that the subject matter was related to an area traditionally considered to fall under the First Pillar area, i.e. environmental law, ultimately gave the Commission the upper hand.

In a nutshell, the facts are as follows: the Commission had asked the Court to annul Council Framework Decision 2003/80/JHA of 27 January 2003 on the protection of the environment through criminal law[318] which required the Member States to provide for criminal sanctions in the case of the offenses against environmental law set out in the Framework Decision, on the grounds that the power to impose such an obligation on the Member States is a matter for a Community instrument and the Commission had in fact proposed the adoption of such an instrument.[319]

---

315 Proposal for a Directive of the European Parliament and of the Council on the fight against fraud to the Union's financial interests by means of criminal law COM(2012) 363 final. See above Chapter 2, section 3.2.

316 See above Chapter 2, section 3.2.

317 Case C-176/03 *Commission v. Council*, Judgment of 13 September 2005.

318 OJ L 29, 5 February 2003, p. 55.

319 Proposal for a Directive of the European Parliament and of the Council on the protection of the environment through criminal law (COM (2001) 139 of 13 March 2001, OJ C 180 E, 26 June 2001, and amended proposal (COM (2002) 544)).

The Court found that although "as a general rule, neither criminal law nor the rules of criminal procedure fall within the Community's competence"[320] "the last-mentioned finding does not prevent the Community legislature, when the application of effective, proportionate and dissuasive criminal penalties by the competent national authorities is an essential measure for combating serious environmental offenses, from taking measures which relate to the criminal law of the Member States which it considers necessary in order to ensure that the rules which it lays down on environmental protection are fully effective".[321] There is certainly a host of comments on this fundamental ruling.[322] Yet from a federal criminal law perspective it is interesting to note certain tendencies embedded in the decisive ECJ ruling.

First and foremost, the ECJ words in similar terms as the US Supreme Court the natural belonging of criminal law to the sphere of the States. A brief comparison between "as a general rule, neither criminal law nor the rules of criminal procedure fall within the Community's competence"[323] (ECJ) and "the States possess primary authority for defining and enforcing the criminal law"[324] (USSC) shows a common logic. Criminal law is closely related to the states' sovereignty and, therefore, the interference of the Unions in states' matters should be interpreted (at least in theory) restrictively.[325]

The Court refers in its analysis to the traditional criterion of the *aim and content* of the act in order to establish whether the legal basis is correct. In this case, the Community policy concerned is environmental protection. However the judgment lays down principles going far beyond the case in question. The same arguments can be applied in their entirety to the other common policies and to the four freedoms (freedom of movement of persons, goods, services and capital).[326] A similar approach is present in the groundbreaking decisions of the

---

320 § 47.

321 § 48.

322 See among many Ester Herlin-Karnell, *Commission v. Council: Some Reflections on Criminal Law in the First Pillar*, European Public Law 13 (2007); Katherine M. Apps, *Case C-176/2003, Commission v. Council: Pillars Askew: Criminal Law EC-Style*, Colum. J. Eur. L. 12 (2006) at 625; Valsamis Mitsilegas, *EU Criminal Law*, 2009 at 70, 72, 75; also Andre Klip, *European Criminal law. An Integrative Approach*, 2nd ed., 2012 at 17, 58, 79, 130, 173–177; Ester Herlin-Karnell, *The Constitutional Dimension of European Criminal Law*, 2012 at 29–31; Samuli Miettinen, *Criminal Law and Policy in the European Union*, 2013 at 37–41, 56–57.

323 § 47.

324 *United States v. Lopez*, 514 U.S. 549, 561 (1995).

325 The following passage is remarkable: "Not only is there no express conferral of power in that regard, but, given the considerable significance of criminal law for the sovereignty of the Member States, there are no grounds for accepting that this power can have been implicitly transferred to the Community at the time when specific substantive competences, such as those exercised under Article 175 EC, were conferred on it" (Case C-176/03 *Commission v. Council*, Judgment of 13 September 2005, at § 27). The situation changed with the Lisbon Treaty and the provisions contained in Article 83(1) and (2) TFEU.

326 Communication from the Commission to the European Parliament and the Council on the implications of the Court's judgment of 13 September 2005 (Case C-176/03 *Commission v Council*), COM (2005) 583 final.

USSC based on the statement: "[l]et the end be legitimate, let it be within the scope of the constitution, and all means which are appropriate, which are plainly adapted to that end".[327] The natural consequence is that the possibilities of the Unions producing criminal legislation grow exponentially.

Finally, the Commission will have to determine, when submitting proposals, whether this test of *necessity* is met on a case-by-case basis. Depending on that necessity, the Commission will determine the degree of Community involvement in the criminal field, whilst giving priority as much as possible to horizontal measures not specific to the relevant sector.[328] Not only by its name, but by its rationale, the *Necessary* and Proper Clause always takes into account, first, whether there is a real need for Union legislation in a certain area; and second, whether federal legislation is the proper means for achieving the goal.[329]

The findings of the 2005 *Commission v. Council* decision were later confirmed in another *Commission v. Council* judgment in 2007. Though the clash of titans was not as spectacular in the so-called *Ship Pollution* case,[330] it is worth noting the consolidation of the aforementioned doctrine. As has been already noted, the Court simply followed the previous case and reiterated the requirement for full-effectiveness of EU law.[331] Against this backdrop it was easy to foresee that the 2008 Lisbon Treaty would contain a provision condensing the findings of the ECJ in the *Commission v. Council* decisions.[332]

The second paragraph of Article 83 TFEU states that: "If the approximation of criminal laws and regulations of the Member States proves essential to ensure the effective implementation of a Union policy in an area which has been subject to harmonisation measures, directives may establish minimum rules with regard to

327 *M'Culloch v. Maryland*, 17 U.S. (4 Wheat) 316, 421 (1819).

328 Communication from the Commission to the European Parliament and the Council on the implications of the Court's judgment of 13 September 2005 (Case C-176/03 *Commission v Council*) COM (2005) 583 final at 3.

329 Expressed in terms of one of the most recent and significant decisions concerning the Necessary and Proper Clause: "Even if the individual mandate is 'necessary' to the Affordable Care Act's other reforms, such an expansion of federal power is not a 'proper' means for making those reforms effective" (*National Federation of Independent Business v. Sebelius*, 567 U. S. ___ (2012) at 27–30).

330 Ester Herlin-Karnell, *The Ship-Source Pollution Case C-440/05, Commission v. Council, Judgment of 23 October 2007 (Grand Chamber)*, European Public Law 14 (2008) at 533.

331 This was done notwithstanding the reluctance expressed in the opinion of AG Mazak in that case: "It ought not be concealed, however, that the competence of the Community in relation to criminal law as established by the Court in Case C-176/03 reveals on closer inspection certain conceptual flaws, which make it difficult, as the present case shows, to ascertain whether in a concrete case the conditions for the exercise of that competence are fulfilled".

332 See Ester Herlin-Karnell, *The Constitutional Dimension of European Criminal Law*, 2012 at 65: "it represents a codification of the Case C-176/03 approach, that criminal law can be harmonised in order to ensure the full effectiveness of EU law": Marta Miglietti, *The New EU Criminal Law in Action: The Proposal for a Directive on Criminal Sanctions for Insider Dealing and Market Manipulation*, IES Working Paper 5 (2013) (available at: www.ies.be/files/Working%20Paper%20Miglietti.pdf) at 14 notes "Article 83(2), conversely, is new in comparison to the previous treaty framework and represents the codification of the ECJ Case Law."

the definition of criminal offences and sanctions in the area concerned." As noted previously, this is a broad grant of power that, fully utilized, would potentially enable EU criminal legislation related to the other common policies and to the four freedoms (freedom of movement of persons, goods, services and capital).[333]

A first approach to this provision seems to suggest that it basically contains a two-prong test:[334] first, EU criminal legislation must be essential to ensure the effective implementation of a Union policy; second, the concrete area must have been subject previously to harmonization measures. In a way, the TFEU provision mimics the Necessary and Proper Clause: EU legislation must be necessary/essential to achieve a certain goal, i.e. effective implementation of EU policies; second, it must be proper in the sense that not every Union policy can be enforced through criminal law; only those that have previously been subject to harmonization measures may now be enforced through criminal law means.

From an academic perspective this conferred power has been labeled as "functional criminalization".[335] In a similar fashion to the Necessary and Proper Clause, "criminal law is thus perceived as a means to an end, the end being the effective implementation of other Union policies".[336] Out of the two requirements set forth in Article 83(2) TFEU, academics signal the "essentiality" requirement as the most controversial that will surely produce substantial litigation in the future.[337] Post-Lisbon academic works have provided interesting insights into how to interpret the essentiality requirement.

Öberg considers that the requirement of "essentiality" implies that the Union legislator and the ECJ need to make a proportionality assessment regarding the need for criminal sanctions. Moreover, it is contended that the ECJ should apply

---

333 Actually, according to Paul Craig and Gráinne De Búrca, *EU Law – Texts, Cases and Materials*, 5th ed., 2011 at 942, the article "enshrines a broad interpretation of the previous jurisprudence". In a recent EU Parliament report, it was noted that "the introduction of EU criminal law provisions is not confined to the area of freedom, security and justice but can relate to many different policies" (Report on an EU Approach on Criminal Law, 2010/2310 (INI) dated 24 April 2012 at 5). This finding is clearly related to Article 83(2) TFEU.

334 See also Valsamis Mitsilegas, *EU Criminal Law Competence after Lisbon: From Securitised to Functional Criminalisation*, in Diego Acosta Arcarazo and Cian C. Murphy, eds., *EU Security and Justice Law*, 2014 at 117; Jacob Öberg, *Union Regulatory Criminal Law Competence after Lisbon Treaty*, in Hans-Jörg Albrecht and André Klip, eds., *Crime, Criminal Law and Criminal Justice in Europe*, 2013 at 298 distinguishes between a "substantial requirement" (the essentiality test) and the "procedural requirement" (the previous harmonization test).

335 Valsamis Mitsilegas, *EU Criminal Law Competence after Lisbon: From Securitised to Functional Criminalisation*, in Diego Acosta Arcarazo and Cian C. Murphy, eds., *EU Security and Justice Law*, 2014 at 117–118.

336 Ibid.

337 Valsamis Mitsilegas, *EU Criminal Law Competence after Lisbon: From Securitised to Functional Criminalisation*, in Diego Acosta Arcarazo and Cian C. Murphy, eds., *EU Security and Justice Law*, 2014 at 117. Jacob Öberg, *Union Regulatory Criminal Law Competence after Lisbon Treaty*, in Hans-Jörg Albrecht and André Klip, eds., *Crime, Criminal Law and Criminal Justice in Europe*, 2013 at 297 (arguing for a strict proportionality requirement).

a strict review of proportionality in relation to criminal law legislation "given that criminal penalties is liable to infringe the individual's fundamental right to freedom to movement and given that a substantial review of the merits of a legislative act is necessary is proportionality is to secure legal safeguards for the individuals affected by the criminal law legislation".[338] *Klip* notes that the necessity of the EU intervention "in essence means the application of the subsidiarity principle"[339] and that the criteria of criminalization included in Article 83(1) and (2) "must be regarded as a more detailed version" of the principle.[340] In conclusion, criminal law, *Herlin-Karnell* notes, "should not be regarded as just another instrument in the EU legal toolbox" and the concept of essentiality shall be seen as the essential need to intervene at EU level, according to the principles of *ultima ratio* and subsidiarity.[341]

The "official" interpretation of this conferred power was produced by the EU Commission in its Communication "Towards an EU Criminal Policy: Ensuring the Effective Implementation of EU Policies through Criminal Law".[342] The Commission acknowledged what is generally considered as common ground: criminal law measures "comprise intrusive rules" and can still be regarded as a "sensitive policy field".[343] Correspondingly, it notes that the role of EU criminal law is defined "as a complement to the national law systems"[344] in the framework provided by the Lisbon Treaty. This implies that "criminal law must always remain a measure of last resort"[345] and the Communication outlines the process that must be followed to assess the need to adopt criminal law measures, and, in the event of a positive answer, *what kind of criminal measures,* i.e. if they are proper.

Most notably the Commission specified that "the legislator needs to analyse whether measures other than criminal law measures, e.g. sanction regimes of administrative or civil nature, could not sufficiently ensure the policy implementation ... This will require a thorough analysis in the Impact Assessments preceding any legislative proposal, including for instance ... an

338 Jacob Öberg, *Union Regulatory Criminal Law Competence after Lisbon Treaty*, in Hans-Jörg Albrecht and André Klip, eds., *Crime, Criminal Law and Criminal Justice in Europe*, 2013 at 323–324.

339 André Klip, *European Criminal Policy*, European Journal of Crime, Criminal Law and Criminal Justice 20 (2012) at 6.

340 Ibid. at 7.

341 Ester Herlin-Karnell, *Subsidiarity in the Area of EU Justice and Home Affairs Law – A Lost Cause?*, European Law Journal 15 (2009) at 356. This author provides the most in-depth discussion of the essentiality requirement in light of the principles of EU law in Ester Herlin-Karnell, *The Constitutional Dimension of European Criminal Law*, 2012.

342 Communication from the Commission to the European Parliament, the Council, the European Economic and Social Committee and the Committee of the Regions. Towards an EU Criminal Policy: Ensuring the effective implementation of EU policies through criminal law. COM (2011) 573 final.

343 Ibid. at 2, 4.

344 Ibid. at 3.

345 Ibid. at 6.

assessment of whether Member States' sanction regimes achieve the desired result and difficulties faced by national authorities implementing EU law on the ground".[346] Moreover, the Commission underlined that the institutions "need to be able to rely on clear factual evidence" regarding the need for the intervention.[347]

Finally, the Commission also specifies the elements that must be taken into account in assessing the necessity of criminal sanctions: the seriousness and character of the breach of law; the importance of stressing strong disapproval in order to ensure deterrence; and the extent to which and the reasons why existing sanctions do not achieve the desired enforcement level.[348] Needless to say, this approach introduces through the back door the "seriousness" criteria that was outlined above and that is so common in the Unions' approach to criminal matters.

From a federal perspective (be it vertical or horizontal) it is worth noting the importance given to the impact assessments in the EU legislation in criminal matters. To be sure, the US counterpart, i.e. congressional findings, have played a major role in justifying federal criminal legislation. But as certain landmark decisions of the US Supreme Court note, "the existence of congressional findings is not sufficient, by itself, to sustain the constitutionality" of federal legislation.[349] The question of the burden of proof, i.e. who has the burden to prove the necessity of the federal legislation, is an issue that frequently arises in federal litigation.

4.4.3. *The Necessary and Proper Clause in the US Constitution*

In the prior discussion of US powers, the Necessary and Proper Clause was pointed out as a vehicle for expanding a strict textual reading of Congress's authority. In other words, the list of federal powers specifically conferred to the Union in the text of the Constitution is opened up by this expanding clause. The wording of the Necessary and Proper Clause provides that Congress has the power "[t]o make all laws which shall be necessary and proper for carrying into execution" both its enumerated powers and "all other powers vested by this Constitution in the government of the United States, or in any department or

346 Ibid. at 7.

347 Ibid. at 8; see also the Report on an EU Approach on Criminal Law, 2010/2310 (INI) dated 24 April 2012 at 5: "necessity of new substantive criminal law provisions must be demonstrated by the necessary factual evidence". Herlin-Karnell considers that consistent analysis and impact-assessments on the respect of the subsidiarity principle have been absent, in general, in the legislative initiatives related to EU criminal law, however, they also correctly underline the need for a stronger application of this principle in this area (Ester Herlin-Karnell, *Subsidiarity in the Area of EU Justice and Home Affairs Law – A Lost Cause?*, European Law Journal 15 (2009) at 351, 361).

348 Communication from the Commission to the European Parliament, the Council, the European Economic and Social Committee and the Committee of the Regions. Towards an EU Criminal Policy: Ensuring the effective implementation of EU policies through criminal law, COM (2011) 573 final at 7.

349 *United States v. Morrison*, 529 U.S. 598 (2000).

officer thereof."[350] Therefore, it becomes evident that, by its own wording, this is *not* an independent source of authority, but "must always be tied to the exercise of some other identifiable constitutional power of the national government."[351]

There are many aspects of the Necessary and Proper Clause that are worth considering when conducting a comparison between the US and the EU systems. Before we explore some interesting similarities in the area of criminal law, it should not go unnoticed that one of the basic contentions of this book, repeated over and over again, is consistent with the findings of this section. The rationale behind the Necessary and Proper Clause (US) coincides with the rationale of the effective policy implementation provision (EU). Yet the US clause reinforces vertical federalism; the EU provision reinforces horizontal federalism. In both cases, it is a source to expand the Unions' power in the area of criminal law.

A first noteworthy consideration is that the iconic US Supreme Court decision concerning the Necessary and Proper Clause came about at the time the Second National Bank of the United States was created.[352] *John Marshall*'s opinion in *M'Culloch v. Maryland* (1819)[353] has influenced the debate surrounding this important clause in the US Constitution for almost two centuries.[354] Although not specifically referring to criminal law, this clause has been used time and time again to extend the Unions' criminal law powers beyond the ones explicitly enumerated in Article I Section 8 of the Constitution. The end result was that the US Supreme Court affirmed that Congress has power to incorporate a bank and, in order to reach such a conclusion, it specifically noted that: "There is nothing

---

350 US Const. Art. I, § 8, cl. 18.

351 Gary Lawson and Patricia B. Granger, *The "Proper" Scope of Federal Power: A Jurisdictional Interpretation of the Sweeping Clause*, Duke L.J. 43 (1993) at 267, 275.

352 The historical context seems relevant as the criminal law powers conferred by the effective implementation of the Union's policy (Article 83(2) TFEU) have been used in the wake of EU sovereign debt crisis not only for the already enacted Directive 2014/57/EU of the European Parliament and of the Council of 16 April 2014 on criminal sanctions for market abuse (market abuse directive), but also for the Proposal for a Directive of the European Parliament and of the Council on the fight against fraud to the Union's financial interests by means of criminal law, COM (2012) 363 final. Although the creation by the EU of a European bank is not at stake, the Article 83(2) TFEU powers in criminal law matters have been used while the EU was creating banking regulation agencies such as the European Banking Authority, the European Systemic Risk Board and, more importantly, the European Single Supervision Mechanism and the Single Resolution Mechanism. Precisely on the occasion of the Commission's European Single Supervision Mechanism's proposal, Commission's former President, José Manuel Barroso, addressing the EU Parliament in Strasbourg, called for the EU to evolve into a "federation of nation-states". Barroso said he was not calling for a "superstate", but rather "a democratic federation of nation states that can tackle our common problems, through the sharing of sovereignty," acknowledging that such a federation "will ultimately require a new treaty."

353 *M'Culloch v. Maryland*, 17 U.S. (4 Wheat) 316, 421 (1819).

354 *John Marshall* was aware of the importance of his decision: As he noted: "The Constitution of our country, in its most interesting and vital parts, is to be considered, the conflicting powers of the Government of the Union and of its members, as marked in that Constitution, are to be discussed, *and an opinion given which may essentially influence the great operations of the Government. No tribunal can approach such a question without a deep sense of its importance, and of the awful responsibility involved in its decision*" (*M'Culloch v. Maryland*, 17 U.S. (4 Wheat) 316, 400 (1819), emphasis added).

in the Constitution of the United States similar to the Articles of Confederation, which exclude incidental or implied powers."[355]

Out of the many sentences for which this ruling is famous,[356] for the purposes of criminal law powers of the Union under this clause there is a guiding principle that strikes us as particularly relevant: "Let the end be legitimate, let it be within the scope of the constitution, and all means which are appropriate, which are plainly adapted to that end, which are not prohibited, but consistent with the letter and spirit of the constitution, are constitutional."[357] Under this approach, Congress is given considerable deference, and courts will "not presume the unconstitutionality of federal criminal statutes".[358] Therefore, the Necessary and Proper Clause seems to leave little constraint on congressional authority[359] or as *Garnett* puts it: "It is difficult to see how the extent of federal regulatory power authorized by this doubly deferential scrutiny is anything but "limitless."[360]

Not surprisingly, the Necessary and Proper Clause is also known as the "elastic clause" or the "sweeping clause"[361] because of its flexibility. The broad reading of the Necessary and Proper Clause and the deferential approach to congressional decisions has allowed vast numbers of federal statutes, so long as there exists some nominal connection to an enumerated power. Given this connection, the legislature is authorized "to provide, by suitable penalties, for the enforcement of all legislation necessary or proper to the execution of powers with which it is intrusted."[362] This is arguably even further removed from the original Article I enumerated powers.[363]

---

355 *M'Culloch v. Maryland*, 17 U.S. (4 Wheat) 316, 406 (1819).

356 Probably, one of the most cited sentences is "That *the power to tax involves the power to destroy*; that the power to destroy may defeat and render useless the power to create" (*M'Culloch v. Maryland*, 17 U.S. (4 Wheat) 316, 431 (1819), emphasis added).

357 *M'Culloch v. Maryland*, 17 U.S. (4 Wheat) 316, 421 (1819).

358 *Sabri v. United States*, 541 U.S. 600, 605 (2004) (upholding the constitutionality of a federal criminal law dealing with bribery under the Spending Clause, even though the statute did not require showing a connection between the criminal activity and federal funds).

359 Gary Lawson and Patricia B. Granger, *The "Proper" Scope of Federal Power: A Jurisdictional Interpretation of the Sweeping Clause*, Duke L.J. 43 (1993) at 267, 271 ("Ever since Chief Justice John Marshall's famous opinion in McCulloch v. Maryland, which construed the Sweeping Clause to require only a minimal 'fit' between legislatively chosen means and a valid governmental end, the clause has not been widely viewed as a significant substantive limitation on congressional authority.").

360 Richard W. Garnett, *The New Federalism, The Spending Power, and Federal Criminal Law*, 89 Cornell L. Rev. 1 (2003) at 82.

361 Already in 1788 Alexander Hamilton termed the Necessary and Proper Clause "the sweeping clause, as it has been affectedly called") (see *The Federalist* No. 33 (Clinton Rossiter, ed., 1961) at 203). In the academic world see among others Gary Lawson and Patricia B. Granger, *The "Proper" Scope of Federal Power: A Jurisdictional Interpretation of the Sweeping Clause*, Duke L.J. 43 (1993) at 267; Lauren E. Marsh, *The Revival of the "Sweeping Clause": An Analysis of Why the Supreme Court Had to "Breathe New Life" into the Necessary and Proper Clause in United States v. Comstock.*, American University Criminal Law Brief 5 (2010) at 23–42.

362 *United States v. Fox*, 95 U.S. 670, 672 (1877).

363 Robin Morse, Note, *Federalism Challenges to the Adam Walsch Act*, B.U. L. Rev. 89 (2009) at 1753, 1769–70.

Now, an interesting point of comparison between the Necessary and Proper Clause (US) and the effective implementation of the Union's policies (EU) is how "necessary" (US) or "essential" (EU) must the enactment of the Unions' criminal legislation be to confer this power to the Union. In *M'Culloch v. Maryland* the US Supreme Court made clear that "necessity" in the absolute sense was not required by the Necessary and Proper Clause. In the wake of the new (restrictive) federalism approach supported by the *Lopez* and *Morrison* cases, some US scholars contended that the US Supreme Court should update the interpretation of the Necessary and Proper Clause pursuant to the new federalism[364] landscape regarding the Commerce Clause. Although that was finally not the case – as we shall explore below – it would seem reasonable to argue, for the purposes of the EU discussion, that the term "essential" as noted in the TFEU seems to be more restrictive than the term "necessary" in the US Constitution.

In this sense, the effective implementation of the Union's policies requires that, before exerting criminal law powers, the area in which purported criminal legislation is to be enacted has been previously "subject to harmonisation measures". In other words, it seems that criminal law cannot be the first choice to provide an effective implementation of EU policies. First, other harmonizing measures, i.e. civil or administrative, must have tried to effectively implement an EU policy. If such harmonizing measures have not achieved effective implementation, then criminal legislation seems to be "essential" to provide the effectiveness.

Be that as it may, the hope of providing a restrictive interpretation of the Necessary and Proper Clause came to an end in *Gonzales v. Raich*. To be sure, for a long period of time, the Necessary and Proper Clause was not at the center of the federalism debate. But with the landmark decision in *Gonzales v. Raich* certain statements of Justice Scalia paved the way for the return of the Necessary and Proper Clause to center stage. In permitting the federal Controlled Substances Act to override California's medical marijuana statutes, Justice Scalia recast much of the 20th-century commerce power case law as turning in fact on the necessary and proper power.[365] The crucial point for Scalia was that in the all-important regulatory arena of activities that substantially affect interstate commerce, the real source of Congress's power was in fact the Necessary and Proper Clause, not the Commerce Clause.

---

364 At the time, the *Lopez* and *Morrison* decisions were regarded as a "federalism revolution" of the Rehnquist court. See Erwin Chemerinsky, *The Federalism Revolution*, N.M. L. Rev. 13 (2001) at 7, 30; Sylvia A. Law, *In the Name of Federalism: The Supreme Court's Assault on Democracy and Civil Rights*, U. Cin. L. Rev. 70 (2002) at 367, 370; Thomas W. Merrill, *The Making of the Second Rehnquist Court: A Preliminary Analysis*, St. Louis U. L.J. 47 (2003) at 569, 618. See generally Jack M. Balkin and Sanford Levinson, *Understanding the Constitutional Revolution*, Va. L. Rev. 87 (2001) at 1045.

365 *Gonzales v. Raich*, 545 U.S. 1, 34 (2005) 33–34 (describing as "mechanical[] recit[ation]" and previous cases' "misleading and incomplete" inclusion of activities that "substantially affect" interstate commerce in the three categories of permissible regulation under the Commerce Clause).

In cases following *Raich*, several Justices picked up Justice Scalia's necessary and proper analysis and applied it in other contexts to uphold congressional regulation, with the result that a distinct body of Necessary and Proper Clause doctrine and commentary appeared to be developing for the first time since *M'Culloch*.[366] The newly prominent Necessary and Proper Clause proved dispositive to the Court's analysis five years later, in *United States v. Comstock*.[367] In *Comstock*, the Court relied on the necessary and proper power in upholding a federal civil commitment[368] statute for persons convicted of federal sex offenses.[369] Writing for the Court, Justice Breyer held that the statute was a valid extension of Congress's authority to establish federal criminal law; the fact that the federal criminal law was itself based on an implied power of Article I did not trouble the Court.[370] The Court rejected the argument that "when legislating pursuant to the Necessary and Proper Clause, Congress's authority can be no more than one step removed from a specifically enumerated power",[371] calling such an argument "irreconcilable with our precedents".[372] As Justice Breyer pointed out, "all Justices of the Supreme Court (even the dissenting Justice), acknowledge that Congress has the implied power to criminalize any conduct that might interfere with the exercise of an enumerated power".[373]

The dissenters' principal objection to the statute at issue in *Comstock* was its attenuated relationship to any particular enumerated power.[374] Absent such a connection, the dissenters appeared to view the case as though Congress had based

366 See H. Jefferson Powell, *The Regrettable Clause: United States v. Comstock and the Powers of Congress*, San Diego L. Rev. 48 (2011) at 713.

367 130 S. Ct. 1949 (2010).

368 Civil commitment is a legal process through which an individual with symptoms of severe mental illness is court-ordered into treatment in a hospital (inpatient) or in the community (outpatient). Article 18 U.S. Code § 4248 establishes the civil commitment of a sexually dangerous person. The wording reads "In relation to a person who is in the custody of the Bureau of Prisons, or who has been committed to the custody of the Attorney General pursuant to section 4241 (d), or against whom all criminal charges have been dismissed solely for reasons relating to the mental condition of the person, the Attorney General or any individual authorized by the Attorney General or the Director of the Bureau of Prisons may certify that the person is a sexually dangerous person, and transmit the certificate to the clerk of the court for the district in which the person is confined. The clerk shall send a copy of the certificate to the person, and to the attorney for the Government, and, if the person was committed pursuant to section 4241 (d), to the clerk of the court that ordered the commitment. The court shall order a hearing to determine whether the person is a sexually dangerous person. A certificate filed under this subsection shall stay the release of the person pending completion of procedures contained in this section."

369 130 S. Ct. 1949 (2010) at 1964–1965.

370 Ibid. at 1964.

371 Ibid. at 1963–1964.

372 Ibid. at 1963 ("from the implied power to punish we have further inferred both the power to imprison and ... the federal civil-commitment power").

373 Ibid. at 1964.

374 Ibid. at 1973, Justices Scalia and Thomas dissenting: "The Government identifies no specific enumerated power or powers as a constitutional predicate for § 4248, and none are readily discernable."

the statute on a bare assertion of the necessary and proper power, and nothing else – that is, as though a decision to uphold the regulation would transform the power from an auxiliary into a primary tool. Indeed, the dissent expressed skepticism that a claim of congressional power grounded in the Necessary and Proper Clause might ever pass constitutional muster.[375]

Extremely interesting to the concerns about national sovereignty and criminal is the concurring judgment in Comstock provided by Justice Kennedy: "It is of fundamental importance to consider whether essential attributes of state sovereignty are compromised by the assertion of federal power under the Necessary and Proper Clause".[376] As some commentators have noted, these cases demonstrate that some of these putative primary underlying powers are themselves non-enumerated, the most notable being Congress's power to establish a body of federal criminal law.

In a post-*Comstock* case, not limited to criminal law, the US Supreme Court continued to develop the breath of the Necessary and Proper Clause. As noted previously in *National Federation of Independent Business* the Court not only addressed the extent to which the Commerce Clause enables Congress to pass legislation, but, moreover, to which extent the Necessary and Proper Clause may be used in such context. In this landmark decision, the USSC concedes substantial leeway to Congress is term of what is "necessary" – therefore departing from the "strictness" of the "essential" requirement of the TFEU. The Supreme Court noted in this 2012 decision: "As our jurisprudence under the Necessary and Proper Clause has developed, we have been very deferential to Congress's determination that a regulation is 'necessary.' We have thus upheld laws that are 'convenient', or 'useful' or 'conducive' to the authority's 'beneficial exercise.'"

Finally, shortly after *National Federation of Independent Business*, the US Supreme Court continued to emphasize its analysis of the Necessary and Proper Clause in *Kebodeaux*,[377] a criminal law-related case. *Kebodeaux* suggests a broader vision of the Necessary and Proper Clause[378] in the sense that it allows Congress

375 Ibid. at 1983 ("Not long ago, this Court described the Necessary and Proper Clause as 'the last, best hope of those who defend ultra vires congressional action'. ... Regrettably, today's opinion breathes new life into that Clause, and – the Court's protestations to the contrary notwithstanding ... – comes perilously close to transforming the Necessary and Proper Clause into a basis for the federal police power that 'we always have rejected.'").

376 Ibid. at 1974.

377 *United States v. Kebodeaux*, 133 S. Ct. 2496, 2496 (2013) relying in *Comstock*. See Casey B. Nathan, *Searching for "Jurisdictional Hook": United States v. Kebodeaux and the Constitutional Limits of the Sex Offender Registration and Notification Act*, Boston College Journal of Law & Social Justice 33 (2013) at 52–62 for an analysis of the previous rulings of the Fifth Circuit, which had declared SORNA to be unconstitutional.

378 *United States v. Kebodeaux*, 133 S. Ct. 2503 (2013): "The scope of the Necessary and Proper Clause is broad". In its concurrent opinion, Chief Justice Roberts provided an interesting angle on the basis for upholding the statute pursuant to the Necessary and Proper Clause and the connection between necessity and rationality: "Maybe so, but those consequences of the registration requirement are irrelevant for our purposes. *Public safety benefits are neither necessary nor sufficient to a proper exercise of the power to regulate the military. What matters – all that matters – is that Congress could have rationally determined* that 'mak[ing] the civil

to "adopt any means, appearing to it most eligible and appropriate, which are adapted to the end to be accomplished and consistent with the letter and spirit of the Constitution."[379] Focusing the attention in federal criminal law, the Court summarized much of what we have been explaining in the previous sections:

> "The Constitution, for example, makes few explicit references to federal criminal law, but the Necessary and Proper Clause nonetheless authorizes Congress, in the implementation of other explicit powers, to create federal crimes, to confine offenders to prison."[380]

The question, therefore, is whether there is sufficient connection between the Necessary and Proper Clause and an enumerated power.[381] This discussion of the US Supreme Court does not seem too far from future EU discussion concerning the conferred powers of Article 83(2) TFEU. Not only how essential criminal legislation is to effectively implement a Union's policy, but also what sort of connection between the Union's criminal legislation on a certain matter and the Union's policy seem to be subjects for future debate that will surely take place in the EU.

---

registration requirement at issue here a consequence of Kebodeaux's offense' would give force to the Uniform Code of Military Justice adopted pursuant to Congress's power to regulate the Armed Forces" (emphasis added).

379 Ibid. This case dealt with the application of the Sex Offender Registration and Notification Act (SORNA) to an individual who had been convicted by a special court-martial of a sex offense.

380 Ibid. Interestingly enough Chief Justice Roberts warned against interpreting *Kebodeaux* as a "federal police power", which, for centuries has been excluded by the USSC: "Here, however, I worry that incautious readers will think they have found in the majority opinion something they would not find in either the Constitution or any prior decision of ours: a federal police power". "I write separately to stress not only that a federal police power is immaterial to the result in this case, but also that such a power could not be material to the result in this case – because it does not exist. See United States v. Morrison, 529 U.S. 598, 618–619 (2000) ('[W]e always have rejected readings of ... the scope of federal power that would permit Congress to exercise a police power' (quoting United States v. Lopez, 514 U. S. 549, 584–585 (1995)."

381 In a similar sense, related to the potential existence of a federal power to police by implication and not by specification, Chief Justice Roberts wrote in his concurring opinion to *United States v. Kebodeaux*, 133 S. Ct. 2503 (2013): "I find it implausible to suppose – and impossible to support – that the Framers intended to confer such authority by implication rather than expression. A power of that magnitude vested in the Federal Government is not 'consist[ent] with the letter and spirit of the constitution,' McCulloch, supra, at 421, and thus not a 'proper [means] for carrying into Execution' the enumerated powers of the Federal Government, U.S. Const., Art. I, § 8, cl. 18."

5. THE ENFORCEMENT FEDERAL DIMENSION IN THE UNIONS' CRIMINAL LAW

5.1. INTRODUCTION

Certainly the law in the books dimension provided by the Unions' legislation in criminal matters is critical to the development of (vertical/horizontal) criminal law. But the law in action perspective has equal – even greater – importance. Here, again, the distinction between vertical and horizontal federalism plays a major role. The enforcement of horizontal federal criminal laws has been traditionally left to the states, while the US system promptly created a body of "federal prosecutors", i.e. US attorneys, to enforce vertical criminal laws. Interestingly, the EU has noticed the need to introduce a more vertical approach to the enforcement of the Union's criminal law – especially to those provisions related to the protection of the Union's financial interests.

Article 86 TFEU contains some basic elements of the European Public Prosecutor's Office. But, to be sure, it leaves it up to the future Regulation to lay out the details of its functioning. It is fair to say that many EPPO models can be proposed, and that the elements set out in Article 86 TFEU are so minimal that the federal nature of this institution will probably vary with time. In this sense, certain elements of Article 86 TFEU point towards horizontal federalism; others to vertical federalism. The final outcome will probably depend on the political willingness of creating an enforcement institution with real "teeth", or reaching a compromise institution based on political correctness.

In the wake of the 2010 sovereign debt financial crisis and the subsequent need to effectively protect EU taxpayers, a strong enforcement agency seemed to be the preferred option. Yet, as the concern over the crisis waned, so did the pressure of the EU in forcing this option. Instead of a model similar to the parameters of EU competition law, i.e. direct enforcement from Brussels with its own staff, its own rules, etc., there is a clear tendency to enact a decentralized model in which the EPPO coordinates action of local prosecutors. In a nutshell, horizontal federalism has again trumped vertical federalism. It seems reasonable to foresee that major enforcement issues will be raised in the future and that the independence of those in charge of enforcing the legislation designed to protect the EU's financial interests will be called into question.

The experience of the US federal prosecutors, i.e. United States attorneys, shows the constant tension between federal and local authorities. The success of the US Attorney's Office relies heavily on the independence and resources available to them. The EU should take due note of the problems embedded in protecting the financial interests of the Union and strive for a system similar to EU competition law.

5.2. EUROPEAN PUBLIC PROSECUTOR'S OFFICE (ARTICLE 86 TFEU): FROM HORIZONTAL TO VERTICAL FEDERALISM?

It can hardly be questioned that one of the most important "criminal law" hallmarks of the Lisbon Treaty is the introduction, in the TFEU itself, of the European Public Prosecutor's Office. As we shall explore, the express enumeration in the Union's "constituent" text is unparalleled in the US system of federal criminal law, i.e. the federal prosecution office in the US (the US Attorney's Office) created by virtue of the Judiciary Act of 1789. In short, the US Constitution does not include the creation of the federal prosecution office. In general, the provisions on the European Prosecutor contained in the Lisbon Treaty seem to draw on the Green Paper on criminal law protection of the financial interests of the Community and the establishment of a European Prosecutor.[382] Hence, there is already abundant literature which provides extensive exposition and (mostly) criticism on the subject.[383]

Given that at the time of writing there are still major discussions as to the structure that will finally take shape on the grounds of the proposed Regulation,[384] we will address some details of the various proposals (both legislative and academic) in a later section.[385] For now we will concentrate on the federal dimension of the EPPO according to the TFEU, which will be reinforced or weakened depending on the final Regulation that will be passed.

As a general statement, the structure of the EPPO in Article 86 TFEU shows some mixed federalism tendencies.[386] On the one hand, there is some horizontal federalism language embedded in the fact that the EPPO "shall exercise the functions of prosecutor in the competent courts of the Member States" (Article 86(2) TFEU). But, on the other hand, the fact that this institution is created through a Regulation, and that such regulation will contain "the rules of procedure applicable to its activities, as well as those governing the admissibility of evidence, and the rules applicable to the judicial review of procedural measures taken by it in the performance of its function" (Article 86(3) TFEU), adds a vertical federalism element.

---

382 COM (2001) 715 final. For a thorough review of the various projects prior to the Regulation see MARTIJN ZWIERS, *The European Public Prosecutor's Office. Analysis of a Multilevel Criminal Justice System*, 2011 at 355–385. See also LORENA BACHMEIER, *The Potential Contribution of a European Public Prosecutor in light of the Proposal for a Regulation of 17th July 2013*, EUROPEAN JOURNAL OF CRIME, CRIMINAL LAW AND CRIMINAL JUSTICE 23 (2015) at 121.

383 For a broad explanation see MARTIJN ZWIERS, *The European Public Prosecutor's Office. Analysis of a Multilevel Criminal Justice System*, 2011, with further references.

384 Proposal for a Council Regulation on the establishment of the European Public Prosecutor's Office, COM (2013) 534 final.

385 See below Chapter 5, section 6.

386 As ANDRE KLIP, *European Criminal Law*, 2nd ed., 2012 at 459 points out: "On the of first things that appears from Article 86 is that a *hybrid* system will be created" (emphasis added).

It seems clear that the intention of Lisbon Treaty Founding Fathers was to create an independent institution that would effectively protect the EU's financial interests. This legislative intent may be drawn from the fact that the primal goal of the EPPO is to "combat crimes affecting the financial interests of the Union" (Article 86(1) TFEU). However, the fact that Article 86(4) TFEU enables an extension of the EPPO's scope of competence to "include serious crime having a cross-border dimension" signals the willingness to spread its area of influence. In this sense, *there are two different spheres of competence are in Article 86 TFEU*: crimes affecting the EU's financial interests (Article 86(1) TEU) and serious crimes having a cross-border dimension (Article 86(4) TFEU). A black-letter law analysis would find that the first is related to Article 325 TFEU and the second to Article 83(1) TFEU. This would leave the offenses contained in Article 83(2) TFEU with no possibility of being prosecuted by the EPPO unless they could be related either to Article 325 TFEU or Article 83(1) TFEU. As mentioned previously, there seems to be some support for linking Article 325 TFEU with the general competence laid out in Article 83(2) TFEU, i.e. the European Necessary and Proper Clause in criminal matters. Yet an argument could also be made as to the connection between Article 83(2) TFEU and Article 83(1) TFEU given that both are located in the Area of Freedom, Justice and Security and both are based on the principle of mutual recognition (including harmonization). In any event, this distinction supports a major premise of this book: that the Lisbon Treaty provides for two sources of federal criminal power: one characterized by gravity and transnationalism – relying more on horizontal federalism – and the other characterized by involvement of EU financial interests – which signals a possible tendency towards vertical federalism.[387]

Against this backdrop, the wording of Article 86(2) TFEU finally makes it clear that horizontal federalism generally trumps vertical federalism in terms of enforcement. The European Public Prosecutor's Office "shall exercise the functions of prosecutor in the competent courts of the Member States in relation to such offences" and not before a truly European court. The Lisbon Treaty does not envisage the existence of federal judicial authority over criminal trials.[388] The courts responsible for enforcing the European "federal" law are strictly national.

387 This matter highlights the importance of the change in structure introduced by the Lisbon Treaty. The European Prosecutor's Office used to be proposed by means of Article 280 *bis* ToA within the Fight against Fraud section (now Article 325 TFEU), and it was to be limited to offenses against European Union interests (see Green Paper Protection at 86–90). The new TFEU has two significant changes: the possible expansion of the EPPO's competence into the field cross-border criminality and the systemic importance of including such provision in that field (under "Judicial Cooperation in Criminal Matters", and not in the chapter on "Combatting Fraud").

388 This is one the main criticisms raised by Schünemann against the model introduced by the Lisbon Treaty. This commentator correctly points out that a European judicial body should have been awarded with powers to impose criminal sanctions. Accordingly, he proposes the creation of a specialized court within the European Court of Justice as per Article 257 of the TFEU. (See Schünemann, 116 ZStW (2004) at 379, footnote 14.)

This coincides with the longstanding tradition in European law, where EU law is regularly applied by national courts. Needless to say, this format is very different from the United States' federal criminal law.

As we shall address in a later section,[389] the fact that the EPPO will have to act before national courts has triggered a decentralized structure where national prosecutors are charged with the responsibility of making the case in their capacity as "delegates" of the EPPO. This, in turn, creates an area of potential conflicts of interests when the interests of the Member States are not aligned with the interests of the EU – which will often be the case. A very simple question shows some deficiencies in this approach: if, until now, basically all Member States have included in their national penal legislation provisions protecting the EU's financial interests and national prosecutors have failed to actively prosecute most EU fraud cases,[390] then why should they be more efficient if the proposed Regulation is passed? Just because they wear a "double hat"?[391]

Regardless of how questionable these previous statements are, one thing remains clear: the Lisbon Treaty is aware of the lack of consistency that the model entails. The Founding Fathers of the Lisbon Treaty try to surmount this deficit by declaring that the Regulation with direct enforcement capacity in all Member States will be "governing … the rules of procedure applicable to its activities, as well as those governing the admissibility of evidence, and the rules applicable to the judicial review of procedural measures taken by it in the performance of its functions."[392] In short, the possibility of creating *something akin to a European Rules of Criminal Procedure* should compensate, at least in the eyes of the Lisbon Treaty, for the enforcement deficit resulting from EPPO action before national courts of the Member States. As we shall see, the Proposed Regulation has not seized the opportunity to establish a comprehensive set of procedural rules that would truly compensate for this deficit.

Given the importance of a European Public Prosecutor in the shaping of a potential European federal criminal law, it would not be surprising if, in the future, the European Public Prosecutor's Office will determine whether a crime is to be prosecuted at the European or national level. This would, again, coincide with the US trends in this area, since there are many who argue, for theoretical or

389 See below Chapter 5, section 6.

390 The OLAF reports, as we shall note below, reflect an outstanding deficit in prosecution of the cases referred by this EU institution to the national authorities.

391 To be sure, the Regulation proposed tries to address this topic by declaring that the Head of the EPPO or the Deputies will instruct national prosecutors, therefore ensuring their independence. Yet it is reasonable to conclude that it is, at best, naïve that national prosecutors will be necessarily independent just because a far-distant Brussels orders them to act in a certain manner. There are many ways in which national prosecutors will be able to "drag their feet" and not prosecute cases that are in the Union's best interests – just as they have been doing so far. As we shall explain below, a key feature of the USAO is its independence from national interests and its focus on truly federal interests.

392 Article 86(3) TFEU.

practical reasons, that the federal prosecutor's office (Attorney-General) should determine federal and state jurisdiction.[393]

5.3. FEDERAL PROSECUTORS IN THE US: THE RAW DISCRETIONARY POWER

Federal prosecution in the US is assigned to the US Attorney's Office (USAO). Yet their competence goes beyond criminal law enforcement, as they are also involved in *civil* litigation where the United States is a party. As a general statement, the 93 United States Attorneys work to enforce federal laws throughout the country ensuring "that the laws be faithfully executed".[394] As noted before, the US Congress enacted the Judiciary Act of 1789. This legislation directed the President to appoint in each federal district "a meet person learned in the law to act as an attorney for the United States".[395] According to the relevant legislation the task of the United States Attorney was "to prosecute in (each) district all delinquents for crimes and offenses cognizable under the authority of the United States, and all civil actions in which the United States shall be concerned."[396]

It is important to note that before the US Civil War, United States Attorneys prosecuted *only the cases mentioned specifically in the Constitution*, namely piracy, counterfeiting, treason, felonies committed on the high seas, or cases resulting from interference with federal justice (perjury, bribery), extortion by federal officers, thefts by employees from the United States Bank, and arson of federal vessels.[397] Over the years, however, the caseloads have changed, as have the responsibilities of the office. There are 93 United States Attorneys with over 350 Assistant US Attorneys. In addition to their main offices, many US Attorneys maintain smaller satellite offices throughout their districts.[398] US Attorneys are appointed by the President and confirmed by the Senate, and they serve terms of four years or at the President's discretion. While the US Attorney him or herself is a political appointee, the Assistants, by law, hold non-partisan jobs, so political affiliations or beliefs *should* play no role in how they are hired, fired, or promoted. This has not always been the case.

In general, the USAO consists of two major divisions: criminal and civil. The criminal division, which is significantly larger than the civil division in most offices, prosecutes violations of the federal criminal laws, such as organized

[393] See generally Dan M. Kahan, *Is Chevron Relevant to Federal Criminal Law?*, Harv. L. Rev. 110 (1996) at 469; Dan M. Kahan, *Three Conceptions of Federal Criminal Lawmaking*, Buff. Crim. L. Rev. 1 (1997) at 5, 17.

[394] U.S. Const., Article II.

[395] Judiciary Act, 1789, Section 35.

[396] Judiciary Act, 1789, Section 35.

[397] James Eisenstein, *Counsel for the United States: U.S. Attorneys in the Political and Legal Systems*, 1978, at 9.

[398] www.justice.gov/usao/districts.

crime, drug trafficking, political corruption, tax evasion, fraud and other financial crimes, bank robbery, cybercrime, human trafficking, and civil rights offenses. Many criminal divisions have specialized units or sections within them. Many criminal divisions now have a national security section or unit and work with state and local governments to combat terrorist activities.

The United States Attorney's Office is included within the Department of Justice Organizational Chart:

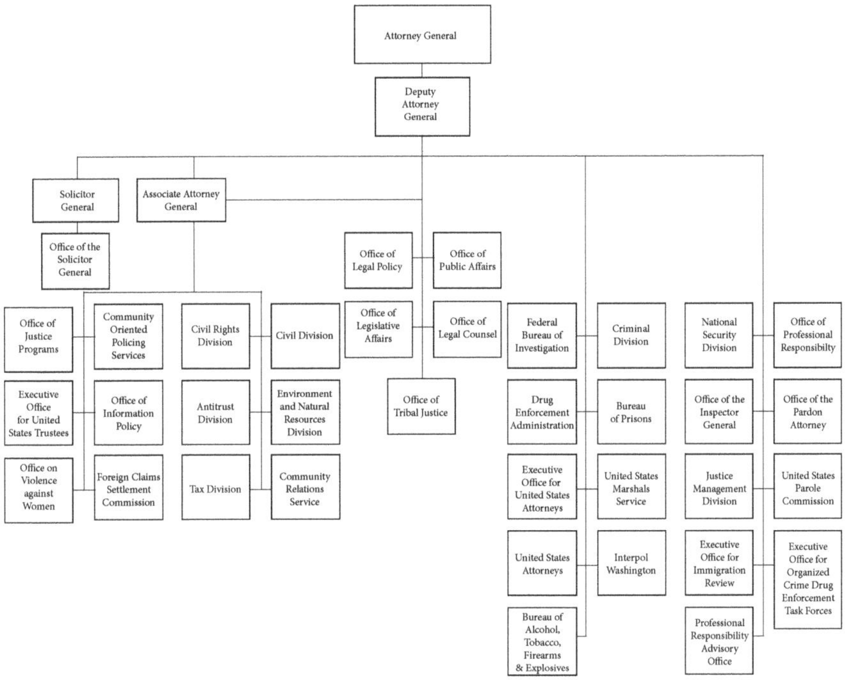

The structure of the criminal division is as follows:

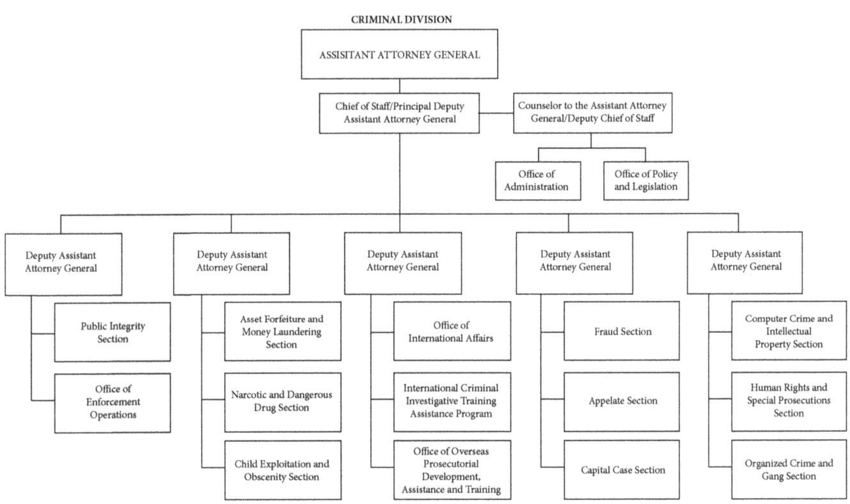

In any event, the United States Attorney retains a large degree of independence and prosecutorial discretion. Obviously United States Attorneys receive direction and policy advice from the Attorney General and other Department officials, but the United States Attorney has wide latitude in determining what cases are taken under consideration in his or her district. "The discretionary power to decide whether to prosecute is awesome," admitted one United States Attorney.[399] So formidable is this power that, "if the United States Attorney abuses this power, the only available remedy is removal."[400]

Therefore, the US system of federal criminal law is based to a great extent in prosecutorial discretion,[401] which goes largely unreviewed. As critics are quick to point out, the alleged gatekeeper function of prosecutors has no real enforcement mechanisms, and instead is dependent upon the ethical personal integrity of the member of the US Attorney's Office.[402] In theory, defendants may make a claim of discrimination under the selective prosecution doctrine, alleging that a prosecutor chose to pursue their case for illegitimate reasons.[403] However, this standard is purposefully high, with a presumption that even the preliminary showing to obtain discovery should "be a significant barrier".[404] On the other hand, there are mechanisms within the DOJ, which in turn have congressional supervision, that provide the necessary doses of control that make the system

---

399 Ibid. at 47.

400 Ibid. at 47.

401 For an introductory view from the Government side see James Gorelick and Harry Litman, *Prosecutorial Discretion and the Federalization Debate*, Hastings L.J. 46 (1995) at 967 explaining why the principle that the federal courts should never, or even rarely, be able to exercise criminal jurisdiction over areas of criminal law that also fall under the concurrent jurisdiction of the state system is flawed. For a general overview see Gerard E. Lynch, *Our Administrative System of Criminal Justice*, Fordham L. Rev. 66 (1998) at 2117, 2138–2142. Some interesting statistics were provided by Richard S. Frase, *The Decision to File Federal Criminal Charges: A Quantitative Study of Prosecutorial Discretion*, U. Chi. L. Rev. 47 (1980) at 246, 257, 278.

402 Though the piece is more than 30 years old, the piece by James Vorenberg, *Decent Restraints in Prosecutorial Power*, Harv. L. Rev. 94 (1981) at 1521, 1559 is worth revisiting. As he noted "prosecutors are not held to anything remotely like what due process would require if they were engaged in an acknowledged rather than a hidden system of adjudication. No uniform, pre-announced rules inform the defendant and control the decision-maker; a single official can invoke society's harshest sanctions on the basis of ad hoc personal judgments. Prosecutors can and do accord different treatment – prison for some and probation or diversion to others – on grounds that are not written down anywhere and may not have been either rational, consistent, or discoverable in advance" (at 1554).

403 See *United States v. Armstrong*, 517 U.S. 456 (1996) (explaining the procedural requirements of a selective prosecution claim).

404 Ibid. at 463–464. Not surprisingly, many consider this threshold to be virtually insurmountable in many cases, leaving prosecutorial discretion effectively unreviewable. See Anne Bowen Poulin, *Prosecutorial Discretion and Selective Prosecution: Enforcing Protection after United States v. Armstrong*, Am. Crim. L. Rev. 34 (1997) at 1081 (referring to this defense right as "The Disfavored Right"); Yaov Sapir, *Neither Intent nor Impact: A Critique of the Racially Based Selective Prosecution Jurisprudence and a Reform Proposal*, Harv. Black Letter L.J. 19 (2003) at 127; Richard H. McAdams, *Race and Selective Prosecution: Discovering the Pitfalls of Armstrong*, Chi.-Kent L. Rev. 73 (1998) at 605.

at least bearable for the citizenry.[405] This prosecutorial leeway raises important issues in a criminal justice system where many crimes fall under concurrent state and federal jurisdiction.[406] Combined with the already discussed proliferation of federal criminal laws in the United States, individual prosecutors in the US perhaps have the most say in whether or not a crime is treated as federal or left to state mechanisms.

There has also been some debate over the political dependence of US Attorneys,[407] who are appointed by the centralized, federal government but serve in decentralized offices throughout the country. It is no easy task to coordinate opposing interests as the perception of certain issues from DC might greatly differ from the more "local" needs that the regional offices face. Add opposing political interests to the mix, and potential for dispute grows. This issue is very relevant to the future system of European Prosecutors, especially since Brussels is perceived as even more of an outsider in the EU than Washington DC is in the US.

The US controversy between local and federal prosecutors could be reduced or avoided in the EU if criminal law were limited to "direct" or "genuine" European offenses, so that the risk of overlapping with states' regulations is hence diminished. Such limitations would also reduce the power (and the problem) of federal prosecutors to invoke a different law and punishment for similar defendants at their discretion. There could still be some local hesitance to prosecute valued members of the local community, and this hesitation will be exacerbated by the fact that they will be tried in state courts applying European standards. Overall, though, the system will have a greater chance of maintaining its integrity if offenses that are perceived to be only of state interest are left to the corresponding authorities of the Member States.

---

405 Daniel C. Richman, *Federal Criminal Law, Congressional Delegation, and Enforcement Discretion*, UCLA L. Rev. 46 (1999) at 757, (noting, however, that Congress cannot use many of the tools for monitoring and managing delegated criminal enforcement authority that it can draw on to constrain bureaucratic discretion in other areas).

406 Robert Heller, Comment, *Selective Prosecution and the Federalization of Criminal Law: the Need for Meaningful Judicial Review of Prosecutorial Discretion*, U. Pa. L. Rev. 145 (1997) at 1309, 1309–1315 (noting that "[c]oncurrent jurisdiction due to the federalization of criminal law introduces into the criminal justice system a potential for prosecutorial abuse that was not an area of concern when crime was primarily a locally regulated phenomenon").

407 Sara Sun Beale, *Rethinking the Identity and Role of US Attorneys*, Ohio St. J. Crim. L. 6 (2009) at 369.

CHAPTER 3

TESTING THE ALLEGED LACK OF FEDERALISM

How Non-Federal is EU Criminal Law?

1. INTRODUCTION

The preceding chapters have shown the gradual establishment of a federal dimension in the area of EU criminal law. Still, many would argue that this approach reads too much into the Lisbon Treaty provisions and the recent communications of the EU institutions. It is true that only recently have EU authorities used the word "federal" to refer to actual developments regarding criminal law. Therefore, it is worth examining whether current, routinely applied European instruments contain federalizing elements. The aim, as throughout the book, is to call attention to the fact that the more reluctant the EU is to clearly acknowledge existing European federal interests that deserve EU federal criminal law protection, the more an ineffective federalization will be taking place.

The analysis starts by examining the hallmark of EU criminal law: the European Arrest Warrant. Initially devised to simply replace existing extradition proceedings between Member States, it has a far broader impact. A comparative approach shows that this instrument is truly federal in nature. Moreover, the current EU system is more federal (in horizontal federalism terms) than its US counterpart, interstate extradition. The mandatory nature and the extensive catalogue of offenses to which the EAW applies stands in contrast to the US system. Reluctance to acknowledge the federal nature of this EU instrument reduces the possibility for a transparent discussion on the rationale for establishing such a system.

Similarly, the EU currently has a powerful (horizontal) federal institution related to the well-known principle of double jeopardy. Article 54 of the Schengen Treaty bars EU Member States from prosecuting the same facts and offender in their own jurisdiction after acquittal, dismissal or conviction by another EU Member State. On the contrary, the dual sovereignty exception in the US system enables other states and the federal government to prosecute the same facts and offender in their respective jurisdiction, regardless of any outcome in another jurisdiction.[1] The horizontal federalization throughout the EU of the decision reached by one EU Member State thus provides for a harmonization across borders which goes far beyond the US system.

Finally, the harmonization of both substantive and procedural law taking place in the EU is reviewed. The EU Member States' obligation to harmonize their national legislation consistently with EU Directives in criminal law stands in sharp contrast with the US, where states' harmonization through the Model Penal Code's provisions is entirely voluntary. Again, the reluctance to distinguish between truly European federal crimes and those offenses that the EU feels should be treated similarly throughout the EU results in a double deficiency: the EU lacks independent and complete power above the Member States to enforce the law against crimes harming its own interests but the EU Member States are forced to establish criminal sanctions in their own legislatures in a way that does not allow for national diversity.

In general it is a fair statement that horizontal federalism in EU criminal law has provided certain checks and balances. The EAW is a clear instrument of horizontal federal criminal law that favors the prosecution. Article 54 of the Convention Implementing the Schengen Agreement (CISA) can be equally considered an institution of horizontal federal criminal law favoring the defense. As to the mandatory harmonization process, a fair assessment would consider the effects as neutral in the prosecution/defense dichotomy. The problem here is the lack of standing of citizens to request judicial review of the harmonizing legal instruments across the EU (individual level) and the curtailment of national diversity to decide how and whether or not to harmonize (state level). This, again, is a consequence of the horizontal federalism nature of EU criminal law.

2. INTERSTATE EXTRADITION

2.1. INTRODUCTION

Extradition is itself not a federal issue; more commonly it is a product of international relations and treaty arrangements. However, special issues can arise where the governments involved are subject to a higher authority. This is the case with both the EU and the US, where state governments are subject to specific rules which dictate their extradition decisions to some degree. Thus international relationships in both systems are replaced by federal ones, dictated from above.

[1] *Heath v. Alabama*, 474 U.S. 82 (1985) (declaring "that successive prosecutions by two States for the same conduct are not barred by the Double Jeopardy Clause").

This comes as no surprise in the US, but yet again highlights the reality of the EU as a federalized system.

2.2. EUROPEAN ARREST WARRANT (EU)

It can hardly be questioned that the EAW is the hallmark of the principle of mutual recognition in criminal law matters. Instituted in the aftermath of 9/11,[2] the number of EAWs issued and executed is staggering.[3] Though the increase has not been always consistent, it has outnumbered the extraditions between EU Member States before the entry into force of the EAW. In this sense, although the aim was merely to replace the system of multilateral extradition built upon the European Convention on Extradition of 13 December 1957 which was simplified between EU Member States in 1995 and 1996,[4] the consequences of the implementation of the EAW system are far reaching.

The aim here is not to conduct an extensive analysis of the EAW,[5] but to demonstrate certain features of this European mechanism that stand in sharp contrast to its American counterpart: interstate rendition, also known as interstate extradition. To be sure, the number of interstate rendition proceedings in the US has decreased significantly over time. This is probably due to, among other factors, the expansion of federal criminal law. But the basics of the American mechanism are still in place, and the notable differences between two institutions that were tailored to serve similar purposes is worth noting.

We start by looking at the EAW. The first salient feature is that, from an institutional perspective, the involvement of government administration has been suppressed.[6] Traditionally, extradition has been a combined proceeding

---

2 See Maria Feltcher, Robin Lööf and Bill Gilmore, *EU Criminal Law and Justice*, 2008 at 112–126.

3 See generally the Report from the Commission to the European Parliament and the Council on the implementation since 2007 of the Council Framework Decision of 13 June 2002 on the European arrest warrant and the surrender procedures between Member States, COM (2011) 17 final at 13.

4 Convention of 10 March 1995 on simplified extradition procedure between the Member States of the European Union and the Convention of 27 September 1996 relating to extradition between the Member States of the European Union.

5 For an extensive review see Libor Klimek, *European Arrest Warrant*, 2014; Nico Keijzer and Elies Van Sliedregt, *The European Arrest Warrant in Practice*, 2009. For a decade review see Luisa Marin, *Effective and Legitimate? Learning from the Lessons of 10 Years of Practice with the European Arrest Warrant*, New Journal of European Criminal Law 5 (2014) at 326. A fundamental rights' perspective in Steve Peers, *The European Arrest Warrant: The Dilemmas of Mutual Recognition, Human Rights and EU Citizenship*, in *The Court of Justice and the Construction of Europe: Analyses and Perspectives on Sixty Years of Case-law - La Cour de Justice et la Construction de l'Europe: Analyses et Perspectives de Soixante Ans de Jurisprudence*, 2013 at 523–538.

6 See also Maria Feltcher, Robin Lööf and Bill Gilmore, *EU Criminal Law and Justice*, 2008, at 112 noting that "the depoliticisation of the process in one of the notable features of the EAW compared to the previous extradition procedures".

of both the executive and the judiciary. Since the enactment of the EAW, the judicial phase is paramount and there is no room for the government to deny extradition of a person within its territory. Although arguably the actual effect of governmental approval had diminished over time – in most cases, judicial approval of extradition was routinely followed by government authorities – the absence of even a requirement of government approval is significant.[7]

Perhaps the most blatant change of the EAW was to suppress the dual criminality requirement.[8] At the time, it was argued that most offenses which enable the issuance and execution of an EAW were already present in the criminal provisions of all EU Member States, more or less. However, a closer look at the catalog contained in Article 1(2) of the Framework Decision shows that the EAW does not deal with specific offenses – which are the basis for the dual criminality requirements – but with certain types of criminality, for instance the "computer-related crime" offense. Numerous specific offenses may fall under this headline.

The lack of specificity within the EAW list of offenses has enabled EU Member States to issue and execute EAWs under certain labels for offenses not clearly contained in their national legislation under the same label. Under the EAW heading of fraud offenses, EAWs have been issued and executed for tax and bankruptcy crimes.[9] The principle of mutual recognition demands that if the issuing state considers that a certain offense in under a certain EAW label, the executing state cannot question such labeling according to its own criminal legislation. National diversity cannot be factored into the equation of the EAW. This has been seen as a problem with the EAW, and a reason to question its existence and strict enforcement.[10] However, given that the EAW is firmly established within the EU, it can also be used as an argument to, in turn, harmonize the substantive criminal law of EU Member States,[11] using the presence of one element of federal authority to justify another.

For over five years, the specifics of the EAW have been questioned before national courts, and, more importantly, before the ECJ. It is worth noting some crucial aspects of the debate, as it clearly shows a tendency to curtail Member States' discretion and to stretch the effects of the principle of mutual recognition. As has been argued a number of times throughout this work, the federal elements

---

7 In this sense, the discretionary governmental powers in extradition cases has been sometimes used in high profile cases in which the State was seeking interests other than cooperation with foreign nations.

8 This tendency has been relatively amended in more recent instruments of the principle of mutual recognition. As Samuli Miettinen, *Criminal Law and Policy in the European Union*, 2013 at 183 notes: "some late period framework decision also, unlike early instrument such as the EAW, offer Member States the opportunity to derogate and in effect reintroduce restrictions based on double criminality".

9 For a recent example, in Case C-399/11 *Melloni v. Ministerio Fiscal*, Judgment of 26 February 2013.

10 See Šugman Stubbs and Gorkič, *Abuse of the European Arrest Warrant System*, in N. Keijzer and E. van Sliedregt, eds., *The European Arrest Warrant in practice*, 2009 at 259–260.

11 See Chapter 4.

embedded in European criminal law clearly surface in certain legal instruments, such as the EAW.

The first major challenge before the European courts came in 2007 with the *Advocaten voor der Wereld* case.[12] The Belgian *Arbitragehof* (Arbitration Court) sought the guidance of the ECJ through a petition for a preliminary ruling in July 2005.[13] The Belgian court posed the following questions:

> "Is [the] Framework Decision ... compatible with Article 34(2)(b) of the [EU] Treaty, under which framework decisions may be adopted only for the purpose of approximation of the laws and regulations of the Member States?
>
> Is Article 2(2) of [the] Framework Decision ... in so far as it sets aside verification of the requirement of double criminality for the offences listed therein, compatible with Article 6(2) of the [EU] Treaty ... and, more specifically, with the principle of legality in criminal proceedings guaranteed by that provision and with the principle of equality and non-discrimination?"

Regarding the first issue, the ECJ denied that the EAW serves the purpose of approximating the law and regulations of the Member States, but rather of facilitating and accelerating judicial cooperation in relation to proceedings and the enforcement of decisions and of facilitating extradition between Member States.[14] Actually, the argument goes, the EAW presupposes that legislation in the various Member States is similar, i.e. "proximate". The key decision-making point here is whether the European Council has authority to use a certain legal instrument, namely the framework decision, to achieve such goals. The response from the ECJ was clear: it does.[15]

The second issue was even more important to the core principles of criminal law; the concern raised by the petitioner was that the list of offenses – more accurately, forms of criminality – is so vague and imprecise that it breaches, or at the very least is capable of breaching, the principle of legality in criminal matters. The ECJ acknowledged that the principle of the legality of criminal offenses and

---

12 Case C-303/05 *Advocaten voor de Wereld VZW v. Leden van de Ministerraad*, Judgment of 3 May 2007. See Florian Geyes, "Case Note", European Constitutional Law Review, 4 (2008) at 149–161. Ester Herlin-Karnell, *In the wake of Pupino: Advocaten voor der Wereld and Dell'Orto*, Germ. L.J. 8 (2007) at 1153. A further development in Ester Herlin-Karnell, *European Arrest Warrant Cases and the Principles of Non-discrimination and EU Citizenship*, Modern Law Review 73 (2010) at 824–835.

13 The relevance of the case was already noted because of the number of Member States that filed allegations in this proceeding before the ECJ: Poland, Finland, Netherlands, Lithuania, Latvia, France, Spain, the Czech Republic and the UK were parties to the proceedings in addition to Belgium, the European Commission and the European Parliament.

14 Case C-303/05 *Advocaten voor de Wereld VZW v. Leden van de Ministerraad*, Judgment of 3 May 2007 at § 31. More specifically, the ECJ notes "it is not the objective of the Framework Decision to harmonise the substantive criminal law of the Member States" (at 59).

15 Case C-303/05 *Advocaten voor de Wereld VZW v. Leden van de Ministerraad*, Judgment of 3 May 2007 at § 41.

penalties (*nullum crimen, nulla poena sine lege*) is one of the general legal principles stemming from the constitutional traditions common to the Member States and also a principle enshrined in Article 7 of the ECHR. Still, the ECJ considered that it is up to the Member States to verify that their national legislation conforms to the principle of legality. Moreover, each Member State must trust that other Member States are also producing legislation in accordance with the principle of legality.

From our perspective, two important conclusions follow from this ruling. First, the ECJ established that the EAW is not intended to harmonize or standardize national legislation; it is technically only a means to achieve the broader goal of judicial cooperation. Second, the ECJ refuses to subject the wording of the 32 "offenses categories" contained in the EAW Framework Decision to the principle of legality; instead, it imposes on other Member States the duty to trust each other on this front. These issues will come up again in our comparison with the US system.

More recently, the ECJ has addressed the difficult issue that arises when a national court sets certain limits on the ability of the national courts of another Member State to try a case and its relationship with the European Charter of Fundamental Rights.[16] In Case C-399/11, *Stefano Melloni v. Ministerio Fiscal*, decided on 26 February 2013, the ECJ reviewed the possibility of conditioning an EAW on a retrial of the case in the issuing state due to the fact that the defendant had been convicted *in absentia*. The issues presented to the ECJ concerned:

> "The interpretation and, if necessary, the validity of Article 4a(1) of Council Framework Decision 2002/584/JHA of 13 June 2002 on the European arrest warrant and the surrender procedures between Member States, as amended by Council Framework Decision 2009/299/JHA of 26 February 2009."

And:

> "Whether a Member State may refuse to execute a European arrest warrant on the basis of Article 53 of the Charter of Fundamental Rights of the European Union ('the Charter') on grounds of infringement of the fundamental rights of the person concerned guaranteed by the national constitution."

---

[16] See STEVE PEERS, *The European Arrest Warrant: The Dilemmas of Mutual Recognition, Human Rights and EU Citizenship*, in *The Court of Justice and the Construction of Europe: Analyses and Perspectives on Sixty Years of Case-law – La Cour de Justice et la Construction de l'Europe: Analyses et Perspectives de Soixante Ans de Jurisprudence*, 2013 at 523–538; LUISA MARIN, *Effective and Legitimate? Learning from the Lessons of 10 Years of Practice with the European Arrest Warrant*, NEW JOURNAL OF EUROPEAN CRIMINAL LAW 5 (2014) at 338 ("The issue of the balance between enforcement, i.e., execution of surrender, and guarantees is a source of continuous litigation", concluding that "[t]he problem of defence rights within the surrender procedure is and remains a weak point in the EAW system" (at 342)). SUOMINEN, *The Principle of Mutual Recognition in Cooperation in Criminal Matters*, 2011 at 88.

As to the first issue, the ECJ decided that the EAW Framework Decision must be interpreted to preclude judicial authorities, in the circumstances specified in that provision, from making the execution of an EAW issued for the purposes of executing a sentence conditional upon the *in absentia* conviction being open to review in the issuing Member State.[17] The ECJ also noted that this approach does not disregard either the right to an effective judicial remedy and to a fair trial or the rights of the defense guaranteed by Articles 47 and 48(2) of the Charter, respectively.[18]

As to the second issue, the ECJ first explains the underlying rationale of the Spanish Constitutional Court:

> "the interpretation envisaged by the national court at the outset is that Article 53 of the Charter gives general authorization to a Member State to apply the standard of protection of fundamental rights guaranteed by its constitution when that standard is higher than that deriving from the Charter and, where necessary, to give it priority over the application of provisions of EU law. Such an interpretation would, in particular, allow a Member State to make the execution of a European arrest warrant issued for the purposes of executing a sentence rendered in absentia subject to conditions intended to avoid an interpretation which restricts or adversely affects fundamental rights recognized by its constitution, even though the application of such conditions is not allowed under Article 4a(1) of Framework Decision 2002/584".[19]

However, the ECJ rejects such an interpretation with the following words:

> "Allowing a Member State to avail itself of Article 53 of the Charter to make the surrender of a person convicted in absentia conditional upon the conviction being open to review in the issuing Member State, a possibility not provided for under Framework Decision 2009/299, in order to avoid an adverse effect on the right to a fair trial and the rights of the defense guaranteed by the constitution of the executing Member State, by casting doubt on the uniformity of the standard of

---

17 The ECJ notes that the objective of the harmonization of the conditions of execution of European arrest warrants issued for the purposes of executing decisions rendered at the end of trials at which the person concerned has not appeared in person, effected by that framework decision, is to enhance the procedural rights of persons subject to criminal proceedings whilst improving mutual recognition of judicial decisions between Member States. Therefore, it seems clear that the ECJ is trying to achieve a fair balance between defendants' rights and effective judicial cooperation.

18 To achieve this result the ECJ noted that although the right of the accused to appear in person at his trial is an essential component of the right to a fair trial, that right is not absolute (see, *inter alia*, Case C-619/10 *Trade Agency*, 2012 ECR I-0000, paras. 52 and 55). Specifically it recalls that violation of the right to a fair trial has not been established by the ECtHR, even where the accused did not appear in person, if he was informed of the date and place of the trial or was defended by a legal counsellor to whom he had given a mandate to do so.

19 Ibid. at § 56.

> protection of fundamental rights as defined in that framework decision, would undermine the principles of mutual trust and recognition which that decision purports to uphold and would, therefore, compromise the efficacy of that framework decision."[20]

The *Melloni* case sets an importance precedent for the future: the principle of mutual recognition is paramount, even when confronted with issues of fundamental rights. The ECJ actually prevents national courts from establishing a higher standard than the one enthroned in the European legislation where such legislation is mandatory. In other words, when dealing with the enforcement of European legislation, the *Spielraum* of national courts is almost nonexistent. When executing an EAW, the national court must limit itself to the grounds provided by such instrument, and no deviation from the European standard is allowed. The significance of *Melloni* is discussed further below, but it clearly demonstrates a powerful federal authority within the EU, one which seemingly trumps even national, constitutional considerations of human rights.[21]

2.3. INTERSTATE RENDITION (US)

With the recent rise of this "federal" instrument in the EU, and the controversy around it, it is worth comparing the EAW with the US analogue: so-called interstate rendition, or interstate extradition, among US states. Interstate extradition in the US is a combined executive and judicial procedure; as noted above, the EAW moved from this model and has become only a judicial proceeding. In this sense, interstate extradition still depends to a great extent on the executive branches of both states involved. It is regulated in Article IV Section 2, clause 2 of the US Constitution, making it a federal law issue.

We have already discussed the greater direct or vertical federalism within the United States in the area of criminal law. The traditional understanding of direct federal interests has always granted a measure of criminal law authority to

---

20 Ibid. at § 63.

21 See Corri Longridge, *In Defence of Defence Rights: The Need for Common Rules of Criminal Procedure in the European Union*, European Journal of Legal Studies 13 (2013) at 138–155 (available at: www.ejls.eu/13/173UK.htm); Tony Marguery, *European Union Fundamental Rights and Member States Action in EU Criminal Law*, Maastricht Journal 20 (2013), at 282 concluding that "The Member States' policy on fundamental rights protection cannot take precedence over EU fundamental rights if it undermines the effectiveness of the European security policy, as illustrated in particular by the principle of mutual recognition" (at 287). For a general perspective Stefano Ruggeri, *Human Rights in European Criminal Law: New Developments in European Legislation and Case Law after the Lisbon Treaty*, 2015 at 139–145. Probably, the most pressing issue will relate to the compatibility of *Melloni* with the ECtHR case law. The final details of the EU accession to the ECHR will determine to a great extent whether the ECtHR or the ECJ has the final word in determining the enforceable scope of human rights across the EU.

the US federal government. Through interpretation of the Necessary and Proper Clause, grants of federal authority to control, in particular, interstate commerce have allowed virtually unfettered federal regulation of criminal activity. Unlike the traditional arrangement of the European Union, the United States government also has executive and judicial resources to directly enforce its criminal law mandates. On the other hand, judicial cooperation and mutual recognition have been the underlying principles which have driven EU "federalism", with the result being a much greater emphasis on horizontal federalism in Europe. Interstate rendition, however, exemplifies the horizontal dimension of federalism in the United States. It is found within Article IV of the Constitution, the so-called States' Relations Article,[22] which regulates interstate relationships within the US federal system. This article also contains the Full Faith and Credit Clause, discussed earlier in Chapter 1, as the closest American equivalent to EU judicial cooperation and mutual recognition. Similarly, interstate rendition is a crucial area for comparing criminal law federalism in the two systems.

The United States Constitution provides that any person charged with a crime in one state who flees and is found in another state "shall on demand of the executive authority of the state from which he fled, be delivered up, to be removed to the state having jurisdiction of the crime."[23] In addition to this constitutional standard for interstate extradition or rendition, there are federal laws which also deal with this issue. On the grounds of Article IV, the US Congress enacted a series of laws to address how to issue and execute extradition petitions over fugitives between American states, codified in § 3182, Title 18 of the United States Code.[24]

22 See e.g. *Baldwin v. Fish & Game Comm'n*, 436 U.S. 371, 378–79 (1978). To a certain extent States' relations are based on the doctrine of equality of the states (Section 3 of Article IV of the US Constitution). Because all states are equal "in power, dignity and authority" (*Coyle v. Smith*, 221 U. S. 559, 567 (1911)) they have the right to be treated as equals not only by the Union, but by sister states. Indeed, "the constitutional equality of the states is essential to the harmonious operation of the scheme upon which the Republic was organized" (at 580). Though the first angle, i.e. the right to be recognized as equal by the federal government, has been explored thoroughly (see lately the US Supreme Court decision in *Shelby County v. Holder*, 570 U.S. ___ (2013) in which the Supreme Court struck down the coverage formula of Section 5 of the Voting Rights Act, a civil rights law that protected the right to vote for people of color since 1965). The right to be treated as an equal by sister states, i.e. the horizontal federalism aspect, does not seem to have been reviewed with "equal" intensity. Again, the vertical federalism dimension is paramount in the American federal system.

23 U.S. Const. art. IV sec. 2 cl. 2.

24 "Whenever the executive authority of any State or Territory demands any person as a fugitive from justice, of the executive authority of any State, District, or Territory to which such person has fled, and produces a copy of an indictment found or an affidavit made before a magistrate of any State or Territory, charging the person demanded with having committed treason, felony, or other crime, certified as authentic by the governor or chief magistrate of the State or Territory from whence the person so charged has fled, the executive authority of the State, District, or Territory to which such person has fled shall cause him to be arrested and secured, and notify the executive authority making such demand, or the agent of such authority appointed to receive the fugitive, and shall cause the fugitive to be delivered to such agent when he shall appear. If no such agent appears within thirty days from the time of the arrest, the prisoner may be discharged."

Early development of extradition in the US was closely tied to the issue of slavery, and particularly fugitive slaves.[25] Although that issue, and the closely linked fugitive slave clause,[26] are obviously no longer relevant, it was a significant indication of the nature of the new American federalism. Cooperation agreements between the states had governed these issues prior to the current Constitution.[27] However, some slaveholding states were concerned that this provided insufficient protection against their "property" interests.[28] Thus, this outdated provision of the American Constitution, coupled with the interstate rendition clause, signaled a shift from comity between the states to a relationship based on federal compulsion.[29]

Beyond the interstate rendition clause, which sets the framework for federal authority in this area, Congress has been regulating extradition between the states since 1793.[30] In 1842, the Supreme Court determined that the authority to regulate this are of law rested exclusively with the federal government, overturning state laws which touched on the issue.[31] Despite this show of federal authority, the case also held that the federal government could not actually compel state action on the issue.[32] This concept was reiterated in the main case dealing with rendition for over a century, *Kentucky v. Dennison*.[33] In that case, Kentucky sought extradition of a free black man who was accused of enticing a slave to run away from her owner.[34] In refusing to force the extradition of this person, the court found that the interstate rendition clause was "declaratory of … [a] moral duty" but that

---

25 See Christopher N. Lasch, *Rendition Resistance*, 92 N.C. L. Rev. 149 (2013) with abundant reference to case law and scholarship.

26 U.S. Const. art. IV sec. 2 cl. 3.

27 Christopher N. Lasch, *Rendition Resistance*, 92 N.C. L. Rev. 149 (2013).

28 For instance, James Madison noted, in regards to the new fugitive slave clause, "This is a better security than now exists. … [A]t present, if any slave elopes in any of those states where slaves are free, he becomes emancipated by their laws; for the laws of the States are uncharitable to one another in this respect …" Paul Finkelman, *An Imperfect Union: Slavery, Federalism, and Comity,* 1981 at 27 (quoting the Debates in the Several State Conventions on the Adoption of the Federal Constitution as Recommended by the General Convention at Philadelphia, in 1787, at 453 (Jonathan Elliot ed., Philadelphia, J.B. Lippincott Co., 2nd ed. 1896)); Robert M. Cover, *Justice Accused: Antislavery and the Judicial Process,* 1975 at 88 (noting that norms of "international" law at the time would not lead to recognition of slave ownership in non-slaveholding states).

29 Christopher N. Lasch, *Rendition Resistance*, 92 N.C. L. Rev. 149 (2013).

30 The Extradition Act of 1793, 1 Stat. 302 (1793).

31 *Prigg v. Pennsylvania*, 41 U.S. 549 (1842).

32 Ibid. at 630 (Taney, C.J., concurring) ("The state officers mentioned in the law are not bound to execute the duties imposed upon them by Congress, unless they choose to do so, or are required to do so by a law of the state; and the state legislature has the power, if it thinks proper, to prohibit them. The act of 1793, therefore, must depend altogether for its execution upon the officers of the United States named in it"); see Paul Finkelman, *Sorting out Prigg v. Pennsylvania*, Rutgers L.J. 24 (1993), at 646–647 (summarizing Justice Story's view that the federal government could not compel state officials to act).

33 *Kentucky v. Dennison*, 65 U.S. 66 (1860), overruled by *Puerto Rico v. Branstad*, 483 U.S. 219 (1987).

34 *Dennison*, 65 U.S. 66 (1860) at 67.

"the Federal Government, under the Constitution, has no power to impose on a State officer, as such, any duty whatever, and compel him to perform it."[35] This was a powerful reflection of the strong view of state sovereignty prevailing at the time; the Court resisted an interpretation which "would place every State under the control and dominion of the General government, even in the administration of its internal concerns."[36] The concept of dual sovereignty of state and federal governments, each with its own independent purview, meant that the federal government had the power to *authorize* the performance of the duty of rendition by statute, but no power to enforce it.

As a result of this interpretation, the next significant moves in establishing interstate rendition procedures came from the states themselves. In 1916, the Court reversed its earlier decision on federal exclusivity, determining that congressional regulation of interstate rendition in fact left room for additional state regulation of the matter.[37] The Uniform Criminal Extradition Act (UCEA) was drafted in 1926 (amended again in 1936) in order to provide a state law framework for extradition.[38] The UCEA, operating within the limits set by the Constitution and federal law, served to expedite interstate rendition with standardized procedures.[39] The lack of an effective enforcement mechanism at the federal level required what was essentially again a relationship of comity between the states, although one eventually codified and compelled by uniform laws. Since passage of the UCEA, the Uniform Extradition and Rendition Act was approved in 1980, although it has not been as widely adopted as the UCEA.[40]

In 1987, there was once again a shift in the approach to interstate extradition from the Supreme Court. *Puerto Rico v. Branstad*[41] overruled the earlier *Dennison* decision and found that federal courts did have the authority to enforce the constitutional duties set out by the extradition clause. In *Branstad*, a man, Ronald Calder, was charged with murder based on an automobile accident in Puerto Rico; however, he had fled to Iowa while on bail, where the governor refused to extradite him.[42] Discussing the importance of interstate cooperation to the national unity of the United States, the Court reaffirmed the holding of *Dennison* that "the commands of the Extradition Clause are mandatory, and afford no discretion to the executive officers or courts of the asylum State."[43]

The change represented by *Branstad* was a conclusion that this duty was in fact enforceable by federal courts. Noting that the years since *Dennison* had seen an expansion of federal power, including the power to enjoin unconstitutional

35 Ibid. at 107.
36 Ibid.
37 *Innes v. Tobin*, 240 U.S. 127 (1916).
38 Uniform Criminal Extradition Act, reprinted in 11 Uniform Laws Annotated 51 (1974).
39 31A Am. Jur. 2d Extradition § 11.
40 31A Am. Jur. 2d Extradition § 10.
41 483 U.S. 219 (1987).
42 Ibid. at 222.
43 Ibid. at 227.

action by state officials, there was "no justification for distinguishing the duty to deliver fugitives from the many other species of constitutional duty enforceable in the federal courts."[44] Crucial for our comparison of federal systems, the court declared that "[t]he fundamental premise of the holding in *Dennison* – 'that the States and the Federal Government in all circumstances must be viewed as coequal sovereigns – is not representative of the law today.'"[45]

On the other hand, states are able to enact legislation which allows extradition under less rigorous standards than those of the Constitution or federal law.[46] Furthermore, it is obviously cumbersome to require intervention of federal courts in order to obtain an order of rendition. Thus the UCEA and other state laws dealing with the extradition of those accused of crimes continue to play a major role in the day-to-day implementation of interstate rendition.

2.4. COMPARISON

The resemblances between the EAW and interstate extradition are clear. What is more, they both deal with important issues of federalism. As noted above, extradition generally has been dealt with through treaties between countries; as such, any limits on sovereignty of the states involved are self-imposed. Both the EAW and the American system of interstate rendition, on the other hand, are mandated above the state/State level, and represent a complete derogation of state sovereignty. The similar evolution of this issue in the two systems points to the truly federal nature of the EU.

It is interesting to note how the US evolution was closely linked to the slavery issue and the EU development was extremely tied to the terrorism issue. National courts tried to eschew the federal duty to provide full cooperation with other Sister States (US)/Member States (EU). Yet, in the end, the US Supreme Court (*Branstad*) and the ECJ (*Melloni*) rejected the states' reluctance to provide full cooperation. Interestingly enough, the US system of interstate rendition seems to provide greater safeguards than the EU system of the EAW. This is consistent with our basic premise: the EU shows a greater degree of horizontal federalism than the US.

Both the EU and the US began from a fairly similar starting point, with extradition (or rendition in the US case) as a relationship of comity between two sovereigns. Although the US Constitution contains an unambiguous command of mandatory extradition among the states, the reality after *Dennison* of a duty without enforceability was no different than the relationship between sovereign nations. However, both the EU and the US would ultimately find the exercise of

44 Ibid. at 228.

45 Ibid. at 227–228 (quoting *FERC v. Mississippi*, 456 U.S. 742, 761 (1982)).

46 31 Am. Jur. 2d Extradition § 9 (2014) (citing *People ex rel. Dimas v. Shimp*, 83 Ill. App. 3d 150, 403 N.E.2d 750 (2d Dist. 1980)).

unchecked discretion at the state level to threaten the unity of their overarching system. The EU, with its emphasis on mutual recognition, obviously utilized the EAW to advance this aim, giving true recognition to "foreign" criminal courts within the EU. The rejection of the dual criminality principle and the limits placed on even fundamental rights protection in *Melloni*[47] force the conclusion that this is truly about federal authority. Similarly, the discretionary relationship that existed in the US under *Dennison* was finally swept away and replaced by federal coercion under *Branstad*. The US Supreme Court acknowledged that the true aim of interstate rendition is to preserve federal unity, and thus there is no room for individual discretion within the states. At this point, acknowledging that the US system of interstate rendition is clearly based on federalism, the fact that the EU, through the EAW, has arrived at the exact same state of law again proves its federal nature.

3. DOUBLE JEOPARDY

3.1. INTRODUCTION

Another question of interstate criminal law federalism arises in reference to repeat punishment of the same crimes, covered by the rules on double jeopardy or *ne bis in idem*. The prohibition against double jeopardy is common to basically every system of criminal law. However, examining the way federal systems deal with this fundamental principle brings an opportunity to realize how much federalism the EU system has already achieved. While all the national systems in Europe and also the United States forbid repeat punishment of the same crime in some way, traditionally the rulings from one sovereign state are not necessarily binding on others. A federal government, therefore, has an interesting question to answer: what is the effect within a union of sovereign entities when one State has already adjudicated a particular crime? A comparison of Europe and the United States yields a telling result. Contrary to what the lack-of-EU-federalism logic would prescribe, national rulings within the European Union are binding on other EU Member States. On the contrary, the admittedly federal US system does not follow the same principles; therefore, acquittals (or even possibly convictions) at the federal or at state level do not preempt prosecutions and convictions in other states.

As we shall see, the European development of the double jeopardy principle – termed *ne bis in idem* in Europe – has resulted in the binding nature of national rulings to other Member States. Probably surprising to American practitioners, the European double jeopardy prohibition applies even to cases dismissed by the

---

[47] Case C-399/11 *Melloni v. Ministerio Fiscal*, Judgment of 26 February 2013, is also discussed below in regards to fundamental rights to due process, in Chapter 4.

prosecutors without any court involvement, and to cases in which the acquittal is obtained due to a lack of evidence. Also, when the dismissal is obtained due to the statute of limitations in a certain Member States, the ruling is with prejudice to other Member States. In turn, it may be surprising to Europeans to learn that the dual sovereignty doctrine in the United States means that federal and state rulings are not binding in terms of double jeopardy for other states or federal prosecutors; in theory, one could be tried for the same crime independently by all fifty states and the federal government (although there are other, non-constitutional limits to avoid such an absurd result).

Again, in this section we will not conduct a thorough review of both institutions, i.e. Article 54 CISA (EU) and dual sovereignty doctrine (US), but only highlight certain elements and evolution that reassert the federal (horizontal) dimension of EU criminal law when compared with US federal criminal law.

3.2. ARTICLE 54 SCHENGEN AGREEMENT AND *NE BIS IN IDEM* (EU)

At the European level, the most important provision dealing with multiple prosecutions is embedded in the Schengen Agreement.[48] Given that the main goal of this international agreement was to create a Europe's borderless area, it was probably not intended initially to provide the cornerstone for transnational *ne bis in idem*. Although it took some time to develop fully, the current state of affairs mandates that once a person is tried in one European Member State, she cannot be tried for the same facts in another Member State – regardless of the applicable legislation. The bedrock principle against which this principle is enshrined is the free movement of persons.[49]

Article 54 contains the following language:

> "A person whose trial has been finally disposed of in one Contracting Party may not be prosecuted in another Contracting Party for the same acts provided that, if a penalty has been imposed, it has been enforced, is actually in the process of

[48] Schengen Agreement of 14 June 1985 between the Governments of the States of the Benelux Economic Union, the Federal Republic of Germany and the French Republic on the gradual abolition of check sat their common borders, signed on 19 June 1990 at Schengen. For an initial overview see WASMEIER and THWAITES, *The Development of ne bis in idem into a Transnational Fundamental Right in EU Law: Comment of Recent Developments*, EUROPEAN LAW REVIEW 31 (2006), 565–578; JOHN VERVAELE, *The transnational ne bis in idem principle in the EU. Mutual recognition and equivalent protection of human rights*, UTRECHT LAW REVIEW 1 (2005) at 100. For an in-depth analysis see Bas VAN BOCKEL, *The Ne Bis in Idem Principle in EU Law, 2010; Christine Janssens, The Principle of Mutual Recognition in EU Law*, 2013. A more recent account in JOHN VERVAELE, *Ne Bis In Idem: Towards a Transnational Constitutional Principle in the EU?*, UTRECHT LAW REVIEW 9 (2013) at 211.

[49] See VALSAMIS MITSILEGAS, *EU Criminal Law*, 2009, at 147–153.

being enforced or can no longer be enforced under the laws of the sentencing Contracting Party."

The groundbreaking[50] case for the development of the transnational *ne bis in idem* principle was the joined cases *Gözütok* and *Brügge*.[51] Here, the ECJ noted that the *ne bis in idem* principle, laid down in Article 54 of the Schengen Convention, also applies to dismissal rulings, that is procedures where by further prosecution is barred. In other words, prejudice attaches to cases in which the Public Prosecutor of a Member State discontinues or dismisses criminal proceedings brought in that State, even without the involvement of a court. That particular instance involved a special provision of the German Code of Criminal Procedure by which proceedings are dismissed once the accused has fulfilled certain obligations and, in particular, has paid a certain sum of money determined by the Public Prosecutor.

A couple of years later, the ECJ produced another ruling on the applicability of Article 54. In the *Miraglia*[52] case, the Court noted that the purpose of this provision is to ensure that no one is prosecuted on the same facts in several Member States on account having exercised his right to *freedom of movement*. In this sense, the ECJ laid down some of the cornerstones for future development. Yet the Court held that Article 54 does not apply to cases in which the dismissal or stay of the proceedings does not contain a determination of the merits of the case.[53] Therefore, according to the ECJ, this does not constitute a final decision within the meaning of Article 54. In other words, *the merits of the ruling closing the case are fundamental to the attachment of prejudice.*

In 2006, the ECJ again dealt with Article 54, showing an increasing concern with the application of this principle. In *Van Esbroeck*,[54] the Court dealt with proceedings in Member States that joined the Convention after the person was

---

50 Christine Janssens, *The Principle of Mutual Recognition in EU Law*, 2013 at 133. In *Gözütok:* "The ECJ rather radically and audaciously introduced the duty of mutual recognition of criminal law decisions in the area of freedom, security and justice, with a strong focus on the law of the member states in which the criminal proceedings were initiated".

51 Joined Cases C-187/01 and C-385/01 *Gözütok and Brügge*, Judgment of 11 February 2003. See Nadine Thwaites, *Mutual Trust in Criminal Matters: the European Court of Justice gives a first interpretation of a provision of the Convention implementing the Schengen Agreement*, German Law Journal 4 (2003) at 253. Norel Neagu, *The Ne Bis in Idem Principle in the Case-Law of the European Court of Justice (II). The Final Judgment and Enforcement Issues*, LESIJ No. XIX, Vol. 2/2012, at 67. Maria Fletcher, *Some Developments to the ne bis in idem Principle in the European Union: Criminal Proceedings Against Hüseyin Gözütok and Klaus Brügge*, Modern Law Review 66 (2003) at 769–780.

52 Case C-469/03 *Miraglia*, Judgment of 10 March 2005. See Bas van Bockel, *The Ne Bis in Idem Principle in EU Law*, 2010 at 131, 157–159.

53 Christine Janssens, *The Principle of Mutual Recognition in EU Law*, 2013 at 134: no double jeopardy is attached where a "judicial authority had closed proceedings without any assessment of the unlawful conduct with which the defendant had been charged."

54 Case C-436/04 *Van Esbroeck*, Judgment of 9 March 2006. Steve Peers, *EU Justice and Home Affairs Law*, 2011, at 839 assigns this great the relevance of initiating a new line of jurisprudence.

convicted. Double jeopardy's effect of Article 54 CISA attaches even though the Convention was not yet in force in the latter state at the time at which that person was convicted. The key issue was whether the Convention was in force in the relevant Contracting States when the assessment of the applicability of the *ne bis in idem* principle took place in the second state.

Yet the most important issue addressed in *Van Esbroeck* was the definition of the term "offence" included in Article 54.[55] According to the Court, for the purposes of the application of that article, it refers to the "material acts", understood as the existence of a set of facts which are inextricably linked together, irrespective of the legal classification given to them or the legal interest protected. Thus, it is not relevant whether the definitions of the offense coincide in both Member States.[56] The application of Article 54 CISA is not made conditional upon harmonization, or even approximation, of the criminal laws of the Member States. The *ne bis in idem* principle thus necessarily implies that the Contracting States have mutual trust in their criminal justice systems; since there is no harmonization of national criminal laws required, each state must recognize the criminal law in force in the others, even when the outcome would be different if its own national law were applied.

That same year, the ECJ delivered another decisive judgment concerning Article 54 CISA. In *Van Straaten et al*,[57] the Court reinforced the basic principle of transnational *ne bis in idem*, i.e. exercise of the right to freedom of movement,[58] and established that double jeopardy effect attaches to cases in which the accused is finally acquitted due to lack of evidence. The key here is a somewhat grammatical interpretation: the main clause of the single sentence comprising Article 54 CISA makes no reference to the content of the judgment that has become final. It is only in the subordinate clause that Article 54 refers to the case of a conviction by stating that, in that situation, the prohibition of further prosecution is subject to a specific condition. The ECJ reasoned that these conditions would be superfluous if the general rule only applied to convictions. Finally, the Court also introduced two further principles that are to be considered in this type of cases: the principle of legal certainty and of the protection of legitimate expectations. The accused

---

55 Bas van Bockel, *The Ne Bis in Idem Principle in EU Law*, 2010 at 161–163, 231–232. According to Van Bockel "the criteria according to which the Community Courts approach a finding of *idem* in competition cases is considerably less clear and precise than those laid down by the ECJ in *Van Esbroeck*".

56 Christine Janssens, *The Principle of Mutual Recognition in EU Law*, 2013 at 137 ("a factual interpretation of idem (the facts are identical) was to be preferred over an interpretation based on the legal qualification (the legal provisions are identical) and over an interpretation based on the protected legal interest"). For some European traditions, the irrelevance of the so-called protected legal interest (*Rechtsgut*) did come as a surprise. Yet, from a problem-solving approach, it seems to have been a more pragmatic decision.

57 Case C-150/05 *Van Straaten and others*, Judgment of 28 September 2006.

58 The ECJ noted that not applying Article 54 of the Convention to a final decision acquitting the accused for lack of evidence would jeopardize the exercise of the right to freedom of movement.

would have to fear a fresh prosecution in another Contracting State despite a final resolution in a case dealing with the same acts.[59]

The *Gasparini* case,[60] also from 2006, noted that the *ne bis in idem* principle applies to a decision of a court of a Contracting State, made after criminal proceedings have been brought, by which the accused is acquitted finally because prosecution of the offense is time-barred.[61] According to the Court, not applying Article 54 where the accused is finally acquitted because prosecution for the offense is time-barred would again undermine the objective to ensure that no one is prosecuted for the same acts in several Contracting States on account of the exercise of the right to freedom of movement. Therefore, such case is regarded as having been finally disposed of for the purposes of that provision.[62] Needless to say, as the ECJ notes, Article 54 does not apply to persons other than those whose trial has been finally disposed of in a Contracting State. Finally, the Court reinforced its interpretation of the term "same acts"; it noted that the only relevant criterion for applying the concept of "the same acts" within the meaning of Article 54 CISA is identity of the material acts, understood as the existence of a set of concrete circumstances which are inextricably linked together. However, the definitive assessment in this regard is a matter for the competent national courts which are charged with the task of determining whether the material acts at issue constitute a set of facts which are inextricably linked together in time, in space, and by their subject matter.

In the 2007 *Kretzinger* case,[63] the Court summarized its previous findings concerning Article 54.[64] First, the relevant criterion for the purposes of the application of that article is identity of the material acts, understood as the existence of a set of facts which are inextricably linked together, irrespective of the legal classification given to them or the legal interest protected. Second, for the purposes of Article 54, a penalty imposed by a court of a Contracting

[59] In other words, an acquittal for lack of evidence cannot be treated as a decision without any determination whatsoever of the merits of the case (Bas van Bockel, *The Ne Bis in Idem Principle in EU Law*, 2010 at 159).

[60] Case C-467/04 *Gasparini and others*, Judgment of 28 September 2006.

[61] As Valsamis Mitsilegas, *EU Criminal Law*, 2009 at 152 notes the content and framing of the questions in *Gasparini* shows the difficulties in precisely defining the concept of *ne bis in idem*.

[62] The ECJ was aware of the different statutes of limitation in various Member States. Responding to this issue it noted that it is true that the laws of the Contracting States on limitation periods have not been harmonized. However, nowhere in Title VI of the EU Treaty, relating to police and judicial cooperation in criminal matters, or in the Schengen Agreement or the Convention implementing the latter is the application of Article 54 made conditional upon harmonization, or at the least approximation, of the criminal laws of the Member States relating to procedures whereby further prosecution is barred or, more generally, upon harmonization or approximation of their criminal laws.

[63] Case C-288/05 *Kretzinger*, Judgment 18 July 2007.

[64] Christine Janssens, *The Principle of Mutual Recognition in EU Law*, 2013 at 139 considers that "[i]n refusing to qualify the short length of time a suspect is in police custody and/or being held on remand pending trial as a penalty that has been enforced or is actually in the process of being enforced the ECJ wisely acknowledged that the ne bis in idem principle should not be taken to reckless extremes".

State "has been enforced" or is "actually in the process of being enforced" if the defendant has been given a suspended custodial sentence. That penalty must be regarded as "actually in the process of being enforced" as soon as the sentence has become enforceable and during the probation period. Once the probationary period comes to an end, the penalty must be regarded as "having been enforced" within the meaning of that provision. Third, a penalty imposed by a court of a Contracting State is not to be regarded as "having been enforced" or "actually in the process of being enforced" where the defendant was briefly taken into police custody and/or held on remand pending trial, even if that detention would count towards any subsequent enforcement of the custodial sentence under the law of the State in which judgment was given. The purpose of detention on remand is very different from that underlying the enforcement condition laid down in Article 54 of the CISA.

2007 was another productive year in terms of Article 54 case law, as the ECJ addressed another substantial case: *Kraaijenbrink*.[65] After reinforcing the established case law on the irrelevance of the legal classification given to the set of facts or the "legal interest" protected by national law provisions, the ECJ determined that it was up to the national court to assess whether the degree of identity and connection between all the facts to be compared is such that they should be considered "the same acts" within the meaning of Article 54. The national court may consider that the facts in their proceedings are not identical to those that constituted the basis of a criminal proceeding in another Member State, even if the national court accounts for penalties imposed in the first set of proceedings when determining the sentence.

In *Bourquain*,[66] the ECJ addressed a delicate matter: the double jeopardy effect attached to in absentia judgments. According the Court, the sole fact that the proceedings in absentia would necessitate reopening proceedings under the national law of the second state does not, in itself, mean that a conviction in absentia cannot be regarded as a final decision within the meaning of Article 54 CISA. Rather, the condition of enforcement is satisfied when it is established that, at the time when the second criminal proceedings over the same act were instituted, the penalty imposed in that first state can no longer be enforced according to the laws of that state.

Thus far, the ECJ had examined cases involving decisions made by judicial or prosecutorial authorities. However, many investigations in EU countries are conducted initially by the police. In a 2008 case, the ECJ addressed the potential binding nature of police decisions to suspend the investigation. In *Turansky*,[67] the Court considered that Article 54 does not apply to decisions suspending criminal proceedings based on the merits of the case *at a stage before the charging of a*

65 Case C-367/05 *Kraaijenbrink*, Judgment of 18 July 2007.

66 Case C-297/07 *Bourquain*, Judgment of 11 December 2008.

67 Case C-491/07 *Turansky*, Judgment of 22 December 2008.

person suspected of a crime, where the suspension decision does not, under the national law of that state, definitively bar further prosecution and therefore does not preclude new criminal proceedings in that state. Therefore, where a police decision suspends criminal proceedings but does not definitively bring the prosecution to an end, the case cannot be considered "finally disposed of".

Finally, in *Mantello*,[68] the ECJ thoroughly addressed the issue of the interpretation of the identity of facts in the specific context of the European Arrest Warrant. First, it noted that the concept of "same facts" contained in the European legislation regulating the EAW is an "autonomous concept of European Union law". Second, following this logic, the Court considered that when a national court authority issuing an EAW expressly states that the earlier judgment delivered under its legal system does not constitute a final judgment covering the acts referred to in warrant and therefore does not preclude the criminal proceedings referred to in that arrest warrant, the executing judicial authority has no reason to apply the ground for mandatory non-execution provided for in Article 3(2) of the Framework Decision.

3.3. DOUBLE JEOPARDY AND THE DUAL SOVEREIGNTY DOCTRINE (US)

In the US system, the double jeopardy clause is contained in the sacrosanct Fifth Amendment, which states that no person "shall ... be subject for the same offence to be twice put in jeopardy of life or limb."[69] Through the incorporation doctrine of the Fourteenth Amendment, this provision became applicable to the states.[70] From a constitutional standpoint, the double jeopardy clause provides three constitutional protections.[71] First, it protects the citizenry against a second prosecution for the same offense after acquittal. In some cases, this prohibition may even apply after certain forms of dismissals, although usually not unless based on the merits of the case.[72] As a consequence, acquittal verdicts cannot be appealed to a higher court. Equally important is protection against a second prosecution after conviction. Third, double jeopardy protects against multiple punishments for the same offense. Crucially important for white-collar litigation, embodied in the prohibition of double jeopardy is the doctrine of collateral estoppel.[73] Thus, issues which have been necessarily adjudicated in an earlier

---

68 Case 261/09 *Mantello*, Judgment of 16 November 2010.

69 U.S. Const amend. V.

70 For more on incorporation, see Chapter 4.

71 *North Carolina v. Pearce*, 395 U.S. 711, 717 (1969).

72 For a greater examination of this issue, which is beyond the scope of this work, see Scott J. Atlas, *Comment, Double Jeopardy and Government Appeals of Criminal Dismissals*, Tex. L. Rev. 52 (1974) at 303.

73 See e.g. *Ashe v. Swenson*, 392 U.S. 436, 443–44 (1970).

criminal prosecution cannot, in some instances, be revisited in later litigation at least between the same two parties.[74]

Jeopardy is said to "attach" "when a jury is empaneled and sworn, or, in a bench trial, when the court begins to hear evidence".[75] Thus, after this point, a defendant may raise double jeopardy as a bar to prosecution. Prior to the empaneling of a jury or hearing of evidence, there is no constitutional bar to retrying a case. Unlike the European system, there is no application of double jeopardy to situations prior to an actual hearing.

The protections afforded by the double jeopardy clause in the US system are only implicated in the crimes themselves, not the conduct. Therefore, a person may be tried multiple times for multiple crimes that are derived the same conduct (within the limits of the aforementioned collateral estoppel doctrine). The focus for US double jeopardy is the statute defining the crime and the elements which much be proven for a conviction. The test for determining whether double jeopardy is applicable to two different charges is whether *each* crime requires proof of an element which the other one does not,[76] referred to as the Blockburger test. As an example, a trial for murder where a person burns down a home resulting in the death of its occupant would not prevent another trial for arson. Murder would require the proof of death of a person, not present in arson, and arson would require proof that a fire were set, not necessary for murder. On the other hand, lesser-included offenses would be excluded by the Blockburger test. A law which punished aggravated arson by adding an element of death *would* be the "same offense" as regular arson for double jeopardy purposes, because only one crime required proof of an element not present in the other.

Collateral estoppel can provide some additional protection against multiple trials for the same conduct where the relitigation of underlying facts is necessary, given the specifics of the trial.[77] However, since juries do not reveal the specifics of their determination, it is frequently no more than a restatement of the Blockburger test, where the final judgment of one case is a required element of proof in another (thus has no additional element).[78]

---

74 Ibid.

75 *Serfass v. United States*, 420 U.S. 377, 378 (1975).

76 *Blockburger v. United States*, 284 U.S. 299, 304 (1932).

77 As the Supreme Court said in *Ashe v. Swenson*, the court must apply collateral estoppel "with realism and rationality" which "requires a court to 'examine the record of a prior proceeding, taking into account the pleadings, evidence, charge, and other relevant matter, and conclude whether a rational jury could have grounded its verdict upon an issue other than that which the defendant seeks to foreclose from consideration.'" 397 U.S. at 444 (quoting DANIEL K. MAYERS and FLETCHER L. YARBROUGH, *Bix Vexari: New Trials and Successive Prosecutions*, HARV. L. REV. 1, 74 (1960) at 38–39).

78 For instance, the Second Circuit Court of Appeals noted that "Since it is usually impossible to determine with any precision upon what basis the jury reached a verdict in a criminal case, it is a rare situation in which the collateral estoppel defense will be available to a defendant." *United States v. Tramunti*, 500 F.2d 1334, 1346 (2d Cir. 1974).

Until 1969, the double jeopardy clause was only applicable to the federal government, and therefore only to federal criminal laws.[79] The discussion of incorporation, below, further examines the process by which fundamental rights from the Bill of Rights were applied to the states; suffice to say here that the Supreme Court in 1937 did not find that double jeopardy would "violate those 'fundamental principles of liberty and justice which lie at the base of all our civil and political institutions'".[80] Eventually, the Court reversed its position, and in 1969, the double jeopardy clause was at last incorporated in the states in the case of *Benton v. Maryland*.[81] At this time, the Court still dealt with the question of two criminal charges or punishments being brought within the same system. Thus a state could not itself convict a defendant for a crime already tried by that state, or two state crimes as defined in the *Blockburger* case. However, the question of whether two states could try a person for the same crime within their respective jurisdictions was left open. The resolution of this question would eventually be resolved by application of the dual sovereignty doctrine.

These issues of double jeopardy are easy enough to apply when the same governmental body is seeking re-prosecution. But what happens when the federal government acquits or convicts a defendant, or when one particular state does so? What is the effect of this decision for other governmental bodies, state or federal, which were not involved in the original proceeding? The doctrine of dual sovereignty developed by the US Supreme Court[82] answers these questions by distinguishing between different sovereigns exercising *ius puniendi* and determining, therefore, that one is not confined by the act of another. In a nutshell, "an act denounced as a crime by both national and state sovereignties is an offense against the peace and dignity of both and may be prosecuted and punished by both."[83] Thus, it is permissible for a distinct sovereign entity – state or federal – to prosecute the same defendant after an earlier prosecution for the same conduct.

The dual sovereignty doctrine was formulated in 1922, when double jeopardy was still held applicable only to the federal government. In the case of *U.S. v. Lanza*,[84] the defendants were initially prosecuted in Washington state court for violation of its Prohibition statute. When later charges were brought under the federal Prohibition statute (the Volstead Act), defendants complained that this was a subsequent prosecution for the same act, that is, the possession, manufacture and transportation of alcohol. Although the lower court agreed, the Supreme Court reversed and rejected the argument that prosecution by the states

---

79 *Palko v. Connecticut*, 319 U.S. 322 (1937) (finding double jeopardy was not fundamental to systems of justice).

80 Ibid. at 328 (quoting *Hebert v. Louisiana*).

81 395 U.S. 784 (1969).

82 *United States v. Lanza*, 260 U.S. 377 (1922). Prosecutions under laws of separate sovereigns are prosecutions of different offenses, not re-prosecutions of the "same offense".

83 *United States v. Lanza*; *Heath v. Alabama*.

84 260 U.S. 377 (1922).

does not preclude federal prosecution for the same acts. In his opinion, Chief Justice William Taft wrote:

> "We have here two sovereignties, deriving power from different sources, capable of dealing with the same subject matter within the same territory. Each may, without interference by the other, enact laws to secure prohibition, with the limitation that no legislation can give validity to acts prohibited by the amendment. Each government in determining what shall be an offense against its peace and dignity is exercising its own sovereignty, not that of the other. It follows that an act denounced as a crime by both national and state sovereignties is an offense against the peace and dignity of both and may be punished by each."[85]

Thus, the American double jeopardy prohibition was one based on the source of the criminal law itself, rather than the actual acts for which a defendant was charged. Because of the American federalism established by the Tenth Amendment, the criminal law of the states was included as a sovereign power left to the states, rather than a grant under broader federal authority. The federal statute, on the other hand, was derived from the Eighteenth Amendment.[86] Thus two prosecutions for the same conduct were allowable, because they were offenses against separate sovereigns.

Subsequent decisions clarified the effect of dual sovereignty on the states, after the incorporation process applied the same Fifth Amendment restrictions beyond the federal government. Crimes created under local government authority were found to "spring from the same organic law that created the state court of general jurisdiction."[87] Since municipalities were themselves creatures of state law, so too were their statutes; since these statutes stemmed from the same source of sovereignty, the dual sovereignty doctrine did not apply. Most importantly for our discussion, this decision highlights the importance of federalism in considering the US double jeopardy doctrine. It is precisely because states are not mere subsets of the US federal government that double jeopardy, while applicable within the states, does not apply to criminal proceedings outside of their jurisdiction. These states retained portions of their sovereignty even with the formation of the United States, a concept emphasized in the related case of *United States v. Wheeler*,[88] which found that trials in Indian tribal courts did not preclude later federal charges, even under the same statute. The decisions of *Waller* and *Wheeler*, while not explicitly settling the issue of double jeopardy's application between states, did underscore the rationale in determining whether the dual sovereignty doctrine applies, and contributed to the resolution of the interstate prosecution question.

85 Ibid. at 382.
86 Ibid. at 381–382.
87 *Waller v. Florida*, 397 U.S. 387.
88 *United States v. Wheeler*, 435 U.S. 313 (1978).

Heath v. Alabama,[89] following the reasoning laid out in *Wheeler*, extended the dual sovereignty doctrine to interstate prosecutions. In *Heath*, the defendant had been convicted in Georgia, after which he was similarly convicted in Alabama. In its opinion, the Court stated the foundation of the dual sovereignty clause was "the common conception of crime as an offense against the sovereignty of the government."[90] In their determination of whether sovereigns are separate, the Court noted that the inquiry turned on "whether the two entities draw their authority to punish the offender from distinct sources of power."[91] This distinction is essential to the dual sovereignty doctrine, as the relation between sovereigns does not bear any relation to the resolution of whether successive prosecutions are permitted. While the relationship may be useful in defining the scope of authority, ultimately the source of that authority is the determining factor. Because American states are viewed as retaining their own sovereignty independent of the federal government, their laws serve to protect separate sovereign interests. The US Supreme Court found that "[a] State's interest in vindicating its sovereign authority through enforcement of its laws by definition can never be satisfied by another State's enforcement of its own laws."[92]

Despite the ability of the federal government to try defendants already convicted in state court, there are some "soft limits". For instance, federal prosecutors follow several guidelines which determine whether or not a prosecution for actions already heard in other courts will be pursued. These guidelines are stated in § 9 – 2031 of the United States Attorneys Manual. The "Petite Policy", so named for the case from which it arose, *Petite v. United States*,[93] states:

> "This policy precludes the initiation or continuation of a federal prosecution, following a prior state or federal prosecution based on substantially the same act(s) or transaction(s) unless three substantive prerequisites are satisfied: first, the matter must involve a substantial federal interest; second, the prior prosecution must have left that interest demonstrably unvindicated; and third, applying the same test that is applicable to all federal prosecutions, the government must believe that the defendant's conduct constitutes a federal offense, and that the admissible evidence probably will be sufficient to obtain and sustain a conviction by an unbiased trier of fact."

Upon these prerequisites being satisfied, subsequent federal prosecution is only permitted once it has been so approved by the US Attorney-General. Federal prosecutors have shown themselves willing to pursue subsequent prosecutions

89 *Heath v. Alabama*, 474 U.S. 82 (1985).
90 Ibid. at 88.
91 Ibid. at 88.
92 Ibid. at 93.
93 *Petite v. United States*, 361 U.S. 529 (1960).

in particular cases following acquittals in state courts, as demonstrated during the civil rights era and in the case of the four Los Angeles Police Department officers who beat Rodney King. Though acquitted in California courts of using excessive force against King, the federal government subsequently convicted two of the four officers for violation of federal civil rights.

In addition to this policy, Congress has also enacted certain crimes where an acquittal or conviction at state level will preclude any subsequent federal prosecution. However, dual sovereignty applies as a rule; federal crimes will only be found to limit re-prosecution where the language in the statute itself so requires. The crimes exempted from the dual sovereignty doctrine on this basis are usually of a particular interstate nature, or involve particular interstate instrumentalities.[94] The states themselves might enact similar policies or restrictions on their own laws, but any such limits would be self-imposed rather the result of federal rules.

3.4. COMPARISON

It is the relative lack of double jeopardy protection against dual state prosecutions in the US that sheds some light over the special *ne bis in idem* regime functioning in the EU. A strong federal system would seem to have the authority to prohibit two states from exercising their criminal powers where prosecution was within their jurisdiction. On the other hand, a non-federal system should have less power to confer any type of binding effect to states' judicial decisions, since such a preemption is a strong restriction on sovereign prerogatives. Maybe surprisingly to some, the CISA provides protection prosecuting the same defendant for the same facts even across national borders. While the CISA is not an EU instrument, it has become closely tied to European law. The Charter contains a general prohibition against double jeopardy and the ECJ has linked the jurisprudence surrounding Article 54 CISA with Article 50 of the Charter. Therefore, claims of double jeopardy violation by Member States in these matters can be channeled as infringement of the Charter rights. Additionally, the ECJ has been heavily involved in this area, developing substantial jurisprudence in this area. Since all EU states (except the UK) are Schengen states, for the purposes of the following discussion we will refer to these states as "European states."

Comparing the European system and the American system, there is an obvious difference. The American system is based on violation of different states' criminal law provisions. The dual sovereignty doctrine applies precisely because the defendant is violating different criminal codes established by different sovereigns. The European system, on the other hand, focuses on facts regardless of the laws governing those facts, so that if a judgment has reviewed whether

---

94 See 18 U.S.C. §§ 659, 660, 1992, 2101, 2117; see also 15 U.S.C. §§ 80a-36, 1282.

those facts constitute a criminal offense, the verdict is binding for all European states. This comparison highlights the (horizontal) federal power embedded in EU criminal law.

The undeniably federal US system defers to the sovereign prerogatives of its Member States, so much so that it neglects to even apply the constitutional double jeopardy prohibition within its own national borders. An argument can be made that in fact the several states of the United States surrendered much of this sovereignty upon ratification of the Constitution, or alternatively that the Full Faith and Credit Clause should apply to decisions in criminal trials and thereby implicate double jeopardy issues.[95] Nevertheless, the federal protection against multiple trials has been found to have minimal impact on state decisions, other than its application within each state's court system. On the other hand, what began as a multilateral treaty agreement, the CISA, has been seemingly elevated to "constitutional" status by the Charter on the Fundamental Rights of the EU and the jurisprudence of the ECJ. While the Member States of the EU are truly sovereign nation-states, the strength of Article 54 CISA is much more restrictive of their authority. In at least this instance, the federalism element of EU criminal law goes beyond that of the American federal system.

4. CRIMINAL LAW HARMONIZATION

4.1. INTRODUCTION

The above discussion of extradition and interstate double jeopardy emphasizes the need for a harmonized standard on what conduct deserves what punishment. Both of these issues require deferral by one government to the criminal law and policy of its neighbor (although less so in the case of American double jeopardy, due to the dual sovereignty doctrine). One might expect that the fact that the States are bound together in the Union reflects a similar (not identical) approach to criminal law, in the definitions of crimes, sanctions, and procedures. However, the federal "connection" between States with divergent legal and social traditions is, in many instances, extremely weak; there remain significant differences between different sub-federal governments. It is one thing to acknowledge the emergence of a federal sovereign; it is another entirely to harmonize legislation horizontally across the state level in order to ensure that the standards of one state meet the standards of others.

As we are about to explore, the harmonization of the states' criminal law (substantive and procedural) has followed two different paths in the US and in the

95 Terrence M. Messonier, *Neo-Federalism, Popular Sovereignty, and the Criminal Law*, Akron L. Rev. 29 (1996), at 549. However, on the issue of Full Faith and Credit, the Supreme Court has long exempted criminal law from many of its considerations. See *Huntington v. Attrill*, U.S. 146 (1892) at 657, 669.

EU. In the US, the main push for harmonization came with an academic project: the Model Penal Code. This was not mandatory, but rather a voluntary approach to incorporate into state and national criminal codes. On the contrary, the EU approach has not been so "conceding". EU Directives harmonizing criminal law are mandatory and the *Spielraum* of the Member States is almost nonexistent. Inadequate incorporation of EU Directives into national legislation will trigger the states' liability in European courts, and the Directive will nevertheless have direct effect (regardless of how it has been transposed). Once again, it seems that the EU has a more coercive approach regarding harmonization of national laws (horizontal federalism), probably due to the lack of a direct European federal criminal law (vertical federalism). The strength of American federal power to protect its own interests may have made coercion of states unnecessary.

4.2. MANDATORY HARMONIZATION (EU): EUROPEAN DIRECTIVES

The need for a harmonized approach to criminal law, both substantial and procedural, has been a constant concern for EU institutions. As the reader is probably aware, harmonization is achieved through the enactment of EU legislation that must subsequently be implemented in the EU Member States. This implementation is not discretionary; the Member States are required to ensure that the norms created are adopted into their national legislation. Moreover, if the implementation is not adopted in conformity with the EU legislation, the Member State can be sanctioned by the EU. Although our discussion centers on criminal law, this mechanism extends to other areas as well.

Harmonizing criminal law throughout the EU has never been an easy task. National resistance has always been present in the discussion surrounding this topic. Still, as time passed a certain consensus was reached over at least some topics. As noted previously, the EU institutions changed their general approach to this matter, in part to accommodate the objections of Member States to expanded EU authority. At first, the European Commission was eager to use the power available in the European Treaties to develop a harmonized criminal law within the so-called First Pillar. After the failure of this approach, the European Council instead initiated a wave of proposals within the Third Pillar through intergovernmental cooperation mechanisms. This new strategy resulted in a number of Framework Decisions being adopted in the course of roughly a decade.[96] This new approach came to an end with the decision of the ECJ in *Commission v. Council*.[97] The Court of Justice concluded that there is an EC (First Pillar) legislative competence in criminal law if this is needed for an effective

[96] See Chapter 1.

[97] Case C-176/03 *Commission v. Council*, 2005 ECR I-7879.

implementation of EU policy.[98] The Lisbon Treaty altered much of this discussion, but ultimately reaffirmed the powers conferred to EU institutions to harmonize certain areas of criminal law through Directives.[99] As a result the European Parliament currently has the power to establish minimum rules concerning the definition of criminal law offenses and sanctions in the area of particularly serious crime with a cross-border dimension resulting from the nature or impact of such offenses or from a special need to combat them on a common basis.[100]

Our focus here is not which areas of criminal law can be harmonized through EU Directives, but the mandatory nature of such harmonization. This is precisely where the strong horizontal federalism nature of EU criminal law comes into play. In short, the EU forces Member States to adopt certain EU legislation, and while it is true that there is theoretically some room for national diversity, in practice the Member States generally stick to the EU-adopted legislation. The following is not addressed exclusively to EU Directives in criminal law, but extends to all matters.

The basic tenet is found in Article 288 TFEU: "A directive shall be binding, as to the result to be achieved, upon each Member State to which it is addressed, but shall leave to the national authorities the choice of form and methods". To be sure, EU Directives are binding on the Member States, but not on private citizens. The ECJ has been quite adamant about the fact that, especially in criminal law matters, EU Directives cannot create obligations for citizens. In *Berlusconi*[101] the Court recalled its traditional case law[102] on the lack of horizontal effect of Directives. The Court held that a Directive cannot of itself impose obligations on an individual and cannot therefore be relied upon as such against an individual. In particular, in a situation in which a directive is relied on against an individual by the authorities of a Member State within the context of criminal proceedings, a Directive cannot, of itself and independently of a national law adopted by a Member State for its implementation, have the effect of determining or aggravating the liability in criminal law of persons who act in contravention of the provisions of that Directive.[103]

Therefore, it has been clearly specified by the EU that the Member States are the ones that have the *obligation* to implement EU Directives. They cannot refuse to reform their national legislation in criminal matters in accordance with the EU legislation. If they do not comply, two important consequences follow: first, they

98 Case C-176/03 *Commission v. Council*, 2005 ECR I-7879 and its follower Case C-440/05 *Commission v. Council*, Judgment of 23 October 2007.

99 See Chapter 2.

100 Article 83 TFEU.

101 Case C-387/02, Judgment of the Court (Grand Chamber) of 3 May 2005.

102 § 73: "The Court has, however, also consistently ruled that a directive cannot of itself impose obligations on an individual and cannot therefore be relied on as such against that individual (see, *inter alia*, Joined Cases C-397/01 to C-403/01 *Pfeiffer and Others* [2004] ECR I-8835, paragraph 108 and the case-law there cited)."

103 *Flaminia Tacconi Casenote* – Berlusconi at the European Court of Justice, Ger. L.J. 7 (2006) at 315.

are sanctioned by the EU institutions; second, the EU Directive will automatically enter into force such that a defendant may directly appeal to any benefit therein. Both aspects deserve closer attention.

As for the sanction, there is a specific mechanism that is triggered by the failure to implement a European Directive into national legislation correctly and in a timely manner. The EU Commission, acting as the EU watchdog on European legislation implementation, initiates a friendly approach to the EU Member State that has failed to implement EU legislation. If the state remains non-compliant, the EU may take the EU Member State to the ECJ.

A recent example relates to the implementation of Directive 2008/99/EC on the protection of the environment through criminal law.[104] In 2012, the European Commission referred Cyprus to the ECJ for failing to take measures to ensure that serious breaches of EU environmental law are considered criminal offenses and punished. The deadline for transposing Directive 2008/99/EC on the protection of the environment through criminal law was 26 December 2010, but Cyprus still had not implemented it in 2012. The Commission asked the Court to impose on Cyprus a *daily* penalty payment of € 5,909.40 until the adoption of all the necessary national measures for a complete transposition. Regarding the same Directive, in that same year, a reasoned opinion – the second stage in the infringement procedure – was sent by the Commission to Belgium urging it to complete the transposition within two months; failure to do so would result in a reference to the ECJ as well. Also that year, the Commission acknowledged that Greece and Finland had transposed this Directive into national law, and the infringement cases against these countries were closed.

The second issue, even where Member States fail to transpose EU Directives, is the so-called direct effect. It has been noted that EU legislation cannot create criminal law obligations for EU citizens, only for the Member States. However, the potential benefits for the defendant contained in the EU legislation may be utilized by defendants regardless of national implementation. For instance, if the EU legislation decriminalizes certain offenses, the Member State will not be able to impose a criminal sanction on the defendant for the national offense. As *Miettinen* puts it, "directives may create rights which can protect individuals from the effects of otherwise applicable national criminal law".[105]

Thus, while an emphasis on judicial cooperation initially was a way to move European power out of the First Pillar of vertical federalism, the result is contrarily to grant a great deal of authority over criminal (or other) law at the national level. On its face, Article 82 TFEU seeks to allow Member States to retain

---

104 Directive 2008/99/EC on the protection of the environment through criminal law.

105 Samuli Miettinen, *Criminal Law and Policy in the European Union*, 2011 at 88 referring to Case C-329/11, Judgment of the Court (Grand Chamber) of 6 December 2011 (Alexandre Achughbabian Préfet du Val-de-Marne) (illegally staying third-country nationals in a Member State cannot have a sentence of imprisonment imposed on them during the return procedure provided for by Directive 2008/115/EC).

power over their legislature and promises to respect national diversity within the EU. The reality is that the passage of Directives at the EU level which are to be harmonized leaves no authority to Member States, other than unauthorized refusal and consequent liability before the ECJ. Furthermore, the provisions themselves become applicable law in domestic legal systems through direct effect: even refusal to implement EU law cannot stop its influence. Whether this is termed vertical or horizontal, it is clearly a mechanism of federalist enforcement.

Looking at this issue over time, it is also clear that this coercion has been steadily increasing. The first attempts to harmonize criminal law through EU Directives faced strong opposition and did not enter into force. The subsequent approach tried a "weaker" harmonization strategy, mostly comprised of Framework Decisions. We term this approach weaker given the lack of state responsibility in the event of non-incorporation into national legislation.

However, the increasing equivalence between Framework Decisions and Directives – clearly signaled in the leading ECJ *Pupino* case – the suppression of Framework Decisions in the Lisbon Treaty, and the approach of EU institutions to criminal matters in the aftermath of the financial crisis have reinforced the coercive nature of EU harmonization in criminal law. The somewhat "timid" approaches in the first decade of the 21st century to harmonize criminal law provisions through Directives have been replaced with a "vigorous" approach in the second decade. The weak harmonization through Framework Decisions has been replaced by Directives on the same subject matters. Furthermore, the EU has expanded the area of its criminal law authority, producing Directives on issues, e.g. criminal sanctions for market abuse, in which no previous criminal law Framework Decisions existed.

4.3. VOLUNTARY HARMONIZATION (US): INTERSTATE COMPACTS AND UNIFORM STATE LAW

As has been pointed out by a leading scholar on US horizontal federalism, one of the several potential disadvantages of a federal system is the lack of national uniformity in laws.[106] Since the US Supreme Court established in 1939 that the Full Faith and Credit Clause could be utilized to mandate a state to replace its statutes with the statutes of other states, the need for cooperation has been clear. States have sought to promote greater uniformity in policies and program by entering into interstate compacts and administrative agreements, and enacting uniform laws. Additionally, states cooperate through informal administrative agreements promoted by regional and national association of state officials.

Interstate compacts are constitutionally authorized contracts between two or more states creating an agreement on a particular policy issue, adopting a certain

[106] Joseph F. Zimmerman, *Horizontal federalism. Interstate relations*, 2011 at 181.

standard or cooperating on regional or national matters.[107] In other words, the US Constitution contains clauses establishing a constitutional framework within which relations between sister states are conducted. It is fair to say that interstate compacts are the most powerful, durable, and adaptive tools for ensuring cooperative action among the states. Unlike federally imposed mandates that often dictate unfunded and rigid requirements, interstate compacts provide a state-developed structure for collaborative and dynamic action, while building consensus among the states and evolving to meet new and increased demands over time. Yet such interstate compacts and agreements must be approved by Congress. As Article I Section 10 of the US Constitution provides, "no state shall enter into an agreement or compact with another state without the consent of Congress".[108]

Yet the Supreme Court has invoked the mantle of federalism to explain increasingly narrow readings of the congressional consent requirement for interstate compacts. In 1893, in *Virginia v. Tennessee*, Chief Justice Field held that Congress's consent could be implied when it had acted with knowledge of an interstate agreement.[109] In dicta, Field introduced the idea that the Constitution would not require congressional consent for all interstate agreements, but only those that involved "the formation of any combination tending to the increase of political power in the states, which may encroach upon or interfere with the just supremacy of the United States."[110] The Court reasoned that:

> "The terms 'agreement' or 'compact' taken by themselves, are sufficiently comprehensive to embrace all forms of stipulation, written or verbal, and relating to all kinds of subjects; to those to which the United States can have no possible objection or have any interest in interfering with, as well as to those which may tend to increase and build up the political influence of the contracting states, so as to encroach upon or impair the supremacy of the United States, or interfere with their rightful management of particular subjects placed under their entire control."

From this landmark decision it seems, then, that the US Supreme Court considers that the US Constitution gives Congress the power to regulate interstate

---

107 For an somewhat early account see Editorial, *The Power of the States to Make Compacts*, YALE L.J. 31 (1921–22) at 635, 638. A review of the evolution of the Interstate Compacts Clause in DUNCAN B. HOLLIS, *Unpacking the Compact Clause*, TEX. L. REV. 88 (2010) at 741.

108 A constitutional perspective in JIM ROSSI, *Constitutional Isolationism and the Limits of State Separation of Powers as a Barrier to Interstate Compacts,* MARQUETTE LAW REVIEW 90 (2007) 721, noting that "Since Congress must approve such compacts, states entering into compacts typically do so against the backdrop of some federal law"; JILL ELAINE HASDAY, *Interstate Compacts in a Democratic Society: The Problem of Permanency*, FLA. L. REV. 741 (1997) at 1, 3–4 nn. 14–18.

109 148 U.S. 503, 522 (1893).

110 Ibid.

agreements when it needs that power. But if that is not the case, let the states otherwise make their own way. Accordingly, it remains an open question when exactly the Court will find that an interstate agreement requires congressional consent. The Court has suggested that form is not the key concept here and that the "pertinent inquiry is one of potential, rather than actual, impact upon federal supremacy."[111] Therefore, the US Supreme Court has suggested that simply creating an administrative body – even one with extensive powers – will not suffice to trigger the need for congressional consent, nor will the mere presence of a federal interest.[112]

Hollis summed up the above discussion as follows:

> "the Court's decisions have produced a very different interstate Compact Clause doctrine than the literal text suggests. Far from requiring congressional consent for 'any agreement or compact' by the states, the Court instead has created a two stage inquiry. First, is the arrangement a compact according to the 'classic' indicia? Second, even if it is a compact, does it encroach on federal supremacy so as to require congressional consent? Given that such encroachment may only occur through a legal requirement from which the State may not extricate itself, the universe for congressional consent becomes small indeed. In fact, no court, at any level, has ever found an interstate agreement lacking congressional approval to encroach on federal supremacy. On the contrary, the Court has indicated that some interstate agreements that did receive congressional approval may not have needed it, thus opening up the possibility of even fewer categories for congressional consent in the future."[113]

Some academics have emphasized the potential use of interstate compacts in the criminal justice area, and specifically outlined (1) compacts providing for the arrest of persons who have fled across state lines, (2) compacts for the return of criminals found in another state, (3) compacts to secure the attendance of non-resident witnesses in criminal cases, and (4) compacts for the supervision of parolees and probationers.[114] In general, interstate compacts have been perceived as a means of advancing cooperation in procedural criminal matters.

The following interstate criminal justice compacts are in effect: (1) Arkansas-Tennessee Criminal Jurisdiction over the Boundary Waters of the Mississippi River (1909), (2) Colorado River Crime Enforcement Compact (Arizona and California, 1934), (3) Crime Control Compact (now Interstate Compact for Adult Offender Supervision, fifty states, Puerto Rico, and US Virgin Islands, 1934), (4) Interstate Corrections Compact (thirty-seven states and the District of Columbia with California 1934), (5) National Crime Prevention and

---

111 *U.S. Steel Corp. v. Multistate Tax Commission*, 434 U.S. 452, 470, 472 (1978).
112 Ibid. at 472–473.
113 Duncan B. Hollis, *Unpacking the Compact Clause*, Tex. L. Rev. 88 (2010) at 760.
114 Gordon Dean, *The Interstate Compact A Device for Crime Repression*, Law and Contemporary Problems 1 (1934) at 460– 71.

Privacy Compact (twenty-nine states with eleven states and two territories signing a memorandum subscribing to the compact, 1998), (6) New England Corrections Compact (six states, 1934), and (7) New England State Police Compact (six states, 1934).[115] It is noteworthy that most of the interstate compacts related to criminal justice were adopted before the great expansion of federal criminal law.

This is not by chance. The growth of interstate commerce and travel prompted another horizontal federalism type of instrument: uniform state laws. To be sure, the vertical federalism response to growing interstate commerce – which ultimately prevailed over any form of horizontal federalism – was to enact federal legislation on issues affecting interstate commerce. But in some instances there was another form of cooperation, based on horizontal federalism, seeking adoption of identical or similar laws by all the states through the uniform state laws.

Uniform state law is based on a non-governmental body, the National Conference of Commissioners on Uniform State Law (NCUSL).[116] Interestingly enough, it was formed in 1892 at the recommendation of the American Bar Association for the purpose of promoting "uniformity in state laws on all subjects where uniformity is deemed desirable and practicable." The Conference oversees the preparation of proposed laws, "Uniform Laws", which the states are *encouraged, but not mandated* to adopt.[117] Commissioners have approved more than two hundred uniform laws,[118] of which more than one hundred have been adopted by at least one state. Yet only a few have been widely adopted and have, as a consequence, approached the hoped-for uniform national law on their subject.

In order to clarify the process, it is important to note that upon approval by the National Conference, a uniform law is not law anywhere in the United States:

---

115 As Joseph F. Zimmerman, *Congress and Crime: The Impact of Federalization of State Criminal Laws*, 2013 at 33.

116 Commissioners are appointed by the fifty states, District of Columbia, Puerto Rico and the US Virgin Islands. The number of commissioners from a state varies, but most states appoint at least three. The governor typically is responsible for appointing the commissioners. The conference is composed of approximately 300 nonpartisan judges, attorneys and law professors who serve without compensation (see Joseph F. Zimmerman, *Horizontal federalism. Interstate relations*, 2011 at 184.

117 To be sure, there are certainly ways to promote adoption of the Uniform Law. As Joseph F. Zimmerman, *Congress and Crime: The Impact of Federalization of State Criminal Laws*, 2013, at 73 writes, "Congress in 1990 promoted the enactment of a uniform highway safety law by all state legislatures by means of an opt-out method respecting their quasi-sovereignty. The Department of Transportation Appropriation Act of 1991, enacted in 1990 mandates each state legislature to enact a statute providing for the automatic revocation of the operator's license of an individual convicted of a drug-related crime or to vote to opt-out of the requirement by a resolution, concurred in by the governor and sending it to the U.S. Secretary of Transportation *A state failing to enact a uniform law or to opt-out is penalized by a 10 percent reduction in its federal highway grants-in-aid*" (emphasis added).

118 According to Joseph F. Zimmerman, *Horizontal federalism. Interstate relations*, 2011 at 185 "since 1892 approximately 310 uniform law have been drafted as of 2009 on a wide variety of topics", including (for criminal law related purposes) the following: rules of criminal procedure (1987), Victims of Crimes (1992).

it is simply a legislative proposal addressed to fifty state legislatures.[119] Now, it is important to note that *the versions of the "uniform laws" passed by the states are rarely uniform*. Variations occur at the outset since prior law or other special local conditions lead states to make changes; rarely do states adopt uniform laws verbatim.[120] This results in multiple versions of some uniform laws, and unless and until the states that adopted an earlier version enact the Commissioners' revisions in multiple versions in effect in the states. The greatest successes of the "uniform law" approach have been in the field of commercial and business law. The Conference, working together with the American Law Institute, later produced the Uniform Commercial Code – which is probably the most successful example of uniform state law.

According to the database of the Uniform Law Commission, i.e. NCUSL, these are the uniform laws in criminal law and procedure matters:[121]

1. *Attendance of Out-of-State Witnesses*[122]
   The Uniform Act to Secure the Attendance of Witnesses from Without a State in Criminal Proceedings was completed in 1936. The Act provides states with statutory authority to secure the attendance of a witness from without the state in which the criminal proceeding or Grand Jury proceeding is pending.
2. *Child Abduction Prevention*[123]
   The Uniform Child Abduction Prevention Act provides courts with guidelines to follow during custody disputes and divorce proceedings in order to help them identify families at risk for abduction and prevent the abduction of children.
3. *Collateral Consequences of Conviction Act*[124]
   The Uniform Collateral Consequences of Conviction Act addresses the penalties and disqualifications that individuals face incidental to criminal sentencing. The Act's provisions are largely procedural, and are designed to rationalize and clarify widely accepted policies and practices.
4. *Controlled Substances Act*[125]
   The Uniform Controlled Substances Act provides fundamental law in the fight against narcotic and dangerous drugs, and achieves uniformity between state and federal drug laws.

119 During the history of the Conference, roughly half its proposals have not been adopted by a single state. In addition, most of those that have enjoyed reasonable success have fallen way short of the goal of adoption by all or even a majority of the states.

120 A second source of variance is the Conference itself. Having adopted a successful Uniform Law, the Commissioners are prompted, just as true legislators are, to revised it from time to time in the light of changing conditions and policies.

121 Available at: www.uniformlawcommission.com/Acts.aspx?category=ULC_Criminal.

122 Adopted by all States except North Dakota and Puerto Rico.

123 Adopted in Alabama, Colorado, District of Columbia, Florida, Kansas, Louisiana, Michigan, Mississippi, Nebraska, Nevada, New Mexico, Pennsylvania, South Dakota, Tennessee, Utah.

124 Adopted only in Vermont.

125 Adopted in 46 states.

5. *Criminal History Records Act*[126]
   The Uniform Criminal History Records Act provides fundamental law to govern "criminal history records information" in any state that adopts it.
6. *Electronic Recordation of Custodial Interrogations*[127]
   The Electronic Recordation of Custodial Interrogations Act requires that law enforcement electronically record the entirety of a custodial interrogation. The Act leaves it to the individual states to decide where and for what types of crimes this mandate applies, as well as the means by which recording must be done. The Act also includes a number of exceptions that excuse nonrecording.
7. *Interstate Enforcement of Domestic Violence Protection Orders Act*[128]
   The Uniform Interstate Enforcement of Domestic Violence Protection Orders establishes uniform procedures that enable courts to recognize and enforce valid domestic protection orders issued in other jurisdictions.
8. *Law Enforcement Access to Entity Information Act*[129]
   This Act preserves the traditional confidentiality of entity ownership and requires the filing of the name of an individual who would be responsible for obtaining, maintaining, and verifying record ownership information.
9. *Mandatory Disposition of Detainers Prevention of and Remedies for Human Trafficking*[130]
   The Mandatory Disposition of Detainers Act is a procedural statute establishing rules for the prompt disposition of detainers (i.e. warrants filed against persons already in custody) by providing that prosecuting officials, upon the request of the prisoner, must move forward with trial of the charge which caused the detainer. Failure to do so within a reasonable time brings about a dismissal of the charge and withdrawal of the detainer.
10. *Prevention of and Remedies for Human Trafficking*[131]
    This Uniform Act is a comprehensive new law directed against human trafficking. It provides the three components necessary for ending human trafficking: comprehensive criminal penalties; protections for human-trafficking victims; and public awareness and prevention methods.
11. *Rules of Evidence*[132]
    The primary object of this Act is to simplify and codify the rules pertaining to what may be introduced in evidence in any civil or criminal trial in a court of law. It reflects closely the federal rules of evidence.

---

126 No state has adopted this uniform law.
127 Adopted only in Indiana and Vermont.
128 Adopted in Alabama, California, Delaware, District of Columbia, Idaho, Indiana, Kansas, Mississippi, Montana, Nebraska, New Mexico, North Dakota, Oklahoma, Rhode Island, South Carolina, South Dakota, Texas, U.S. Virgin Islands, Utah, West Virginia.
129 No state has adopted this uniform law.
130 Adopted in Alabama, Arizona, Colorado, Kansas, Minnesota, Missouri, North Dakota, Utah.
131 Adopted in Delaware, Louisiana, New Hampshire, Pennsylvania.
132 No state has adopted this uniform law.

12. *Victims of Crime Act, Model*[133]
    This Act provides rights of victims of crime to certain protections in the criminal justice system, and a system of compensation for victims personally injured by criminal action.

It is worth noting that most of the uniform laws have not been widely adopted. This shows that the lack of a mandatory duty to adopt uniform laws ultimately results in a clear reluctance of the states to enact legislation that does not originate within in own constituency. It also signals quite bluntly the strong preference for vertical over horizontal federalism in criminal law matters.

Against this backdrop it is necessary to review one of the most well-known efforts to harmonize American criminal law: the Model Penal Code (MPC). The MPC, which seeks to harmonize state criminal law statutes, is in effect a uniform act but it was developed by the American Law Institute rather than the NCUSL. In 1962 the American Law Institute (ALI) produced the MPC, which contained a detailed set of rules concerning the General Part and specific provisions related various crimes of the Special Part.[134] The Code resulted in a wave of state reforms in the 1960s and 1970s, influenced to some extent by the Code.[135] These reforms were not undertaken out of an obligation by the Union's states, but by a voluntary decision of those states to update their respective criminal law legislation. It is up to the discretion of the states to adopt all or only some of the provisions contained in the MPC.

When the ALI undertook to provide a systematic codification of the criminal law, criminal codes throughout the US were largely just an assortment of ad hoc statutes passed without rhyme or reason.[136] Unlike some other projects of the ALI, like the Restatements, the Model Penal Code was meant to actually create a new way of organizing and defining criminal laws, not simply to consolidate and explain the laws already in existence.[137] The MPC had great success, at least compared to other attempts at criminal law harmonization across the fifty US states: as of 2011, only fourteen states had not incorporated any of the MPC into their criminal law.[138] However, when it came to the federal law, reformers were unable to implement any broad consolidation and organization of criminal law at the national level.[139] Instead, the American federal criminal code remains

---

133 Only Montana has adopted this uniform law.

134 Paul H. Robinson and Markus D. Dubber, *The American Model Penal Code: A Brief Overview*, New Crim. L. Rev. 10 (2007) at 319.

135 Ibid.

136 Ibid. at 322–323.

137 Gerald E. Lynch, *Revising the Model Penal Code: Keeping it Real*, Ohio State Journal of Criminal Law 1 (2003), at 219.

138 Anders Walker, *The New Common Law: Courts, Culture, and the Localization of the Model Penal Code*, Hastings L.J. 62 (2011) 1633.

139 Gerald E. Lynch, *Revising the Model Penal Code: Keeping it Real*, Ohio State Journal of Criminal Law 1 (2003) at 219.

completely disorganized, beyond alphabetization.[140] As a result, at least some would consider the MPC as a tool of reform to be finished, although its continued presence across the US is still felt.[141]

Despite these successes, the MPC has by no means provided uniform harmonization of criminal law across the United States. In addition to the states which did not implement any portion of the MPC, there remains great diversity among the fifty-two American criminal codes.[142] States are completely free to adopt, reject, or amend the MPC as they choose, and many controversial subjects were not widely implemented.[143] The result is that many state have criminal laws influenced by the MPC, but in reality "lack the conceptual integrity of the model statute".[144] Furthermore, great portions of the MPC had no real effect anywhere, such as regulations of sentencing and treatment.[145]

Also notable is the fact that the MPC did not broadly attempt to deal with the rules governing criminal procedure and evidence, although many of the rules therein touch on these subjects.[146] Much of the harmonized criminal procedure in the United States, where it exists, has come out of fundamental rights and due process jurisprudence, addressed in the next chapter.

4.4. COMPARISON

Once again, it is reasonable to assert that, at least concerning criminal law, the EU mandatory harmonization mechanism reveals stronger (horizontal) federalization than the discretionary US discretionary harmonization mechanism. Although the American federal government has a much greater power to create and enforce its own criminal law, the longtime resistance to create an independent system of European federal criminal law has resulted in greater pressure by the Union to harmonize criminal legislation. This harmonization is also important for EU

140 See above, Chapter 1 (discussing the American criminal law, and its state of expansive disorganization); Paul H. Robinson and Markus D. Dubber, *The American Model Penal Code: A Brief Overview*, New Crim. L. Rev. 10 (2007) 319 at 327 ("the lack of a modern federal criminal code us considered a matter of some embarrassment among criminal law scholars in the United States").

141 Gerald E. Lynch, *Revising the Model Penal Code: Keeping it Real,* Ohio State Journal of Criminal Law 1 (2003) at 219; Paul H. Robinson and Markus D. Dubber, *The American Model Penal Code: A Brief Overview*, New Crim. L. Rev. 10 (2007) 319 at 326 (suggesting that even yet, some states where the MPC was used to draft new codes which were not approved may yet reconsider them).

142 Paul H. Robinson and Markus D. Dubber, *The American Model Penal Code: A Brief Overview*, New Crim. L. Rev. 10 (2007) 319 at 320.

143 Ibid.

144 George P. Fletcher, *Dogmas of the Model Penal Code*, 2 Buff. Crim. L. Rev. 3, 3 (1998) (referring specifically to the codes of New York and Illinois).

145 Paul H. Robinson and Markus D. Dubber, *The American Model Penal Code: A Brief Overview*, New Crim. L. Rev. 10 (2007) 319 at 327–328.

146 Ibid. at 324.

extradition and *ne bis in idem* principles discussed above. Given the significant deference to the domestic law of neighboring countries mandated by the EAW and the Schengen Treaty, harmonized criminal law across the EU states is almost a requirement for the smooth operation of these federal instruments. Interestingly enough, the refusal of EU Member States to give up sovereignty in order to provide federal protection of the Union's interests has resulted in greater horizontal federalism. While not letting the EU handle its federal business itself, horizontal federalism requires a usurpation of Member State sovereignty in these areas through a strictly mandatory system of harmonization.

In the United States, the federal system operates directly in the criminal law arena, and thus states are left free to maintain their own internal priorities and traditions. EU countries, on the other hand, are certainly waiving their right to protect certain national interests the way they see fit according to their national diversity. Given this result, it is important to note that the offenses in which the EU is imposing harmonization are considered federal offenses in the US system: drug trafficking, money laundering, currency counterfeiting – all classic examples of federal crimes. It seems, then, that the underlying rationale in the EU's approach is to impose a certain standard (the so-called "minimum rules") concerning offenses that are considered federal in other systems. If we see mandatory harmonization and a loss of national diversity as a result of this system, it is an especially significant cost for the restriction of EU competence in those areas where truly direct EU interests are involved.

CHAPTER 4

THE FEDERAL DIMENSION OF FUNDAMENTAL RIGHTS

Incorporation of Due Process Rights in the EU

1. INTRODUCTION

Having discussed the harmonization of the substantive criminal law in both the US and the EU, there is another important element of the criminal process which has been an issue for both. Beyond the definitions of crimes themselves, both Unions are concerned with the fundamental rights of individuals charged with a crime. We have already reviewed some federalizing aspects of one such right – the protection against double jeopardy. However, there are a panoply of recognized criminal defense rights in Europe and the United States. In both of these Unions, these rights are protected both at and above the state level. Obviously, the United States government has federal authority to protect the rights of its citizens, even when those rights are threatened by the constituent states. The similar development of criminal rights protection in Europe emphasizes the federal nature of the EU as well.

In modern legal thinking, at least in the western world, the concept of "due process" has become ubiquitous as a requirement for state action. All European constitutions include some sort of due process clause, and the Fifth Amendment to the United States Constitution, from the core Bill of Rights, states that "[n]o person shall be ... deprived of life, liberty, or property without due process of law."[1] In particular, the criminal trial, particularly because of the *ultima ratio* nature of criminal law, exemplifies the full extent of due process. Over time, "due process" across countries has solidified into a specific set of guarantees, whether spelled out in domestic legal texts, interpreted as a necessary corollary of general justice or other specific guarantees, or imposed by superior legal orders.

1 US CONST. amend. V.

The European Union has experienced a standardization of due process rights, as found in the European Convention on Human Rights, as well as in the case law of the European Court of Justice and later the Charter of Fundamental Rights of the European Union. Similarly, in the 20th century, the United States experienced an expansion of the scope of its constitutional due process rights, once applicable only to the federal government, to the individual states. These parallel developments in European and American human rights law are yet another example of growing European federalism, particularly in criminal law.

Indeed, the EU experience of "constitutionalizing" criminal defense standards across state borders is similar to the incorporation process of the American system. Both systems now have a federal level of "due process protection" which is binding on states, even when those states would prefer to offer different standards within their domestic borders. Even more remarkable is the fact that the EU federalizing standards at times prohibit Member States from offering greater protection, another instance of federal power beyond that of the United States. We will again see that this result stems from the hesitance to grant direct federal authority to the EU, with an ironic effect. Beyond this constitutional level of federal standardization, Europe at least has seen legislative reforms aimed at harmonizing standards of due process protections at the statutory level. These are discussed below.

Finally, we address as a case study a very specific example related to the Spanish legislation. Pursuant to a concept of European due process it is interesting to note how national due process is being gradually enriched by the case law of the European maximum courts. Although a major caveat regarding the different impact on national systems of ECtHR and ECJ must be drawn, the intrinsic relationship between the ECHR, the Charter and the case law of the ECtHR thanks to the Lisbon Treaty justifies a combined treatment of the issues at hand.

To be sure, much of the discussion that follows is currently heading to an unknown future. The EU Accession to the ECHR has generated discussion and controversy. The recent Opinion 2/13 of the ECJ[2] on the draft agreement on the accession of the EU to the ECHR signals certain incompatibilities with EU law.[3] Depending on the final content of the agreement, some of the tendencies here noted will probably experience a dramatic change in the near future. Therefore, our aim, again, is not to provide an in-depth review of the fundamental rights debate in the US and Europe, but just to highlight certain similarities in such an important area.

---

2 Press release: http://curia.europa.eu/jcms/upload/docs/application/pdf/2014-12/cp140180en.pdf. Opinion 2/2013 (Full Court) delivered on 18 December 2014.

3 See generally the contributions in Vasiliki Kosta, Nikos Skoutaris and Vassilis Tzevelekos, eds., *The EU Accession to the ECHR*, 2015. See also the contributions of Daniel Halberstam, Christoph Krenn, Stian Øby Johansen, Adam Lazowski, Ramses A. Wessel and Steve Peers in the German Law Journal 16 (2015).

2. THE BILL OF RIGHTS AND THE INCORPORATION DEBATE (US)

2.1. INTRODUCTION

As already noted, the Bill of Rights of the United States guarantees "due process" when the government takes action that threatens the life, liberty, or property of its citizens. Specific protections for individuals facing criminal charges – what would be included in the broader concept of due process – can be found in the Fifth and Sixth Amendments in the Bill of Rights. Early in the history of the United States, the Supreme Court declared that the Bill of Rights of the US Constitution was not applicable against state governments.[4] An eventual change to this practice was made possible with the passage of the Fourteenth Amendment to the Constitution following the American Civil War, which provided *inter alia*: "No State shall make or enforce any law which shall abridge the privileges or immunities of citizens of the United States; nor shall any State deprive any person of life, liberty, or property, without due process of law; nor deny to any person within its jurisdiction the equal protection of the laws."[5] This new wording, with specific reference to "States", along with the background to this amendment (a federal government subduing its rebelling states), provided a new avenue for enforcing fundamental rights against the states.

Litigators began to argue that the Bill of Rights should restrict the states through this new framework. Early attempts to incorporate the Bill of Rights through the "privileges and immunities" clause were rejected in 1872[6] (a widely criticized decision,[7] yet affirmed as recently as 2010).[8] Finally, in 1925, the Supreme Court recognized that freedom of speech and press, found in the First Amendment, are "among the fundamental personal rights and 'liberties' protected by the due process clause of the Fourteenth Amendment from impairment by the States."[9] With this, the floodgates were opened to use the due process clause as a vehicle for protecting Bill of Rights guarantees against state encroachment.

2.2. BACKGROUND CONCEPTS

As we examine the specifics of the American process of incorporation under the due process clause, it is worth expounding upon some related topics in American

4 *Barron v. City of Baltimore*, 32 U.S. 243 (1833).
5 U.S. Const. amend. XIV, 00A7 2.
6 *Slaughterhouse Cases*, 83 U.S. 36 (1872).
7 Kenneth Katkin, *"Incorporation" of the Criminal Procedure Amendments: the View from the States*, Neb. L. Rev. 84 (2005) 397, 402–403 (with additional citations at footnote 22).
8 *McDonald v. Chicago*, 130 S. Ct. 3020 (2010).
9 *Gitlow v. New York*, 268 U.S. 652 (1925).

law. To begin with, "due process" in American law has both a procedural and a substantive understanding, as developed by the federal courts. Procedural due process is that set of rights which is literally guaranteed (although without specifics) under the due process clauses of the Fifth and Fourteenth Amendments: it is the actual procedures required by the government whenever it seeks to deprive individuals of their life, liberty, or property. The reader should bear in mind, however, that many of the procedural guarantees of the criminal process are specifically spelled out for the federal government in the Fifth and Sixth Amendments, and thus the term "procedural due process" generally refers to civil matters.[10] On the other hand, substantive due process is a judicially created doctrine through which the federal courts have recognized that specific fundamental rights, although not explicitly listed, are nevertheless protected under due process; in this regard, the Supreme Court has asked whether such rights are "implicit in the concept of ordered liberty".[11] This process was used to incorporate Bill of Rights protections – "enumerated rights" – as well as to create rights beyond the text of the Constitution – "unenumerated rights".[12]

"Incorporation" refers to the process by which the courts have applied the specific guarantees of the Bill of Rights to the individual states. There was a debate in the court over whether the individual freedoms from the Bill of Rights should be incorporated fully against the states (total incorporation), or examined as they arose to see if they fell under "due process" (selective incorporation). Despite the arguments of some justices, namely *Hugo Black*, the court rejected total incorporation, opting instead for selective incorporation. With this understanding, the court used its "substantive due process" to assess whether specific protections within the bill of rights are "fundamental" and incorporated by the Fourteenth Amendment.

Criminal due process falls under "substantive due process" when applied to the states, because these are not explicitly applicable to the states and thus must be created under the due process clause of the Fourteenth Amendment. However, they are explicitly listed in the Fifth and Sixth Amendments, so the Court simply had to find them fundamental and thus binding on the states through the Fourteenth Amendment "due process" clause. By now virtually all of these guarantees, as well as the rest of the Bill of Rights, are applicable to state government actions

---

10 Of course, many of these protections are similar to those provided in criminal trials, such as a right to notice and reasons for the deprivation, an opportunity to defend including a hearing and the right to confront witnesses, a right to an attorney, and a neutral fact-finder.

11 *Palko v. Connecticut*, 302 U.S. 319, 325 (1937) (although in that case rejecting the application of the double jeopardy provision to the states, a decision which was later reversed in *Benton v. Maryland*, 395 U.S. 784 (1969)).

12 These include the rights to raise a family, to marriage, to contraception, to work in a selected occupation, to abortion, to private sexual conduct, etc.

as well as federal.[13] There are minor exceptions not applied to the states, like the right to a grand jury indictment,[14] or specifically a twelve-person jury.[15]

2.3. THE EVOLUTION OF INCORPORATION

Although many would argue that the Bill of Rights should have been applied to the states under the "privileges and immunities" clause of the Fourteenth Amendment, the use of the "due process" clause as an alternative has widely been understood as an example of judicial activism. Indeed, early uses of "substantive due process" were commonly used to overrule legislatively enacted economic regulation, under the Supreme Court's conception of economic or contract freedoms;[16] this line of cases was abandoned by the court following the Great Depression and remains obsolete.[17] Much less contested has been the incorporation of enumerated defense rights against the states, ensuring that the criminal defendant "is entitled to the full panoply of the relevant protections which due process guarantees in state criminal proceedings."[18]

The bulk of criminal defense rights guaranteed in the federal Constitution were also present in some form in the constitutions of the constituent states, yet the line of cases incorporating the federal criminal defense protections necessarily occurred in instances where the Supreme Court found that the state-level protections were lacking.[19] While in some instances this could be the result of a lack of explicit protection, in others it was the result of disparate interpretations of due process concepts. As a general rule, the rights and interpretations in the

---

13 See *McDonald*, 130 S. Ct. 3020 (demonstrating that the majority of the Bill of Rights is applicable now against the states, and itself incorporating the Second Amendment right to bear arms for the first time).

14 *Hurtado v. California*, 110 U.S. 516 (1884).

15 *Ballew v. Georgia*, 435 U.S. 223 (1978).

16 See e.g. *Lochner v. New York*, 198 U.S. 45 (1905) (overturning a New York law limiting the allowable work hours for bakers). The period when the Supreme Court was overturning labor laws in the interest of freedom of contract rights found under substantive due process has been termed the "Lochner era" after this case.

17 e.g. *Nebbia v. New York*, 291 U.S. 502 (1934); *West Coast Hotel v. Parrish*, 300 U.S. 379 (1937); et al.

18 *Specht v. Patterson*, 386 U.S. 605, 609 (1967) (citing *U.S. ex rel. Gerchman v. Maroney*, 355 F.2d 302, 312 (3rd Circuit, 1965)). During the tenure of Chief Justice Earl Warren, the Supreme Court of the United States incorporated the majority of the Bill of Rights criminal justice procedural rights. Jerold H. Israel, *Selective Incorporation: Revisited*, 71 Geo. L. J. 253, 253 (1982).

19 See generally Kenneth Katkin, *"Incorporation" of the Criminal Procedure Amendments: the View from the States*, Neb. L. Rev. 84 (2005) 397 (noting that, while in some instances the Court did truly change the substantive law of the states with its due process jurisprudence, the bulk of criminal defense rights were equally protected under state law, and even the "incorporation" of specific rights at the federal level tended to follow, rather than oppose, trends of state interpretation).

Bill of Rights and their Fourteenth Amendment "due process" counterparts are coextensive and interpreted the same,[20] although this was not always the case.[21]

Thus, over time, the United States federal courts have come to effectively standardize the criminal defense rights across state lines. Early cases that did not find these due process guarantees to be fundamental under substantive due process were eventually overruled, slowly eliminating the distinctions between procedural rights in different contexts.[22] At this point, the majority of the Fifth and Sixth Amendments, containing the constitutional basis for criminal defense rights against the federal government, have been incorporated through the Fourteenth Amendment due process clause. These two Amendments provide:

> "No person shall be held to answer for a capital, or otherwise infamous crime, unless on a presentment or indictment of a Grand Jury ...; nor shall any person be subject for the same offence to be twice put in jeopardy of life or limb; nor shall be compelled in any criminal case to be a witness against himself, nor be deprived of life, liberty, or property, without due process of law ..."[23]

> "In all criminal prosecutions, the accused shall enjoy the right to a speedy and public trial, by an impartial jury of the State and district wherein the crime shall have been committed, which district shall have been previously ascertained by law, and to be informed of the nature and cause of the accusation; to be confronted with the witnesses against him; to have compulsory process for obtaining witnesses in his favor, and to have the Assistance of Counsel for his defence."[24]

Unlike the bulk of the Bill of Rights, the grand jury requirement from the Fifth Amendment has not been incorporated under Fourteenth Amendment due process,[25] although there are other notice requirements found in the Sixth Amendment. However, the remainder of the Fifth Amendment procedural protections have been applied against the states, such as the protection against double jeopardy[26] and the right against self-incrimination.[27] The actual "due process" clause of the Fifth Amendment has been used to apply the substantive

20 *Malloy v. Hogan*, 378 U.S. 1 (1964).

21 See e.g. *Betts v. Brady*, 316 U.S. 455 (1942) (holding that the Fourteenth Amendment right to counsel was less extensive than that of the Sixth Amendment). This case was overruled by *Gideon v. Wainwright*, 372 U.S. 335 (1963), which eliminated the distinction between federal and state proceedings.

22 For instance, *Twining v. New Jersey*, 211 U.S. 78 (1908), found that a right against self-incrimination was not applicable in state criminal proceedings, but *Malloy v. Hogan*, 378 U.S. 1 (1964), overturned that decision and incorporated this right; similarly, *Palko v. Connecticut*, 302 U.S. 319 (1937) held that double jeopardy – akin to the European *ne bis in idem* principle – was not "of the very essence of ordered liberty", a decision later overruled in *Benton v. Maryland*, 395 U.S. 784 (1969).

23 U.S. Const. amend. V.

24 U.S. Const. amend. VI.

25 *Hurtado v. California*, 110 U.S. 516 (1884).

26 *Benton v. Maryland*, 395 U.S. 784 (1969).

27 *Malloy v. Hogan*, 378 U.S. 1 (1964).

due process rights from the Supreme Court's jurisprudence as well as the requirements of the anti-discrimination "equal protection" clause[28] from the Fourteenth Amendment to the federal government.[29]

The right to a trial by jury, although incorporated to apply to the states as well as the federal government,[30] remains one of the few Bill of Rights guarantees which is applied differently against the states. While the Sixth Amendment requires a twelve-person jury and a unanimous verdict,[31] the Fourteenth Amendment due process version of this right allows states to utilize six-person juries[32] and does not always require unanimity.[33]

The Supreme Court has noted generally that the remaining guarantees of the Sixth Amendment, which it describes as "a compact statement of the rights necessary to a full defense",[34] "are basic to our adversary system of criminal justice, [thus] they are part of the 'due process of law' that is guaranteed by the Fourteenth Amendment to defendants in the criminal courts of the States."[35] The right to an attorney was one of the earliest rights to be incorporated against the states, initially in limited circumstances,[36] since expanded to require the provision of an attorney in all cases where the defendant could face incarceration (even when the sentence is suspended).[37] The right "to be informed of the nature and cause of the accusation"[38] – notice – is incorporated as well; this requires both a sufficiently specific law prior to the imposition of criminal punishment[39] as well as notice of the particular criminal act alleged sufficient to allow preparation by

28 U.S. Const. am. XIV, § 1 ("nor shall any State ... deny to any person within its jurisdiction the equal protection of the laws.").

29 See e.g. *Bolling v. Sharpe*, 347 U.S. 497 (1954) (applying concepts of equal protection under the Fifth Amendment due process clause to a school desegregation case from Washington, DC, which is governed by federal law). This process has become known as "reverse incorporation," since it essentially applies state requirements to the federal government. See for example Peter J. Rubin, *Taking its Proper Place in the Constitutional Cannon: Bolling v. Sharpe, Korematsu, and the Equal Protection Component of Fifth Amendment Due Process*, Va. L. Rev. 92 (2006) at 1879 (describing and defending the application of equal protection standards to the federal government, as well as addressing some of the critiques of the reverse incorporation rationale).

30 *Duncan v. Louisiana*, 391 U.S. 145 (1968).

31 *Patton v. United States*, 281 U.S. 276 (1930).

32 *Williams v. Florida*, 399 U.S. 78 (1970) (allowing a six-person jury in a non-capital case); *Ballew v. Georgia*, 435 U.S. 223 (1978) (rejecting the use of a five-person jury).

33 *Johnson v. Louisiana*, 406 U.S. 356 (1972) (allowing a 9–3 jury verdict); *Apodaca v. Oregon*, 406 U.S. 404 (1972) (allowing 11–1 and 10–2 verdicts). However, the Supreme Court does require a unanimous verdict where juries are as small as six persons. *Burch v. Louisiana*, 441 U.S. 130 (1979).

34 *Faretta v. California*, 422 U.S. 806, 818 (1975).

35 Ibid.

36 *Powell v. Alabama*, 287 U.S. 45 (1932) (granting the right to an attorney in state capital criminal proceedings)

37 *Alabama v. Shelton*, 535 U.S. 654 (2002).

38 U.S. Const. art. VI.

39 *Connally v. General Construction Co.*, 269 U.S. 385 (1926).

the defendant.[40] Also incorporated are the Sixth Amendment rights to present evidence and compel witnesses,[41] the right to confront and cross-examine witnesses (in large part serving to limit hearsay evidence),[42] the right to a public trial,[43] and the right to a speedy trial.[44] While not present in the text of the Sixth Amendment, the court has also found that the presumption of innocence is a fundamental liberty, applicable to the federal government[45] and secured against the states through the Fourteenth Amendment.[46]

Also going beyond the text of the Fifth and Sixth Amendments, the Supreme Court has provided additional procedural protections to criminal defendants through "substantive due process" creation of unenumerated rights. Chief among these is the requirement found in *Miranda v. Arizona* that police inform suspects of their constitutional rights to remain silent and to an attorney and that forbade further questioning without a waiver of these rights.[47] Similarly, the some remedies for constitutional violations, like the exclusionary rule, are not found in the text of the Constitution, but have been raised to constitutional status and applied to the state and federal governments alike under Supreme Court jurisprudence.[48]

3. THE GROWTH OF EUROPEAN DUE PROCESS

3.1. DUE PROCESS FROM THE ECJ AND THE ECHR

The legal landscape of Europe is vastly different than that of the United States, but there has been a similar process of standardization of defense (and other) rights. The United States is a federal system, where the component states retain some autonomy but are nevertheless expressly subordinate to the national government;[49] on the other hand, the European Union is made up of independent nation states, though arguably the European Union has indeed become a supranational federal government.

---

40 *United States v. Debrow*, 346 U.S. 374, 376 (1953) (applying only the Sixth Amendment, as this case dealt with a federal prosecution).

41 *Washington v. Texas*, 388 U.S. 14 (1967).

42 *Pointer v. Texas*, 380 U.S. 400 (1965).

43 *In re Oliver*, 333 U.S. 257 (1948).

44 *Klopfer v. North Carolina*, 386 U.S. 213 (1967).

45 *Coffin v. United States*, 156 U.S. 432 (1895).

46 *Estelle v. Williams*, 425 U.S. 501 (1976).

47 *Miranda v. Arizona*, 384 U.S. 436 (1966).

48 *Mapp v. Ohio*, 367 U.S. 643 (1961).

49 As guaranteed by the "Supremacy Clause" in the United States Constitution which states that: "This Constitution, and the Laws of the United States which shall be made in pursuance thereof; and all treaties made, or which shall be made, under the authority of the United States, shall be the supreme law of the land; and the judges in every state shall be bound thereby, anything in the constitution or laws of any state to the contrary notwithstanding." U.S. CONST. art. VI cl. 2.

Just as the protection of individual rights and freedoms increased federal control over state governments in the United States, human rights have played a significant role in the consolidation of EU power. In particular, two international institutions have effectively standardized the protection of fundamental rights across national borders, in a similar fashion to the American process of incorporation: the ECHR and the EU. Among the rights that were established as international norms are criminal defense rights, or "due process". Although once limited in scope, these rights, through the actions of supranational bodies, have become standardized through European "incorporation" of due process.

The European Union initially began as a treaty organization with fairly limited powers, although it has been steadily expanding in competence since. Some of the greatest leaps in this expansion came through decisions of the ECJ. What may have been the most significant development in EU expansion was the establishment of the supremacy of European law over that of the Member States by the ECJ in *Costa v. ENEL.*[50] In turn, however, these Member States, and their constitutional courts in particular, expressed concern over the lack of fundamental rights protection provided by the EU. This arguably leads the ECJ to begin finding fundamental rights protection in the general principles of European law[51] and taking inspiration from the constitutional traditions of its Member States.[52] Thus, over time the ECJ, having declared EU law supreme (despite lacking specific textual basis, perhaps), outlined a regime of fundamental rights, referring to common Western political philosophy and increasingly to the European Convention on Human Rights. Additionally, the ECJ has expanded coverage of these protections to include actions by Member States implementing EU law, and even beyond.[53]

Prior to any codification in the European Treaties, the ECJ had already determined that "respect for the rights of defence is ... a fundamental principle of Community law which must be guaranteed even in the absence of any rules governing the proceedings in question."[54] These defense rights are described as "deriv[ing] from the right to a fair hearing guarantee by Article 6 of the European Convention for the Protection of Human Rights and Fundamental Freedoms."[55]

---

50 Case 6/64 *Costa v. ENEL*, 1964 ECR 585.

51 Case 29/69 *Stauder v. City of Ulm*, 1969 ECR 419.

52 Case 4/73 *Nold v. Commission*, 1974 ECR 491.

53 Daniel Sarmiento, *Who's Afraid of the Charter? The Court of Justice, National Courts and the New Framework of Fundamental Rights Protection in Europe*, Common Market Law Review 50 (2013) at 1267, 1269.

54 Case C-462/98 P *Mediocurso v. Commission*, 2000 ECR I-7183, para. 36. See also Case 85/76 *Hoffmann-La Roche v. Commission*, 1979 ECR 461, para. 9; Joined Cases C-48/90 and C-66/90, *Kingdom of the Netherlands v. Commission*, 1992 ECR I-565, para. 44; Case 234/84 *Kingdom of Belgium v. Commission*, 1986 ECR 2263, para. 27.

55 Case C-14/07, *Ingenieurbüro Michael Weiss und Partner GbR v. Industrie und Handelskammer Berlin*, OJ C 158/5 (2008), para. 47. See also Case 257/85 *Dufay v. European Parliament*, 1987 ECR 1561, para. 10 (recognizing the right to a fair trial from Article 6 ECHR, although dismissing the particular application).

While the European Union was and is limited in its criminal law powers – although its competence in criminal matters seems to be on the rise – the ECJ long ago concluded that though "in principle criminal legislation and the rules of criminal procedure are matters for which the Member States are responsible, it does not follow that this branch of law cannot be affected by Community law."[56] Since these earlier cases, the Lisbon Treaty and others have reworked the TEU to include specific binding reference to the Charter of Fundamental Rights of the European Union,[57] and has made more explicit the prior ECJ practice of finding fundamental rights in constitutional traditions and the ECHR.[58] Thus, what was once a movement of judicial activism has become codified in European instruments.

Unlike the experience of the European Union, the ECHR was always an explicit and purposeful instrument of fundamental rights protection, operating at a supranational level. Established in the aftermath of the Second World War, the ECHR was intended to protect civil liberties against the abuses of government power, in response to the oppressive fascist regimes of the prior decade. Among the guarantees included in the Convention were the specific guarantees that comprise due process in a criminal context.[59]

Although it was always thought of as an institution of international human rights law, the ECHR and the European Court of Human Rights which hears cases under the Convention have grown in influence in the years since their creation.[60] Since 1990 the number of countries who have ratified the ECHR has grown by 24.[61] In 1998, Protocol 11 entered into force, further advancing the power of the ECtHR and the influence of the due process guarantees of the ECHR. With this, the European Commission, which served as a filter between complainants and the Court, was abolished and a full-time court was established to hear all referrals. Additionally, this Protocol allows individuals to bring complaints to the ECtHR,[62] expanding the reach of the Court and truly cementing its role as a supranational enforcer, rather than a mere treaty agreement. At this point, acceptance of individual applications and compulsory jurisdiction of the ECtHR

56 Case C-226/97 *Lemmens*, 1998 ECR I-3711, para. 19.

57 Article 6(1) TEU.

58 Article 6(3) TEU.

59 Article 6 ECHR (entitled "Right to a fair trial"). The ECHR does, however, explicitly grant these guarantees to individuals in "the determination of… [their] civil rights and obligations" as well. Article 6(1) ECHR.

60 See Helen Keller and Alec Stone Sweet, *A Europe of Rights: the Impact of the ECHR on National Legal Systems*, 2008 ("The High Contracting Parties have steadily upgraded the regime's scope and capacities … They have added new rights, enhanced the powers of the European Court of Human Rights (ECtHR), and strengthened the links between individual applicants and the regime.").

61 Helen Keller and Alec Stone Sweet, *A Europe of Rights: the Impact of the ECHR on National Legal Systems*, 2008 at 5.

62 Prior to Protocol 11, the contracting parties, the European countries themselves, could opt to disallow individual complaints.

is required.[63] As caseload increases with the acceptance of individual applications, the Court, largely of its own initiative, has begun using "pilot judgments"[64] to deal with systemic rights failures in national systems, blurring the line between specific judgments and broader judicial lawmaking. For their part, "most States have clarified and enhanced the nature and status of the Convention through the incorporation of the Convention into domestic law."[65]

Although technically the ECHR is a treaty system and the ECtHR is theoretically limited to retrospective damages for human rights violations, in reality it also "works to identify and to consolidate universal standards of rights protection".[66] The cumulative case law has a precedential effect,[67] expanding due process as required throughout Europe. Contracting States to the ECHR are obligated to comply with the judgments of the ECtHR,[68] a requirement which arguably requires changes in domestic law to ensure future compliance. In the context of due process, the court has noted that "Article 6 para. 1 (art. 6-1) imposes on the Contracting States the duty to organise their legal systems in such a way that their courts can meet each of its requirements."[69]

The evolution of the ECtHR case law itself highlights its role in standardizing criminal procedure. Where a new decision sets higher standards for due process rights, it will require adjustment of domestic practices, even though the ECtHR may have earlier declared these practices to be in compliance with the ECHR. For instance, we may look at the recent case of *Salduz v. Turkey*, which determined that "as a rule, access to a lawyer should be provided as from the first interrogation of a suspect by the police."[70] On the contrary, an earlier case found Switzerland in compliance with Article 6 where a lawyer was *not* provided during police interrogation.[71] This sort of development of due process standards within the case law of the ECtHR itself highlights the significance of the ECHR on domestic legal orders. Even were European countries to have conformed their own legal systems

63 Helen Keller and Alec Stone Sweet, *A Europe of Rights: the Impact of the ECHR on National Legal Systems*, 2008 at 6.

64 European Court of Human Rights, Rules of the Court 31, Rule 61.1 (2014) (available at: www.echr.coe.int/Documents/Rules_Court_ENG.pdf).

65 Helen Keller and Alec Stone Sweet, *A Europe of Rights: the Impact of the ECHR on National Legal Systems*, 2008 at 7. For a discussion of the effect of the ECHR and the ECtHR on UK human rights through the domestically enacted Human Rights Act in the counterterrorism context, citing "the enormous influence of article 6 ECHR", see Aileen Kavanagh, *Constitutionalism, Counterterrorism, and the Courts: Changes in the British Constitutional Landscape*, 9 Int'l J. Const. L. 172 (2011).

66 Helen Keller and Alec Stone Sweet, *A Europe of Rights: the Impact of the ECHR on National Legal Systems*, 2008.

67 Dinah Shelton, *The Boundaries of Human Rights Jurisdiction in Europe*, Duke J. Comp. & Int'l L. 95, 13 (2003) at 126–127.

68 Article 46 ECHR.

69 *Abdoella v. The Netherlands*, App. No. 12728/87, 25 Nov. 1992, § 24.

70 49 Eur. Ct. H.R. 421, para. 55 (2008).

71 *Imbrioscia v. Switzerland*, App. No. 13972/88, 24 Nov. 1993.

and due process interpretations to those of the ECtHR at a given time, evolving norms of European due process may mandate additional changes.

As a result of *Salduz*, there has been notable activity at the domestic level in Europe in order to bring criminal justice systems into conformity with the new ECHR standard.[72] Thus the Supreme Court of the United Kingdom, despite noting that it was not a party to the *Salduz* decision,[73] concluded that the consistent line of case law demanded changes in the Scottish criminal justice regime.[74] Similarly, the Supreme Court of the Netherlands concluded that a suspect had a right to an attorney before questioning,[75] as did the French *Conseil Constitutionnel*;[76] in 2011, the Belgian legislature passed the "Salduz law" to provide expanded access to defense counsel.[77] Clearly, at this point, the ECHR has a powerful effect on the due process guarantees of domestic European legal systems.

There remains a question over what the interaction between European due process and the fundamental rights of the Member States will be. Recent cases of the ECJ suggest different possibilities in different situations.[78] Firstly, Article 51 of the Charter defines its scope of application as "to the Member States only when they are implementing Union law."[79] Thus, although now explicitly applicable to EU Member States, there remains a situation where no EU interest comes into play and there is no obligation to observe EU rights at all under the Charter. Where there is an EU-level order which is to be implemented by the Member States with some level of discretion, the Member States will be free to use either their own constitutional protections or those found in the Charter.[80] However, in this situation the Charter will establish a minimum level of protection; should the Member State's own fundamental rights protection fall below this level, they must instead comply with the greater protection from the EU level.[81] They remain free, presumably, to offer a higher level of protection instead.[82] On the other hand, where EU law *completely* determines the action of Member States, the Charter and EU fundamental rights are to be the sole source of fundamental

---

72 www.opensocietyfoundations.org/voices/case-watch-salduz-fever-sweeps-europe.
73 *Cadder v. Her Majesty's Advocate (Scotland)* [2010] UKSC 43, 26 Oct. 2010, para. 45.
74 Ibid. at para. 51.
75 LJN BH3079, 30 June 2009.
76 Decision No 2010-14/22 QPC, 30 July 2010 (deciding on French constitutional grounds).
77 European Agency for Fundamental Rights, *Fundamental Rights: Challenges and Achievements in 2011*, at 205 (2012) (available at: http://fra.europa.eu/sites/default/files/fra_uploads/2211-FRA-2012_Annual-Report-2011_EN.pdf).
78 Daniel Sarmiento, *Who's Afraid of the Charter? The Court of Justice, National Courts and the New Framework of Fundamental Rights Protection in Europe*, Common Market Law Review 50 (2013) at 1267, 1269.
79 Charter of Fundamental Rights of the European Union, Article 51(1), 2000 OJ C 364/1, 21.
80 *Åkerberg Fransson*, Judgment of 26 February 2013 (617/10), nyr.
81 Daniel Sarmiento, *Who's Afraid of the Charter? The Court of Justice, National Courts and the New Framework of Fundamental Rights Protection in Europe*, Common Market Law Review 50 (2013) at 1294–1295 (citing *Åkerberg Fransson* at para. 29).
82 Ibid.

rights protection.[83] This means that the Charter provides a maximum level of protection, and Member States will be unable to apply their own constitutional standards even if such standards provide greater protection. Despite the fact that this seems directly counter to Article 53 of the Charter,[84] the ECJ confirmed this clearly in *Melloni*.[85]

3.2. SPECIFIC EUROPEAN DUE PROCESS RIGHTS

As noted above, due process rights in international, European law are contained within ECHR Article 6. The ECtHR has interpreted paragraph 1 of Article 6 to guarantee an overall right to a fair trial, with the specific requirements in paragraph 3 as considerations in this overall fairness test.[86] Still, the specific procedural rights of a criminal defendant are explicitly spelled out by the ECHR itself, and reinforced in the case law of the ECtHR.

Thus, the ECHR guarantees: a public hearing; a speedy trial (within a reasonable time); an independent and impartial fact finder; the presumption of innocence; notice of the nature and cause of the accusation; the opportunity to prepare a defense; assistance of an attorney; right to examine witnesses; compulsory process to obtain witnesses; and an interpreter, if needed. Article 7 ECHR further includes the principle of legality.[87] Additionally, Protocol 7, which has been ratified by all but three Member States, provides for a right to an appeal[88] and a protection of the *ne bis in idem* principle (akin to the American double jeopardy prohibition).[89] Additionally, the ECtHR has interpreted Article 6 to provide for unlisted, i.e. unenumerated, rights, such as the right to remain silent.[90]

The Charter of Fundamental Rights of the European Union also provides for explicit protection of criminal defense rights since the entry into force of the Lisbon Treaty, although the ECJ was enforcing some human rights standards

---

83 Daniel Sarmiento, *Who's Afraid of the Charter? The Court of Justice, National Courts and the New Framework of Fundamental Rights Protection in Europe*, Common Market Law Review 50 (2013) 1267, 1269 at 1289–1292; Case C-399/11, *Melloni v. Ministerio Fiscal*, Judgment of 26 February 2014.

84 Charter of Fundamental Rights of the European Union, Article 53 ("Nothing in this Charter shall be interpreted as restricting or adversely affecting human rights and fundamental freedoms as recognized ... by the Member States' constitutions.").

85 Case C-399/11, *Melloni v. Ministerio Fiscal*, Judgment of 26 February 2014 at §§ 57 et seq.

86 See e.g. *Rowe and Davis v. United Kingdom*, App. No. 28901/95, 16 February 2000, § 59; *Szabo and others v. Romania*, App. No. 8193/06, 18 March 2014, § 50.

87 Article 7(1) ECHR ("No one shall be held guilty of any criminal offence on account of any act or omission which did not constitute a criminal offence under national or international law at the time when it was committed. Nor shall a heavier penalty be imposed than the one that was applicable at the time the criminal offence was committed.").

88 ECHR Protocol 7, Article 2.

89 ECHR Protocol 7, Article 4.

90 *Saunders v. United Kingdom*, 24 Eur. Ct. H.R. at 2044.

before then.[91] The relevant provisions from the Charter are set out in Chapter IV of the Charter, titled "Justice". This section includes Articles 47–50.

These protections largely mirror those of Article 6 ECHR and the other "due process provisions", although with different wording. Even though there are some differences, those rights which are also expressed in the ECHR will typically have the same meaning in the Charter, which provides that "the meaning and scope of those rights shall be the same as those laid down by the [ECHR]",[92] although the Charter also makes clear that it might grant greater protection to these rights.[93] Thus, the Charter mirrors many of the rights from the ECHR, including: a fair hearing; a public trial; a trial within a reasonable time; an independent fact-finder; an attorney (provided by the state, if necessary); the presumption of innocence; the principle of legality; and the *ne bis in idem* principle. Although some specific rights from the ECHR are not laid out in the Charter, given the "special significance" that the ECJ has attached to the ECHR,[94] and the significance of the ECJ's own case law in the interpretation of the Charter,[95] these rights are nevertheless incorporated into the EU legal order.[96] To illustrate the significance of the overlap between the two international instruments, it is notable that the ECJ has incorporated a right to silence into its pre-Charter case law on the basis of Article 6(1) ECHR,[97] although, as noted above, that right was the product of judicial interpretation by the ECtHR.[98] On the other hand, the Charter does contain a specific requirement of proportionality in criminal punishment,[99] something which is not found in the ECHR or the case law of the ECtHR.[100, 101]

---

91 *Infra.*

92 Charter of Fundamental Rights of the European Union, Article 52(3).

93 Ibid.

94 *Kadi & Al Barakaat International Foundation v. Council of the European Union*, 2008 ECR I-6351, para. 283.

95 Charter of Fundamental Rights of the European Union, Preamble ("This Charter reaffirms … the rights as the result, in particular, from the … case-law of the Court of Justice of the European Communities").

96 For instance, the ECJ has discussed the right to an interpreter from Article 6(3)(e) ECHR (*Ingenieurbüro Michael Weiss und Partner GbR v. Industrie und Handelskammer Berlin*, at para. 71); as well as the right to examine witnesses from Article 6(3)(d) ECHR (*HFB Holding and Others v. Commission*, 2002 ECR II-1487, paras. 389–391) (finding that the Commission is not a tribunal within the meaning of the ECHR, but that it must still follow the general principles of Community law).

97 Case T-112/98 *Mannesmannröhren-Werke AG v. Commission*, 2001 ECR II-729, para. 49.

98 *Saunders v. United Kingdom*, 24 Eur. Ct. H.R. at 2044.

99 Charter of Fundamental Rights of the European Union, Article 49.3.

100 See Leena Kurki, *International Standards for Sentencing and Punishment*, in Michael Tonry and Richard S. Frase, eds., *Sentencing and Sanctions in Western Countries*, 2001 at 331, 361–366 (finding little ECtHR protection for extreme punishments, other than those amounting to inhumane treatment or torture under Article 3, which the court has indicated may include disproportionate punishment (citing *Weeks v. United Kingdom*, 2 March 1987, Series A, No. 114), or punishments for activities which are protected under other civil and political freedoms in the ECHR).

101 Although not contained in the Fifth and Sixth Amendments, the US Constitution also places limits on punishment. US Const. amend. VIII (prohibiting excessive bail, excessive fines, and

Although European countries also have due process protections provided for in their domestic law, these may differ in certain respects from those provided in international law, just as the international legal instruments themselves contain differing language. For instance, Article 24 of the Spanish Constitution reads as follows:

> "1. All persons have the right to the effective protection of the judges and courts in the exercise of their rights and legitimate interests, and in no case may there be a lack of defence.
>
> 2. Likewise, all have the right to the ordinary judge predetermined by law, to defence and assistance of an attorney, to be informed of the accusation made against them, to a public trial without delays and with all the guarantees, to utilize the means of proof pertinent to their defence, to refrain from self-incrimination, to refrain from pleading guilty, and to the presumption of innocence.
>
> The law shall regulate the cases in which for reasons of family relationship or professional secrecy it shall not be obligatory to make declarations concerning allegedly criminal actions."

Thus Spanish constitutional law provides for most of the same rights seen in the ECHR – arguably missing only the explicit right to an impartial and independent tribunal and to an interpreter – but in different words. Despite the differences between these provisions, and indeed between the legal traditions of European countries,[102] the ECHR, and to a lesser degree the Charter and the ECJ, effectively impose at least baseline obligations regardless of domestic provisions, which Member States must comply with in some form or another or face sanction. As a result, international standards become incorporated into domestic law, through passage of additional laws and amendments,[103] or the reinterpretation of domestic

cruel and unusual punishment); *Solem v. Helm*, 463 U.S. 277 (1983) (finding life imprisonment without parole disproportionate under the Eighth Amendment for a charge of writing a $100 worthless check). At the same time, this protection is very limited, because the US Supreme Court has been hesitant to find punishments disproportional. See *Rummel v. Estelle*, 445 U.S. 263, 272 (1980) ("Outside of the context of capital punishment, successful challenges to the proportionality of particular sentences have been exceedingly rare"). There are some examples, like those involving the death penalty (e.g. *Coker v. Georgia*, 433 U.S. 584 (1977) (finding that capital punishment for adult rape was unconstitutional under the Eighth Amendment)), or cases involving juveniles (e.g. *Graham v. Florida*, 560 U.S. 48 (2010) (finding that the Eight Amendment prohibits sentences of life without parole for non-homicidal juvenile offenders)).

102 It is often noted, however, that these differences are shrinking as a result of what we are calling European due process incorporation. See Diane Marie Amann, *Harmonic Convergence? Constitutional Criminal Law in an International Context*, Ind. L.J. 75 (2000) at 809, 825–30 (noting the effect of the ECHR on criminal justice systems and procedures, causing a general harmonization, and the EU (830–839)).

103 e.g. Human Rights Act 1998 (UK law requiring interpretation of domestic law to be "[s]o far as it is possible to do so ... read and given effect in a way which is compatible with the Convention rights."). Ibid. at section 3(1).

due process by courts.[104] In the case of Spain, the Spanish Constitution also mandates an interpretative approach which ensures that Spanish due process will be in line with that of international human rights treaties.[105]

4. COMPARING SYSTEMS

The above discussion of the incorporation process in American law and the more recent rise to prominence of a supranational, European due process demonstrates yet another parallel between the two systems. It is already hard to argue that a "treaty organization" which mandates domestic law change over fundamental questions of human rights is completely non-federal. The similarity between American incorporation and the European experience emphasizes this point. Some differences, specifically the *Melloni* situation, suggest that European federal power is even greater.

4.1. EVOLVING STANDARDS AND JUDICIAL ACTIVISM

Probably the most marked similarity between the incorporation of due process in the United States and Europe is the very concept of evolving standards which, over time, have gained importance and acceptance in state level legal orders. In particular, the role of judicial activism to advance fundamental rights was crucial in both systems. In the United States, the Supreme Court's substantive due process essentially involved the invention of fundamental rights with minimal textual basis.[106] While "due process" has been read to include many fundamental rights, some of which have little or no textual foundation in the US Constitution, at least the criminal due process rights which have been incorporated against the states are largely based on the clear provisions of the Fifth and Sixth Amendments, albeit through a circuitous path of judicial interpretation.

Whether one believes that criminal due process should have initially applied to all levels of US government or that it was only made applicable to states by the Fourteenth Amendment, the time of full due process enforcement was significantly after the drafting of the underlying legal provisions. The Fourteenth Amendment entered into force in 1868, but the beginning of "substantive due process" was not until the early 20th century, and (mostly) full incorporation of

---

104 See also Giuseppe Martinico, *Is The European Convention Going To Be "Supreme"? A Comparative-Constitutional Overview of ECHR and EU Law Before National Courts*, European Journal of International Law (2012), at 401–424 (discussing the various ways in which EU and ECHR law have become integrated into domestic systems, and noting that although the approaches differ the results are similar).

105 Spanish Constitution, Article 10(2).

106 Indeed, the test itself looks to "history and tradition" rather than the Constitution.

criminal due process from the Bill of Rights was not completed until the late 1960s.

The European experience similarly experienced a lag between the drafting of legal instruments and the full enforcement of the fundamental rights of due process. In the case of the ECHR, while the initial treaty contained the bulk of modern due process guarantees when it came into force in 1953,[107] there was a long period before the ECtHR began to aggressively assert Convention rights against the signatory states, issuing only thirty-six opinions in the first twenty-seven years of its existence.[108] In addition to increasing the volume of cases, the ECtHR established its power to expand the scope of due process rights, by declaring in 1978 that "the Convention is a living instrument",[109] a power confirmed by the finding new rights beyond the text of the ECHR – what in the US context could be called "unenumerated rights" – such as the right to remain silent.[110] By the 1990s, the ECtHR had taken on a role similar to that of the US Supreme Court at the height of its due process incorporation, becoming "a Warren Court in the midst of Europe".[111] Beyond the judicial sphere, the ECHR itself was made more powerful, particularly with the entry into force of Protocol 11 which cemented the right to individual petition and the mandatory acceptance of ECtHR jurisdiction.[112]

In the context of the European Union, the role of judicial activism in advancing due process rights was even more pronounced. Where the US Supreme Court at least had the Bill of Rights to suggest a starting point for new federal powers conferred under the Fourteenth Amendment, the ECJ founded its human rights jurisprudence on minimal textual basis: non-discrimination plus "unwritten Community law" in the early European treaties,[113] later influenced by "constitutional traditions of the member states".[114] What is more, the ECJ effectively asserted these rights only after expanding its own competencies, declaring the supremacy of EU law where none had existed before.[115] Although

107 Protocol 7, which provides for a right to appeal and the *ne bis in idem* principle was not drafted until 1984 and came into force in 1988.

108 Gerda Kleijkamp, Transnat'l L. & Contemp. Probs. 12 (2002) 307, fn. 10. Compare this to 3,659 judgments issued in 2013. European Court of Human Rights, *Statistics 2013* (available at: www.echr.coe.int/Documents/Stats_annual_2013_ENG.pdf).

109 *Tyrer v. United Kingdom*, EHRR 2 (1978) 1, para. 31.

110 *Saunders v. United Kingdom*, 24 Eur. Ct. H.R.

111 Gordon Van Kessel, *European Perspectives on the Accused as a Source of Testimonial Evidence*, W.Va. L. Rev. 100 (1998) at 799, 802 (referencing Chief Justice Earl Warren, who was the head of the US Supreme Court from 1953–1969 when the bulk of the Bill of Rights was incorporated against the states).

112 Council of Europe, *Explanatory Report to Protocol 11 to the Convention for the Protection of Human Rights and Fundamental Freedoms, Restructuring the Control Machinery Established Thereby*, para. 85 (available at: http://conventions.coe.int/Treaty/EN/Reports/HTML/155.htm).

113 *Stauder v. City of Ulm*, 1969 ECR 419, at 422 (referring to Articles 7 and 40(3) in the Treaty Establishing the European Economic Community as well as general principles).

114 *Nold v. Commission*, 1974 ECR.

115 *Costa v. ENEL*, 1964 ECR 585.

the US Supreme Court had also moved into competencies previously denied to it with the incorporation of the Bill of Rights, this power was created by the passage of a new constitutional amendment explicitly limiting the states,[116] and with a federal government which was explicitly supreme over its constituent parts.[117] It is interesting to note that, although judicial interpretation and activism has been understood as a predominantly American, or at least common law, concept, it is the European Court which has displayed the most judicial activism of all in its development and incorporation of due process.

Significantly, however, some of these parallels between American and European judicial activism may be less relevant due to more recent legal developments in Europe. With the entry into force of the Charter of Fundamental Rights, the ECJ no longer has to "interpret" fundamental rights out of thin air, but can refer directly to the Charter. Thus, while the US Supreme Court continues to operate with little textual limitation, European due process law has become increasingly codified.[118] In turn, the Charter itself refers directly to the ECHR and ECtHR jurisprudence.[119] It has already been noted that EU and ECHR approaches and relationships with Member States are converging;[120] with the pending accession of the EU to the ECHR, the co-development of these two forms of due process incorporation will be cemented.[121]

4.2. FEDERAL/"FEDERAL" RELATIONSHIPS

Another distinction to be made between American incorporation of criminal due process and that of Europe arises from the different relationships between states and the overarching government, be it expressly federal or the more *sui generis* organization of the EU. While the United States is comprised of semi-autonomous states, the US Constitution makes clear that federal actions of any sort will trump state actions or standards, "anything in the constitution or laws of any state to the contrary notwithstanding".[122] On the other hand, the European organizations which have helped to incorporate international standards of due process, the

116 U.S. Const. amend. XIV, § 2 (containing the crucial language, "No state shall …" which has been interpreted to vastly increase the authority of the federal government).

117 U.S. Const., art. 6, cl. 2 (the Supremacy Clause).

118 As the EU expands its power, more of this codification is happening at the legislative level. See e.g. Roadmap for Strengthening Procedural Rights.

119 Charter of Fundamental Rights of the European Union, Article 52(3).

120 See generally also Giuseppe Martinico, *Is The European Convention Going to be "Supreme"? A Comparative-Constitutional Overview of ECHR and EU Law Before National Courts*, European Journal of International Law (2012) at 401–424.

121 Article 6(2) TEU ("The Union shall accede to the Convention for the Protection of Human Rights and Fundamental Freedoms"). Recall, however, that the Charter does provide criminal due process protection beyond that found in the ECHR in at least one context, the proportionality of punishment to the crime.

122 Supremacy Clause.

ECHR/Council of Europe and the European Union, began as treaty organizations and remain something short of a state themselves; the European Member States remain strongly autonomous nations in their own right. While there are strong similarities in the way in which federal power has been consolidated in both systems – like the use of judicial activism by courts to declare their own supremacy[123] – the relative weakness of American states in their federal system has created differences between American and European incorporation.

One interesting consequence of this balance of power in the European Union is that the initial push for fundamental rights protection at an international level, including criminal due process, came from the states themselves. After the ECJ asserted the supremacy of European law, a number of national courts in Europe expressed concern over the lack of human rights protection at the European level;[124] it seems that these concerns may have in fact pushed the ECJ to expand its human rights jurisprudence.[125] In any event, the expansion of fundamental rights protection at the EU level led to greater acceptance by some domestic, constitutional courts.[126] Of course, the ECHR was established by European nations with the intent of international monitoring of human rights, although it has grown in significance since its founding. On the contrary, American incorporation of fundamental rights against the states grew out of the Fourteenth Amendment, a federal level instrument passed directly in response to the rebelling states of the American Civil War; expanded protection of criminal due process happened in spite of – in some cases directly against – the will of the states. In Europe, without cooperation at various points from the particular members of the European Union, supranational organizations could never have consolidated the power to mandate changes in state law. The US federal government has always had the power to do so, at least in certain areas.

Beyond the historical context of incorporation in Europe and the United States, the greater federal authority in the American legal system affects the implementation of criminal due process standards. As repeatedly noted, the

---

123 See *Costa v. ENEL* (securing the primacy of EU law through judicial activism, and in the process, declaring the power of the ECJ to review Member State actions). In the American context, the Supreme Court has definitely expanded the understanding of federal power at points, including the process of incorporation of the Bill of Rights which was not considered applicable to the states before.

124 See e.g. BVerfG 37, 271 ("*Solange I*") (reserving the German Constitutional Court's power to review European Community law so long as there was insufficient European protection of human rights); Italian Constitutional Court, *Frontini v. Ministero delle Finanze*, Case 183/73 (1973) (setting out the "counter-limits" doctrine to review European action for compliance with core constitutional requirements).

125 Daniel Sarmiento, *Who's Afraid of the Charter? The Court of Justice, National Courts and the New Framework of Fundamental Rights Protection in Europe*, Common Market Law Review 50 (2013) 1267, 1269 at 1269.

126 See e.g. BVerfG 73, 339 ("*Solange II*") (citing the increased protection of fundamental rights by the European Communities and the ECJ in particular in a decision to stop reviewing Community action under the Solange I doctrine); Italian Constitutional Court, *Granital v. Amministrazione delle Finanze dello Stato*, Case 170/84 (1984).

Supremacy Clause of the US Constitution ensures that once federal rights were incorporated to the states there was no further discussion: all state government actors were obligated to follow the new standards in all cases. Furthermore, the US Bill of Rights, through the Fourteenth Amendment, is applied to states in (almost always) the exact same way as it applies to the federal government.[127] Although due process rights established by supranational organizations in Europe have been incorporated against European nations, they remain subject to more restrictions due to the less powerful nature of European level entities.

For instance, in the context of European Union law, Article 51 of the Charter, while now providing fundamental rights protection to EU Member States, applies the Charter "only when they [Member States] are implementing Union law."[128] While it is established that fundamental rights also apply whenever a country is acting "within the scope of Community law",[129] which is considerably broader, there remains an area where the national government is not limited by the Charter or ECJ fundamental rights review. The ECHR, on the other hand, applies to all actions within the jurisdiction of the signatory countries; however, certain rights allow for exceptions and reservations by European countries.[130] Still other criminal due process rights are contained in additional protocols which have not been ratified by some countries.[131]

Furthermore, the interpretation of both EU and ECHR rights reflects further deference to state governments, unlike in the US system. The ECJ in its interpretation is limited by the principles of proportionality and subsidiarity, which limit when the EU may act and the scope of action.[132] Since the fundamental rights from the EU order only apply when Member States are acting in the scope of EU law, these limits in turn limit the applicability of due process standards. In the ECHR context, the "margin of appreciation" doctrine grants flexibility to states in the protection of fundamental rights;[133] in at least one recent case,

---

127 *Malloy v. Hogan*, 378 U.S. 1, 10–11 (1964) (noting a number of cases where the Court utilized the same standards for fundamental rights in the state context as the federal and rejecting "'a watered-down, subjective version of … the Bill of Rights'") (citing *Ohio ex rel. Eaton v. Price*, 364 U.S. 263, 275 (1960)).

128 Charter of Fundamental Rights of the European Union, Article 51(1).

129 *ERT*, 1991 ECR I-2925, para. 42.

130 Council of Europe Treaty Office, *List of declarations made with respect to treaty No. 005* (available at: http://conventions.coe.int/Treaty/Commun/ListeTraites.asp?CM=8&CL=ENG (click on #005, "Convention for the Protection of Human Rights and Fundamental Freedoms," then click on "List of declarations, reservations and other communications")).

131 For instance, Protocol 7 to the ECHR, providing for a right to appeal and the *ne bis in idem* principle has not been ratified by Germany, the Netherlands, Turkey, and the United Kingdom. Council of Europe Treaty Office, Protocol No. 7 Chart of Signatures and Ratifications (available at: http://conventions.coe.int/Treaty/Commun/ListeTraites.asp?CM=8&CL=ENG (click on #117, "Protocol No. 7 to the European Convention on Human Rights and Fundamental Freedoms," then click the link "Chart of signatures and ratifications")).

132 Article 5 TEU.

133 *Handyside v. United Kingdom*, 1976 Eur. Ct. H.R. 5 (first introducing the concept of the "margin of appreciation" in ECtHR jurisprudence).

the ECJ has also referenced the ECtHR's use of the margin of appreciation when examining an alleged violation of fundamental rights.[134] Protocol 15 amending the ECHR, currently awaiting signatures from all the high contracting parties before going into effect, proposes adding language referencing both subsidiarity and the margin of appreciation into the ECHR itself.[135]

One area where both the US and European human rights law grants deference to states is in the offering of more protection than is provided at the federal or supranational level. While the incorporation process holds all states to the same standards as the federal government in the protection of (most) criminal due process rights, the US Supreme Court has allowed states to offer greater protections than those found in the US Constitution.[136] Similarly, European law generally allows individual nations to offer greater human rights guarantees than those offered at an international level. Article 53 ECHR provides that "[n]othing in this Convention shall be construed as limiting or derogating from any of the human rights and fundamental freedoms which may be ensured under the laws of any High Contracting Party or under any other agreement to which it is a party." The Charter similarly states that "nothing in this Charter shall be interpreted as restricting or adversely affecting human rights and fundamental freedoms as recognized ... by the Member States' constitutions."[137] In its case law, the ECJ confirms that, "where action of the Member States is not entirely determined by European Union law ... national authorities and courts remain free to apply national standards, provided that the level of protection provided for by the Charter ... [is] not thereby compromised."[138] In these situations, the US Constitution, the ECHR, and the Charter all provide a constitutional floor, a baseline protection of criminal due process rights which is applicable at all levels of government.

---

134 *Kadi & Al Barakaat International Foundation v. Council of the European Union*, 2008 ECR I-6351, para. 360.

135 Protocol 15 Amending the Convention on the Protection of Human Rights and Fundamental Freedoms, 24 June 2013, CETS 213, Article 1 (adding to the preamble to the ECHR the following language: "Affirming that the High Contracting Parties, in accordance with the principle of subsidiarity, have the primary responsibility to secure the rights and freedoms defined in this Convention and the Protocols thereto, and that in doing so they enjoy a margin of appreciation, subject to the supervisory jurisdiction of the European Court of Human Rights established by this Convention".

136 See *Cooper v. California*, 386 U.S. 58 (1967) ("Our holding, of course, does not affect the State's power to impose higher standards on searches and seizures than required by the Federal Constitution if it chooses to do so"); William J. Brennan Jr., *State Constitutions and the Protection of Individual Rights*, 90 Harv. L. Rev. 489 (1977) (encouraging the use of state law to expand civil liberties beyond the federal constitutional floor).

137 Charter of Fundamental Rights of the European Union, Article 53.

138 *Åklagaren v. Åkerberg Fransson*, at para. 29.

4.3. GREATER EUROPEAN FEDERALISM: MAXIMUM STANDARDS

It is here that the human rights law of the EU takes an ironic twist, given the relative weakness of the European Union compared to the American federal government: as noted above, EU law as interpreted by the ECJ provides that in certain situations European nations are prohibited from offering a greater level of constitutional protection than found in the Charter, Article 53 notwithstanding.[139] Significantly, it seems that the ECHR will provide no help in this situation either, given the deference the ECtHR has granted to EU law.[140] In this situation, the ECJ is concerned that allowing Member States to utilize Article 53 of the Charter would "undermine the principles of mutual trust and recognition"[141] and threaten "the primacy, unity and effectiveness of EU law".[142] Surprisingly, the weaker EU therefore prohibits its Member States from applying their own constitutional protections where EU law allows no discretion, while the unquestionably supreme US government allows greater human rights protections so long as they rest on an "independent and adequate state ground".[143]

The cooperative, horizontal federalism approach of the EU makes it all the more important that criminal due process be standardized across Member States. Just as the harmonization of substantive law is important for the operation of federal legal institutions, like the EAW described above, it is also crucial that European nations respect the integrity of their neighbors' criminal process. One step towards that goal is the standardization of due process rights, through "incorporation" as described above as well as through EU legislative action, discussed below. Still, in the pursuit of such mutual respect, the ECJ has gone further. Where international standards are not enough, and Member States still find their neighbors lacking in due process protections, *Melloni* requires compliance with the results of criminal trials across the EU, regardless. Here, the court has been explicit in stating what we have repeatedly observed throughout this chapter: where European law is based on mutual recognition

139 See below Chapter 4 (discussing the *Melloni* case (Case C-399/11 *Melloni v. Ministerio Fiscal*, 26 February 2013)). It seems that this decision also runs counter to the spirit of Article 82(2) TFEU ("Adoption of the minimum rules referred to in this paragraph shall no prevent Member States from maintaining or introducing a higher level of protection for individuals").

140 Bosphorous (laying out the "equivalent protection doctrine", wherein the ECtHR will defer to the action of the EU on the basis of EU human rights protection). How much of this will survive the accession of the EU to the ECHR is questionable; it would be contrary to the very purpose of the ECHR to grant an actual party to the Convention a general reprieve from human rights review.

141 Case C-399/11 *Melloni v. Ministerio Fiscal*, Judgment of 26 February 2013, § 63.

142 Ibid. at § 60.

143 *Fay v. Noia*, 372 U.S. 391, 428 (1963); see also *Murdock v. City of Memphis*, 87 U.S. (Wall) 590, 634–35 (1874).

and harmonization,[144] resistance to such law would "undermine the principles of mutual trust and recognition ... and would, therefore, compromise the efficacy of that [law]."[145] The horizontal focus of European federalism ends up making domestic compliance even more "mandatory" than in the American system. It becomes hard in this case to deny that the new Europe resembles a federal state.

5. OTHER CRIMINAL PROCEDURE HARMONIZATION

5.1. INTRODUCTION

Given the prior discussion of the similar experiences of "incorporation" of fundamental due process rights within the US and the EU, it is fitting to also mention the federal standardization of criminal procedure that has happened at the legislative level. While the EU has recently turned its attention to the standardization of procedural rights with its Roadmap on procedural rights,[146] American criminal procedure is still rarely governed at the federal level, other than incorporated fundamental rights, discussed above.

5.2. THE EU ROADMAP ON PROCEDURAL RIGHTS

The EU's Roadmap for strengthening procedural rights of suspected or accused persons in criminal proceedings has resulted in a number of EU Directives on criminal defense rights, with more to come.[147] The EU has already issued Directives on the right to translation,[148] the right to information in criminal proceedings,[149] and the right to an attorney.[150] There are current proposals being debated on the

---

144 As is the EAW, see Case C-399/11 *Melloni v. Ministerio Fiscal*, Judgment of 26 February 2014, § 62.

145 Ibid. at § 63.

146 Resolution of the Council on a Roadmap for strengthening procedural rights of suspected or accused persons in criminal proceedings, 30 November 2009, 2009 OJ C 295/1.
Reforms have been considered by EU bodies for at least the last decade. See Green Paper on procedural safeguards for suspects and defendants in criminal proceedings throughout the EU, 19 February 2003, COM (2003) 75 final; and the ensuing Proposal for a Council Framework Decision on certain procedural rights in criminal proceedings throughout the European Union, 28 April 2004, COM (2004) 328 final.

147 Resolution of the Council on a Roadmap for strengthening procedural rights of suspected or accused persons in criminal proceedings, 30 November 2009, 2009 OJ C 295/1.

148 Directive 2010/64/EU of the European Parliament and of the Council of 20 October 2010 on the right to interpretation and translation in criminal proceedings.

149 Directive 2012/13/EU of the European Parliament and of the Council of 22 May 2012 on the right to information in criminal proceedings.

150 Directive 2013/48/EU of the European Parliament and of the Council of 22 October 2013 on the right of access to a lawyer in criminal proceedings and in European arrest warrant

procedural rights of vulnerable persons,[151] the presumption of innocence,[152] and the provision of legal aid in certain situations,[153] with more plans for the future.[154]

Without examining the specifics of these directives and proposals, the significance is that the EU is clearly actively working to harmonize rules of criminal procedure across national borders. This activity at a "federal" legislative level in the EU stands in contrast to the US system.

5.3. THE (LACK OF) SUB-CONSTITUTIONAL CRIMINAL PROCEDURE IN THE US

Already noted, there is a large body of criminal procedure law which is applicable to all American states as well as the federal government: that promulgated by the US Supreme Court through the Fourth, Fifth and Sixth Amendments to the Constitution. Through incorporation, the limits on searches and seizures, the rights to silence and attorneys, and so on, have generated specific requirements of state criminal procedure. What is more, the Supreme Court's willingness to go beyond broad statements of the law has made "due process" jurisprudence truly more akin to criminal procedure than fundamental rights in many regards.

The requirement by the court of specific treatment of due process rights and remedies, and certain "prophylactic" measures, affect even minor procedural details of criminal investigations and trials. It is beyond the scope of this chapter to examine the full range of constitutional criminal procedure in the US, but some examples are in order: violations of fundamental protections in the Fourth Amendment against search and seizure are dealt by constitutional-level exclusionary remedies;[155] the right to silence in the Fifth Amendment is accompanied by a ban on commenting on this silence at trial.[156] Probably most illustrative of this judicial foray into constitutional criminal procedure was the case of *Miranda v. Arizona*, where the Fifth Amendment was found to require a specific set of warnings be given to criminal suspects prior to police

---

proceedings, and on the right to have a third party informed upon deprivation of liberty and to communicate with third persons and with consular authorities while deprived of liberty.

151 Commission recommendation of 27 November 2013 on procedural safeguards for vulnerable persons suspected or accused in criminal proceedings, 2013 OJ C 817/8.

152 Proposal for a directive of the European Parliament and of the Council on the strengthening of certain aspects of the presumption of innocence and of the right to be present at trial in criminal proceedings, COM (2013) 821 final.

153 Proposal for a directive of the European Parliament and of the Council on provisional legal aid for suspects or accused persons deprived of liberty and legal aid in European arrest warrant proceedings, COM (2013) 824 final, 27 November 2013.

154 Green Paper, Strengthening mutual trust in the European judicial area – A Green Paper on the application of EU criminal justice legislation in the field of detention, COM (2011) 327 final.

155 For instance, the "exclusionary rule", excluding evidence obtained in violation of Fourth Amendment search and seizure rules, was applied to the states in *Mapp v. Ohio*, 367 U.S. 643 (1961).

156 *Grifin v. California*, 380 U.S. 609 (1947); *Doyle v. Ohio*, 426 U.S. 610 (1976).

interrogation.[157] Violations of these requirements themselves mandate exclusion of evidence.[158] Although the Court later claimed that this requirement was not itself a constitutional right but merely a set of "prophylactic standards",[159] this was in turn clarified by a case which reaffirmed its constitutional standing.[160]

As a result of this judicial practice, American criminal procedure textbooks are largely grounded in constitutional law. Although the ALI which drafted the Model Penal Code, also promulgated a Model Code of Criminal Procedure in 1930,[161] it has received minimal treatment in comparison. It is not relevant for our discussion whether or how disparate state criminal procedure rules are in the US, it is simply important that this is not an area subject to lots of federal, legislative regulation. It emphasizes again that while the US has a more supreme federal government than the EU, it is also more willing or able to leave many criminal law issues to the states.

6. CONCLUSION

Earlier in this book, we noted the significance of mutual recognition and judicial cooperation to the EU legal order. Where the EU in many ways lacks some of the federal powers present in the US system, its law focuses on cooperation between its states and horizontal federalism. We saw that even strongly "European" instruments of criminal law, like the European Public Prosecutor's Office and the regulation of EU financial crimes, happen through national implementation and indirect enforcement. In contrast, the United States was shown to be a federal system with supreme, direct powers, including criminal law authority. Thus, the US has its own (sprawling) criminal law, its own enforcement, and its own courts; states are not necessarily involved in federal criminal priorities.

In this chapter, we have taken a closer look at some of the strongly federal elements of the EU and the US, those dealing with interstate relationships within the unions and with federal authority over criminal laws within the states. The different foci of the two systems, mutual recognition versus direct federal supremacy, have resulted in different treatment of federal issues. As a result of this, we have suggested that the EU is lacking in its direct control over criminal law, at least in some areas, and the US is overcriminalized at a federal level. This chapter illustrates the flip side of the federalism issue, demonstrating that the EU truly does represent a federal state of some sort. A repeated theme of this chapter has been how the lack of direct federal control in Europe ultimately

157 *Miranda v. Arizona*, 384 U.S. 436 (1966).

158 Ibid. at 479.

159 *Michigan v. Tucker*, 417 U.S. 433, 443–44 (1974).

160 *Dickerson v. United States*, 530 U.S. 428, 438 (2000).

161 Kenneth Katkin, *"Incorporation" of the Criminal Procedure Amendments: the View from the States*, Neb. L. Rev. 84 (2005) 397 at 461.

results in more invasive regulation at the Member State level, while the US federal government takes a more hands-off approach to its interstate relations.

Although it proves the EU federalism that some would deny, this result is not actually that surprising. Mutual recognition itself requires that the EU Member States honor the results of foreign criminal processes, as illustrated by the EAW and Schengen rules on *ne bis in idem*. The US also mandates some cooperation in these areas, also providing for a system of compulsory "extradition" between states (although of surprisingly recent vintage), although the double jeopardy provision of the Constitution skirts the issue of dual criminality through its framing of crimes. In turn, the creation of EU level norms and the harmonization of criminal law across borders is a requirement of functioning mutual recognition as well. As the Roadmap – a federal legislative approach to procedural harmonization with no parallel in the US system – notes in its recitals, "[m]utual recognition presupposes that the competent authorities of the Member States trust the criminal justice systems of the other Member States."[162] In order to foster the necessary trust, EU standardization of the substance and procedures of criminal law goes beyond anything in the US in terms of its interference with state sovereignty.

A few examples drive the point home. As discussed, the US Constitution grants limited powers to its federal government, but through the evolution of case law and the Necessary and Proper Clause, the US government remains free to pass many laws which are directly applicable and enforceable by federal agencies.[163] Conversely, the bulk of European law leaves implementation to the Member States through their own legal procedures.[164] Phrased in those terms, the EU is avoiding expanding its own competence and leaving powers vested in the nations of Europe. However, it is interesting to note that the US federal government is actually denied this very power on federalism grounds because it is too invasive of state sovereignty. The American Congress is in fact forbidden from forcing its constituent states to legislate themselves, referred to as "commandeering".[165] These cases overturned federal statutes compelling state action under the Tenth Amendment, perhaps the most explicit constitutional reference to federalism as a controlling idea; the Supreme Court finds such action

162 Roadmap, recitation no. 8, p. 2.

163 In theory, the federal government is limited to those powers enumerated in the Constitution. See *Gregory v. Ashcroft*, 501 U.S. 452, 457 (1991) ("The Constitution created a Federal Government of limited powers"). However, through interpretation and perhaps necessity, there arguably remain few true limits on the subject matter of federal action. See *Gonzales v. Raich*, 545 U.S. 1, 58 (2005) (Thomas, J., dissenting) ("Respondents Diane Monson and Angel Raich use marijuana that has never been bought or sold, that has never crossed state lines, and that has had no demonstrable effect on the national market for marijuana. If Congress can regulate this under the Commerce Clause, then it can regulate virtually anything").

164 Article 288 TFEU (providing that directives are binding as to result but "leave to the national authorities the choice of form and methods); Article 291 TFEU (requiring Member States to "adopt all measures of national law necessary to implement legally binding Union acts").

165 *New York v. United States*, 505 U.S. 144 (1992); *Printz v. United States*, 521 U.S. 898 (1997).

"fundamentally incompatible with … [the] system of dual sovereignty."[166] Since the federal US government has its own legislative competence, interference with state lawmaking, routine in the EU, is unnecessary and invasive.

One more glaring example of the more extreme federalism of the EU is found in the *Melloni* case, where EU Member States are actually forbidden from applying constitutional, fundamental rights protection that goes beyond that of the "incorporated" European instruments. Some comparison of the *Melloni* situation may be made to US federal preemption,[167] but this sort of fundamental rights preemption simply does not arise in the United States. States are free to apply their own standards within their own sovereign spheres. It is the differences in the US federal system which may explain the "freedom" of states to act – and also illustrate the relative power of the US federal government. Where the US federal government seeks to charge an individual with a crime, it may do so under federal law, with federal agents, and federal courts – the fact that the state holds itself to a higher criminal due process standard is irrelevant. Thus it is the relative weakness of the EU, its inability to act directly, which creates a threat to European policy were Member States free to disregard clear direction from the EU level for national reasons. In fairness, American states would still be unable to resist surrendering criminals under the interstate rendition clause due to concerns over due process in the courts of another state, as was the case in *Melloni*.[168] However, we may at a minimum say that the EU arrives at the same coercive result, and in some ways applies federal coercion, which is forbidden under the US system.

What is clear from the foregoing is that the EU has federal powers and deals with many of the same issues that are present in other federal states like the US. For this reason, it is important to carefully consider and plan for the future development of EU power, by acknowledging the reality of federal concerns which drive expansion and by taking lessons from the American experience. For instance, previous chapters have outlined how American criminal law, initially limited at the federal level, has expanded to overwhelming proportions, often criticized by scholars and practitioners. What is more, this expansion happened even while theoretically considering that the federal government was limited to those powers specifically listed in Article I of the Constitution. Similarly, we have noted that the competence of the EU has been on the rise, even in terms of substantive, European crimes. As in the US, this growth is probably inevitable to some degree – those interests that have true federal dimensions are appropriately addressed at a federal level. By resisting considered expansion in areas of genuine federal interest, opponents may eventually force the EU to expand in unexpected

---

166 *Printz v. United States*, 521 U.S. 898, 935 (1997).

167 Daniel Sarmiento, *Who's Afraid of the Charter? The Court of Justice, National Courts and the New Framework of Fundamental Rights Protection in Europe*, Common Market Law Review 50 (2013), at 1291 fn. 95.

168 In *Melloni*, Spain resisted extradition under a European Arrest Warrant on the basis of an *in absentia* conviction, which violated its constitutional due process.

ways. For examples, we may look to the development of Commerce Clause powers under the Necessary and Proper Clause in the US, which eventually became unmoored from their theoretical foundation; alternatively, EU bodies have shown the willingness and ability to expand their own competence when it appeared necessary to the EU system, from the earlier ECJ cases introducing human rights in the first place to the *Melloni* decision which eviscerates the plain language of Article 53 of the Charter.

In addition to the wisdom of allowing for well-defined and thought-out powers for necessary EU action in order to prevent less sensible expansion, this chapter has also shown that EU power, once granted, may in some instances be more invasive of national sovereignty than in the US. This very interference with state prerogatives may actually occur *because of* the focus on horizontal rather than direct federalism. As acknowledged in *Melloni* and the Roadmap on Procedural Rights, mutual recognition as a cornerstone of EU cooperation makes harmonized procedures and laws especially important. Where the US has the ability to address its own interests without "commandeering" state government, the implementation of EU law pretends to leave sovereignty in the hands of state governments to enact law, while in reality leaving them no choice but to comply. Particularly where criminal law issues are appropriate for European regulation, like dealing with fraud in regards to EU funds, direct EU criminal laws and enforcement powers will allow the reasonable/inevitable regulation of this area while actually leaving the Member States more autonomy to operate in their domestic spheres.

7. CASE STUDY: EUROPEAN DUE PROCESS IN ACTION: THE CASE OF SPANISH SECRECY COURT PROCEEDINGS[169]

7.1. INTRODUCTION

The Spanish system of criminal justice is a relic, drafted in the Victorian era (1882). For more than a century, patchwork reforms have updated an outmoded approach, but an extremely peculiar institution remains: the ability of an investigating court to declare the proceedings secret from the defense but not the Public Prosecutor. The court conducting the investigation may then issue warrants, wiretap conversations, and order detention without informing the defendants that are party to the proceedings. Defendants with no access to the case file therefore find the possibility of exercising their defense rights curtailed.

This section contends that this practice violates what we term European due process, comprised of the European Convention on Human Rights and the

[169] This section has been written by Carlos Gómez-Jara and Nathan Schaal Wilson.

Charter of Fundamental Rights of the European Union, as well as the case law of the European Court of Human Rights and the European Court of Justice. For one thing, individuals are guaranteed a European right to prompt information on the nature and cause of the offense with which they are charged, and these rights are violated by a court procedure which remains hidden. Furthermore, the fact that these proceedings curtails the European right to information mandates a higher burden on the state to respect other rights. Specifically, the reasonable time of secrecy proceedings must be understood to be shorter than the reasonable time in a regular criminal investigation; in practice, secrecy proceedings can drag on for years.

Consistent enforcement of fundamental rights throughout the EU is paramount in an era of increased cooperation across national borders. The case law of the ECtHR and the ECJ regarding European due process is being steadily incorporated into the national legal systems. The beauty of this evolution is that it strengthens human rights even in national systems that have otherwise upheld suspect institutions, like Spanish secret court proceedings, that violate European due process. Similar to the American incorporation experience, greater human rights protection at the European level is being "incorporated" into national systems which fall below the new European due process standard.

7.2. SPANISH SECRECY PROCEEDINGS

The "secrecy proceedings" (*secreto de sumario*) referred to in this section are those conducted under the authority of a court of law, not those conducted by the police or the Public Prosecutor without the knowledge of the suspect. The remarkable feature of the Spanish inquisitorial system is that the *secreto de sumario* is conducted by an Investigation *Court*, the *Juez de Instrucción*, i.e. these are judicial proceedings, not mere police investigations. A procedure declared secret from the defense clearly favors the prosecution, shattering the already precarious balance between prosecution and defense.

Spanish legislation acknowledges the intrusive nature of secrecy court proceedings. As a result, Article 302 of the Spanish Rules of Criminal Procedure (L.E. Crim. 302) provides that criminal proceedings can be declared secret for only one month.[170] However, this intended limit may be undone through the possibility of extending secrecy time, in some cases for years. This practice conflicts with the European due process envisioned in Article 6 ECHR. Both the right to prompt information and the right to a trial within a reasonable time stand in sharp contrast to the Spanish system of secret investigation and its blatant asymmetry between prosecution and defense. The current reality in Spain is that secrecy proceedings are utilized far more than their exceptional nature

170 Article 302 Ley de Enjuiciamiento Criminal (L.E. Crim.) (Spain).

would suggest.[171] Given the potential abuse of this system, through rote extension of a supposedly limited period, there is a clear need for stricter limits, either in legislation or case law.

7.3. EUROPEAN DUE PROCESS AND SECRECY PROCEEDINGS

We turn now to the law relevant to the *secreto de sumario*. The primary point of reference for this case study is the ECHR as the most developed institution of European due process. Additionally, other international rights standards like the Charter are expressly tied to ECHR interpretation.[172] In light of the recent deadline for the implementation of the EU Directive on the right to information in criminal proceedings,[173] this is clearly a pressing issue.

The modern approach of the ECtHR is to consider potential violations under Article 6(3) – such as whether sufficient information was given to a defendant – "in the light of the more general right to a fair hearing guaranteed by Article 6 § 1."[174] Thus Article 6(1)'s guarantee of overall fairness overlaps with the specific guarantees of Article 6(3), and these provisions are considered together in determining "whether the proceedings in their entirety were fair".[175] This approach suggests that the bundle of rights created by all of Article 6 is interconnected;[176] "any difficulties caused to the defence by a limitation on its rights must be sufficiently counterbalanced".[177] In particular, the court has found "that denying the applicant access to the case file ... constituted a substantial impairment of the right to a fair trial in view of the breach of the principle of equality of arms."[178]

"The principle of equality of arms ... [is] one of the features of the wider concept of a fair trial."[179] This requirement demands that both parties be given the opportunity to present their case without "substantial disadvantage".[180] Only

---

171 Alex Tinsley, *Protecting Criminal Defence Rights through EU Law: Opportunities and Challenges*, New J. of Eur. Crim. L. 4 (2013) at 461, 477–78 (citing reports by practitioners of excessive use of secrecy procedures in Spain).

172 Charter of Fundamental Rights of the European Union, Article 52(3).

173 Directive 2012/13/EU, of the European Parliament and of the Council, of 22 May 2012 on the right to information in criminal proceedings, 2012 OJ L 142/1.

174 *Szabo and others v. Romania*, App. No. 8193/06, 18 March 2014, § 50.

175 *Rowe and Davis v. United Kingdom*, App. No. 28901/95, 16 February 2000, § 59.

176 See *Golder v. the United Kingdom*, App. No. 4451/70, 21 February 1975, § 28 ("Article 6 para. 1 (art. 6-1) ... enunciates rights which are distinct but stem from the same basic idea and which, taken together, make up a single right ...").

177 *Jasper v. UK*, App. No. 27052/95, 16 February 2000, § 52 (notably, this case dealt with secrecy at the trial stage).

178 *Foucher v. France*, App. No. 22209/93, 18 March 1997, § 27 (referencing the opinion of the Commission which was ultimately affirmed with the finding of a violation of Article 6(1) taken together with Article 6(3)).

179 *Foucher v. France*, App. No. 22209/93, 18 March 1997, § 34.

180 *Dombo Beheer B.V. v. the Netherlands*, App. No. 14448/88, 27 October 1993, § 33.

those restrictions on the defense "which are strictly necessary are permissible under Article 6 § 1."[181] This clashes with a procedure that allows only one party – the prosecution – access to the evidence and indeed the court itself. In one case finding that equality of arms was not respected, the ECtHR specifically noted that "it is ... unfair for the prosecution to make submissions to a court without the knowledge of the defense."[182]

While law enforcement authorities or prosecutors commonly investigate potential crimes without informing every suspect, Spanish secrecy proceedings are actually conducted under the authority of a judge. When a court of law gets involved, the urgency of informing the defendants of the accusation becomes self-evident on at least two interconnected grounds. First, legal action before a court signals a more pressing need for defendants to begin formulating their defense; second, since a court may impose precautionary measures such as pretrial detention, freezing of assets, etc., defendants must be given enough information to contest these measures.

Furthermore, one key function of the judiciary is to protect individuals from precisely the sort of actions represented by the Spanish secret investigations; a judicial check on the police power of the state is a fundamental value that the European legal tradition holds dear. For this reason, the ECtHR has been particularly protective of the requirement of "an independent and impartial tribunal".[183] Beyond questions of actual bias, the court requires "an appearance of independence" and "sufficient guarantees to exclude legitimate doubt in this respect".[184] The ECtHR has become increasingly sensitive to the appearance of the court procedures in the eye of the public[185] and "the confidence which the courts in a democratic society must inspire".[186] Confidence in an unbiased judiciary is clearly undermined by a secret procedure where a judge and prosecutor operate behind closed doors without the involvement of the defendant.

Against this background, we believe that the specific provisions of Article 6 ECHR set fundamental boundaries that the Spanish secret proceedings do not respect. Article 6 ECHR provides for the right of citizens to be informed of that which they are accused of. The correlative obligation of the state to provide such information is clearly applicable earlier than the trial itself, regardless of later disclosures at trial. This right to information from Article 6(3)(a) ECHR is directly

181 *Edwards and Lewis v. UK* (fourth section), App. Nos. 39647/98 & 40461/98, 22 July 2003, § 53 (affirmed by the Grand Chamber, 27 October 2004).

182 *Bulut v. Austria*, App. No. 17358/90, 22 February 1996, § 49.

183 The court considers the concepts of independence and impartiality closely linked and often considers the two together. See e.g. *Findlay v. UK*, App. No. 22107/93, 25 February 1997, § 73.

184 *Findlay v. UK*, App. No. 22107/93, 25 February 1997, at § 73.

185 *Borgers v. Belgium*, App. No. 12005/86, 30 October 1991, § 24 (noting "considerable evolution in the Court's case law, notably in respect of the importance attached to appearances"); *Findlay v. UK*, App. No. 22107/93, 25 February 1997, at § 76 (stating that "appearances may be of importance").

186 *Henryk Urban and Ryszard Urban v. Poland*, App. No. 23614/08, 30 November 2010, § 45.

threatened by secret investigations under Spanish law. Furthermore, because these limits on Article 6(3) rights threaten the equality of arms, and therefore overall fairness of the criminal process, such measures – if allowable at all – must be strictly limited. Specifically, Article 6 ECHR's guarantee of "reasonable time" for criminal procedure must be especially applicable to Spanish secrecy proceedings; a practice of *ad eternum* secret investigations violates the rights of criminal defendants. Recalling the considerations of overall fairness, equality of arms, and the appearance of judicial independence, we look at the specific ECtHR treatment of the right to information in criminal proceedings and the right to a trial within a reasonable time.

7.4. THE RIGHT TO INFORMATION IN ARTICLE 6(3)(A) ECHR

The right to prompt information is crucial to the ability of an individual to mount an effective defense in response to criminal charges, as guaranteed by Article 6(3)(b) ECHR.[187] "[P]rovision of full, detailed information concerning the charges against a defendant, and ... the legal characterization that the court might adopt in the matter, is an essential prerequisite for ensuring that the proceedings as a whole are fair."[188] Equality of arms, thus overall fairness, is threatened where defendants are denied access to information at the pretrial stage.[189]

There is little case law available to specifically define "promptness" in this context. The ECtHR continues to rely on the basic premise that "any relevant information, whether of fact or law, must obviously be given to the accused in sufficient time to enable him to prepare his defense in accordance with his entitlement under Article 6(3)(b)."[190] In *Mattoccia v. Italy*, the ECtHR takes particular note of an interview of a suspect by the public prosecutor prior to his indictment, noting that, due to a lack of information, the suspect was unable to adequately address the charges against him.[191] The court's concerns over this early stage of the proceedings imply that the right to information about a criminal accusation is relevant as early as a pre-indictment interview by the authorities. Failure to provide such information has led to findings of violations of Article 6(3)(a) during judicial investigations in other contexts, even when a formal accusation was never brought.[192]

[187] *Pélissier and Sassi v. France* (GC), App. No. 25444/94, 25 March 1999, § 54.

[188] Ibid. at § 52.

[189] See e.g. *Foucher v. France* (finding a violation of the principle of equality of arms and Article 6(1) ECHR where defendant has no access to his case file).

[190] Interrights Manual for Lawyers, *Right to a Fair Trial under the European Convention on Human Rights (article 6)*, 2009 at 63 (citing *Chichlian and Ekindjian v. France*, App. No. 10959/84, 16 March 1989).

[191] *Mattoccia v. Italy*, App. No. 23969/94, 25 July 2000, § 63.

[192] e.g. *Casse v. Luxembourg*, App. No. 40327/02, 27 April 2006.

These cases make clear that the right to information on charges may attach even at the investigation stage of criminal procedure. The ECtHR has noted "the importance of the investigation stage for the preparation of the criminal proceedings, as the evidence obtained during this stage determines the framework in which the offence charged will be considered at trial."[193] In order for a proceeding to be fair as a whole, a failure to abide by the requirement of Article 6(3)(a) ECHR cannot simply be remedied by later disclosure; in some cases the fairness of the trial as a whole will be prejudiced by such an initial failure.[194] Although the information which must be given to prepare a defense under Article 6(3)(b) is more extensive than that of Article 6(3)(a), there is still no justification for withholding all information during the pretrial investigation stage. A lack of earlier disclosure can still constitute a violation of the defendant's rights, even if such information is given at trial.[195] A brief examination of ECtHR case law on the right to information is useful to shed light on the specific context of the Spanish *secreto de sumario.*

7.4.1. Information for the Preparation of Defense

"The essence of the right to receive information under Article 6(3)(a) is that it should be sufficient to enable an accused to begin formulating his defence."[196] This standard does not require the details of all the evidence in the prosecutor's file; a fuller disclosure will be required later to satisfy the requirements of Article 6(3)(b) which specifically guarantees the ability to prepare a defense. Still, the ECtHR has increasingly stressed the connection between Article 6(3)(a) and Article 6(3)(b). In a decision from March 2014, the Court stated the following:

> "The Court considers that in criminal matters the provision of full, detailed information concerning the charges against a defendant, and consequently the legal characterisation that the court might adopt in the matter, is an essential prerequisite for ensuring that the proceedings are fair. *As regards the complaint under Article 6 § 3 (b) of the Convention, the Court reiterates that sub-paragraphs (a) and (b) of Article 6 § 3 are connected and that the right to be informed of the nature and the cause of the accusation must be considered in the light of the accused's right to prepare his defence.*"[197]

---

193 *Salduz v. Turkey*, App. No. 36381/02, 27 November 2008, § 54.
194 See *Imbrioscia v. Switzerland*, App. No. 13972/88, 24 November 1993, § 36.
195 *Mattoccia v. Italy*, at § 52 (finding that even if an imprecise charge were to be remedied at trial, there was still a violation of the applicant's rights).
196 Interrights Manual for Lawyers, *Right to a Fair Trial under the European Convention on Human Rights (article 6)*, 2009 at 61.
197 *Szabo and others v. Romania*, at § 50 (emphasis added).

Similar wording may be found in another case, this one brought against the Spanish government.[198]

Underlying the disclosure requirements of Article 6(3)(a) ECHR is a need to allow defendants to fully participate in their own trial. This fundamental need is supported by a number of considerations, both practical and theoretical. From a judicial efficiency perspective, preliminary negotiations about the case cannot be effectively conducted without both parties. If informed, the suspect could speed the entire process by admitting guilt or providing exculpatory evidence. Furthermore, the right to information is crucial to allow the exercise of other defense rights that are meaningless without knowledge of the charges (or worse yet, without knowledge of the investigation at all). Essentially, knowledge is a prerequisite for the effective exercise of defense rights. For example, a right to refuse questioning cannot be effectively exercised by a suspect who does not know the matter on which he is being questioned. Such rights are crucial even at a pretrial stage to protect individuals from abuse of government powers. The involvement of the defendant can avoid lasting prejudice which invalidates a subsequent trial. An informed defendant can object to illegally obtained evidence, which in some cases raises "a strong presumption that the use of items of evidence obtained [as the result of such illegal evidence] ... renders a trial as a whole unfair."[199]

7.4.2. Article 6(3)(a) ECHR in the Context of Secrecy Proceedings

If Article 6(3)(a) ECHR applies to those under secret investigation in Spain then the incompatibility of the *secreto de sumario* with such a requirement is obvious: under such procedures defendants are given no information whatsoever. Thus, the main issue to address is the applicability of the right to information in pretrial secrecy proceedings.

While technically still "investigation", it is clear that the ECtHR applies defense rights to even these early stages of the criminal process.[200] Over two decades ago, the Court had special concern for the requirements of Article 6(3) which may prejudice a subsequent trial due to an initial failure to comply,[201] indicating the direction of the ECtHR; that case has since been overruled in favor

[198] *Varela Geis v. Spain*, App. No. 61005/09, 5 March 2013, § 44 ("Enfin, quant au grief tiré de l'article 6 § 3 b) de la Convention, la Cour estime qu'il existe un lien entre les alinéas a) et b) de l'article 6 § 3 et que le droit à être informé sur la nature et la cause de l'accusation doit être envisagé à la lumière du droit pour l'accusé de préparer sa défense.").

[199] *Gäfgen v. Germany* (Fifth Section), App. No. 22978/05, 30 June 2008, § 105 (affirmed by the Grand Chamber, 1 June 2010) (referring in that case to confessions obtained in violation of Article 3 ECHR and the so-called "fruit of the poisonous tree" doctrine).

[200] *Imbrioscia v. Switzerland*, at § 36 ("the primary purpose of Article 6 ... is to ensure a fair trial by a 'tribunal' competent to determine 'any criminal charge', but it does not follow that the Article (art. 6) has no application to pre-trial proceedings.").

[201] *Imbrioscia v. Switzerland.*

of greater protections as early as police interrogation.[202] In the specific context of Article 6(3)(a), the *Mattoccia* case suggests that some information must be given to defendants even during interrogation at an investigatory stage.[203] The ECtHR in that case reasoned that the applicant was not "provided with sufficient information as is necessary ... to preparing an adequate defense."[204] The court notes that Mattoccia, in dealing with pretrial investigation, "adopted a line of defense which was manifestly inadequate" because he did not know the full details of the crime of which he was accused.[205] If such logic is applied to Spanish secrecy proceedings, where the investigation is actually conducted by a court of law with its judicial powers, surely there must be greater disclosure of the "nature and cause" as required under the ECHR.[206]

The fact that Spanish secrecy proceedings are conducted by a court makes the need to protect the accused even more significant. The ECHR demands an independent and impartial judiciary in the examination of crimes, a requirement which is threatened by secret proceedings between the prosecution and the court. Furthermore, a court brings to bear those investigatory and compulsory powers of the judiciary that extend beyond those of the police. Most significantly, the courts are able to imprison the target of secrecy proceedings pending their conclusion; to do so without an explanation as to why is patently counter to Article 6 (and incidentally, Article 5) ECHR. Other powers include freezing or seizure of personal assets and subpoenas of personal information. All of these powers implicate personal rights which cannot be protected without knowledge of what is happening and why; as discussed above, basic information about charges is a prerequisite to the effective exercise of other defense rights. These judicial powers also make the risk of illegal action by the government, in search or seizure, more significant. Information is crucial to allow individuals to challenge state action in a timely fashion and prevent subsequent actions based on illegally obtained material. This is important since such actions could ultimately taint the fairness of the trial as a whole. Failure to respect these rights at an early stage – more likely

202 *Salduz v. Turkey*, at § 55 ("as a rule, access to a lawyer should be provided as from the first interrogation of a suspect by the police." This is in contrast with the Imbrioscia case, which found no violation where the accused was not given access to an attorney when questioned by police.).

203 See *Mattoccia v. Italy.*

204 *Mattoccia v. Italy*, at § 60.

205 *Mattoccia v. Italy*, at § 63.

206 We must admit that there are specific concerns in the context of interrogation, such as protection against self-incrimination, which might explain some of the ECtHR's actions in applying a right to information or an attorney in these situations. However, given the guarantee of equality of arms and the purpose of the ECHR as a check on government power, it would be unreasonable and circular to provide lower standards for informing the targets of court action precisely because the government has chosen not to alert the accused of their jeopardy. This logic would allow the government to opt out of any disclosure requirement under Article 6 ECHR.

without defense involvement – at best requires more time and effort to rectify at a later date and at worst leaves the defendant irreparably harmed.

All of these points demonstrate that true protection of individual rights in criminal procedure is based on information being given to the defendant, but there is also an independent value in transparency and fairness. A process which empowers and informs the prosecutor while leaving the defendant in the dark threatens these values. Clearly, the Spanish *secreto de sumario* does not provide the necessary information for defendants to effectively prepare a defense, the guiding principle of Article 6(3)(a) ECHR. That this unfairness happens with support from a judiciary which is bound to remain independent and neutral goes against the basic guarantees of Article 6 in general.

7.5. TRIAL WITHIN A REASONABLE TIME IN ARTICLE 6 ECHR

It is clear from the foregoing that there are serious questions about the basic legitimacy of Spanish secrecy proceedings, given the threat to Article 6(3)(a) rights. If such proceedings are allowable in some limited form, the interference with the rights of the defense must be "sufficiently counterbalanced" to protect the equality of arms and fairness as a whole.[207] If defendants are not granted the full information which is their right, there must be a special urgency on the part of the state to end secret proceedings as soon as is possible.[208] Surely secret investigations must be limited more than investigations which are conducted in the public eye and with the knowledge of defendants. Establishing appropriate "length of proceedings" limits in any given case is a difficult task, given the principle of proportionality and the need to serve conflicting interests. The fact that the Spanish Criminal Code itself sets one month as an initial limit for declaring the proceedings secret gives a good starting point. However, the Spanish government's unwillingness to comply with the spirit of its own legislation is demonstrated by the routine extension of this time far beyond its intended limit, illustrating the need for more exacting standards from European due process.

---

207 *Jasper v. UK*, at § 52.

208 In an analogous situation, dealing with limitations on the right to an attorney during investigation, the ECtHR has noted that "any exception to this right should be clearly circumscribed and its application strictly limited in time." *Salduz v. Turkey*, at § 54. It seems reasonable to apply the same strict time limits to a situation where other defense rights are threatened.

7.5.1. *Length of Proceedings: the Law*

Much has been written about the "reasonable time" provision of Article 6 ECHR, the source of the most commonly found violation by the ECtHR.[209] The fact that there is no case law on the extension of secrecy proceedings is probably due to the distinct nature of Spanish secrecy proceedings, not found in the rest of Europe. However, there are many principles in ECtHR case law on the Article 6 right to a trial in a reasonable time which are relevant to the Spanish system and secrecy proceedings.

7.5.1.1. Beginning of the "Reasonable Time" Measure

In judging the speediness of a criminal trial, the ECtHR must initially determine what period of time to assess for "reasonableness". "In criminal matters, the 'reasonable time' referred to in Article 6 par. 1 (art. 6-1) begins to run as soon as a person is 'charged'; this may occur on a date prior to the case coming before the trial court, such as ... the date when preliminary investigations were opened."[210] Despite the term "charged", the Court uses functional tests; even where there is no official notification of a charge, "other measures which carry the implication of such an allegation and which likewise substantially affect the situation of the suspect"[211] may trigger the requirement of reasonable length under Article 6(1) ECHR.

The ECtHR has clearly stated that the "reasonable time" of Article 6(1) is applicable during pretrial proceedings,[212] and violations of the reasonable length requirement have been found even in cases that have not made it past the investigation stage.[213] In fact, the court has taken particular note that "proceedings remained at the preliminary investigation stage".[214] One significant element of pretrial proceedings is self-evident: any time spent prior to the trial will necessarily form only part of the procedure as a whole.

---

209 European Court of Human Rights, *Violations by Article and State 1959–2013* (available at: www.echr.coe.int/Documents/Stats_violation_1959_2013_ENG.pdf) (showing length of proceedings as almost 1/3 of total violations, 30.9%); The European Court of Human Rights, *50 years of activity* (available at: www.echr.coe.int/Documents/Facts_Figures_1959_2009_ENG.pdf) (showing 26.37% of the cases in which the Court finds an infringement of the ECHR concern the length of proceedings).

210 *Eckle v. Germany*, App. No. 8130/78, 15 July 1982, § 73 (citation omitted).

211 *Corigliano v. Italy*, App. No. 8304/78, 10 December 1982, § 34.

212 *Imbrioscia v. Switzerland*, at § 36.

213 *Viezzer v. Italy*, App. No. 12598/86, 19 February 1991, §§ 15–17.

214 *Vachev v. Bulgaria*, App. No. 42987/98, 8 July 2004, § 96. See also *Karamitrov and Others v. Bulgaria*, App. No. 53321/99, 10 January 2008, § 55; *Ivan Hristov v. Bulgaria*, App. No. 32461/02, 20 March 2008, § 54.

7.5.1.2. Factors Considered by the Court

The question of what constitutes reasonable time "must be assessed in the light of the particular circumstances of the case".[215] Four broad issues have been identified as important when assessing the reasonableness of the length of proceedings:[216] the complexity of the case; the conduct of the applicant; the conduct of state authorities; and the nature of the proceedings, i.e. what is at stake for the defendant.[217]

Insofar as the ECtHR has specifically defined it, complexity can refer to a large number of evidentiary issues to be examined, multiple defendants, or multiple charges.[218] Overall, the court seems to take a common sense approach to complexity rather than spelling out specific factors. Regardless, a finding of complexity may justify a longer criminal process, while a case that is not complex must be shorter.

Conduct of the parties to a trial is also considered by the ECtHR in determining reasonable length. Delays that are the result of actions by the applicant will not be counted against the government in a complaint over the length of proceedings. At the same time, defendants will not be punished for fully pursuing legal remedies and defenses:[219] there is no duty "actively to co-operate with the judicial authorities".[220] At the same time, the conduct of the government stands in contrast to that of the defense. Actions by the state not designed to fully respect the right to a trial in a reasonable time undermine the government's explanations for overly long proceedings. In particular, "Article 6 para. 1 (art. 6-1) imposes on the Contracting States the duty to organise their legal systems in such a way that their courts can meet each of its requirements."[221]

Lastly, the ECtHR considers what is at stake for the applicant.[222] The court has held that certain matters of particular importance to the applicants call for special expediency, and shorter periods may constitute a violation of the reasonable time requirement.[223] Surely the human rights guaranteed under the

215 *H. v. France*, App. No. 10073/82, 24 October 1989, § 50.

216 The ECtHR frequently refers to three considerations, those being "the complexity of the case, the behaviour of the applicant and the conduct of the relevant authorities." *H. v. France*, at § 50. More recent cases have included consideration of what is at stake for the applicant as well.

217 *László Magyar v. Hungary*, App. No. 73593/10, 10 May 2014, § 64.

218 See *Mattilla v. Finland*, App. No. 77138/01, 23 May 2006, § 15.

219 *Girardi v. Austria*, App. No. 50064/99, 11 December 2003, § 56.

220 *Eckle v. Germany*, at § 82.

221 *Abdoella v. The Netherlands*, App. No. 12728/87, 25 November 1992, § 24.

222 Pieter Van Dijk et al., *Theory and Practice of the European Convention on Human Rights*, 4th ed., 2006 at 608.

223 Christoph Grabenwarter, *Europäischen Menschenrechtskonvention*, 2nd ed., 2005 at 313. See e.g. *Docevski v. The Former Yugoslav Republic of Macedonia*, App. No. 66907/01, 1 March 2007, § 35 (pension disputes); *Niederboster v. Germany*, App. No. 39547/98, 27 February 2003 (child custody cases); *Dumanovski v. The Former Yugoslav Republic of Macedonia*, App. No. 13898/02, 8 December 2005, § 48 (labor disputes after the applicant is dismissed); *Gana v. Italy*, App. No. 13024/87, 1 January 1990, § 17 (disputes regarding civil status and capacity); *Kreps v.*

ECHR are important enough to call for expedited review;[224] for instance, cases where defendants are detained require special diligence by the state under Article 6 ECHR, as these cases deal with instances where rights under Article 5 ECHR are being restricted pending the outcome of their cases.[225] This relationship between different rights is apparent in the ECtHR's approach to specific violations of Article 6(3), examining cases under the overall right to a fair trial. Equality of arms also demands that "difficulties caused to the defense by a limitation on its rights must be sufficiently counterbalanced by the procedures followed by the judicial authorities."[226] In this case, the court was reviewing a case of information being withheld from defendants at trial.

7.5.2. *Length of Proceedings in the Context of Secrecy Proceedings*

Because of the obvious impairment of the right to information under Article 6(3)(a) ECHR, we believe that the time limit in secrecy proceedings should be governed by the following principle: whatever constitutes "reasonable time" in regular criminal proceedings must be shorter in secret criminal proceedings. ECtHR jurisprudence has reflected increasing awareness of the interconnectedness of individual rights and equality of arms in the criminal process, such that restrictions on one right (if allowable at all) must be limited and counterbalanced.[227] Furthermore, the court's assessment of "reasonable time" in different contexts also supports the argument for a stricter application to Spanish secrecy proceedings.

Initially, there is the question of when the length of proceedings period begins to run prior to a trial. The earlier discussion on the right to information on charges makes clear that due process rights apply at the pretrial stage. Specifically, the length of proceedings is measured from the moment a defendant is "charged",[228] which includes effects other than an official delivery of accusation. Again, Spanish secrecy proceedings are unlike typical investigations by police or prosecutors, which may not require the full application of ECHR rights. Rather, the Spanish *secreto de sumario* is conducted under the authority of a court of

Poland, App. No. 34097/96, 26 July 2001, §§ 52–54 (cases where defendant is detained); *Silva Pontes v. Portugal*, App. No. 14940/89, 23 March 1994, § 39 (cases determining compensation for victims of road accidents).

224 Among those situations calling for expedited review, many are linked to other ECHR guarantees: custody of children, as protected by Article 8 ECHR and Article 5 of Protocol 7 to the ECHR; decisions of mental capacity, linked to the guarantees of Article 5 ECHR which may be limited under Article 5(1)(e) due to "unsound mind"; cases where defendants are deprived of liberty, as guaranteed by Article 5 ECHR.

225 *Kreps v. Poland*, at §§ 52–54. This is distinct from the review of pretrial detention itself, which of course also calls for especially speedy review under Article 5(4) ECHR. *Hutchison Reid v. the United Kingdom*, App. No. 50272/99, 20 February 2003, § 79.

226 *Jasper v. UK*, § 52.

227 *Jasper v. UK*, at § 43 ("Any such restriction on the rights of the defence should, however, be strictly proportionate and counterbalanced by procedural safeguards adequate to compensate for the handicap imposed on the defence").

228 *Eckle v. Germany*, at § 73.

law. This distinction elevates the status of those under investigation from that of a mere suspect under investigation to a defendant charged by a criminal court. While there is no official charge, this is not due to uncertainty over whether court action will be ultimately appropriate. On the contrary, it is a function of the general lack of information given to defendants in what is already a criminal case before a court with full judicial powers. The targets of secrecy proceedings may be subject to measures affecting their freedom and property, not to mention the anxiety and reputational cost that judicial scrutiny entails.[229] Obviously this "substantially affect[s] the situation of the suspect",[230] triggering considerations of the length of proceedings.

Earlier in this case study we demonstrated that secrecy proceedings curtail defense rights guaranteed under Article 6(3)(a) ECHR. At the very least, the *secreto de sumario* comes at a cost to the defendant, threatening the equality of arms between prosecution and defense. Like the review of cases where rights under Article 5 are threatened, secret proceedings should demand a more rapid resolution than a standard criminal investigation. On the contrary, the Spanish government has shown a willingness and habit of extending secrecy proceedings far beyond a reasonable time, suggested at the first instance by the one-month limit set out in 302 L.E. Crim. However, this period is routinely extended in practice. An obvious similarity may be observed in a length of proceedings case where the court found a violation because "compliance [with a thirty-day time limit] had become the exception".[231] Even a reasonable requirement under the law is meaningless if the state authorities do not respect its intent, and clearly Spain's practice does not meet its "duty to organise their legal systems in such a way that their courts can meet each of its [Article 6(1) ECHR's] requirements."[232]

7.6. CONCLUSION

The past decade has seen an increasing awareness of the importance of procedural rights throughout Europe.[233] As the European Union increases cooperation and

229 See *Kart v. Turkey* (GC), 8917/05, 3 December 2009, §§ 68 and 70 (noting that the right to a speedy trial "is based on the need to ensure that accused persons do not have to remain too long in a state of uncertainty as to the outcome of the criminal accusations against them", and that "the vicissitudes of criminal proceedings ... generally also harm the reputation of the alleged offender"). We realize that in some ways, secrecy could at the very least protect the reputation of defendants, but experience shows that some investigations still become public. Regardless, the use of judicial powers will alert some of those closest to the accused that they are the target of an investigation.

230 *Corigliano v. Italy*, at § 34.

231 *Abdoella v. The Netherlands*, at § 24.

232 Ibid.

233 See e.g. Resolution of the Council of 30 November 2009 on a Roadmap for Strengthening Procedural Rights of Suspected or Accused Persons in Criminal Proceedings, 2009 OJ C 295/1; Directive 2010/64/EU of the European Parliament and of the Council, of 20 October 2010

integration among the Member States, the government of one country expects to be able to rely on the fundamental rights protection of its neighbors and standardization of rights has become a priority. Some of this action has been legislative,[234] but there is no denying the increased significance of European due process as described above: the power of international rights instruments like the ECHR and the Charter.

There is an obvious parallel in the American system, where, through "incorporation", the protections found in the Bill of Rights were applied to the individual states, until virtually all those protections were given power at the state level, guaranteeing a minimum threshold of "due process" even at a local level.[235] While European due process is rooted in early cases of the ECJ,[236] the entry into force of the Charter provides a clear European mandate of human rights protection across national borders.[237] Thus, just as the American courts used the federal Bill of Rights to raise the due process standards of constituent states, the ECJ and the ECtHR (which is given greater force over EU Member States through the Charter as well)[238] are in a position to promote human rights in European countries by reviewing even domestic legislation which national courts have allowed.

Clearly, the secret investigations conducted by judges and prosecutors in the Spanish system are an area where the national laws are falling below the guarantees of European due process under the ECHR and consequently the Charter. If the *secreto de sumario* is not completely disallowed, there must at least be stricter limits on the time of such investigation. While it falls first to the Spanish government to make sure that due process rights are "secured by the authorities through all appropriate means, including change of practice or legislative amendments if necessary",[239] a failure of the national authorities to uphold criminal defense rights can now be rectified at an international level. The current regime of lengthy and secret investigations, under the auspices of

on the Rights to Interpretation and Translation in Criminal Proceedings, 2010 OJ L 280/1; Directive 2013/48/EU of the European Parliament and of the Council, of 22 October 2013 on the Right of Access to a Lawyer in Criminal Proceedings, 2013 OJ L 294/1; Proposal for a Directive of the European Parliament and of the Council on the Strengthening of Certain Aspects of the Presumption of Innocence and of the Right to be Present at Trial in Criminal Proceedings, COM (2013) 821 final, 27 November 2013.

234 For instance, EU Member States are now obliged to provide certain information to criminal suspects as of 2 June 2014. Directive 2012/13/EU, at 6.

235 *McDonald v. Chicago*, 130 S. Ct. 3020 (2010) (demonstrating that the majority of the Bill of Rights is applicable now against the states, and itself incorporating the Second Amendment for the first time).

236 *Stauder v. City of Ulm*, 1969 ECR 419 (29/69) (applying "general principles of European law" to limit state action with fundamental rights protection).

237 See Tony Marguery, *European Union Fundamental Rights and Member States Action in EU Criminal Law*, Maastricht J. 20 (2013) at 282, 283 (noting the increasing significance of EU law on criminal justice, particularly since the Lisbon Treaty).

238 Charter of Fundamental Rights of the European Union, Article 52(3).

239 *Kitov v. Bulgaria*, App. No. 37104/97, 3 Apr. 2003, § 73.

a supposedly neutral court, threatens a fundamental right of European citizens. If the Spanish government does not recognize this on its own, the international community has the authority and duty to do so.

CHAPTER 5

THE SOVEREIGN DEBT CRISIS AND THE FUTURE OF EU CRIMINAL LAW

1. INTRODUCTION

When the Lisbon Treaty entered into force, the attitude of the EU towards the criminal law remained business as usual. The existing Framework Decisions were transformed into Directives, and the EU's initiative followed the same guidelines that existed previously. However, a dramatic set of events pursuant to the 2010 EU sovereign debt crisis triggered unheard-of reactions by the EU. Starting with the (in)famous bailouts of EU Member States on the brink of bankruptcy, the EU became aware of fragility of the current system and the need to protect its own financial interests. Since 2011 the communications produced by EU institutions clearly show a change in not only the rhetoric but also the actual means to be used to efficiently protect EU financial interests.

This final chapter first deals with the reaction of both Unions to financial crisis. Though from an economic perspective historical circumstances explain the different approach to the current financial crisis, a common ground can be observed when it comes to the financial interests of the Unions. In the US, the first federal criminal law provisions, i.e. federal crimes prosecuted by US attorneys, were enacted in the wake of the late 18th-century US sovereign debt crisis when the federal government had to assume the debt of the Union's member states. In a similar fashion, the EU is enacting criminal law provisions protecting EU financial interests to be enforced by European Public Prosecutors. The pressure of modern financial markets has forced the EU to take "immediate" action in this field to reassure financial investors of the soundness of EU sovereign debt.

This chapter next addresses the communications of the EU underscoring the rationale behind its approach: protecting EU taxpayers' monies, designing an anti-fraud policy and implementing a criminal law policy. There is a clear intent by EU institutions to provide a roadmap for future action. Although the language related to harmonized protection throughout the EU is used constantly, the federal "taint" can be perceived all over the EU message. The deficiencies of the approach undertaken so far have been acknowledged, and the need for an overhaul of the system is presented. The success of such an endeavor will depend on the determination of the EU institutions.

The middle portion of this chapter addresses the transition from the well-intended language of EU *communiqués* to the actual provisions proposed over the past couple of years. Three main proposals are covered: the Directive imposing criminal sanctions on market abuse, the Directive imposing criminal sanctions to protect EU financial interests and the Regulation establishing the European Public Prosecutor's Office. The key principles supporting legislative action are integrity of the EU financial markets and protection the EU budget. Being aware of the lack of adequate protection provided by the law in the books alone, the EU has established a law-in-action institution: the EPPO. Though the proposal of the EPPO only confers prosecuting powers related to the EU budget, it is reasonable to believe that in the near future market abuse with a cross-border dimension could also be included in its jurisdiction.

These developments add up to a clear indication that the EU is trying to restore investors' confidence, which makes perfect sense in the current financial climate. Comparative research shows that there is a close relationship with the level of enforcement of investor protecting provisions and the confidence of those investors in the markets, i.e. securities markets or sovereign debt markets. This is why the final portion of this chapter is devoted to proposing certain guidelines as to how to design an institutional framework that serves two purposes: strengthening the vertical dimension, while weakening the horizontal federal dimension.

2. UNITED STATES VERSUS EUROPE: DIFFERENT APPROACHES TO THE SAME PROBLEM?

From an economic perspective, the US and the EU have adopted different approaches to the 21st-century financial crisis. The US has lowered interest in an unprecedented maneuver, pumping liquidity into the system through massive injections of capital, i.e. quantitative easing programs, and a strong determination to increase debt as necessary to avoid recession. In sharp contrast, the EU has been cautiously conserving its reserves, injecting liquidity as a last resort. Only after major struggles and accepting draconian budgetary restrictions to prevent inflation have EU Member States been able to tap into the all too needed EU funds.[1] The opposing goals of avoiding recession versus avoiding inflation seem to underlie the two "federal" policies.

1 For a general consideration of the relationships between sovereign debt crisis and bailouts see Francisco Roch and Harald Uhlig, *The Dynamics of Sovereign Debt Crises and Bailouts* (available at: ec.europa.eu/economy_finance/events/.../day2-paper1_en.pdf).

The reasons for this divergent approach are manifold. It may be simplistic, but historic memory could explain these differences. The American collective memory of the Great Depression may still be very present.[2] The German hyperinflation in the Weimar Republic may also have had an impact on the approach the EU-dominant nation is taking to the crisis.[3] Notwithstanding the importance of these considerations, another significant difference appears whenever a comparison is drawn between the US and the EU: the latter is not a federal state. Even if the EU (not specific Member States) wanted to pursue a policy similar to that of the US, its structure and powers have important limitations that prevent authentic EU action.[4]

The EU has become aware of this fundamental deficit, and recent proposals (including treaty reform) are aimed at surmounting such limitations. As outlined below, those proposals include (as they must) mechanisms to enhance protection of EU financial interests from a legal point of view. Normally, criminal law sanctions and their enforcement have been left out of the EU financial policy as a result of the Member States' sovereignty concerns.[5] Given the current state of affairs, with billions of euros pouring from EU facilities to ailing Member States, sovereignty warnings have become less audible and liquidity needs more palpable. It would be unreasonable to completely entrust management of bailout funds to the same countries that mismanaged EU funds in the first place.

It has become increasingly clear that if the EU is to solve the sovereign debt problem once and for all a movement towards unification is needed. This trend in thinking is quickly catching on in the banking system, to the extent that on 13 December 2012, the Council of the EU agreed to establish the ECB as a European Supervision Authority.[6] Yet the point to be made is that something similar is needed at the enforcement level, including criminal sanctions. Notwithstanding the timid attempts made so far, a more consistent and determined step needs to be taken in the face of a rapidly changing financial environment. To the same extent

---

2 It has often been pointed out that the deep knowledge of the Great Depression by Ben Bernanke, Chairman of the Federal Reserve during the financial crisis, has impacted decisively on the American approach to the 2008 crisis. See LAURENCE BALL, *Ben Bernanke and the Zero Bound*, NBER Working Paper No. w17836 (February 2012). See also the reflections of Ben Bernanke himself in BEN BERNANKE and HAROLD JAMES, *The Gold Standard, Deflation, and Financial Crisis in the Great Depression: An International Comparison*, in R. GLENN HUBBARD, ed., *Financial Markets and Financial Crises*, 1991 at 33–68.

3 See THEO BALDERSTON, *Economics and Politics in the Weimar Republic*, 2002.

4 The strong federal power that now permeates US economic and legal policy provides the necessary tools to act promptly against economic downturns and their underlying causes. Not only does it enable rapid massive capital injections that do not burden state and local budgets (but the federal budget); it also entitles the federal government to immediate action with an array of enforcement possibilities yet unknown to the EU structure. If the EU is willing to achieve such immediate action enforcement capabilities, it must acquire a similar structure.

5 For a classic account of the critics see PETER ALEXIS ALBRECHT and STEPHAN BRAUM, *Deficiencies in the Development of European Criminal Law*, EUROPEAN LAW JOURNAL 5 (1999) at 293–310.

6 17739/12. PRESSE 528.

that sovereignty is being transferred to the EU for the purposes of advancing a unified banking supervision authority,[7] Member States should enable sovereignty transfer in matters concerning the protection of the EU financial interests against criminal misconduct. Again, some work is already in progress and will be outlined in the remainder of this chapter. Still, if "a good crisis should never to go waste",[8] then the EU should seize the opportunity of gaining enforcement power in the area of criminal law – restricted, however, to the protection of EU financial interests.

2.1. THE FINANCIAL MARKETS' PRESSURE

If anything, the financial crisis has made it clear that markets outpace politics. The liquidity crisis affecting financial institutions has turned into a credit crunch affecting the ability of entire nations to fund their budgets. Politicians throughout the EU have been constantly concerned with the risk premium of their sovereign debt. Even as markets have relentlessly pounded their sovereign debt, the political action of the EU has remained dormant. Solidarity of wealthier EU nations has been the recurrent theme in and outside the political scenario of less favored states, but decisive action by the EU itself has been delayed.

It is not surprising, therefore, that the spike in borrowing costs forced once-proud EU nations to kneel down and request a bailout. While the spread of the contagious financial disease[9] has triggered bailout requests by modern Western nations like falling dominoes,[10] the patchwork solutions have made the necessity of a long-term solution requiring a new institutional design in the EU clear. The European Financial Stability Facility (EFSF),[11] the European Financial Stabilisation Mechanism (EFSM) and the recent European Stability Mechanism (ESM) are clear examples of the EU's attempts to stabilize the financial markets

---

7 The Symposium on *The Sovereign Debt Crisis: Towards Fiscal Union in Europe?*, held on Thursday 7 June 2012, clearly signaled the path to overcome the current situation.

8 This well-known citation is used by John C. Coffee, *The Political Economy of Dodd-Frank: Why Financial Reform Tends to be Frustrated and Systemic Risk Perpetuated*, Cornell Law Review 2012 (available at: http://papers.ssrn.com/sol3/papers.cfm?abstract_id=1982128) to justify "that only after a catastrophic market collapse, can legislators and regulators overcome the resistance of the financial community and adopt comprehensive 'reform' legislation." In a similar fashion Jürgen Habermas, *The Crisis of the European Union. A response*, 2012, sees "crisis as opportunity" to deepen Europe's democratic credentials.

9 See Sebastian Missio and Sebastian Watzka, *Financial Contagion and the European Debt Crisis*, CESifo Working Paper No. 3554, August 2011.

10 See Roberto A. De Santis, *The Euro Area Sovereign Debt Crisis: Safe haven, Credit Rating Agencies and the Spread of the Fever from Greece, Ireland and Portugal*, European Central Bank, Working Paper Series No. 1419, February 2012.

11 See among many Harry Huizinga and Bálint Horváth, *Does the European Financial Stability Facility Bail Out Sovereigns or Banks? An Event Study* (10 November 2011), European Banking Center Discussion Paper No. 2011-031 (available at: http://ssrn.com/abstract=1957584).

with an eye on a more permanent solution.[12] The decision in December 2012 to establish the ECB as a European Banking Supervision Authority for the oversight of credit institutions confirms this trend.[13]

One circumstance seems evident in the *quid pro quo* trade between bailout countries and the EU. In order to have access to the much-desired funds, the Member States have to give up some sovereignty. National budgets have to be trimmed, control over financial decisions handed over to the EU and certain EU economic goals become national policy. In some cases even obvious signs of sovereignty such as national elections have to be temporarily put aside. The cases of Greece and Italy show that, when push comes to shove, an EU-friendly politician must govern the country. In other words the political will of the EU has temporarily replaced the political will of EU citizens who were reluctant to accept major reductions of the welfare state.

In the wake of such sovereignty transfers, another equally important step seems to be in process. The EU is slowly becoming conscious of the importance of a traditional expression of state sovereignty: criminal law. Thus the question of developing an effective European criminal law has become more pressing since the sovereign debt crisis of 2010.[14] Moreover, the current state of affairs confers on the EU the necessary legitimacy to enact criminal legislation in order to protect the European taxpayers' and foreign investors' money that is already being poured into some Member States. The main reason for this assertion is that a long-term solution to the threat to the EU – through the eurozone – posed by the financial markets must include a criminal oversight mechanism enforced by the EU itself. The injection of European funds into ailing countries can only be guaranteed if there is proper supervision of the final destination of those funds.

Real criminal enforcement by EU institutions is a must if the system is to have a chance of succeeding. To be sure, the mismanagement of European funds has been a recurring theme in recent EU history. The lack of a strong law enforcement authority in the EU with competence in criminal matters that monitors how these funds are applied can be considered one of the main reasons behind the disastrous spending of certain EU Member States. Just as US bailout funds for ailing US companies were closely monitored by the Department of Justice (DOJ),[15] there is

12 See the extensive analysis by Rodrigo Olivares-Caminal, *The EU Architecture To Avert a Sovereign Debt Crisis* (available at: www.oecd.org/finance/financialmarkets/49191980.pdf) which was presented at the Symposium on Financial Crisis Management and the Use of Government Guarantees, held at the OECD in Paris on 3 and 4 October 2011.

13 17739/12. PRESSE 528.

14 An interesting approach to the origins to the crisis, the political challenges of the EU to solve it and the consequences of the (potential) Greek departure is conducted by Martin Feldstein, *The Euro and the European Economic Conditions*, NBER Working Paper No. 17617 (2011).

15 The Trouble Assets Release Program (TARP) and additional bailout programs are closely monitored by the DOJ. The amount of money and federal agents deployed for the task of protecting the federal funds has increased since the enactment of the programs in 2008. See just for the FY 2010 the $62.6 million and the 379 positions (54 agents and 165 attorneys) requested by the DOJ at www.justice.gov/jmd/2010factsheets/pdf/cff-fisc.pdf.

a real need for similar mechanisms in the EU. To put it simply, EU funds should be treated as federal funds, and mismanagement of them has to be prosecuted and punished by the EU.

In short, the question raised by the financial markets is quite simple: can investors be confident that their investments in European sovereign debt are secure when enforcement is lacking? Moreover, can EU taxpayers be certain that their painful effort to rescue failing Member States will be worth it when the EU lacks full enforcement mechanisms to avoid mismanagement of bailout funds? There is clearly a moral hazard when EU funds are rescuing ailing nations, but mismanagement of those funds cannot be prosecuted at the EU level. If egregious misconduct affecting EU financial interests should not go unpunished, then full enforcement, including the criminal dimension, should be available at the EU level to protect those interests.

2.2. THE EUROPEAN APPROACH

The typical EU response to these concerns has been to let Member States determine the appropriate enforcement of the provisions dealing with the financial interest of the EU. However, everything has a limit, and the naïveté of EU institutions, resembling willful blindness, cannot go on any longer. There has been too much waste of EU assets[16] and it would certainly be reassuring for the international financial markets to know that a truly effective EU watchdog will be ensuring proper allocation of these now extremely highly valued funds. No longer can the EU institutions trust the EU Member States to vigorously enforce the proper use of the funds. National institutions have failed time and again to punish the misappropriation of EU funds. The undetected/unreported fraud is staggering, and with upcoming injections that add up to hundreds of billions of euros, no more leeway can be afforded.

Interestingly enough, the Lisbon Treaty already contains the necessary provisions to give the EU the arsenal it needs. A European Public Prosecutor's

16 The numbers of fraud affecting the financial interests of the EU are staggering and increasing. Just for the FY 2010, the financial impact of the irregularities detected by control systems in the area of expenditure amounted to €1.8 billion (1.27% of the allocations), as compared to €1.4 billion (1.13% of total allocations) in 2009. On the revenue side, the overall financial impact of irregularities was also higher than in 2009: €393 million (1.88% of total collected Traditional Own Resources, gross) as compared to €357 million (1.84% of total collected Traditional Own Resources, gross). In short "Overall figures for 2010 indicate that the number of irregularities reported has increased for all sectors" (Report from the Commission to the European Parliament and the Council, *Protection of the European Union's financial interests – Fight against fraud – Annual Report 2010* (available at: http://ec.europa.eu/anti_fraud/reports/commission/2010/EN.pdf)). Two additional factors must be taken into account. First, these numbers only reflect reported fraud; the undetected fraud is even greater. Second, the potential increase of EU fraud in light of the amount that will be poured into the ailing EU countries is just breathtaking.

Office in conjunction with the strengthened agencies of Eurojust and Europol[17] represent the optimal tool to ensure compliance with the parameters set forth by Brussels.[18] Full protection of financial interests has become an essential ingredient of the bailout recipe that the EU is trying to work out presently. If the EU refuses to enact legislation for this purpose, it will miss a great opportunity to advance the protection of one of its vital components, its European coffers. It is not by chance that federal states have always considered it to be a matter of their incumbency to watch over federal monies. The fact that EU federalism is not state but rather supranational federalism[19] does not diminish the EU's prerogative to guard its funds. It is matter of design, not of principle.

2.3. THE AMERICAN APPROACH

Against this backdrop, the experience of some federal systems, especially the US, in protecting their financial interests with criminal sanctions can shed light on how to implement these provisions. Recognizing the European idiosyncrasy is one thing; neglecting the need for serious EU punishment of misconduct affecting EU funds is another.[20] If the structure the EU already has in terms of protecting fair competition,[21] i.e. the sacrosanct pillar of EU integration, is insufficient, it just begs the question how much longer the EU can survive without taking a hands-on approach to governmental misspending. This chapter tries to highlight recent developments that point in this direction and provide additional arguments based on the way in which financial markets, including sovereign debt markets, operate.

Without doubt, the American system of federal criminal law should not be imported *cum grano salis* into Europe. There are too many deficiencies[22] and too many idiosyncrasies that must be taken into account. These reflections pretend

[17] For an overview of the proposed structural relationship between Eurojust and the EPPO, see Jorge Ángel Espina Ramos, *Towards a European Public Prosecutor's Office: the Long and Winding Road*, in André Klip, ed., *Substantive Criminal Law of the European Union*, 2011.

[18] For an overview of these agencies and proposed agencies see André Klip, *European Criminal Law: An Integrative Approach*, 2nd ed., 2012 at 383–414.

[19] On this concept see Armin von Bogdandy, *Founding principles*, in Armin von Bogdany and Jürgen Blast, eds., *Principles of European Constitutional Law*, 2009 at 11.

[20] For an overview of American punishment practices and a comparison with Europe see James Q. Whitman, *Harsh Justice: Criminal Punishment and the Widening Divide between America and Europe*, 2003 at 41–64.

[21] "Competition law is the only area where the European Union currently has direct enforcement powers at its disposal. Competition law has its origins in the internal market from the very beginnings of the European Communities." André Klip, *European Criminal Law: An Integrative Approach*, 2nd ed., 2012 at 454.

[22] As Sullivan puts it, drawing from other sources, the current US federal criminal "code" is an "incomprehensible," random and incoherent, "duplicative, ambiguous, incomplete, and organizationally nonsensical" mass of federal legislation that carries criminal penalties. Julie E. Sullivan, *The Federal Criminal Code is a Disgrace: Obstruction Statutes as a Case Study*, J. Crim. L. & Criminology 96 (2006) 643.

to stay at arm's length with the US system, while at the same time try to obtain as much benefit as possible from one of the systems with a greater degree of enforcement experience and political significance. Questions about federal criminal law in the US often turn out to be questions about federalism. Similarly, the question of EU criminal law is mostly about whether the EU has competence in criminal matters. Similarities between the two systems go far beyond this issue. The overreaching enactment of federal criminal law in the US on behalf of the Commerce Clause[23] is similar to the proliferation of EU instruments on behalf of the principle of "free movement of goods", as the EU has established that judicial rulings should be considered as "goods" that may freely move within the EU pursuant to the principle of mutual recognition.[24] Interestingly enough, the EU's reluctance to acknowledge its powers in criminal matters has created a *sui generis* system that, to a certain extent, is more federal than the US system.[25] This is the final "curtain call" for EU institutions and they have to be up to the task of providing an adequate and uniform response to the ongoing fraud affecting EU financial interests.

2.4. THE FUTURE AHEAD

It will take plenty of political will and determination to adopt measures of criminal enforcement at an EU level. Many Member States will be reluctant to confer such powers to the EU. However, the current situation enables the EU to play a *quid pro quo* with the Member States: if European nations want the funds, they must agree to the creation of adequate enforcement mechanisms including criminal sanctions when signing the (in)famous Memorandums of Understanding.[26] Great nations have required the onset of a crisis to empower some of their more fundamental structures. It may be time to finally acknowledge that, although not a sovereign state, the EU has the same problems as if it were. Quite frequently similar problems demand similar solutions.

---

23 Norman Abrams, Sara Sun Beale and Susan Riva Klein, *Federal Criminal Law and its Enforcement*, 5th ed., 2010.

24 Wording of the Framework decision establishing the European Arrest Warrant (Official Journal of the EU L 190, 18 July 2002, at 1): "Traditional cooperation relations which have prevailed up till now between Member States should be replaced by a system of free movement of judicial decisions in criminal matters, covering both pre-sentence and final decisions, within an area of freedom, security and justice", available at: http://eur-lex.europa.eu/LexUriServ/LexUriServ.do?uri=CELEX:32002F0584:en:HTML.

25 See Introduction and Findings.

26 Actually, it is clear that the conditions set forth in these MOUs entail a surrender of national sovereignty. See, for instance, the MOU with Greece at http://ec.europa.eu/economy_finance/eu_borrower/mou/2012-03-01-greece-mou_en.pdf. A limited cession of sovereignty in criminal matters, i.e. limited to cases involving the protection of EU financial interests, would be perfectly consistent with the current trend and Article 325 TFEU. Especially taking into consideration that these are not "genuine" national interests, but interests of a supranational institution: the EU.

As this book is being written, the EU is in deep discussion regarding a potential reform of the EU treaties that would result in a more unified fiscal policy with automatic sanctions for countries that do not comply with the debt ratios imposed by Brussels.[27] This opportunity for treaty reform should be used to foster the creation of the European Public Prosecutor's Office pursuant to Article 86 TFEU[28] and establish a special court within the European Court of Justice enabled by Article 257 TFEU that could provide adequate criminal law enforcement, as in the US system. As long as compliance with these fiscal reforms is left exclusively to the Member States – leaving individual and corporate enforcement to them – the system will be flawed.

3. RECENT DEVELOPMENTS IN THE EU APPROACH

Since the sovereign debt crisis hit the EU with the Greek Episode in May 2010, EU institutions have developed a greater sense of urgency regarding protection of the EU budget. However, the final wording of the communications of the EU Commission and EU Council does not address the real problem. Though they clearly acknowledge the problem and even use the correct wording to describe it, they fail time and again to provide the solution that the problem demands. Just like the snail pace at which EU institutions react to adverse market conditions – triggering strong reprimands from the US and China – the slow-motion approach of the EU towards effective criminal law enforcement of EU funds is anything but reassuring.

3.1. SAFEGUARDING TAXPAYERS' MONEY?

The failure to act vigorously in this field is exemplified by the recent communication from the EU Commission to various EU institutions "on the protection of the financial interests of the European Union by criminal law and by administrative investigations. An integrated policy to safeguard taxpayers' money."[29] While it acknowledges that "[t]he Treaty sets a clear framework for the EU to reinforce its action in the field of criminal law",[30] that "more effective

---

[27] For the details see HERMAN VAN ROMPUY, *Towards a Genuine Economic and Monetary Union*, EUCO 120/12, 26 June 2012.

[28] For a discussion of the legislative process by which the EPPO will be formed, see ANDRÉ KLIP, *European Criminal Law: An Integrative Approach*, 2nd ed., 2012 at 463.

[29] Communication from the Commission to the European Parliament, the Council, the European Economic and Social Committee and the Committee of the Region. On the protection of the financial interests of the European Union by criminal law and by administrative investigations. An integrated policy to safeguard taxpayers' money, COM (2011) 293 final, 26 May 2011.

[30] Ibid. at 3.

means are also needed to fight criminal activities against the EU Budget"[31] and that there is both "[i]nsufficient protection against criminal misuse of the EU Budget" and "[i]nsufficient legal action to fight criminal activity",[32] the end result is somewhat mild. This is all the more surprising when the text makes clear that the EU Commission has a thorough enough understanding of the necessary mechanisms to articulate the solution. The Commission specifically refers to the following four ways to protect EU financial interests under the TFEU:

(1) Measures on procedural judicial cooperation in criminal matters (Article 82).
(2) Directives containing minimum criminal law rules (Article 83).
(3) Legislation on fraud affecting the financial interests of the Union (Articles 310(6), 325(4)).
(4) Article 85 allows granting Eurojust investigative competences and Article 86 allows for the establishment of a European Public Prosecutor Office from Eurojust to combat crimes affecting the financial interests of the Union.

Now, after recognizing the situation, the need for action and the available resources, it proceeds with the following low-key language: "Should criminal law, including further developed definitions of offences and minimum rules on sanctions, be deemed necessary to achieve the legitimate purpose of fighting fraud against the EU budget, certain guiding principles will need to be observed".[33] Then it proceeds to detail procedural safeguards regarding fundamental rights, the approximation of criminal law regimes and the need to reflect on the strengthening of EU institutions. Given the current situation regarding sovereign debt in the EU, with spiking interests, skyrocketing costs to insure it against default, i.e. the costs of credit default swaps, and the difficulties with its allocation (a German government debt auction in November 2012 drew some of the weakest demand since the introduction of the euro),[34] decisive action must be taken.

3.2. THE SO-CALLED ANTI-FRAUD STRATEGY

The immediate follow up to this communication was, unsurprisingly, another communication. The Commission addressed the same institutions on its next "Anti-fraud Strategy".[35] The overall objective of the new Commission Anti-Fraud Strategy is to "improve prevention, detection and the conditions for investigations

31 Ibid. at 5.
32 Ibid. at 4–5.
33 Ibid. at 9.
34 Wall Street Journal, Thursday 24 November 2011, "German Bond Sale Spurs Worries".
35 Communication from the Commission to the European Parliament, the Council, the European Economic and Social Committee, and the Committee of the Regions and the Court of Auditors, On the Commission Anti-Fraud Strategy, COM (2011) 376 final.

of fraud and to achieve adequate reparation and deterrence, with proportionate and dissuasive sanctions, and respecting the due process, especially by introducing anti-fraud strategies at Commission Service level respecting and clarifying the different responsibilities of the various stakeholders".[36] This communication states that in 2011, several initiatives will be taken to step up the fight against fraud and corruption affecting EU public money. These initiatives are as follows:

> "The Commission's proposal for amending the legal framework of OLAF aims at increasing the efficiency and speed of OLAF investigations, at strengthening procedural guarantees, at reinforcing OLAF's cooperation with Member States and at improving its governance.
>
> The Communication on the protection of EU financial interests by criminal law and administrative investigations sets out how the Commission intends to safeguard taxpayers' money at EU level against illegal activities, including threats posed by corruption inside and outside the EU institutions. The Communication points to opportunities for improving the criminal law framework and the procedural tools for investigators and prosecutors, and to possible institutional developments such as the setting up of a European Public Prosecutor's Office.
>
> Complementing those initiatives, the Communication on Fighting Corruption in the EU15 sets an EU anti-corruption reporting mechanism for periodic assessment of Member States ('EU Anti-Corruption Report').
>
> The Commission Work Programme for 2011 also includes a Proposal for a new legal framework on the confiscation and recovery of criminal assets under the heading 'Initiatives on Protecting the Licit Economy'."

After all this well-intended language, the final guiding principles for action are once again watered down concerning the criminal law. In addition to reinforcing areas of ethics, transparency, fraud detection and cooperation between Member States, i.e. business as usual, the Commission considered that in the field of EU sanctions for misconduct affecting EU funds:

> "Justice must be achieved with due process and in reasonable time. Procedures must provide for enhanced standards of due process using mechanisms that enable swift and independent action. In addition to adequate sanctions, convicted and administratively sanctioned persons must be effectively deprived of the proceeds of their offence and defrauded resources must be recovered."

In developing the sanctions it will use, the Commission only considers "financial and/or administrative penalties".[37] The question is then: what happened to criminal sanctions?[38]

---

36 COM (2011) 376 final at 3, 24 June 2011.

37 Ibid. at 15.

38 The short answer is that the Commission has no authority to impose such sanctions. The longer answer is that the most powerful EU institution, the European Commission, is still

3.3. TOWARDS AN EU CRIMINAL POLICY

Notwithstanding what has been noted in Chapter 1, the response may be found in a recent communication of the EU Commission dated 29 September 2011 in which the Commission once again addresses other EU institutions. The title of the communication sounds promising: "Towards an EU Criminal Policy: Ensuring the effective implementation of EU policies through criminal law".[39] The problem may actually lie in the sweeping breadth of its objective, which moves from the narrow scope of EU financial interests currently of serious concern to the broader subject of implementation of EU policies through criminal law. The Commission lost its focus, and in doing so it also lost the persuasiveness of the arguments favoring a strong EU criminal law but only in a narrowly tailored area such as the protection of the financial interests of the EU. Instead, wishful policies and rationales are outlined in the communication when explaining why the EU should act in the area of criminal law.[40]

> "EU criminal law fosters the confidence of citizens in using their right to free movement and to buy goods or services from providers from other Member States through a more effective fight against crime and the adoption of minimum standards for procedural rights in criminal proceedings as well as for victims of crime.
>
> Today, many serious crimes, including violations of harmonized EU legislation, occur across borders. There is thus an incentive and possibility for criminals to choose the Member State with the most lenient sanctioning system in certain crime areas unless a degree of approximation of the national laws prevents the existence of such 'safe havens'.
>
> Common rules strengthen mutual trust among the judiciaries and law enforcement authorities of the Member States. This facilitates the mutual recognition of judicial measures as national authorities feel more comfortable recognizing decisions taken in another Member State if the definitions of the underlying criminal offences are compatible and there is a minimum approximation of sanction level. Common rules also facilitate cooperation with regard to the use of special investigative measures in cross-border cases.

---

reluctant to test the waters of criminal sanctions. Without doubt, as an administrative authority, it will never have the necessary power to use criminal sanctions. But most certainly, it can definitely focus its actions in enforcing that criminal courts across the EU impose those sanctions based on European Rules of Criminal Procedure and pursuant to the charges filed by European Prosecutors. These features will be explored in greater detail below, but the point to make at this stage is that clearly, the European Commission is not making full use, even in its communication strategy, of the deterrence effect associated with its communications.

39 Communication from the Commission to the European Parliament, the Council, the European Economic and Social Committee and the Committee of the Regions. Towards an EU Criminal Policy: Ensuring the effective implementation of EU policies through criminal law, COM (2011) 573 final, 20 September 2011.

40 Ibid. at 5.

> EU criminal law helps to prevent and sanction serious offences against EU law in important policy areas, such as the protection of the environment or illegal employment."

The language used makes it clear that protection of EU financial interests is not the driving force behind this communication. Indeed, reference is constantly made to the legal basis provided by Article 83 TFEU, which focuses on serious cross-border criminality, and little attention is paid to Article 325 TFEU, which deals with the protection of EU financial interests. In short, EU protection of the EU budget and taxpayers' money through criminal law seems to be included as only one of the elements in a much broader approach to criminal law, despite specific language in the TFEU targeting financial crimes against the EU budget.

3.4. WILL THIS WELL-INTENDED LANGUAGE SUFFICE?

This is clearly not what the current situation demands. A strong message of vigorous supervision at the EU level, including criminal sanctions, is necessary not only to appease the markets, but to provide deserved reassurance to EU citizens that the strain that they will be subject to will be validated. Why should some EU citizens' sacrifices enable other EU citizens to waste their money? It would be more reasonable and fair for the EU to closely supervise the funds raised to ensure that they are spent correctly and that misappropriation is heavily punished. Indeed, EU citizens cannot trust the existing mechanisms that led to the current situation.

Luckily this is nothing new to federal systems. The need for federal enforcement against local misappropriation or mismanagement of federal funds is a common theme in federal systems. It is precisely the independent enforcement by federal (external) agencies that provide equilibrium. If the EU continues to leave supervision and enforcement powers over EU funds to the states, the result will be the same as before. Local prosecution of the mismanagement of EU funds is unlikely, tending to be non-existent.[41] There is diminished incentive for local enforcement officials to prosecute and the local courts to convict prominent public officials for mismanaging "foreign" funds. A sense of responsibility is surely present in many members of the enforcement community, but to trust that sense with the only enforcement power is plain wishful thinking. Again, the best evidence of the need for change is that the existing mechanisms have not provided adequate protection in the past. There is no reason to think they will do so in the future.

---

[41] This tension between Member States and the EU will be crucial in defining the relationship between the EPPO and Member States. For a discussion of this relationship and three possible models, see André Klip, *European Criminal Law: An Integrative Approach*, 2nd ed., 2012 at 459–464.

These and other rationales are behind the federal supervision of proper spending of the TARP funds in the US. Officials who misspent federal funds to the point of technically bankrupting an entity cannot be trusted, especially if no investigation, prosecution and conviction by the local authorities followed. Often these local authorities request that federal enforcement officials intervene, as they are perfectly aware of their limited power to adequately investigate, prosecute and get convictions for these crimes. Local authorities may have the manpower to conduct the investigations, but in many cases they lack either the knowledge or the necessary authorization to proceed with such cases. Recognizing these deficiencies, the US government created the Office of the Special Inspector General for the Troubled Asset Relief Program (SIGTARP), an office specifically charged with monitoring TARP funds. SIGTARP is only a temporary government agency meant to supplement the work done by the Treasury Department and the Justice Department. The high level of supervision of federal funds in the US should serve as an indication to the EU of the level of financial oversight which is needed.

At the EU level, a deficiency in this area is evident from the findings of the EU Anti-Fraud Office (OLAF).[42] The report for the FY 2010 reports the number of investigations referred to the local authorities that resulted in non-prosecution.[43] The figure presented of 68 million euros recovered is dwarfed by the fraud that is detected. This discrepancy was verified by OLAF's FY 2011 report, which stated that 691.4 million euros had been recovered. OLAF itself discounted the figure as an anomaly, citing an investigation in Italy's Calabria region that resulted in the recovery of 389 million euros. Even discounting the amount from that single investigation, 2011 still saw an increase of over 400% in recovered fraudulent funds. OLAF also cited a change in the form in which recovered funds are calculated as a reason for the shocking difference, but as the new reporting system will not be used until FY 2012, 2010 and 2011's figures were calculated using the same metrics. In their FY 2011 report, it states "OLAF's experience, underpinned by statistical and analytical evidence, shows that there is insufficient deterrence concerning criminal misuse of the EU budget … Additionally, practitioners have

---

42 The role of OLAF in the EPPO would likely be quite significant. "Currently OLAF has the expertise and the know-how as regards the investigation of offences against Union's financial interest. It is not conceivable that any future perspective in this field could be without bringing them on board, and the Action Plan for the Stockholm Programme acknowledges this." Jorge Ángel Espina Ramos, *Towards a European Public Prosecutor's Office: the Long and Winding Road*, in Andre Klip, ed., *Substantive Criminal Law of the European Union*, 2011.

43 For illustrative purposes, in Spain, between 1999 and 2007, OLAF sent 79 cases to Spanish prosecutors, 28 of which were decided on the merits. 11 of 28 were handled by the Special Anticorruption Prosecutor's Office, of which three resulted in convictions. The other 17 were territorial prosecutions, and resulted in only one conviction. "Two conclusions can be extracted from these figures: a) specialisation is a clear added value that increases the efficiency, and b) the overall figures of convictions are quite low and there is, therefore, ground for improvement." Jorge Ángel Espina Ramos, *Towards a European Public Prosecutor's Office: the Long and Winding Road*, in Andre Klip, ed., *Substantive Criminal Law of the European Union*, 2011.

pointed out that mutual legal assistance has its limits, that the use of evidence in cross-border cases is sometimes problematic and that there is a tendency to limit prosecutions to domestic cases and disregard the European dimension".[44] In so many words, OLAF has succinctly made the case for greater oversight of EU funds.

4. THE FIRST BENCHMARK: THE DIRECTIVE ON CRIMINAL SANCTIONS FOR INSIDER DEALING AND MARKET MANIPULATION – FINANCIAL MARKETS AND THE STABILITY OF THE EU

A quick review of the development of EU criminal law shows that the pendulum of criminal enforcement has oscillated from the protection of the EU financial interests in the late 1990s to the fights against transnational criminality in the early 21st century;[45] it has swung back again to address concerns of white collar criminality related to the European financial markets. This should not be interpreted as a lack of attention towards the transnational dimension but as an increased understanding that the sovereign debt crisis and its threat to the eurozone requires real criminal law enforcement in the financial markets area. This time, it should be clear to the EU institutions that merely referring the issue to the national authorities of the Member States is not enough, particularly because a lack of supervision from the EU contributed to the problem. The EU reveals itself as a lame duck trying to achieve the status of a real watchdog, but without criminal enforcement capacity, it will ultimately be a toothless one.

It is worth noting that the Directive on criminal matters pursuant to the new powers embedded in the Lisbon Treaty[46] has been on criminal sanctions for insider dealing and market manipulation.[47] The importance of this first step should be stressed. For the first decade of the 21st century, the EU institutions were particularly concerned with fighting drug trafficking, human trafficking, money laundering, etc. However, since the entry into force of the Lisbon Treaty, the attention of the EU has focused on the protection against of financial markets

---

44 OLAF FY 2011 report at 35.

45 For an overview of these developments see generally the contributions in André Klip, ed., *Substantive Criminal Law of the European Union*, 2011.

46 See Christian Schröder, *Europa in der Finanzfalle. Irrwege internationales Rechtsangleichung*, 2012, at 89 (concluding that "in any event, from a German perspective, the conditions for exercising this power in the Market Manipulation area are not present".

47 Directive 2014/57/EU of the European Parliament and of the Council of 16 April 2014 on criminal sanctions for market abuse (Market Abuse Directive), OJ L 173/179, 12 June 2014 at 179. See Christian Schröder, *Europa in der Finanzfalle. Irrwege internationales Rechtsangleichung*, 2012 at 88–90 (noting that, in his opinion, "it is dubious whether the EU has the competence to make criminal-law decisions in area of financial markets").

from certain forms of criminality. This shift clearly shows that the main concern these days revolves around how to protect the European financial markets from offenses that could ultimately destabilize the economy of Member States and threaten the existence of the eurozone.

To a certain extent, this development notes the relationship that the EU is making between criminal law protection of the financial markets and the increasing importance of the European economy. Put simply, there seems to be a connection between the protection of financial markets through EU criminal law and investors' confidence. Yet some academics have already voiced their concerns on such a relationship. *Herlin-Karnell*[48] notes that "there is no obvious connection between criminal law and 'confidence' in the market. More specifically there is no clear relationship between the confidence in the market argument and the need to criminalise in order to boost such confidence". In her opinion, criminalizing these fields leads to an unbearable overcriminalization. And, in essence, the "confidence" argument reveals the same diffuse contours as the "efficiency" argument.[49] Though such criticism is exceptionally constructed, it is based primarily on the overreaching nature of money laundering Directives and national statutes. Yet the relationship between market manipulation and investors' confidence seems to be anchored in a realm of economic and financial activity quite distant from money laundering operations. Not by chance does the aforementioned Directive clearly follow the path of linking criminal law protection and investors' confidence (in the EU financial markets). As becomes clear in the recitals of the Directive:[50]

> "An integrated and efficient financial market and stronger investor confidence requires market integrity. The smooth functioning of securities markets and public confidence in markets are prerequisites for economic growth and wealth.

---

48 Herlin-Karnell, *The Constitutional Dimension of European Criminal Law*, 2012 at 185–186.

49 Ibid. at 106–110.

50 Moreover, in the context of the Proposal of the Directive (COM (2011) 654 final), the EU Commission was even more adamant about the relationship between criminal law protection and boosting investors' confidence/market integrity: "The Directive aims to increase investor confidence and market integrity by prohibiting those who possess inside information from trading in related financial instruments, and by prohibiting the manipulation of markets through practices such as spreading false information or rumours and conducting trades which secure prices at abnormal levels.
The European Commission has assessed the application of the national rules implementing the MAD and has identified a number of problems which have negative impacts in terms of market integrity and investor protection.
Market abuse can occur across borders and harms the integrity of financial markets which are increasingly integrated in the Union. The divergent approaches to the imposition of criminal sanctions for market abuse offences by Member States leave a certain scope for perpetrators who can often make use of the most lenient sanction systems. This undermines both the deterrent effect of each national sanction regime and the effectiveness of enforcement of the Union's legislative framework on market abuse. EU-wide minimum rules on the forms of market abuse that are considered to be a criminal conduct contribute to addressing this problem."

> Market abuse harms the integrity of financial markets and public confidence in securities, derivatives and benchmarks.[51]
>
> Due to the adverse effects of attempted insider dealing and attempted market manipulation on the integrity of the financial markets and on investor confidence in those markets, those forms of behaviour should also be punishable as a criminal offence.[52]
>
> In order to ensure effective implementation of the European policy for ensuring the integrity of the financial markets set out in Regulation (EU) No 596/2014, Member States should extend liability for the offences provided for in this Directive to legal persons through the imposition of criminal or non-criminal sanctions or other measures which are effective, proportionate and dissuasive, for example those provided for in Regulation (EU) No 596/2014."[53]

But probably even more important, in Article 1 of the Directive the actual goal of this legislation is clearly established:

> "1. This Directive establishes minimum rules for criminal sanctions for insider dealing, for unlawful disclosure of inside information and for market manipulation *to ensure the integrity of financial markets in the Union and to enhance investor protection and confidence in those markets.*"

Impact assessments conducted by the Commission have led to a conclusion that the recommended criminal legislation "will have a positive impact on investors' confidence and will further contribute to the financial stability of financial markets".[54] This fits with the previous JHA Council conclusions on economic crisis prevention and support for economic activity, which stressed that consideration should be given to whether it is possible or appropriate to harmonize criminal laws on the handling of serious stock market price manipulations and other misconduct relating to securities markets.[55] As the proposal itself pointed out, the criminal laws on insider trading are notably divergent between Member States, and these differences create opportunities to exploit the common European market while avoiding criminal prosecution.[56]

The recent LIBOR scandals have, if anything, stressed the importance of a centralized system of enforcement – and, we may add, criminal law enforcement. The EU has realized that a major part of its weakness comes from abuses by financial institutions of its own Member States, and the timid reaction of national law enforcement has proven to be insufficient. A centralized system of criminal

51 OJ L 173/179, 12 June 2014 at 179.
52 Ibid. at 181.
53 Ibid. at 181.
54 SEC (2011) 1217 final, 20 October 2011 at 64.
55 See Docc. 8920/10 of 22 April 2010 and 7881/10 of 29 March 2010.
56 COM (2011) 654 final: "The divergent approaches to the imposition of criminal sanctions for market abuse offences by Member States leave a certain scope for perpetrators who can often make use of the most lenient sanction systems".

enforcement is necessary, and, as *Viviane Reding* worded it: "This will end the often too 'cozy' relationship that exists today between national supervisors and banks in their home country".[57]

The reaction of the EU was an amended proposal for a Directive on criminal sanctions for insider dealing and market manipulation (submitted in accordance with Article 83(2) TFEU).[58] The amended proposal is modified to suggest that benchmark manipulation be made a criminal offense in Member States. That these amendments are needed demonstrates the speed with which financial crimes may adapt in new forms. It is therefore unsurprising that the biggest problem (and probably paradoxically the solution) is time. Financial markets do not abide by political timing. The need to act is pressing and even a delay of months, let alone years, could be too slow. Prompt response to immediate threats has proven to be the only way to appease the markets and give confidence to investors seeking safe harbors for their money.

5. THE SECOND BENCHMARK: THE PROPOSAL FOR A DIRECTIVE TO PROTECT EUROPEAN FINANCIAL INTERESTS THROUGH CRIMINAL LAW – GENUINE EU INTERESTS

Shortly after the Proposal for a Directive on Insider Dealing and Market Manipulation was issued, the Parliament and the Council proposed a Directive on the fight against fraud to the Union's financial interests by means of criminal law,[59] based on Article 325 TFEU.[60] Both EU institutions recognized that fraud and related illegal activities affecting the Union's financial interests pose a serious problem for the Union budget and thereby for taxpayers.[61] The proposal acknowledged that the Union needs to defend taxpayers' money in the most efficient way, utilizing all possibilities offered by the Treaty on the European Union.[62] The divergent rules and levels of protection between Member States

57 Viviane Reding, Amended Proposal for a Directive on Criminal Sanctions for Insider Dealing and Market Manipulation, Joint press conference with Commissioner Barnier/Brussels, 25 July 2012, SPEECH/12/569, at 3.

58 2011/0297 (COD).

59 COM (2012) 363 final.

60 To be sure, there was a heated discussion for years concerning the wording of former Article 280(4) of the TEU – predecessor to Article 325 TFEU. Though there were divergent interpretations of what this paragraph meant, the truth is that the current view held by the EU institution is that "Article 325 therefore includes the power to enact criminal law provisions in the context of the protection of the Union's financial interests against all angles of illegal attacks, which was not the case in the corresponding Article 280 (4) in the EC-Treaty" (COM (2012) 363 final at 7).

61 COM (2012) 363 at 2.

62 Ibid. at 2.

has triggered action by the EU itself. In the opinion of the European Parliament and Council, i.e. two important bodies of the EU, "[e]quivalent protection of its financial interests is also a *matter of credibility of the Union's* institutions, bodies, offices and agencies, and of ensuring a *legitimate budget execution*".[63]

In Chapter 2 we reviewed at length certain aspects of the criminal law protection of EU financial interests. In this sense, we have referred the current discussion on whether Article 325(4) TFEU or Article 83(2) TFEU – or a combination of both – should be the legal basis for enacting such legislation. Our goal now is to show that this proposal may be certainly linked to the EU sovereign debt crisis, the need to protect taxpayers' monies and the lack of sufficient protection of EU financial interests by Member States. Although a Directive to protect such interests was proposed at the turn of the century,[64] the current financial crisis has certainly potentiated the perception that legislative action was needed.

In this context, the proposed Directive defines the type of offenses: fraud affecting the Union's financial interests (Article 3) and fraud-related offenses affecting the Union's financial interests (Article 4). Probably the most controverted piece of the legislation related to the latter, the so-called ancillary offenses. As the Directive clearly points out "Not only fraud in its strict sense should be covered by this proposal, but also *other fraud-related forms of illegal behaviour through which the EU budget is damaged, including corruption, money laundering and obstruction of public procurement procedures*. The decisive element is that a profit is made at the expense of the EU budget, and thus at the expense of all taxpayers".[65]

Against the backdrop of the sovereign debt financial crisis, it is interesting to note that the taxpaying dimension of EU citizenry has become paramount. While it is a centerpiece in the currently proposed legislation, no explicit reference was made in the 2001/2002 proposals to protect EU financial interests. The current proposal makes abundantly clear that this element is decisive for EU action. To a certain extent, therefore, the justification of EU action relies more on the protection of European citizens and less in the institutions themselves.

In any event, the impact assessments and the overall perception of the EU institutions make equally clear that an enactment of this substantive legislation without (at least) control of its enforcement by the EU will serve no real purpose. It is not by chance that the Proposal for a Directive on the fight against fraud to the Union's financial interests by means of criminal law and the Proposal for a Directive establishing the European Public Prosecutor's Office are closely interrelated. It is hard to envision a scenario in which one is enacted without the other.

---

63 Ibid. at 4.

64 Proposal for a Directive of the European Parliament and of the Council on the criminal-law protection of the Community's financial interests (OJ C 240 E of 28 August 2001). Amended proposal for a Directive of the European Parliament and of the Council on the criminal-law protection of the Community's financial interests (COM (2002) 577 final – OJ C 71 E of 25 March 2003).

65 COM (2012) 363 final at 4.

6. THE THIRD BENCHMARK: THE EUROPEAN PROSECUTOR OFFICE – "BLUE HELMETS" IN THE WAR AGAINST CRIME?

As noted, substantive regulation without an adequate procedure is doomed to failure. Therefore, it is easily comprehensible that the proposals on criminal laws to protect financial markets, whether European or harmonized national laws, should be complemented by measures in the procedural field to respond to enforcement deficiencies.[66] Not surprisingly, the possible creation a European Public Prosecutor's Office has been heavily discussed.[67] The *Corpus Iuris* already contained certain provisions regulating this proposed institution, although the breadth of the proposal might have been a bit premature for the political willingness at the time.[68] Shortly after, a Green Paper linking the protection of the EU financial interests to the establishment of the European Prosecutor was produced.[69] Even so, the actual legislative proposal at the time focused on protection of financial interests without any new European enforcement power.[70] In any event, it never was enacted. A few years later, the first drafts of the "Constitution for Europe" foresaw a European prosecutor with jurisdiction in cases involving not only EU financial interests but other serious cross-border criminality as well. The final text confined the EPPO to the protection of EU financial interests[71] and the current Lisbon Treaty has maintained this approach in Article 86 TFEU.[72]

Times have changed, and the need for real law enforcement action by the EU has become extremely palpable. Recently, the EU Commission proposed a Regulation establishing the European Public Prosecutor's Office.[73] Needless to say, this is a qualitative leap as it creates a supranational authority in criminal law with competence over the EU territory.[74] This initiative is inexorably linked to the proposed Directive on the protection of EU financial interests through criminal

---

66 "A central theme of the different models suggested for the creation of the EPPO is to define in how far it is necessary to adopt a harmonized set of procedural rules for the functioning of the supranational EPPO, and to which extent it is possible to rely on mutual recognition." These procedural measures would have to take into account the need for harmonization, as well as mutual recognition. See Katalin Ligeti, *The European Public Prosecutor's Office: Which Model?*, in André Klip, ed., *Substantive Criminal Law of the European Union*, 2011.

67 See Valsamis Mitsilegas, *EU Criminal Law*, 2009, at 229 noting that it has been one of the most controversial issues in the development of EU criminal law.

68 http://ec.europa.eu/anti_fraud/documents/fwk-green-paper-corpus/corpus_juris_en.pdf.

69 COM (2001) 715 final.

70 COM (2001) 272 final.

71 Article III-274. CIG 87/1/04.

72 For a comparison of two other proposed procedural frameworks for the EPPO, the Corpus Juris and the Green Paper, see Katalin Ligeti, *The European Public Prosecutor's Office: Which Model?*, in André Klip, ed., *Substantive Criminal Law of the European Union*, 2011.

73 COM (2013) 534 final.

74 See already J.A.E. Vervaele, *Quel statut pour le ministère public?, in Quelles perspectives pour un ministère public européen? Protéger les intérêts financiers et fondamentaux de l'Union*, 2010 at 189.

law,[75]and would grant the EPPO jurisdiction over the crimes contained in the directive. Before this legislation is finalized, it is worth mentioning certain issues that should be amended to avoid problems that are fairly well-known in other federal systems.

First, the federal nature at the core of this institution should always be stressed. As Commissioner Reading adequately worded this idea in her speech presenting the Regulation establishing the EPPO, "a federal budget needs federal protection". This implies that national interests cannot continue to play a decisive role in these matters. The emergence of a truly European federal interest should be clearly acknowledged to avoid weakening an institution that must have the necessary power to fulfill its primary function.

Second, using a Regulation – specifically prescribed in Article 86 TFEU – is aimed at ensuring unified enforcement throughout the EU. The advantages of this type of legal instrument should not be wasted. Although the relationship with Eurojust and OLAF should be clarified to a greater extent,[76] the opportunity to implement the full mandate contained in Article 86 TFEU should be seized, especially regarding the evidence law as discussed below.

Third, the decentralized model that the EU Commission has chosen creates coordination difficulties.[77] Although European delegated prosecutors must comply with the guidelines issued by the European Public Prosecutor, sooner or later this dual structure will lead to conflicts between the orders of the European Public Prosecutor and of the national Attorneys General. The fact that Member States remain secondarily civilly liable in case of conviction poses a clear conflict of interests that already accounts for the current lack of enforcement of national provisions protecting EU financial interests. A centralized model with sufficient deputies of the EPPO is preferable from a technical point of view. The long-term value of EPPO independence outweighs the short-term cost of setting up the structure.[78]

---

75 COM (2012) 363 final.

76 See Jorge Ángel Espina Ramos, *Towards a European Public Prosecutor's Office: the Long and Winding Road*, in André Klip, ed., *Substantive Criminal Law of the European Union*, 2011. Already noting the need Annika Suominen, *The Past, Present and the Future of Eurojust*, Maastricht Journal of European and Comparative Law 15 (2008) 229. On the new role of OLAF see Valentina Covolo, *From Europol to Eurojust – Towards a European Public Prosecutor. Where Does OLAF Fit In?*", Eucrim 2/2012, at 83.

77 Also, the lack of democratic control over the EPPO has already been voiced by Martin Zwiers, *The European Public Prosecutor's Office*, 2011 at 373.

78 Budgetary concerns in the era of austerity are outright legitimate. The possibility of using national prosecution services and therefore minoring the budget that will be needed to establish the EPPO is clearly tempting (see also Simone White and Nicholas Dorn, *Towards a Decentralized European Public Prosecutor's Office?*, Amicus Curiae 89(7) (2012)). Also, linguistic diversity throughout the EU might play a significant role in the option chosen by the EU Commission. However, both of this issues dwarf in comparison with the possibility of establishing a centralized enforcement authority that only serves the interests of the EU.

Fourth, there is a clear risk of forum shopping by the EPPO, as many academics have previously warned.[79] The current proposal would allow the European prosecutor to bring its case in the jurisdiction most favorable to its interests. Forum differences may arise not only because the Directive governing the crimes over which the EPPO has jurisdiction might be implemented differently across the EU, but also because the lack of standardized evidentiary law in the EU Regulation establishing the EPPO will certainly create various regimes among the Member States. In short, the EPPO will be able to maneuver accordingly, seeking jurisdiction in the countries it perceives as more friendly to its interests.

Fifth, the Directive that establishes the crimes over which the EPPO has jurisdiction expands the traditional notion of EU fraud crimes in the Member States. Under the title of "Fraud related criminal offenses affecting the Union's financial interests", the Directive contains in Article 4 public corruption (active and passive) and misappropriation offenses. This will imply that national public officials that deal with the EU funds will theoretically be prosecuted by supranational authorities, but the delegated representatives of such authority will be local. Needless to say, this creates a clear conflict of interest.

Sixth, judicial review, a key feature in every criminal justice system, is problematic under the current proposal.[80] The proposal explains that judicial review will lie with national judicial authorities, with a generic warning concerning the need (and actual obligation) to request prejudicial rulings from the ECJ pursuant to Article 267 TFEU. In theory, whenever there is no further appeal against a decision from the national courts, then a prejudicial ruling from the ECJ should be granted. However, legal practitioners around the EU are well aware of the reluctance of national courts in many Member States to file such requests. Some academics[81] have proposed a special chamber for criminal matters within the ECJ on the basis of Article 257 TFEU to deal with judicial review of EPPO decisions. This would provide more adequate relief for defendants across EU territory and would ensure a uniform interpretation of EPPO powers and limitations.[82]

Seventh, and probably the most pressing issue, the Commission's proposal did not seize the opportunity to establish a thoughtful and consistent body of

79 Jorge Ángel Espina Ramos, *Towards a European Public Prosecutor's Office: the Long and Winding Road*, in André Klip, ed., *Substantive Criminal Law of the European Union*, 2011. The report that was produced pursuant to the Greenbook also reflected this deficit (COM (2003) 128 final).

80 Jorge Ángel Espina Ramos, *Towards a European Public Prosecutor's Office: the Long and Winding Road*, in André Klip, ed., *Substantive Criminal Law of the European Union*, 2011 at 43.

81 See Carlos Gómez-Jara Díez, *Models for a System of European Criminal Law: Unification vs. Harmonization*, New Journal of European Criminal Law 1 (2010) at 398. See also www.eppo-project.eu/.

82 At least, the proposed legislation should make good use of the possibility provided by Article 86 TFEU to introduce the "rules applicable to the judicial review of procedural measures taken by it in the performance of its functions" and establish the standards governing judicial review.

evidentiary law governing EPPO action.[83] In Article 30 of the proposal, evidence should be admitted unless it would "adversely affect the fairness of the procedure or the rights of defence as enshrined in Articles 47 and 48 of the Charter of Fundamental Rights of the European Union". Though probably well intended, the provision falls short of providing an effective standard, especially if judicial review rests in the hands of national judicial authorities. This is known to be an extremely controversial area of law,[84] given national differences concerning admissibility of evidence and the natural reluctance of courts to admit evidence produced in other states. It would be wise to take the opportunity to determine the general rules "governing the admissibility of evidence" pursuant to Article 86 TFEU and elaborate a comprehensive set of rules similar to the US Federal Rules of Evidence.[85]

The Commission's proposal should be more than welcome, but we should make sure it provides the response needed. As the head of the EU Anti-fraud Office (OLAF), Giovanni Kessler recently stated, "We need to have a European reaction, a European answer, and the answer is to have a European Public Prosecutor's Office in charge. This is in the European treaty, the Commission is working on it, and I hope the Parliament is also on track".[86] From this the willingness of the EU institutions to follow through on the creation of the EPPO seems clear, especially if we consider that the fight against corruption is closely related to the protection of the EU financial interests.[87] The final push might come from a more practical need to encourage confidence in the European sovereign debt. As noted below, financial markets will react positively to an EU with (criminal) enforcement capacities.

Still, the path to the creation of the EPPO is far from over. On 28 October 2013, 14 national chambers, totaling 19 votes, issued "reasoned opinions" on the EPPO proposal, i.e. negative votes, stating that they found it in breach of the subsidiarity principle. These opinions were issued by the Dutch Senate, the Czech Senate, the Dutch House of Representatives, the Cypriot House of Representatives, the UK

---

83 Some had already noted the need and convenience of establishing a body of evidence law in this respect (see Carlos Gómez-Jara Díez, *Models for a System of European Criminal Law: Unification vs. Harmonization*, 1 New Journal of European Criminal Law 398 (2010); Helmut Satzger, *International and European Criminal Law*, 2012 at 116). Others have considered the possibility of entrusting the principle of mutual recognition with the task of providing an adequate solution to the evidence problem (Katalin Ligeti, *The European Public Prosecutor's Office: Which Model?*, in André Klip, ed., *Substantive Criminal Law of the European Union*, 2011 at 61), though finally conclude that it is unrealistic to believe it will be up to the task.

84 See Katalin Ligeti and Michele Simonato, *The European Public Prosecutor's Office: Towards a Truly European Prosecution Service?*, New Journal of European Criminal Law Review 4 (2013) at 19.

85 See Henning Radtke, *The Proposal to Establish a European Prosecutor*, in Husabo and Strandbakken, eds., *Harmonization of Criminal Law in Europe*, 2005 at 113, who was extremely reluctant to the institution of a EPPO if it was not accompanied by a set of criminal procedure rules.

86 Available at: www.euractiv.com/justice/olaf-chief-pleads-european-publi-news-516487.

87 If the Union is unable to address the issue of corruption properly and in an efficient way "the European Union as such is at stake", he pleaded (available at: www.euractiv.com/justice/olaf-chief-pleads-european-publi-news-516487).

House of Commons, the Hungarian Parliament, the Swedish Parliament, the Irish Parliament, the Romanian Chamber of Deputies, the Slovenian Parliament, the French Senate, the Maltese Parliament, and the UK House of Lords. Their concerns generally focused on the Commission not sufficiently demonstrating the need for or added value of the proposed EPPO and failing to satisfactorily explore alternative mechanisms or existing ones. Dissenters also complained that the protection of the EU financial interests could be better obtained by strengthening and deepening existing mechanisms of cross-border cooperation between criminal justice authorities.[88]

On 27 November 2013, the Commission issued a communication in response to the so-called "yellow card" procedure that had been initiated by the national parliaments against the Commission's proposal for a regulation on the establishment of the EPPO.[89] The Commission rebutted the objections raised by the Member States by stating that the impact assessment report is sufficient to demonstrate respect for the principle of subsidiarity, supplementing the reasons given in the explanatory memorandum and in the legislative financial statement. The Commission also acknowledged that proposed changes to the existing structures of Eurojust and Europol are expected to lead to some improvements, but they cannot address the insufficient level of investigations and prosecutions in the Member States. Among the arguments demonstrating the added value of the proposed EPPO, the Commission points to the pooling of expertise and knowledge, the avoiding of time-consuming mutual legal assistance procedures and the proposed method of handling cross-border evidence.

Besides defending the organizational structure of the proposed EPPO, the Commission stresses that the nature and the scope of the proposed EPPO competences will be compatible with the principle of subsidiarity.[90] To put it simply, including all cases of EU fraud in the EPPO's competence is the most effective way to ensure a consistent investigation and prosecution policy, and it avoids parallel action at the EU and national levels.

More importantly, the communication of the Commission clearly differentiates protection of the EU's financial interests from cross-border criminal conduct:

> "The need to grant the European Public Prosecutor's Office exclusive competence for all crimes affecting the financial interests of the Union, including

---

88 On 21 November 2013 the Academic Services of the German Parliament (Wissenschaftliche Dienst des Deutschen Bundestags) signaled a strong opposition (available at: www.bundestag.de/dokumente/analysen/2013/Europaeische_Staatsanwaltschaft.pdf).

89 Communication from the Commission to the European Parliament, the Council and the National Parliaments, on the review of the proposal for a Council Regulation on the establishment of the European Public Prosecutor's Office with regard to the principle of subsidiarity, in accordance with Protocol No. 2, COM (2013) 851 final.

90 For a thorough review of this issue see Fuglsang Madsen and Thomas Elholm, *EPPO and the Principle of Subsidiarity*, in Peter Asp, ed., *The European Public Prosecutor Office's Office. Legal and Criminal Policy Perspectives*, 2015 at 31–49.

> non-cross-border cases, arises out of the nature of the crimes in question, which have an intrinsic Union dimension. It implies Union-level steering and coordination of investigations and prosecutions because these criminal offences affect the Union's own financial interests."[91]

A recent Opinion of the Prosecutors General of Bulgaria, Italy, Portugal and Spain on the Commission's Proposal on the European Public Prosecutor's Office stresses the importance of the exclusive competence of the EPPO regarding the protection of its own financial interests: "EPPO's exclusive competence seems a correct solution as a way to enhance efficiency. Its rationale is that community budget is a good which pertains to the Union and therefore is better protected by the Union itself."[92]

As a final note in the development of this process,[93] it is worth noting that the Council has laid out an alternative proposal containing significant differences[94] with the Commission's proposal. It is difficult to foresee how this tension will evolve, but one thing seems clear: the Council's proposal stresses the horizontal federalism perspective by way of relying to a greater extent on the prosecution authorities of the Member States; the Commission's proposal tries to introduce a (timid, as always) vertical federalism dimension given the lack of effective enforcement that national authorities have shown so far.

7. THE ESMA CASE: A PREQUEL IN TERMS OF QUESTIONING ENFORCEMENT POWERS?

From this perspective, it is noteworthy that the proposal of a Regulation implementing the mandate of the Lisbon Treaty on the EPPO came at a time were numerous European agencies with remarkable doses of traditional state sovereignty have been created: the Single Supervision Mechanism (SSM), the Single Resolution Mechanism (SRM) and the European Supervision Markets Authority (ESMA). The subsequent litigation concerning the SSM, SRM and the

---

91 COM (2013) 851 final, S. 11.

92 Opinion of the Prosecutors General of Bulgaria, Italy, Portugal and Spain on the Commission's Proposal on the European Public Prosecutor's Office (on file with the author), page 3. It should be added that it is not only more efficient, but also more legitimate that the EU protects its own financial interests.

93 For an in-depth analysis see Simon Drew, *How will the European Public Prosecutor's Office (EPPO) be Born?*, in Peter Asp, ed., *The European Public Prosecutor Office's Office. Legal and Criminal Policy Perspectives*, 2015 at 13–29.

94 Simon Drew, *How will the European Public Prosecutor's Office (EPPO) be Born?*, in Peter Asp, ed., *The European Public Prosecutor Office's Office. Legal and Criminal Policy Perspectives*, 2015 at 17.

ESMA[95] anticipates that, in case the EPPO proposal is finally passed, some heavy litigation will come to light.

It therefore pays to review some highlights in the Case C-270/12, *UK v. Council of the European Union and European Parliament.* Here, the new powers granted to ESMA[96] have been heavily questioned. Out of the various grounds on which the new ESMA regulation has been challenged, Advocate General *Niilo Jääskinen* considered that the legal basis for the new sanctioning powers, i.e. the recurring Article 114 TFEU, was flawed:

> "In my opinion, at the heart of this case lies the fact that Article 28 of Regulation No 236/2012 does not entail a delegation of authority by either of the EU executive institutions, that is the Commission or, exceptionally, by the Council to an agency, but is rather concerned with a direct conferral of power to an agency by the legislature pursuant to an Article 289(3) TFEU legislative act. To my mind, in the light of amendments wrought by the Lisbon Treaty, and particularly the confirmation in primary law that the acts of agencies are subject to judicial review in EU law, the principles established in *Romano* and *Meroni* do not support the conclusions the United Kingdom draws from these rulings. However, in my opinion the United Kingdom's action should nonetheless succeed, but on its fourth ground of challenge. This is so because Article 114 TFEU is not an appropriate legal basis for Article 28 of Regulation No 236/2012."[97]

The arguments distinguished between the EU powers to create the regulatory agency[98] and the internal harmonization that affects third parties,[99] on the one

[95] To be sure, the first agency was created within the already existing European Central Bank, the second agency was established at the EU Commission and the third is the reformulation of the CESR, i.e. the Committee of European Securities Regulators. Yet, as the subsequent litigation regarding the creation of the ESMA clearly shows (*United Kingdom v Parliament and Council*, Judgment of 22 January 2014 in Case C-270/12), the new powers afforded to these institutions are being heavily challenged. Not surprisingly, in July 2014 five German academics launched another challenge at the *Bundesverfassungsgericht* – the German Constitutional Court – against the proposals for a banking union based on the Single Supervisory Mechanism (SSM) at the ECB and the Single Resolutions Mechanism (SRM) at the Commission, with a Single Resolution Fund (SRF) set up via a separate intergovernmental treaty (available at: http://openeuropeblog.blogspot.com.es/2014/07/banking-union-challenged-at-german.html). The basic contention is that the banking union plans overstep power given in Article 127 TFEU and that the amount of power transferred to the ECB is more than desirable.

[96] Article 28, with the title 'ESMA intervention powers in exceptional circumstances', of Regulation No. 236/2012.

[97] Case C-270/12 *UK v. Council of the European Union and European Parliament*, § 6.

[98] "Consequently, in my opinion there can be no in principle objection to the establishment of ESMA and regulation of its tasks and powers on the legal basis of Article 114 TFEU. In general terms, and from the perspective of its broader functions (53) the role of ESMA in the context of approximation of the Member States rules on short selling fulfills the conditions that the Court set down in *ENISA*."

[99] "As I have already mentioned, there can be no *in principle* objection to recourse to Article 114 TFEU as the legal basis empowering agencies to adopt legally binding decisions with respect to third parties. The touchstone, however, for assessing whether the conferral of such powers on an agency falls within the scope of Article 114 TFEU is whether or not the decisions of the

hand, and the specific intervention powers through binding decisions against national judiciaries,[100] on the other. In Advocate General Jääskinen's opinion, the appropriate legal basis for the first powers is Article 114 TFEU. In turn, the intervention powers can only derive from Article 352 TFEU. In this sense, "ESMA is intervening on the conditions of competition in a particular financial market, falling within the remit of a national competent authority, when it is confronted with certain exceptional circumstances".[101] In light of the foregoing he concludes that:

> "A centralised emergency decision making process that replaces the decision of the competent Member State authority, without its consent, or which provides a substitution for the absence of one, cannot be considered to be encompassed by the concept of 'approximation of the provisions laid down by law, regulation or administrative action in Member States' under Article 114 TFEU."[102]

It could be argued that the discussion is moot given that in both cases there is a legal basis in the TFEU to provide the ESMA with such intervention powers, but there are relevant differences between the two provisions. In order to pass legislation on the basis of Article 352 TFEU, unanimity is required. And precisely such unanimity was lacking when Regulation No 236/2012 was adopted. The UK did not vote for the proposal.

The Court ruling on 22 January 2014 rejects the arguments laid by the UK and the Advocate General. A helpful aid to understand the position of the ECJ is the distinction between national financial markets and those of the EU. Recent history has shown that certain measures adopted by national authorities, while targeted at protecting national financial interests, can affect the stability of the

---

agency concerned either contribute or amount to internal market harmonisation, in the sense this notion is used in EU law."

100 "For the sake of completeness, I would add that in my opinion Article 352 TFEU would have been an appropriate legal basis for Article 28 of Regulation No 236/2012. This is so because there is clearly a need for action at the EU level since, in an integrated market of financial instruments, inaction or inadequate action by a competent national authority in relation to short selling may have significant cross-border effects. These might include distortions in the banking systems of other Member States other than that of the marketplace where short selling takes place. Hence, in situations posing a threat to the orderly functioning and integrity of financial markets or to the stability of whole or part of the financial system in the European Union, a centralised decision making procedure enabling uniform application of EU rules on short selling would seem to be both necessary and proportionate. But for the reasons I have explained above, a centralised emergency decision making process that replaces the decision of the competent Member State authority, without its consent, or which provides a substitution for the absence of one, cannot be considered to be encompassed by the concept of 'approximation of the provisions laid down by law, regulation or administrative action in Member States' under Article 114 TFEU" (at § 40).

101 At § 54. He continues noting that: "In my opinion, the closest analogy in EU law to ESMA's powers under Article 28 of Regulation No 236/2012 is provided by the Commission intervention powers in the field of agriculture and anti-dumping, that is in areas where the Commission implements a common EU policy".

102 At § 54.

Union's financial system. In extraordinary circumstances, a clear conflict between both interests may arise. It is in precisely in this case that the protection of the EU financial interests should prevail over national financial interests. The wording of the ruling is not so blunt:

> "114. Therefore, the harmonisation of the rules governing such transactions is intended to prevent the creation of obstacles to the proper functioning of the internal market and the continuing application of divergent measures by Member States.
>
> 115. It should be added that, as stated in recital 33 in the preamble to Regulation No 236/2012, while competent national authorities will often be best placed to monitor and react immediately to an adverse development, ESMA should also have the power to take measures where short selling and other related activities threaten the orderly functioning and integrity of financial markets or the stability of the whole or part of the financial system in the Union, where there may be cross-border implications and competent national authorities have not taken sufficient measures to address the threat.
>
> 116. It follows that the purpose of the powers provided for in Article 28 of Regulation No 236/2012 is in fact to improve the conditions for the establishment and functioning of the internal market in the financial field."

The key, again, is the cross-border implications of certain measures. In the recent past, the EU financial system has suffered episodes of great instability. The EU lacked the authority to appease the markets and could only rely on coordination measures by various Member States. It seems reasonable to expect that the EU has the power to adopt certain measures that ensure the orderly functioning and integrity of its own financial system. Though not easy to digest by some Member States, the severity of the recent financial crisis has shown the need for direct EU intervention, regardless of coordinated EU Member States' action.

Though the questioning of ESMA intervention powers is not specifically related to criminal law, case C-236/2012 highlights the willingness of EU institutions to create new agencies with enforcement powers. This could be indicative of the European Public Prosecutor's Office's future. Not surprisingly, a number of Member States have opted out of the EPPO proposal.[103] Although in comparison to the ESMA debate the EPPO has to its advantage that the TFEU specifically foresees its creation, the enforcement nature of the institution will generate strong opposition. And this not only from countries who will participate in the EPPO system, but most probably from Member States who have opted out. A fundamental reason for this questioning will surely be that even if a Member State chooses to opt out, it will still have to cooperate with information requests

[103] For a review of the current status of the legislative process see Simon Drew, *How will the European Public Prosecutor's Office (EPPO) be Born?*, in Peter Asp, ed., *The European Public Prosecutor Office's Office. Legal and Criminal Policy Perspectives*, 2015 at 13–30.

concerning proceedings initiated by the EPPO from the authorities of Member States which "opted in".

8. LAW ENFORCEMENT AND INVESTORS RATIONALITY: SOME LESSONS FROM THE LAW AND FINANCE DEBATE

For years, the prestigious Law and Finance school of thought has studied the relationship between legal regulation of financial markets and the reaction it triggers in investors around the world.[104] Using a sample of some 49 countries, they found a statistically significant relationship between the origins of a country's laws and its level of financial development.[105] According to their findings, common law origin countries had grown at a faster rate (4.3% per capita) than French civil law origin countries (3.2% per capita).[106] As they noted, "the evidence on the importance of the historically determined legal origin in shaping investor rights … suggests at least tentatively that many rules need to be changed simultaneously to bring a country with poor investor protection up to best practice."[107]

These studies focused heavily on the law in the books and found that adequate regulations protecting investors' rights promotes a more rapid and solid development of financial markets. This suggests that if the EU institutions are able to provide the adequate regulatory framework, market credibility could be restored rapidly.[108] However, recent studies have shown that focusing solely on the laws on the books fails to adequately consider the most decisive factors in the development of a sound market place: securities and sovereign debt.

As Columbia University Law School Professor Coffee points out,[109] what really seems to be the deciding factor in the development of solid financial markets is

---

[104] See among many Rafael La Porta, Florencio Lopez-de-Silanes, Andrei Shleifer and Robert W. Vishny, *Law and Finance*, J. Pol. Econ. 106 (1998) at 1113.

[105] Ibid. at 1151.

[106] Ibid. at 1138, table II.

[107] Rafael La Porta et al., *Investor Protection and Corporate Governance*, J. Fin. Econ. 28 (2000) at 3, 20.

[108] Howell E. Jackson, *Regulatory Intensity in the Regulation of Capital Markets: A Preliminary Comparison of Canadian and U.S. Approaches*, in *The Task Force To Modernize Securities Legislation in Canada, Canada Steps Up: Research Studies: Strengthening Market Credibility and Integrity* 75, 98 (2006) (available at: www.tfmsl.ca/docs/V6(2)%20Jackson.pdf).

[109] John C. Coffee, *Law and the Market: The Impact of Enforcement*, U. Pa. L. Rev. 156 (2007) at 229. The basic tenet of Coffee's article is to suggest that only one legal variable – the level of enforcement intensity – distinguishes jurisdictions in a manner that can explain national differences in the cost of capital and therefore determine the decision-making process of investors. See also John C. Coffee, Jr., *The Rise of Dispersed Ownership: The Roles of Law and the State in the Separation of Ownership and Control,* Yale L.J. 111 (2001) at 1, 8–9 (arguing that the level of state control over the economy, rather than the nature of a country's legal system, most influences its financial development).

the degree of enforcement financial regulations in a specific jurisdiction.[110] In this sense, if the EU insists on providing adequate regulation but thereinafter leaves enforcement to the national authorities of the Member States, the attempt to promote market confidence will miss its mark. The enactment of the proposed Directive without the simultaneous creation of an EPPO will fall short of providing investors with the much needed peace of mind that if there is misconduct within financial institutions in the EU, the EU will prosecute the persons responsible.

A clear example of a system where vigorous prosecution encourages market growth can be seen around the intense litigation in the US regarding foreign-cubed securities.[111] Why do investors around the world flock to the US system of federal law to file their claims for misrepresentation and other fraud related issues pursuant to Section 11 of the Exchange Act of 1933 and Rule 10b-5? The answer is quite simple. With its level of enforcement, this system provides the necessary guarantees to make investors feel safe, confident that any prohibition of misconduct will be subject to real enforcement. To be fair, the US system has been a victim of its own success, and the abundance of litigation in this field for years has resulted in a recent setback by the US Supreme Court which reduces the availability of US enforcement to foreign investors.[112]

The empirical fact that foreign investors are attracted to the legal system that provides the highest standards of enforcement should serve as a guiding factor for the difficult decision that is before EU institutions. If the EU is able to provide a uniform system of enforcement at the supranational EU level in matters concerning criminal misconduct affecting EU financial interests, investors will surely regain their lost confidence in the sovereign debt issued by EU Member States, as they will feel that no excess will go unpunished.[113]

110 The literature on securities regulation has long underplayed this public-regarding role, but non-investors as well as investors depend on the efficiency of securities regulation, as the costs of underenforcement fall on the economy as a whole.

111 See the explanation of this type of litigation provided in Stephen J. Choi and Linda J. Silberman, *Transnational Litigation and Global Securities Class Actions*, Wis. L. Rev. (2009) at 465, 476 (2009).

112 See John C. Coffee, *Extraterritoriality After Morrison: Gray Areas Remain*, New York Law Journal (2012). As Professor Coffee lays out, the goals in *Morrison v. National Australia Bank*, 130 S. Ct. 2869 (2010) were both (1) to reduce legal uncertainty (because the Second Circuit's prior "conduct" and "effect" tests had proven murky), and (2) to minimize US interference with the regulatory affairs of other countries (in part because the extraterritorial application of Rule 10b-5 could threaten the solvency of foreign corporations that had no more than a legal toe in US waters).

113 As the referred Proposal for a Directive on criminal sanctions for insider dealing and market manipulation (2011/0297 (COD)) points out: "An integrated and efficient financial market requires market integrity. The smooth functioning of securities markets and public confidence in markets are prerequisites for economic growth and wealth. Market abuse harms the integrity of financial markets and public confidence in securities and derivatives". This consideration is a result of the impact assessments conducted by the Commission that clearly conclude that the legislation "will have a positive impact on investors' confidence and will further contribute to the financial stability of financial markets". This dovetails with the previous JHA Council conclusions on economic crisis prevention and support for economic activity, in which it was

They will be confident that no connivance between national authorities and national banks will take place.[114]

Needless to say, resorting to criminal law to rebuild investors' confidence is a last resort. Whatever the approach, it must be consistent with the *ultima ratio* nature of criminal law. Before using the state's greatest weapon, the enforcement powers of EU market's regulatory agencies should be strengthened. To be sure, the ESMA should play a similar role in the EU to the one exercised by the SEC in the US. Still, the strength of any EU agency established in this area depends on the content of its enforcement powers. Without sanctioning powers, the ESMA will be all bark and no bite.

In any event, it did not take long for the ESMA to reveal its attitude towards some of the problems at the heart of the EU sovereign debt crisis: the credit rating agencies. Since the outset of the crisis in 2007, the CRAs have played a decisive role that has not gone unnoticed or unquestioned.[115] The recent study conducted by ESMA[116] has raised certain concerns that should be addressed promptly.

---

stressed that consideration could be given to whether it is possible or, as the case may be, appropriate to harmonize criminal laws regarding the handling of serious stock market price manipulations and other misconduct relating to securities markets. See Docs. 8920/10 of 22 April 2010 and 7881/10 of 29 March 2010.

114 The connection between both has been obvious (see generally ARTURO ESTRELLA and SEBASTIAN SCHICH, *Sovereign and banking debt interconnections through guarantees*, OECD JOURNAL: FINANCIAL MARKET TRENDS, Volume 2011, at 21); especially in countries like Spain where national Banks purchase the highest percentage of Spanish sovereign debt. This causes a natural tendency for the government to relax standards for banks.

115 See RAQUEL GARCÍA CUBILLA and JAVIER RUIZ DEL POZO, *Credit Rating Agencies on the Watchlist. Analysis of European Regulation*, 2012. As to the US discussion see EDUARD ALTMAN, SABRI ÖNCÜ, MATTHEW RICHARDSON, ANJOLEIN SCHMEITS and LAWRENCE WHITE, *Regulation of Rating Agencies*, in VIRAL ACHARYA, THOMAS COOLEY and MATTHEW RICHARDSON, eds., *Regulating Wall Street. The Dodd Frank Act and the New Architecture of Global Finance*, 2010 at 443; FABIAN AMTENBRINK and KLAUS HEINE, *Regulating Credit Rating Agencies in the European Union: Lessons from Behavioural Science*, THE DOVENSCHMIDT QUARTERLY 1 (2013). In the most recent EU Regulation (Regulation (EU) No. 462/2013 of the European Parliament and of the Council of 21 May 2013 amending Regulation (EC) No 1060/2009 on credit rating agencies, it specifically notes the conflicts of interests derived from the issuer pay model: "As a result, credit ratings issued under the issuer-pays model may be perceived as the credit ratings that suit the issuer rather than the credit ratings needed by the investor. It is essential to reinforce the conditions of independence applying to credit rating agencies in order to increase the level of credibility of credit ratings issued under the issuer-pays model." Furthermore, in Article 8 *bis*, the EU Regulation pays close attention to sovereign debt rating because "the need to review transparency, procedural requirements and the timing of publication specifically for sovereign ratings was highlighted by the current sovereign debt crisis" became obvious (recital 1). Cross-references between the US and the EU discussion in JOHN COFFEE, *Ratings Reform: The Good, the Bad, and the Ugly*, HARV. BUS. L. REV. 1 (2011), at 232 noting the pros and cons of a *subscriber pays* model.

116 *Credit Rating Agencies, Sovereign ratings investigation. ESMA's assessment of governance, conflicts of interest, resourcing adequacy and confidentiality controls*, ESMA/2013/1775. The investigation was conducted in February and October 2013 with a supervision plan. See Credit Rating Agencies (CRAs) 2013 Supervision and Policy Work Plan (available at: www.esma.europa.eu/system/files/2013-87.pdf.). The investigation was triggered by the potential conflicts of interests underlying the CRAs rating that the subsequent impact of sovereign debt rating in other ratings. It also addressed the capability of such agencies to produce a high number of

9. THE CURRENT GREEK CRISIS: WOULD IT LOOK DIFFERENT WITH AN INDEPENDENT EPPO EFFECTIVELY ENFORCING THE PROTECTION OF THE EU FINANCIAL INTERESTS?

If the findings of the Law and Finance debate are to be considered seriously, an interesting questions surface in the current EU crisis generated by Greece's intention to renegotiate the terms of the past years bailouts. Would the financial interests of the EU be more effectively protected if a truly independent EPPO were already in place? What type of tensions would arise between national Greek prosecutors and the EPPO if instructions were given to prosecute Greek officials and relevant businessmen? Would investors' confidence increase if prosecution of crimes against the financial interests be prosecuted directly by European prosecutors (without relying on national prosecutors)?

To be sure, the turmoil generated by the implosion of the Greek sovereign debt crisis in 2010 can hardly be questioned. Not only did it precipitate *de facto* interventions of EU authorities in a number of Member States, but it also brought to light certain power struggles among Member States. The debate has escalated to a point that old reminiscences dating post-Second World War have come into play. It could be argued that emotions are running high, and that the final solution will depend more on the political willingness to hold together a common project than a cold financial assessment of the alternatives at hand.

Yet as these pages are written a general mistrust of the EU institutions and other Member States towards Greece permeates the environment. This is the reason why it pays to review how the EPPO should function in a climate in which the EU is reluctant to rely on national authorities to provide an adequate solution to the problems that have been detected in the past concerning EU fraud and corruption. Of course, it might be argued that this will by no means be the classical example of how the EPPO works. But it is in extreme cases that the general rationale behind the EPPO should be put to the test.

Against this backdrop it seems reasonable to conclude that the greater the independence of the EPPO from the national authorities, the greater the possibilities of providing an effective enforcement of the protection of EU financial interests. To the extent that European institutions are able to effectively prosecute this type of offense without relying on cooperation by national authorities, there will be greater confidence in the overall compliance with the guidelines set out by the European institutions. Needless to say, an independent EPPO would not solve the general lack of confidence of European institutions in the willingness

ratings in a period of great instability. Finally, issues such as confidentiality and ratings timing were also of concern.

of Greek institutions to adopt the measures called for, but it would certainly add material component.

10. A PROPOSED SYSTEM OF EU CRIMINAL LAW: THE BALANCE BETWEEN VERTICAL AND HORIZONTAL FEDERALISM

10.1. INTRODUCTION

We hope to have convinced the reader so far that the current system of EU criminal law has some distinct features of federalism. Acknowledging this fact should provide valuable insights into how to develop a coherent system for the future, avoiding some of the mistakes that are traditionally made in federal systems of criminal law. The EU, consistent with its nature, has developed a system of criminal law based on horizontal federalism with some timid elements of vertical federalism. For a long time this has worked to a certain extent. The sovereign debt crisis, if any, has shown the need to foster a more vertical approach, especially in the area of enforcement.

That the EU should directly protect its intrinsic interests through EU institutions seems not only a matter of legal reasoning, but of common sense. The sovereignty concerns of EU Member States over accepting EU enforcement of EU criminal legislation protecting EU interests start to become obsolete in an era in which sovereignty concessions have been made at much more fundamental levels. Still, the question of how to allow EU sovereignty (in criminal law) while securing national diversity in the same area remains a great challenge that is not easily resolved.

Our proposal tries to strike a fair (probably imperfect) balance between the EU and the Member States in criminal law matters. Pursuing exclusively the avenue of horizontal federalism will, in our opinion, lead to unwanted results: the EU will still depend on Member States to protect EU interests and the Member States will be forced to modify and enforce their national criminal legislation in matters in which they can legitimately raise concerns over suppression of national diversity. The purpose of our proposal is to make good use of the provisions embedded in the Lisbon Treaty to differentiate between genuine EU interests and shared common interests with the Member States. Once the distinction is made, a more strict vertical federalism approach should be undertaken regarding the first; and a more relaxed horizontal federalism approach towards the latter. Instead of Directives and double-hat prosecutors to protect EU financial interests, Regulations and truly European prosecutors to protect such interests are proposed. Instead of expanding the matters subject to EU harmonization, a more contained approach should be put to test.

It is easy to see that one of the main problems is to determine which offenses are to be included in the stronger federal state-like system and which to leave up to the progressive harmonization of national criminal law. Yet the option of not clearly distinguishing between both types of criminal law has unbearable consequences. If we only plead for the existence of harmonized national criminal laws, then the truly European interests will only receive a mediated protection that actually runs contrary to the interest of the Member States. On the other hand, solely establishing a federal European criminal law will prompt vigorous opposition from Member States as they will sense that the EU is usurping their competences in very sensitive matters. Moreover, such a proposal would erase many differences that have longstanding traditions in the Member States and that respond to their national history and idiosyncrasies, i.e. their national diversity.

10.2. ENHANCING THE VERTICAL FEDERALISM DIMENSION

At a time when the enactment of the EPPO Regulation is being discussed it is worthwhile to propose a model that seeks maximum efficiency while providing the necessary checks and balances that are inherent to a sound understanding of due process. Additionally, it seems reasonable to use the resources nowadays available and resort to the experience of both EU current institutions performing enforcement functions and US institutions that have dealt with similar issues for a number of years. To be sure, criticism is granted from the start as the actual proposals laid out by the Commission and the Council are far distant from most of the elements of our proposal.

The following pages only contain a brief outline of certain key elements of the proposal to reinforce the vertical dimension. All of them deserve greater development and, in doing so, many legal and political objections would arise. Because of time and space considerations, such development and the subsequent impact on the current trend of EU horizontal federalism cannot be pursued here. Yet if some of these thoughts serve the overall discussion, then our goal will have been more than achieved.

10.2.1. Rethinking the Model: Towards an EU Competition Law Model with the Necessary Checks and Balances

In a brilliant contribution to the EPPO discussion of which model should be adopted, *Satzger* advances a model based on the principle of complementarity as laid out in the International Criminal Court.[117] Interestingly, *Satzger* draws

[117] Helmut Satzger, *The Future European Public Prosecutor and the National Prosecution: Potential Conflicts and How they Could be Avoided*, in Peter Asp, ed., *The European Public*

on the considerable experience of the ICC to resolve conflicts of jurisdiction and proposes a similar model to govern the relationships between national courts and the EPPO.

In our opinion, although it is surely fruitful to take into account existing models of international criminal justice, the EPPO model should be based on a system that has clearly rendered outstanding results in terms of protecting what is considered to be a bedrock interest of the EU: fair competition. The quick response to this proposal will be to pinpoint the deficiencies of the EU competition law model and warn that adopting such a proposal would only lead to introducing undesired elements into the EPPO model. However, with a careful review of the basic elements of the EU competition law model, we believe that a satisfactory result can be achieved.

Our initial contention is that safeguarding fair competition within the EU has been an intrinsic interest of the EU. It is hard to imagine another area of law that has been so influenced by EU law (in the books and in action). It is well known that national authorities have cooperated with EU authorities in the protection of fair competition. And although the results are far from completely satisfactory, they can at least be considered promising. On top of this, EU and national authorities have a track record that they can relate to when addressing potential issues referred to the EPPO in the future, i.e. conflicts of jurisdiction, etc.

In this model, the EPPO has no double hat, i.e. they are not blue helmet prosecutors. Independence is a key factor for the EPPO to work effectively. EPPO staff should be fully independent from local authorities. The function of national prosecutors would be to *assist* the EPPO, but not to perform its functions. Coordination between the EPPO and national authorities should take place at two levels: a higher level at Eurojust and a lower on-the-ground level in the national criminal proceedings.

The role of Eurojust regarding the EPPO would then be similar to the European Competition Network. To the same extent that the European Commission and the national competition authorities in all EU Member States cooperate with each other through the European Competition Network (ECN), the EPPO and national enforcement authorities could cooperate with each other through Eurojust. This cooperation at a higher level would smooth on-the-ground cooperation between the EPPO and the national prosecutors.

OLAF would also play a key role in the system. With its current 435 staff and a wide experience in fraud investigations, it can provide the necessary workforce to effectively investigate the fraud affecting EU financial interests. OLAF should be instructed by the EPPO and instead of referring the cases to national prosecutors, it would refer those cases to the EPPO which would, in turn, pursue the investigation and trial with the assistance of national prosecutors. It is in this sense that we label OLAF the "European FBI".

Prosecutor's Office. Legal and Criminal Policy Perspectives, 2015 at 69.

As noted, the role of national prosecutors would be to assist the EPPO. This assistance will be key in two areas: gathering of evidence that affect fundamental rights of the defendant (and, therefore, must be authorized by the judiciary); and trying the case to obtain conviction of the defendant. National prosecutors will not have a dual status, i.e. double hat, but will provide the necessary assistance for the EPPO to perform its functions. Their role would be similar (with the necessary adjustments) to the Assistant US Attorneys in the US system of federal criminal law.

Uniformity in enforcement of EU law is a constant concern in many instances. For this reason, two EU Regulations should be enacted: one delineating the offenses against EU financial interests (Article 325 TFEU); one establishing the Rules of Criminal Procedure (Article 86(3) TFEU). Although it might be argued that producing such Regulation would mean a broad reading of the competences in criminal law matters embedded in the Lisbon Treaty, we believe that this is the only way to ensure consistency and foreseeability throughout the EU.

As should be clear from the explanation so far, national courts would serve a dual function: first, at the investigation stage, by authorizing measures that affect fundamental rights; second, at the trial stage, by adjudicating cases brought before them by the EPPO with the assistance of national prosecutors. To properly serve these goals, specialized courts within the national systems of criminal justice should be created – a practice that is already taking place in many EU Member States.

Finally, the ECJ should play a judicial review function at two levels: first, reviewing the decision of the EPPO to proceed to trial; second, reviewing the conviction of the defendant. An Article 257 TFEU specialized court should be created to properly perform this function. Given the number of EU fraud cases per year in which OLAF has sought continuance (approx. 300 cases), the workload of this specialized court would be manageable.

10.2.2. Regulation Protecting EU Financial Interests through Criminal Law

In Chapter 2 we reviewed the existing debate concerning the Proposal for a Directive of the European Parliament and of the Council on the fight against fraud to the Union's financial interests by means of criminal law.[118] As we noted, the initial EU Commission proposal adopted Article 325 TFEU as its legal basis. Yet the European Parliament's amendment clearly indicates that they are not willing to consider, for now, that Article 325(4) TFEU provides an autonomous source of criminal law powers to the EU.

Our model favors a strong reading of Article 325(4) TFEU, independent from Article 83(2) TFEU. Although in terms of uniformity much ground has been gained through the doctrine of interpretation-in-conformity, a Regulation

118 COM (2012) 363 final.

would leave no room for Member State divergence in this area. An EU Regulation would reinforce the vertical federalism element that should be present in this particular area of protection of EU financial interests. To the same extent that EU competition law is mostly comprised of Regulations that ensure an effective protection of EU competition, the EU financial interests deserve no less.

10.2.3. Regulation Introducing European Rules of Criminal Procedure

Our proposal makes good use of the possibility contained in Article 86(4) TFEU to enact a Regulation containing "the rules of procedure applicable to" the activities of the EPPO, "as well as those governing the admissibility of evidence, and the rules applicable to the judicial review of procedural measures taken by it in the performance of its function". A unified criminal procedural is as fundamental to effective enforcement as a unified substantive criminal law.

Instead of providing a general statement that evidence shall be admitted unless there is a violation of the due process rights contained in the Charter, we believe that a full set of rules of criminal procedure should be detailed in the Regulation. The model here would be to follow the US Federal Rules of Criminal Procedure. Crafting such rules would certainly take some time, but a great deal could be advanced just by synthesizing the abundant case law of the ECtHR regarding Article 6 of the ECHR and the jurisprudence so far produced by the ECJ concerning the Charter.

10.2.4. EPPO: Single-Hat Prosecutors

It is hard to overstate the importance of having a truly independent EPPO. The potential conflicts of interests embedded in the EU/Member States relationship has become clear over the years. The number of cases that are referred by OLAF and not thoroughly prosecuted by the enforcement authorities is a clear indication. As the proposed Regulation of the EPPO notes, "[a]s Member States' criminal investigation and prosecution authorities are currently unable to achieve an equivalent level of protection and enforcement, the Union not only has the competence but also the obligation to act".

A good starting point would be to designate a General European Public Prosecutor and a European Public Prosecutor for each Member State. They would work closely with assistant national prosecutors, but the decisions, authority and responsibility would rest alone in the European Public Prosecutors. They would be the ones deciding which cases are subject to investigation and which cases proceed to trial. Also, they would appear before the Article 257 ECJ specialized court in terms of judicial review of their decisions.

10.2.5. Eurojust: Coordination between EPPO and National Enforcement Authorities

The relationship between Eurojust and the EPPO has been heavily discussed. Our proposal considers that the Eurojust should serve a parallel function (with the necessary adjustments) like the one performed by the European Competition Network in EU competition law. It is well known that the ECN's basic purpose is to facilitate the enforcement of EU competition law. As Regulation 1/2003 provides, the national competition authorities become primary enforcers of EC competition rules, alongside the Commission. Either the Commission or any national competition authority can begin an investigation into an alleged breach of EC competition rules. Without ironclad rules on the division of jurisdiction or policy competence, the ECN becomes necessary as a coordination mechanism in a system of dispersed regulatory authority. This philosophy should be embedded in the functioning of Eurojust.

As a consequence, instead of exclusive competence, a concurrent competence is preferred. To be sure, some ironclad rules of the division of jurisdiction should be laid out to avoid ineffective enforcement. But following the guideline of the ECN should prove to be fruitful. In some cases, national enforcement authorities may be better positioned to prosecute certain misconducts.

10.2.6. The Role of National Prosecutors: Assisting the EPPO

Given that certain parts of the investigation, i.e. gathering evidence that affects fundamental right must be subject to judicial authority, and that trials must take place before national courts, an effective enforcement by the EPPO must rely on the assistance of national prosecutors. *Servata distantia* the role national prosecutors would perform would be similar to the Assistant US Attorneys in the US federal criminal law system. They would not serve as double-hat prosecutors, but would assist the EPPO in performing its functions.

To the same extent that Assistant US Attorneys must live within 25 miles of the district represented by their supervisory US Attorneys, Assistants of the EPPO should be national prosecutors with experience in EU fraud cases. There are 93 US Attorneys and over 350 Assistant US Attorneys. A similar balance could be reached concerning the EPPO structure: one European Public Prosecutor per country with three assistant national prosecutors.

10.2.7. OLAF: The European FBI

OLAF has proven over a decade that it is well suited to conduct investigations related to EU Fraud. OLAF's mission is threefold. It consists of (a) protecting the financial interests of the European Union by investigating fraud and other illegal activities, (b) detecting and investigating serious matters relating to the discharge of professional duties by staff of the EU institutions that could result in disciplinary or criminal proceedings, and (c) supporting in general the EU in the development and implementation of anti-fraud legislation and policies.[119]

While OLAF is not a prosecuting authority, it is empowered to conduct internal investigations, i.e. inside any European institution or body funded by the EU budget, and external investigations, i.e. at national level, wherever and whenever the EU budget is at stake. For this purposes, OLAF may conduct on-the-spot checks and inspections on the premises of economic operators, in close cooperation with the member state at issue. OLAF may acquire access to confidential information, to photocopy documents, to invite employees to testify and, in general, to conduct all the investigatory acts, similar to those that national authorities are allowed to conduct.[120]

10.2.8. The Role of National Courts: Creating Specialized Courts to Authorize Measures Affecting Fundamental Rights and to Try EPPO Cases

Though vertical federalism would require a truly European jurisdiction, the current structure of the Lisbon Treaty and the wording of Article 86(2) TFEU, i.e. the EPPO "shall exercise the functions of prosecutor in the competent courts of the Member States", leaves little room in this respect. National courts will have jurisdiction to authorize measure affecting fundamental rights and to adjudicate cases involving EU fraud.

Relying on national courts for the purposes of safeguarding fundamental rights and performing adjudicate functions in EU fraud cases should be accompanied by a specialization that will be much needed. In our proposal they will be in charge of applying both Regulations (substantial and procedural). For this, a thorough knowledge of EU law and ECJ/ECtHR case law will be decisive. Although in theory all national courts must have grown accustomed to such issues, practice shows, at least in the criminal law area, that this is not the case. In some Member States, certain national courts have been assigned the task of dealing with EAW, EEW, etc. cases. This proposal simply reinforces this tendency to assign cases related to EU enforcement to specialized courts.

10.2.9. Judicial Review before the ECJ: Article 257 TFEU to Review the Decision to Proceed to Trial and to Review the Convictions

The cornerstone of uniform and consistent enforcement of EU law protecting the financial interests of the EU relies on the ECJ. Given the limitations of the Lisbon Treaty to afford the ECJ a trial function in criminal matters, a judicial

---

119 Constantin Stefanou, Simone White and Helen Xanthaki, *OLAF at the crossroads – action against EU fraud*, 2011.

120 Michail Rodopoulos and Katerina Pantazatou, *Judicial Protection Against Olaf's Acts: In Search of Effectiveness*, Hellenic Review of European Law (2013) at 133–152.

review function may be awarded instead. Creating a specialized court pursuant to Article 257 TFEU at the ECJ would serve two functions: first, it would have the specialization needed for EU fraud cases and such delicate matters as the ones dealt with by criminal law; second, it would set the necessary distance to national jurisdictions in order to avoid cozy relationships between national authorities.

www.ingramcontent.com/pod-product-compliance
Ingram Content Group UK Ltd.
Pitfield, Milton Keynes, MK11 3LW, UK
UKHW051921100926
8556IPUK00021B/1308

9 781780 681207